WHAT'S ON THE CD-ROM

Test Engine   The CD-ROM supplied with this book contains a Java program written by Simon Roberts, a key player in the development of the Java Certification Program. The program simulates the actual Java Certification Exam, and allows you to test your knowledge of Java, and to make a reasonable estimate of whether you are sufficiently prepared for the exam. Our tester uses some of the questions from each chapter; you can impose a time limit, and control the number of questions and the categories of the questions. When you are done, the program will explain the correct answer.

Java Developers Kit Version 1.1.3   The CD-ROM also contains the JDK Version 1.1.3, the full development package from Sun Microsystems, Inc. for creating Java applications and applets. Versions are released periodically, and can be downloaded from `http://www.javasoft.com/products/jdk/1.1/index.html`.

* The CD-ROM will run on Windows 95, Windows NT, and Solaris.

Java 1.1 Certification Study Guide

Java™ 1.1 Certification Study Guide

Simon Roberts and Philip Heller

SYBEX®

San Francisco • Paris • Düsseldorf • Soest

Associate Publisher: Gary Masters
Acquisitions Manager: Kristine Plachy
Acquisitions & Developmental Editor: Suzanne Rotondo
Editor: Nancy Conner
Project Editor: Davina Baum
Technical Editor: Tim Russell
Book Designer: Catalin Dulfu
Graphic Illustrator: Steve Brooks
Electronic Publishing Specialist: Bob Bihlmayer
Production Coordinator: Amy Eoff
Proofreaders: Katherine Cooley, Charles Mathews,
Eryn L. Osterhaus, Duncan J.A. Watson
Indexer: Ted Laux
Cover Designer: Design Site
Cover Illustrator: Design Site

Screen reproductions produced with Collage Complete.

Collage Complete is a trademark of Inner Media Inc.

SYBEX is a registered trademark of SYBEX Inc.

TRADEMARKS: SYBEX has attempted throughout this book to
distinguish proprietary trademarks from descriptive terms by
following the capitalization style used by the manufacturer.

The author and publisher have made their best efforts to prepare
this book, and the content is based upon final release software
whenever possible. Portions of the manuscript may be based upon
pre-release versions supplied by software manufacturer(s). The
author and the publisher make no representation or warranties of
any kind with regard to the completeness or accuracy of the contents herein and accept no liability of any kind including but not
limited to performance, merchantability, fitness for any particular
purpose, or any losses or damages of any kind caused or alleged
to be caused directly or indirectly from this book.

Library of Congress Card Number: 97-69201
ISBN: 0-7821-2069-5

Manufactured in the United States of America

10 9 8 7 6 5 4 3 2

*For my family, especially Bethan, who arrived
just in time for the first printing.*
—Simon

To my family: Ruth, Richard, and Paul.
—Phil

ACKNOWLEDGMENTS

Simon would like to thank Annie Colvin, Mike Bridwell, Ray Moore, Gary Taylor, and Brian Couling—all of Sun Microsystems—who made it possible for him to work on the certification project (and enjoy three months in the sunshine at the same time!).

Phil would like to thank Jen Volpe, Tom McGinn, Mike Bridwell, Mike Ernest, Josh Krasnegor, Paulette Washington, and everybody at Pastis.

Both authors would like to thank Nancy Conner and Tim Russell, as well as everybody at Sybex who worked on the project, including Suzanne Rotondo, Davina Baum, Amy Eoff, Bob Bihlmayer, Katherine Cooley, Charles Mathews, Eryn Osterhaus, and Duncan Watson.

CONTENTS AT A GLANCE

TABLE OF CONTENTS

A Foreword from Sun Microsystems

Over 60 percent of large companies today are developing applications in the Java™ language. The reasons why are obvious: with Java's "Write Once, Run Anywhere™" capability, programmers and developers can write applications that run on all platforms. In addition, Java technology enables developers to write programs faster and more reliably, cutting down time-to-market by slashing development times by as much as half. The competitive edge Java technology gives companies has led to its explosive growth worldwide.

As a result, there is a tremendous need for people knowledgeable and skilled in Java application designs. Being a relatively new language, companies can't recruit Java professionals with "five years of Java expertise," and developers can't use their experience level to set themselves apart from the crowd. Instead, Java professionals must be able to demonstrate their proficiency.

For this reason, Sun developed the Sun™ Java Certification program to provide a validated means to distinguish among the different levels of Java proficiency. I believe the industry will soon demand certification of the Java workforce and that Java products be 100% Pure Java™. For the certified Java professional, this will translate into greater demand and improved employment opportunities.

Sun certifies Java software professionals at two levels: as a programmer, which tests for a strong working knowledge of Java, and as a developer, which assesses the ability to implement real-world solutions. The Sun Certified Java Programmer exam tests for overall Java knowledge as well as programming concepts and applet development skills. The Sun Certified Java Developer exam tests the ability to perform complex programming through an application assignment which is followed by another exam on the knowledge required to perform the assignment.

As this book explains, becoming a Sun Certified Java Programmer or Developer is not easy. It wasn't meant to be! Familiarity with the Java language will not be enough to pass, you must be prepared to step into real-world programming problems and provide real-world Java solutions. I believe that passing Sun Java certification challenge will enable you to do just that.

Only your own time and experience can provide a better working knowledge of Java technology. However, this book can augment your understanding of the Java language. I strongly recommend taking Sun's "Java Programming" and "Java Programming Workshop" courses to prepare for certification and your role as a Java professional.

Additional information on the Java Certification program and Java courses is available on the World Wide Web at:

```
www.sun.com/sunservice/suned/certif_programs/html
```

Good Luck!

Dr. Bill Richardson,
Vice President and General Manager
Sun Educational Services
SunService Division, Sun Microsystems, Inc.

INTRODUCTION

It looks like you're ready.

Ready to *get* ready, at least, which is practically the same thing. Now all that's left to do is the work.

And there is work to be done. If you want to pass the Java Certification Exam, you will probably need to do some preparation. By now you've heard the news: The exam is difficult. Not everybody passes, even on repeated attempts. (There is no penalty for repeating the exam, if you don't count time and money.)

We want to change those statistics. It wouldn't hurt to get a little help—and we're the ones to help.

Since this is, after all, the Introduction, allow us to introduce ourselves: Simon and Phil. We are Java instructors by day, and by night we write.

What we teach (by day) are Sun Microsystems' Java courses. Between the two of us, we have taught Java to more than 1,000 people. We do not teach anything else; we are committed to Java. And the Java courses that we teach are Sun's own courses. We have been through our own certification process for instructors, and Sun trusts us to teach people the Java facts that Sun considers important. Recently Simon has been influential in the development of new course material. We want you to know all this, because we want to be the ones to help you pass the Certification Exam.

What we write (by night) are Java books. (Phil keeps talking about a novel; we will just have to wait and see.) We wrote the *Java 1.1 Developer's Handbook* (Sybex, 1997), and we contributed to *Mastering Java 1.1* (Sybex, 1997). And now this: the *Java 1.1 Certification Study Guide*.

We thought we were the best team to write this book, for one very simple reason: Simon led the team that wrote all of the questions for the exam. Phil was a consultant for developing the exam, so he also has the inside view of things.

Simon's unique position places a few restrictions on us. We can't give away any answers to the questions on the exam. (We wouldn't want to do that anyway; we want you to pass because you're good at Java, not because we slipped you a crib.)

We had to make sure that the sample questions did not accidentally match any of the real test questions. It took a bit more work, but we think the benefit to you is tremendous: Everything in this book is here for a very good reason. If it's here, then it's here because we know you need to know about it. We understand that buying a book like this costs you money, and reading it costs you time, and absorbing it costs you effort. We appreciate your investment, and we believe it will pay off.

If you read this book, and absorb it, and solve the practice questions at the end of each chapter, and work through the practice exams on the CD-ROM, you will be in the best possible position when you walk through the doors of your local testing center and the time clock starts to tick.

Let's just take care of a few standard formalities, and then we can really get started.

Taking the Exam

You can take the Java Certification Exam whenever you like, just by making an appointment with Sylvan Prometric or Sun Educational Services. Sylvan Prometric administers the exam on Sun's behalf; they have test centers throughout the world, so hopefully you won't have to travel far. The cost of taking the exam is $150.

> **NOTE**
>
> The telephone number for Sylvan Prometric is 800-795-EXAM; their URL is `http://www.sylvanprometric.com`. The number for Sun Educational Services is 800-422-8020; their URL is `http://www.sun.com/sunservice/suned/certif_programs.html`. For people outside the United States, information on registration in any of the eighty-eight countries that Sylvan services is available at this site: `http://www.hibbertco.com/sun/suncontacts/contacts.html`.

You can make an appointment for any time during regular business hours. You will be given two hours and fifteen minutes, and you will probably need every minute. You will not be allowed to bring food or personal belongings into the test area. One piece of scratch paper is permitted; you will not be allowed to keep it after you have finished the exam. (See the end of Chapter 12, *Layout Managers*, for a suggestion about how to use the scratch paper.) Most sites have security cameras.

You will be escorted to a cubicle containing a PC. The exam program will present you with randomly selected questions. Navigation buttons take you to the next question, or to previous questions for review and checking. When you have finished the test, the program will immediately present you with your score and a pass/fail indication. In the 1.1 exam you will be given feedback that indicates how well you performed in each of the dozen or so categories of the objectives. You will not be told which particular questions you got right or wrong.

Formalities of the Exam

There are no trick questions on the exam, but every question requires careful thought. The wording of the questions is highly precise; the exam has been reviewed not just by Java experts, but also by language experts whose task was to eliminate any possible ambiguity. All you have to worry about is knowing Java; your score will not depend on your ability to second-guess the examiners.

It is not a good idea to try to second-guess the question layout. For example, do not be biased toward answer C simply because C has not come up recently. The questions are taken from a pool and presented to you in a random order, so it is entirely possible to get a run of a particular option; it is also possible to get the answers neatly spread out.

Most of the questions are multiple choice. Of these, some have a single answer while others require you to select all the appropriate responses. The Graphical User Interface of the test system indicates which kind of answer you should supply. If a question only has one correct answer, you will be presented with radio buttons, so that selecting a second answer cancels the selection of a previous answer. With this kind of question, you have to select the most appropriate answer. If, on the other hand, you are presented with check boxes, then you may need to make more than one selection, so every possible answer has to be considered on its own merits—not weighed against the others.

You should be aware that where multiple answers are possible, you are being asked to make a decision about each answer, rather as though the question were five individual true/false questions. This requires more effort and understanding from you, but does not actually mean that more than one answer is correct. Think carefully, and always base your answer on your knowledge of Java.

The short-answer type-in questions often cause undue concern. How are they marked? What happens if you omit a semicolon? These worries stem from the knowledge that the questions are marked electronically, and the belief that an answer might be marked wrong simply because the machine didn't have the sense to recognize a good variation of what it was programmed to accept.

As with all exam questions, you should be careful to answer precisely what is asked. However, you should also be aware that the system does accept a variety of different answers; it has been set up with all the variations that the examination panel considered to be reasonable.

Some of the type-in questions provide specific instructions concerning the format of the answer. Take this guidance seriously. If, for example, a question says, "Answer in the form `methodname()`", then your answer should be

```
method()
```

and not any of

```
object.method()
method();
method(a, b)
method
```

Some of the other answers might well be accepted, but programming is a precision job and you should be accustomed to following precise directions.

The test is taken using a windowed interface that can be driven almost entirely with the mouse. Many of the screens require scrolling; the scroll bar is on the right-hand side of the screen. Always check the scroll bar, so that you can be sure you have read a question in its entirety. It would be a shame to get a question wrong because you didn't realize you needed to scroll down a few lines.

The exam contains about 60 questions. On average, this gives you a little more than two minutes per question. Some of the questions are easier than others, and undoubtedly there will be some that you can answer faster than others. However, you really do need to answer all the questions if you possibly can. The test system allows you to review your work after you reach the end. The system will explicitly direct your attention toward any multiple-choice questions that have no items selected. So if you find a particular question difficult, consider moving on and coming back to the difficult ones later.

If you pass, you will be given a temporary certificate. A few weeks later you will receive by mail a permanent certificate, along with an artwork sheet. The artwork shows the "Sun Certified Java Programmer" logo at various magnifications. By passing the exam, you have earned the right to display the logo. Printers know how to reproduce the artwork onto business cards, stationery, and so on. The lettering is legible (just barely, by people who eat carrots) down to a reduction of about ⅝" wide by ⅜" high.

Focus on the JDK 1.1

This book is based entirely on the 1.1 release of the Java Developer's Kit. These days there is little value in convincing a potential employer that you have mastered 1.0. If another candidate comes along who has mastered 1.1, then the jig is up, the case is closed, and your goose is cooked. If, on the other hand, your 1.1 knowledge is certified, then the jig plays on, the case is wide open, and your goose can lay golden eggs. (Release 1.2 is not expected for a while, so 1.1 is definitely the one to focus on.)

Release 1.1 contains a vast collection of useful new features. The most important addition is the new event delegation model. There are also Readers, Writers, Beans, Jars, and Inner Classes. There is Printing and Commerce and Security, as well as Serialization and Remote Method Invocation. In short, there is more than one person can possibly master in any reasonable amount of time.

Fortunately, Sun publishes "objectives" for the exam. These are specific topics that you will be tested on; to see them, browse to `http://www.sun.com/sunservice/suned/certif_programs.html`. This book strongly emphasizes the objectives. In fact, each chapter begins with a list of the objectives that are covered in that chapter. All the objectives are covered somewhere in this book.

At the end of each chapter you will find a set of questions. The answers, along with detailed explanations are in the back of the book, in Appendix A. Some of the questions are theoretical, and some present you with specific code. Here is a typical theoretical question:

Which one of the following statements is true?

   A.   An abstract class may not have any final methods.

   B.   A final class may not have any abstract methods.

Here is a typical code-related question:

Will the following code compile?

```
1. byte b = 100;
2. byte b1 = 101;
3. b = b * b1;
```

If you're intrigued, feel free to look up the answers in Appendix A. The first question is #3 from Chapter 3; the second question is #3 from Chapter 4.

Conventions Used in This Book

This book uses a number of conventions to present information in as readable a manner as possible. Tips, Notes, and Warnings, shown below, appear from time to time in the text in order to call attention to specific highlights.

TIP   This is a Tip. Tips contain specific programming information.

NOTE   This is a Note. Notes contain important side discussions.

WARNING   This is a Warning. Warnings call attention to bugs, design omissions, and other trouble spots.

This book takes advantage of several font styles. **Bold font** in text indicates something that the user types. A monospaced font is used for code, output, URLs, and file and directory names.

These style conventions are intended to facilitate your learning experience with this book—in other words, to increase your chances of passing the exam.

Let's begin.

CHAPTER

ONE

Language Fundamentals

- Source files

- Keywords and identifiers

- Primitive data types

- Literals

- Arrays

- Class fundamentals

- Parameter passing

- Garbage collection

In this chapter you will cover the following Java Certification Exam objectives:

- Use standard "javadoc" format documentation to identify and use variables and methods in classes. Employ such documentation to identify variables and methods that are inherited from a superclass.

- Distinguish legal and illegal orderings of package declarations, import statements, public class declarations, and non-public class declarations.

- State the correct declaration for a main() method.

- Select specific elements from the command line arguments of the main() method by using the correct array subscript value.

- Identify Java keywords from a list of keywords and non-keywords.

- Determine the value of a member variable of any type when no explicit assignment has been made to it.

- Determine the value of an element of an array of any base type, when the array has been constructed but no explicit assignment has been made to the element.

- Recognize source code that fails to insure definite initialization before use of method automatic variables and modify that code to correct the error.

- State the range of primitive data types byte, short, int, long, and char.

- Distinguish between legal and illegal identifiers.

- Construct literal numeric values using decimal, octal, and hexadecimal formats.

- Construct literal char values using quoted format.

- Construct literal String values using quoted format.

- Construct a literal value, of char type, using Java's Unicode escape format, for a specified character code.

- Declare variables of type array of X, for any type X. Identify the legal positions for the [] part of an array declaration.

- Construct arrays of any type.

- Write code to initialize an array using loop iteration.

- Write code to initialize an array using the combined declaration and initialization format.

This book is not an introduction to Java. Since you are preparing for certification, you are obviously already familiar with the fundamentals. The purpose of this chapter is to make sure you are 100 percent clear on those fundamentals covered by the Certification Exam objectives.

Source Files

All Java source files must end with the .java extension. A source file may contain at most one top-level public class definition; if a public class is present, the class name must match the unextended file name. For example, if a source file contains a public class called RayTraceApplet, then the file must be called RayTraceApplet.java. A source file may contain an unlimited number of non-public class definitions.

There are three "top-level" elements that may appear in a file. None of these elements is required. They must appear in the following order:

1. package declaration

2. import statements

3. class definitions

Whitespace and comments may appear before or after any of these elements. For example, a file called Test.java might look like this:

```
1. // Package declaration
2. package exam.prepguide;
3.
4. // Imports
5. import java.awt.*
6. import java.util.*;
7.
8. // Class definition
9. public class Test {...}
```

Keywords and Identifiers

The Java language specifies 49 keywords and other reserved words, which are listed in Table 1.1.

TABLE 1.1: Java keywords

abstract	class	extends	if	native	return	throws
boolean	const	false	implements	new	short	transient
break	continue	final	import	null	static	true
byte	default	finally	instanceof	package	super	try
case	do	float	int	private	synchronized	void
catch	double	for	interface	protected	this	volatile
char	else	goto	long	public	throw	while

The words `goto` and `const` are reserved words: Although they have no meaning in Java, programmers may not use them as identifiers.

An *identifier* is a word used by a programmer to name a variable, method, class, or label. Keywords and reserved words may not be used as identifiers. An identifier must begin with a letter, a dollar sign ($), or an underscore (_); subsequent characters may be letters, dollar signs, underscores, or digits. Some examples are

```
1. foobar                 // legal
2. BIGinterface           // legal: embedded keywords are OK.
3. $incomeAfterExpenses   // legal
4. 3_node5                // illegal: starts with a digit
5. !theCase               // illegal: must start with letter, $ or _
```

Identifiers are case-sensitive. For example, `radius` and `Radius` are two distinct identifiers.

Primitive Data Types

Java's primitive data types are

- boolean
- char
- byte
- short
- int
- long
- float
- double

The sizes of these types are defined in the Java language specification and are listed in Table 1.2.

TABLE 1.2: Primitive data types and their sizes

Type	Size (bits)	Type	Sixe (bits)
boolean	8	char	16
byte	8	short	16
int	32	long	64
float	32	double	64

Variables of type boolean may only take the values true and false.

The four signed integral data types are

- byte
- short
- int
- long

Variables of these types are two's-complement numbers. Their ranges are given in Table 1.3. Notice that for each type, the exponent of 2 in the minimum and maximum is one less than the size of the type.

TABLE 1.3: Ranges of the integral primitive types

Type	Size	Minimum	Maximum
byte	8 bits	-2^7	2^7-1
short	16 bits	-2^{15}	$2^{15}-1$
int	32 bits	-2^{31}	$2^{31}-1$
long	64 bits	-2^{63}	$2^{63}-1$

The char type is integral but unsigned. The range of a variable of type char is from 0 through $2^{16}-1$. Java characters are in Unicode, which is a 16-bit encoding. If the most significant nine bits of a char are all 0, then the encoding is the same as seven-bit ASCII.

The two floating-point types are

- float
- double

These types conform to the IEEE 754 specification. Many mathematical operations can yield results that have no expression in numbers (infinity, for example). To describe such non-numerical situations, both doubles and floats can take on values that are bit patterns which do not represent numbers. Rather, these patterns represent non-numerical values. The patterns are defined in the Float and Double classes, and may be referenced as

- Float.NaN
- Float.NEGATIVE_INFINITY
- Float.POSITIVE_INFINITY
- Double.NaN
- Double.NEGATIVE_INFINITY
- Double.POSITIVE_INFINITY

(*NaN* stands for *Not a Number*.)

The code fragment below shows the use of these constants:

```
1. double d = -10.0 / 0.0;
2.   if (d == Double.NEGATIVE_INFINITY) {
3.     System.out.println("d just exploded: " + d);
4.   }
```

In this code fragment, the test on line 2 passes, so line 3 is executed.

NOTE   All the numerical primitive types (that is, all except boolean and char) are signed.

Literals

A *literal* is a value that may be assigned to a primitive or string variable or passed as an argument to a method call.

boolean Literals

The only valid literals of boolean type are true and false. For example

```
1. boolean isBig = true;
2. boolean isLittle = false;
```

char Literals

A char literal can be expressed by enclosing the desired character in single quotes, as shown here:

```
char c = 'w';
```

Of course, this technique only works if the desired character is available on the keyboard at hand. Another way to express a character literal is as four Unicode hexadecimal digits, preceded by \u, with the entire expression in quotes. For example

```
char c1 = '\u4567';
```

Java supports a few escape sequences for denoting special characters:

- '\n' for Newline
- '\r' for Return
- '\t' for Tab
- '\b' for Backspace
- '\f' for Formfeed
- '\'' for Single Quote
- '\"' for Double Quote
- '\?' for Question Mark

Integral Literals

Integral literals may be expressed in decimal, octal, or hexadecimal. The default is decimal. To indicate octal, prefix the literal with 0 (zero). To indicate hexadecimal, prefix the literal with 0x or 0X; the hex digits may be upper or lower case. The value *twenty-eight* may thus be expressed six ways:

- 28
- 034
- 0x1c
- 0x1C
- 0X1c
- 0X1C

By default, an integral literal is a 32-bit value. To indicate a long (64-bit) literal, append the suffix L to the literal expression. (The suffix can be lower case, but then it looks so much like a 1 that your readers are bound to be confused.)

Floating-Point Literals

A *floating-point literal* expresses a floating-point numerical value. In order to be interpreted as a floating-point literal, a numerical expression must contain one of the following:

- A decimal point: 1.414

- The letter E or e, indicating scientific notation: 4.23E+21

- The suffix F or f, indicating a 32-bit float literal: 1.828f

- The suffix D or d, indicating a 64-bit double literal: 1234d

A floating-point literal with no F or D suffix defaults to a 64-bit double literal.

String Literals

A *string literal* is a run of text enclosed in double quotes. For example

```
String s = "Each character in this string is a 16-bit Unicode value.";
```

Java provides many advanced facilities for specifying non-literal string values, including a concatenation operator and some sophisticated constructors for the String class. These facilities are discussed in detail in Chapter 8, *The java.lang Package*.

Arrays

A Java *array* is an ordered collection of primitives, object references, or other arrays. Java arrays are homogeneous: All elements of an array must be of the same type.

To create and use an array, you must follow three steps:

1. Declaration

2. Construction

3. Initialization

Declaration tells the compiler what the array's name is, and what the type of its elements will be. For example

```
1. int ints[];
2. double dubs[];
3. Dimension dims[];
4. float twoDee[][];
```

Lines 1 and 2 declare arrays of primitive types. Line 3 declares an array of object references (Dimension is a class in the java.awt package). Line 4 declares a two-dimensional array: that is, an array of arrays of floats.

The square brackets can come before or after the array name. This is also true in method declarations. A method that takes an array of doubles could be declared as `myMethod(double dubs[])` or as `myMethod(double[] dubs)`.

Notice that the declaration does *not* specify the size of an array. Size is specified at run time, when the array is allocated via the new keyword. For example

```
1. int ints[];           // Declaration to the compiler
2. ints = new int[25];   // Run time construction
```

Since array size is not used until run time, it is legal to specify size with a variable rather than a literal:

```
1. int size = 1152 * 900;
2. int raster[];
3. raster = new int[size];
```

Declaration and construction may be performed in a single line:

```
1. int ints[] = new int[25];
```

When an array is constructed, its elements are automatically initialized. Numerical elements are initialized to zero; non-numerical elements are initialized to values similar to zero, as shown in Table 1.4.

TABLE 1.4: Array element initialization values

Element Type	Initial Value	Element Type	Initial Value
byte	0	short	0
int	0	long	0L
float	0.0f	double	0.0d
char	'\u0000'	boolean	false
object reference	null		

If you want to initialize an array to values other than those shown in Table 1.4, you can combine declaration, construction, and initialization into a single step. The line of code below creates a custom-initialized array of five floats:

```
1.    float diameters[] = {1.1f, 2.2f, 3.3f, 4.4f, 5.5f};
```

The array size is implicit from the number of elements within the curly braces.

Of course, an array can also be initialized by explicitly assigning a value to each element:

```
1. long squares[];
2. squares = new long[6000];
3. for (int i=0; i<6000; i++)
4.    squares[i] = i * i;
```

When the array is created at line 2, it is full of default values (0L); the defaults are immediately replaced. The code in the example works, but can be improved. If the array size changes (in line 2), the loop counter will have to change (in line 3), and the program could be damaged if line 3 is not taken care of. The safest way to refer to the size of an array is to apply .length to the array name. Thus our example becomes

```
1. long squares[];
2. squares = new long[6000];
3. for (int i=0; i<squares.length; i++)
4.    squares[i] = i * i;
```

NOTE   Java's array indexes always start at 0.

Class Fundamentals

Java is all about classes, and a review of the Certification objectives will show that you need to be intimately familiar with them. Classes are discussed in detail in Chapter 6; for now there are a few fundamentals to examine.

The *main()* method

The main() method is the entry point for Java applications. To create an application, you write a class definition that includes a main() method. To execute an application, you type **java** at the command line, followed by the name of the class whose main() method is to executed.

The signature for main() is

```
public static void main(String args[ ])
```

The `main()` method must be declared public so that the Java Virtual Machine has access to it. It must be static so that it may be executed without the necessity of constructing an instance of the corresponding class.

The `args` array contains any arguments that the user might have entered on the command line. For example, consider the following command line:

```
% java Mapper France Belgium
```

With this command line, the `args[]` array has two elements: `"France"` in `args[0]`, and `"Belgium"` in `args[1]`. Note that neither the class name (`"Mapper"`) nor the command name (`"java"`) appears in the array. Of course, the name `args` is purely arbitrary: Any legal identifier may be used.

Variables and Initialization

Java supports variables of two different scopes:

- A *member variable* of a class is accessible from anywhere within the class.

- An *automatic variable* of a method is only accessible within the method.

All member variables that are not explicitly assigned a value upon declaration are automatically assigned an initial value. The value depends on the member variable's type. Values are listed in Table 1.5.

TABLE 1.5: Initialization values for member variables

Element Type	Initial Value	Element Type	Initial Value
byte	0	short	0
int	0	long	0L
float	0.0f	double	0.0d
char	'\u0000'	boolean	false
object reference	null		

The values in Table 1.5 are the same as those in Table 1.4; member variable initialization values are the same as array element initialization values.

A member value may be initialized in its own declaration line:

```
1. class HasVariables {
2.    int x = 20;
3.    static int y = 30;
```

When this technique is used, non-static instance variables are initialized just before the class constructor is executed; here x would be set to 20 just before invocation of any HasVariables constructor. Static variables are initialized at class load time; here y would be set to 30 when the HasVariables class is loaded.

Automatic variables (also known as *local variables*) are not initialized by the system; every automatic variable must be explicitly initialized before being used. For example, this method will not compile:

```
1. public int wrong() {
2.    int i;
3.    return i+5;
4. }
```

The compiler error at line 3 is, "Variable i may not have been initialized." This error often appears when initialization of an automatic variable occurs at a lower level of curly braces than the use of that variable. For example, the method below returns the fourth root of a positive number:

```
1. public double fourthRoot(double d) {
2.    double result;
3.    if (d >= 0) {
4.        result = Math.sqrt(Math.sqrt(d));
5.    }
6.    return result;
7. }
```

Here the result is initialized on line 4, but the initialization takes place within the curly braces of lines 3 and 5. The compiler will flag line 6, complaining that "Variable result may not have been initialized." The solution is to initialize result to some reasonable default as soon as it is declared:

```
1. public double fourthRoot(double d) {
2.    double result = 0.0;   // Initialize
3.    if (d >= 0) {
4.        result = Math.sqrt(Math.sqrt(d));
5.    }
6.    return result;
7. }
```

Now `result` is satisfactorily initialized. Line 2 demonstrates that an automatic variable may be initialized in its declaration line. Initialization on a separate line is also possible.

javadoc Documentation

The `javadoc` utility creates HTML pages based on source code. The API pages for the standard JDK were all generated by `javadoc`. Since the API pages are practically the only official Sun documentation on how to use the JDK classes, the ability to navigate `javadoc` pages is essential to the success of any Java programmer.

Figure 1.1 shows the top of the page that documents the `Float` class.

At the top of the page are links to various top-level reference pages, including the list of all packages and the comprehensive index. This invariant list of links appears at the top and the bottom of every class page.

FIGURE 1.1:

Float class API: top of the page

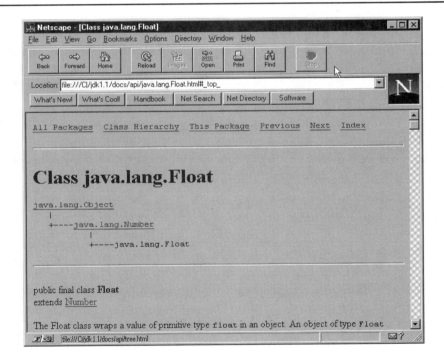

Below the links is the name of the class in a large font. Below the class name is the class hierarchy. The elements of the hierarchy are links, so it is easy to navigate to the superclasses of the current class. This is especially handy when you are certain that a class contains a particular method, but you cannot find the method on the class' page. The reason, of course, is that the method is inherited, and you have to navigate up the class' inheritance hierarchy until you come to the superclass that provides the method. For example, to retrieve the contents of a text field, you need to call getText(). However, getText() is not documented on the TextField API page. To read about what getText() does, you need to navigate to the page for TextComponent, which is the superclass of TextField.

Below the class hierarchy comes the full class signature, followed (optionally) by a text description of the class. This text can be absent, terse, or quite lengthy; some APIs contain extensive sample code.

Below the description are up to three indexes, for the class' non-private data fields, constructors, and methods. The indexes are alphabetical and contain brief descriptions. Figure 1.2 shows the Constructor Index and part of the Method Index for the Float class API.

FIGURE 1.2:

Float class API: indexes

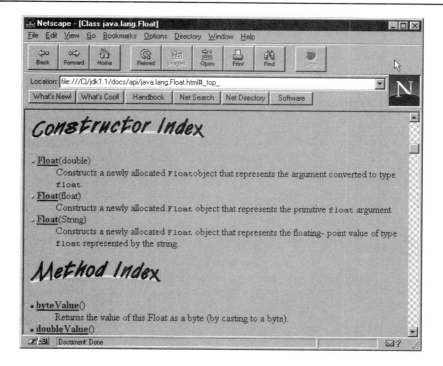

The index entries contain links to full descriptions, which appear farther down on the same page. Figure 1.3 shows a small portion of the Method descriptions for the Float class API.

FIGURE 1.3:

Float class API: method descriptions

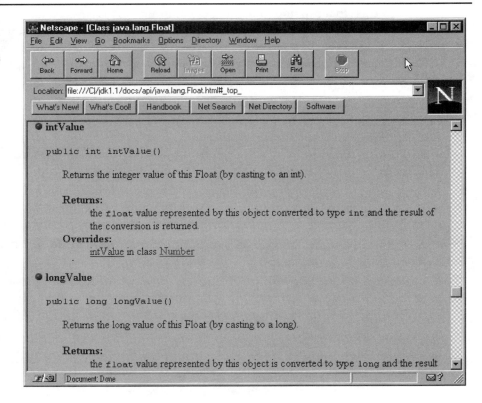

Argument Passing

When Java passes an argument into a method call, it is actually a *copy* of the argument that gets passed. Consider the following code fragment:

```
1. double radians = 1.2345;
2. System.out.println("Sine of " + radians + " = " + Math.sin(radians));
```

The variable radians contains a pattern of 64 0s and 1s that represent the number 1.2345. On line 2, a copy of this bit pattern is passed into the Java Virtual Machine's method-calling apparatus.

When data is passed into a method, the method may modify its copy of the data to its heart's content; the original data is untouched. Consider the following method:

```
1. public void bumper(int bumpMe) {
2.    bumpMe += 15;
3. }
```

Line 2 modifies a copy of the parameter passed by the caller. For example

```
1. int xx = 12345;
2. bumper(xx);
3. System.out.println("Now xx is " + xx);
```

On line 2, the caller's xx variable is copied; the copy is passed into the bumper() method and incremented by 15. Since the original xx is untouched, line 3 will report that xx is still 12345.

The situation is similar when the argument to be passed is an object rather than a primitive. In order to really understand the process, you have to understand the concept of the *object reference*.

Java programs never deal directly with objects. When an object is constructed, the constructor returns a value—a bit pattern—that uniquely identifies the object. This value is known as a reference to the object. For example, consider the following code:

```
1. Button btn;
2. btn = new Button("Ok");
```

In line 2, the Button constructor returns a reference to the just-constructed button; this reference is stored in the variable btn. In many implementations of the JVM, a reference is simply the 32-bit address of the object; however, the JVM specification gives wide latitude as to how references are to be implemented. You can think of a reference as simply a pattern of bits that uniquely indicates an object. When Java code appears to store objects in variables or pass objects into method calls, it is really object *references* that get stored or passed.

Consider this code fragment:

```
1. Button btn;
2. btn = new Button("Good");
3. replacer(btn);
4. System.out.println(btn.getLabel());
5.
6. public void replacer(Button replaceMe) {
7.    replaceMe = new Button("Evil");
8. }
```

Line 2 constructs a button and stores a reference to that button in `btn`. In line 3, a copy of the reference is passed into the `replacer()` method. Before execution of line 7, the value in `replaceMe` is a reference to the "Good" button. Then line 7 constructs a second button and stores a reference to the second button in `replaceMe`, thus overwriting the reference to the "Good" button. However, the caller's copy of the reference is not affected, so on line 4 the call to `btn.getLabel()` calls the original button; the string printed out is `"Good"`.

When a copy of an object reference is passed to a method, the caller and the method each have their own copy of a reference to the same object. If the method modifies the object (as opposed to the reference), then the changes will be visible to the caller. For example

```
1. TextField tf;
2. tf = new TextField("Yin");
3. changer(tf);
4. System.out.println(tf.getLabel());
5.
6. public void changer(TextField changeMe) {
7.    changeMe.setText("Yang");
8. }
```

In this example there is a single-text field. The caller refers to it as `tf`; the `changer()` method refers to it as `changeMe`. The text field originally contains the string `"Yin"`; the call to `changer()` changes the contents to `"Yang"`. Thus line 4 prints out `"Yang"`, not `"Yin"`.

Arrays are like objects in the sense that programs deal with references to arrays, not with arrays themselves. What gets passed into a method is a copy of a reference to an array.

Garbage Collection

Most modern languages permit you to allocate data storage. In Java this is done when you create an object with the new operation. The point of this type of storage allocation is that the storage can remain allocated longer than the lifetime of any one method call. This increased lifetime raises the question of when the storage can be released. Some languages require that you, the programmer, explicitly release the storage when you have finished with it. This approach is quite error-prone, since you might easily release the storage too soon (causing corrupted data), or forget to release it altogether (causing a memory shortage).

In Java, you never free memory that you have allocated; Java provides automatic garbage collection. The runtime system keeps track of the memory that is allocated and is able to determine whether or not that memory is still in use. This work is usually done in the background by a low-priority thread that is referred to as the *garbage collector*. When the garbage collector finds memory that is definitely no longer in use, it takes steps to release it back into the heap for re-use.

Garbage collection can be done in a number of different ways; each has advantages and disadvantages, depending upon the type of program that is running. A real-time control system, for example, needs to know that nothing will prevent it from responding quickly to interrupts; this requires a garbage collector that can work in small chunks or that can be interrupted easily. On the other hand, a memory-intensive program might work better with a garbage collector that stops the program from time to time but recovers memory more urgently as a result. At present, garbage collection is hardwired into the Java runtime system; most garbage collection algorithms use an approach that gives a reasonable compromise between speed of memory recovery and responsiveness. In the future, you will probably be able to plug in different garbage collection algorithms according to your particular needs.

This all leaves the one crucial question unanswered: When is storage recovered? The best you can answer at present is that storage is not recovered unless it is unused. That's it. Even though you are not using an object any longer, you cannot say if it will be collected in 1 millisecond, in 100 milliseconds—or even if it will be collected at all. There are methods, System.gc() and Runtime.gc(), that look as if they "run the garbage collector." Even these cannot be relied upon in general, since some other thread might prevent the garbage collection thread from running. In fact, the documentation for the `gc()` methods states:

"Calling this method *suggests* that the Java Virtual Machine expend effort toward recycling unused objects" (this author's italics).

Chapter Summary

A source file's elements must appear in this order:

1. `package` declaration
2. Then `import` statements
3. Then class definitions

There may be at most one public class definition per source file; the file name must match the name of the public class.

An identifier must begin with a letter, a dollar sign, or an underscore; subsequent characters may be letters, dollar signs, underscores, or digits.

Java's four signed integral primitive data types are `byte`, `short`, `int`, and `long`; all four types use two's-complement notation. The two floating-point primitive data types are `float` and `double`. The `char` type is unsigned and represents Unicode characters. The `boolean` type may only take on the values `true` and `false`.

Arrays must be

1. Declared
2. Then allocated
3. Then initialized

The default initialization values are zero for numerical types, the null character for `char`, and `false` for `boolean`. Applying `.length` to an array returns the number of elements in the array.

A class with a `main()` method can be invoked from the command line as a Java application. The signature for `main()` is `public static void main(String args[])`. The `args[]` array contains all command-line arguments that appeared after the name of the application class.

Method arguments are copies, not originals. For arguments of primitive data type, this means that modifications to an argument within a method are not visible to the caller of the method. For arguments of object or array reference type, modifications to an argument within a method are still not visible to the caller of the method; however, modifications to the object or array referenced by the argument are permanent.

Java's garbage collection mechanism recovers unused memory. It is not possible to force garbage collection reliably. It is not possible to predict when a piece of unused memory will be collected.

Test Yourself

1. True or False: A signed data type has an equal number of non-zero positive and negative values available.

2. Choose the valid identifiers from those listed below.

   A. `BigOlLongStringWithMeaninglessName`

   B. `$int`

   C. `bytes`

   D. `$1`

   E. `finalist`

3. Which of the following signatures are valid for the `main()` method entry point of an application?

   A. `public static void main()`

   B. `public static void main(String arg[])`

   C. `static void main(String [] arg)`

   D. `public static void main(String[] args)`

   E. `static void main(String [] arg)`

4. If all three "top-level" elements occur in a source file, they must appear in which order?

    A. Imports, package declaration, classes

    B. Classes, imports, package declarations

    C. Package declaration must come first; order for imports and class definitions is not significant.

    D. Package declaration, imports, classes

    E. Imports must come first; order for package declaration and class definitions is not significant.

5. Consider the following line of code:

    ```
    int x[] = new int[25];
    ```

    After execution, which statement or statements are true?

    A. x[24] is 0.

    B. x[24] is undefined.

    C. x[25] is 0.

    D. x[0] is null.

    E. x.length is 25.

6. Consider the following application:

    ```
    1. class Q6 {
    2.   public static void main(String args[]) {
    3.     Holder h = new Holder();
    4.     h.held = 100;
    5.     h.bump(h);
    6.     System.out.println(h.held);
    7.   }
    8. }
    9.
    10. class Holder {
    11.   public int held;
    12.   public void bump(Holder theHolder) { theHolder.held++; }
    13. }
    ```

What value is printed out at line 6?

A. 0

B. 1

C. 100

D. 101

7. Consider the following application:

```
1. class Q7 {
2.   public static void main(String args[]) {
3.     double d = 12.3;
4.     Decrementer dec = new Decrementer();
5.     dec.decrement(d);
6.     System.out.println(d);
7.   }
8. }
9.
10. class Decrementer {
11.   public void decrement(double decMe) { decMe = decMe - 1.0; }
12. }
```

What value is printed out at line 6?

A. 0.0

B. −1.0

C. 12.3

D. 11.3

8. How can you force garbage collection of an object?

A. Garbage collection cannot be forced.

B. Call System.gc().

C. Call System.gc(), passing in a reference to the object to be garbage-collected.

D. Call Runtime.gc().

E. Set all references to the object to new values (null, for example).

9. What is the range of values that can be assigned to a variable of type short?

   A. It depends on the underlying hardware.

   B. 0 through $2^{16}-1$

   C. 0 through $2^{32}-1$

   D. 2^{15} through $2^{15}-1$

   E. 2^{31} through $2^{31}-1$

10. What is the range of values that can be assigned to a variable of type byte?

   A. It depends on the underlying hardware.

   B. 0 through $2^{8}-1$

   C. 0 through $2^{16}-1$

   D. 2^{7} through $2^{7}-1$

   E. 2^{15} through $2^{15}-1$

CHAPTER

TWO

Operators and Assignments

- Shifting

- String concatenation

- Comparison

- Short-circuit operators

- Ternary operator

In this chapter, you will cover the following Java Certification Exam objectives:

- Determine the result, in terms of a bit pattern, of applying the >>, >>>, and << operators to an int value specified as a bit pattern.

- Determine the result of the + operator applied to a combination of variables or constants of any type.

- Determine the result of applying the == comparison operator to any two objects of any type.

- Determine at run time if an object is an instance of a specified class or some subclass of that class using the instanceof operator.

- Determine the result of applying the equals() method to any combination of objects of the classes java.lang.String, java.lang.Boolean, and java.lang.Object.

- In an expression involving the operators &, |, &&, and ||, state which operands are evaluated and determine the resulting value of the expression.

- Determine the effect of assignment and modification operations upon variables of any type.

Java provides a fully featured set of operators, most of which are taken fairly directly from C or C++. However, Java's operators differ in some important aspects from their counterparts in these other languages, and you need to understand clearly how Java's operators behave. This chapter describes all the operators: Some are described briefly, while others receive significantly more attention. Operators that sometimes cause confusion are described in detail. You will also learn about the behavior of expressions under conditions of arithmetic overflow.

Java's operators are shown in Table 2.1. They are listed in precedence order, with the highest precedence at the top of the table. Each group has been given a name for reference purposes. That name is shown in the left column of the table.

TABLE 2.1: Operators in Java

Unary	++ -- + - ! ~ ()
Arithmetic	* / % + -
Shift	<< >> >>>
Comparison	< <= > >= instanceof == !=
Bitwise	& ^ |
Short-circuit	&& ||
Ternary	?:
Assignment	= "op="

The rest of this chapter examines each of these operators, but before we start let's consider the general issue of evaluation order.

In Java, unlike many other languages, the apparent order of evaluation of operands in an expression is fixed. Specifically, all operands are evaluated left to right, even if the order of execution of the operations is something different. This is most noticeable in the case of assignments. Consider this code fragment:

```
1. int [] a = new int[2];
2. int b = 1;
3. a[b] = b = 0;
```

In this case, it might be unclear which element of the array is modified: What is the value of b used to select the array element, 0 or 1? An evaluation from left to right requires that the leftmost expression, a[b] is evaluated first, so it is a reference to the element a[1]. Next b is evaluated, which is simply a reference to the variable called b. The constant expression 0 is evaluated next, which clearly does not involve any work. Now that the operands have been evaluated, the operations take place. This is done in the order specified by precedence and associativity. So, the value 0 is assigned to the variable called b, and then the value 0 is assigned into the last element of the array a.

The following sections examine each of these operators in turn.

Although Table 2.1 shows the precedence order, the degree of detail in this precedence ordering is rather high. It is generally better style to keep expressions simple, and to use redundant bracketing to make it clear how any particular expression should be evaluated. This approach reduces the chance that less experienced programmers will find it difficult trying to read or maintain your code. Bear in mind that the code generated by the compiler will be the same despite redundant brackets.

The Unary Operators

The first group of operators in Table 2.1 consists of the *unary operators*. Most operators take two operands. When you multiply, for example, you work with two numbers. Unary operators, on the other hand, take only a single operand and work just on that. Java provides seven unary operators:

- The increment and decrement operators: ++ --
- The unary plus and minus operators: +   –
- The bitwise inversion operator: ~
- The boolean complement operator: !
- The cast: ()

Strictly, the cast is not an operator. However, we discuss it as if it were for simplicity, because it fits well with the rest of our discussion.

These operators are discussed in the following sections.

The Increment and Decrement Operators ++ and –

These operators modify the value of an expression by adding or subtracting 1. So, for example, if an int variable x, which is a trivial expression, contains 10, then ++x results in 11. Similarly --x, again applied when x contains 10, gives a value of 9. Since, in this case, the expression --x itself describes storage (the value of the variable x) the resulting value is stored in x.

The preceding examples show the operators positioned before the expression. They can, however, be placed after the expression instead. To understand how the position of these operators affects their operation, you must appreciate the difference between the value stored by these operators and the result value they give. Both x++ and ++x cause the same result in x. However, the apparent value of the expression itself is different. For example, you could say y = x++; then the value assigned to y is the original value of x. If you say y = ++x; then the value assigned to y is 1 more than the original value of x. In both cases, the value of x is incremented by 1.

Let us look more closely at how the position of the increment and decrement operators affects their behavior. If one of these operators is to the left of an expression, then the value of the expression is modified *before* it takes part in the rest of the calculation. This is called pre-increment or pre-decrement, according to which operator is used. Conversely, if the operator is positioned to the right of an expression, then the value that is used in the rest of the calculation is the *original* value of that expression, and the increment or decrement only occurs after the expression has been calculated.

Table 2.2 shows the values of x and y, before and after particular assignments, using these operators.

TABLE 2.2 Examples of pre-modify and post-modify with the increment and decrement operators

Initial value of x	Expression	Final value of y	Final value of x
5	y = x++	5	6
5	y = ++x	6	6
5	y = x--	5	4
5	y = --x	4	4

The Unary + and – Operators

The unary + and – operators are distinct from the more common binary + and – operators, which are usually just referred to as + and – (*add* and *subtract*). Both the programmer and the compiler are able to determine which meaning these symbols should have in a given context.

Unary + has no effect beyond emphasizing the positive nature of a numeric literal. Unary − negates an expression. So, you might make a block of assignments like this:

```
1.  x = -3;
2.  y = +3;
3.  z = -(y + 6);
```

In such an example, the only reasons for using the unary + operator are to make it explicit that y is assigned a positive value, and perhaps to keep the code aligned more pleasingly. At line 3, notice that these operators are not restricted to literal values but can be applied to expressions equally well, so the value of z is initialized to −9.

The Bitwise Inversion Operator: ~

The ~ operator performs *bitwise inversion* on integral types.

For each primitive type, Java uses a virtual machine representation that is platform-independent. This means that the bit pattern used to represent a particular value in a particular variable type is always the same. This feature makes bit manipulation operators even more useful, since they do not introduce platform dependencies. The ~ operator works by converting all the 1 bits in a binary value to 0s and all the 0 bits to 1s.

For example, applying this operator to a byte containing 00001111 would result in the value 11110000. The same simple logic applies, no matter how many bits there are in the value being operated on.

The *Boolean* Complement Operator: *!*

The ! operator inverts the value of a boolean expression. So !true gives false and !false gives true.

This operator is often used in the test part of an if() statement. The effect is to change the value of the affected expression. In this way, for example, the body of the if() and else parts can be swapped. Consider these two equivalent code fragments:

```
1.  public Object myMethod(Object x) {
2.    if (x instanceof String) {
3.      // do nothing
```

```
4.   }
5.   else {
6.      x = x.toString();
7.   }
8.   return x;
9. }
```

and

```
1. public Object myMethod(Object x) {
2.   if (!(x instanceof String)) {
3.      x = x.toString();
4.   }
5.   return x;
6. }
```

In the first fragment a test is made at line 2, but the conversion and assignment only occurs, at line 6, if the test failed. This is achieved by the somewhat cumbersome technique of using only the else part of an if/else construction. The second fragment uses the complement operator, so that the overall test performed at line 2 is reversed—it may be read as, "If it is false that x is an instance of a string" or more likely, "If x is not a string". Because of this change to the test, the conversion can be performed at line 3 in the situation that the test has succeeded; no else part is required, and the resulting code is cleaner and shorter.

This is a simple example, but such usage is common, and this level of understanding will leave you well armed for the Certification Exam.

The Cast Operator: *(type)*

Casting is used for explicit conversion of the type of an expression. This is only possible for plausible target types. The compiler and the runtime system check for conformance with typing rules which are described below.

Casts can be applied to change the type of primitive values, for example forcing a double value into an int variable like this:

```
int circum = (int)(Math.PI * diameter);
```

If the cast, which is represented by the (int) part, were not present, the compiler would reject the assignment. This is because a double value, such as is returned by the arithmetic here, cannot be represented accurately by an int variable. The cast is the programmer's way to say to the compiler, "I know this is risky, but trust me—I'm a programmer." Of course, if the result loses value or precision to the extent that the program does not work properly, then you are on your own.

Casts can also be applied to object references. This often happens when you use containers, such as the Vector object. If you put, for example, String objects into a Vector, then when you extract them, the return type of the elementAt() method is simply Object. To use the recovered value as a String reference, a cast is needed, like this:

```
1. Vector v = new Vector();
2. v.addElement("Hello");
3. String s = (String)v.elementAt(0);
```

The cast here occurs at line 3, in the form (String). Although the compiler allows this cast, checks occur at run time to determine if the object extracted from the Vector really is a String. Casting, the rules governing which casts are legal and which are not, and the nature of the runtime checks that are performed, are covered in Chapter 4, *Converting and Casting*.

Now that we have considered the unary operators, which have the highest precedence, we will discuss the five arithmetic operators.

The Arithmetic Operators

Next highest in precedence, after the unary operators, are the *arithmetic operators*. This group includes, but is not limited to, the four most familiar operators, which perform addition, subtraction, multiplication and division. Arithmetic operators are split into two further subgroupings, as shown in Table 2.1. In the first group, you will see *, /, and %. In the second group, at lower precedence, are + and −. The following sections discuss these operators and also what happens when arithmetic goes wrong.

The Multiplication and Division Operators: * and /

The operators * and / perform multiplication and division on all primitive numeric types and char. Integer division can generate an ArithmeticException from a division by zero.

You probably understand multiplication and division quite well from years of rote learning at school. In programming there are, of course, some limitations imposed by the representation of numbers in a computer. These limitations apply to all number formats, from `byte` to `double`, but are most noticeable in integer arithmetic.

If you multiply or divide two integers, the result will be calculated using integer arithmetic in either `int` or `long` representation. If the numbers are large enough, the result will be bigger than the maximum number that can be represented, and the final value will be meaningless. For example, `byte` values can represent a range of −128 to +127, so if two particular bytes have the values 64 and 4 respectively, then multiplying them should, arithmetically, give a value of 256. Actually, when you store the result in a `byte` variable you will get a value of 0, since only the low-order eight bits of the result can be represented.

On the other hand, when you divide with integer arithmetic, the result is forced into an integer, and typically, a lot of information that would have formed a fractional part of the answer is lost. For example, 7 / 4 should give 1.75, but integer arithmetic will result in a value of 1. You therefore have a choice in many expressions: Multiply first then divide, which risks overflow, or divide first then multiply, which almost definitely loses precision. Conventional wisdom says that you should multiply first then divide, because this at least might work perfectly, whereas dividing first almost definitely loses precision. Consider this example:

```
1.  int a = 12345, b = 234567, c, d;
2.  long e, f;
3.
4.  c = a * b / b;
5.  d = a / b * b;
6.  System.out.println("a is " + a +
7.    "\nb is " + b +
8.    "\nc is " + c +
9.    "\nd is " + d);
10.
11. e = (long)a * b / b;
12. f = (long)a / b * b;
13. System.out.println(
14.   "\ne is " + e +
15.   "\nf is " + f);
```

This output from this code is

```
a is 12345
b is 234567
c is -5965
d is 0

e is 12345
f is 0
```

Do not worry about the exact numbers in this example. The important feature is that in the case where multiplication is performed first, the calculation overflows when performed with int values, resulting in a nonsense answer. However, the result is correct if the representation is wide enough—as when using the long variables. In both cases, dividing first has a catastrophic effect on the result, regardless of the width of the representation.

Although multiplication and division are generally familiar operations, the modulo operator is perhaps less well known. The next section discusses this operator.

The Modulo Operator: %

The modulo operator gives a value which is related to the remainder of a division. It is generally applied to two integers, although it can be applied to floating point numbers, too. So, in school, we would learn that 7 divided by 4 gives 1 remainder 3. In Java, we say x = 7 % 4;, and expect that x will have the value 3.

The previous paragraph describes the essential behavior of the modulo operator, but additional concerns appear if you use negative or floating point operands. In such cases, follow this procedure: Reduce the *magnitude* of the left-hand operand by the *magnitude* of the right-hand one. Repeat this until the magnitude of the result is less than the magnitude of the right-hand operand. This result is the result of the modulo operator. Figure 2.1 shows some examples of this process.

FIGURE 2.1:

Calculating the result of the modulo operator for a variety of conditions

17 % 5

$17 - 5 \to 12$
$12 - 5 \to \ 7$
$7 - 5 \to \ 2$

$2 < 5$ so $17 \% 5 = \underline{2}$

21 % 7

$21 - 7 = 14$
$14 - 7 = \ 7$
$7 - 7 = \ 0$

$0 < 7$ so $21 \% 7 = \underline{0}$

7.6 % 2.9

$7.6 - 2.9 = 4.7$
$4.7 - 2.9 = 1.8$

$1.8 < 2.9$ so $7.6 \% 2.9 = \underline{1.8}$

–5 % 2

Here, to reduce absolute value by 2, we must <u>add</u>

$-5 + 2 = -3$
$-3 + 2 = -1$

Absolute value of –1 is 1 and 1 < 2

so $-5 \% 2 = \underline{-1}$

–5 % –2

Again, we must reduce absolute value of –5 by the absolute value of –2 which is 2

$-5 - (-2) = -3$
$-3 - (-2) = -1$

so again, $-5 \% -2 = \underline{-1}$

Note that the sign of the result is entirely determined by the sign of the left-hand operand. When the modulo operator is applied to floating point types, the effect is to perform an integral number of subtractions, leaving a floating point result that might well have a fractional part.

A useful rule of thumb for dealing with modulo calculations that involve negative numbers is this: Simply drop any negative signs from either operand and calculate the result. Then, if the original left-hand operand was negative, negate the result. The sign of the right-hand operand is irrelevant.

The modulo operation involves division during execution. Because of this, it can throw an `ArithmeticException` if applied to integral types and the second operand is zero.

Although you might not have learned about the modulo operator in school, you will certainly recognize the + and – operators. Although basically familiar, the + operator has some capabilities beyond simple addition.

The Addition and Subtraction Operators: + and –

The operators + and – perform addition and subtraction. They apply to operands of any numeric type but, uniquely, + is also permitted where either operand is a `String` object. In that case, the other operand is used to create a `String` object, whatever its original type. Creating a `String` object in this way is always possible, but the resulting text might be somewhat cryptic and perhaps only useful for debugging.

The + Operator in Detail

Java does not allow the programmer to perform operator overloading, but the + operator is overloaded by the language. This is not surprising, because in most languages that support multiple arithmetic types the arithmetic operators (+, −, *, / and so forth) are overloaded to handle these different types. Java, however, also overloads the + operator to support clear and concise *concatenation*—that is joining together—of String objects. The use of + with String arguments also performs conversions, and these can be succinct and expressive if you understand them. First we will consider the use of the + operator in its conventional role of numeric addition.

NOTE

Overloading is the term given when the same name is used for more than one piece of code, and the code that is to be used is selected by the argument or operand types provided. For example the println() method can be given a String argument, or an int. These two uses actually refer to entirely different methods; only the name is re-used. Similarly, the + symbol is used to indicate addition of int values, but the exact same symbol is also used to indicate the addition of float values. These two forms of addition require entirely different code to execute; again, the operand types are used to decide which code is to be run. Where an operator can take different operand types, we refer to *operator overloading*. Some languages, but not Java, allow the programmer to use operator overloading to define multiple uses of operators for their own types. Overloading is described in detail in Chapter 6, *Objects and Classes*.

Where the + operator is applied to purely numeric operands, its meaning is simple and familiar. The operands are added together to produce a result. Of course some promotions might take place, according to the normal rules, and the result might overflow. Generally, however, numerical addition behaves as you would expect.

If overflow or underflow occurs during numeric addition or subtraction, then meaning is lost but no exception occurs. A more detailed description of behavior in arithmetic error conditions appears in the next section, *Arithmetic Error Conditions*. Most of the new understanding to be gained about the + operator relates to its role in concatenating text.

Where either of the operands of a + expression is a `String` object, the meaning of the operator is changed from numeric addition to concatenation of text. In order to achieve this, both operands must be handled as text. If both operands are in fact `String` objects, this is simple. If, however, one of the operands is not a `String` object, then the non-string operand is converted to a `String` object before the concatenation takes place.

How Operands Are Converted to String Objects

Although a review of the Certification objectives will show that the Certification Exam does not require it, it is useful in practice to know a little about how + converts operands to `String` objects. For object types conversion to a `String` object is performed simply by invoking the `toString()` method of that object. The `toString()` method is defined in `java.lang.Object`, which is the root of the class hierarchy, and therefore all objects have a `toString()` method. Sometimes, the effect of the `toString()` method is to produce rather cryptic text that is only suitable for debugging output, but it definitely exists and may legally be called.

Conversion of an operand of primitive type to a `String` is typically achieved by using, indirectly, the conversion utility methods in the wrapper classes. So, for example, an `int` value is converted by the static method `Integer.toString()`.

The `toString()` method in the `java.lang.Object` class produces a `String` that contains the name of the object's class and some identifying value—typically its reference value, separated by the at symbol (@). For example, this might look like `java.lang.Object@1cc6dd`. This behavior is inherited by subclasses unless they deliberately override it. It is a good idea to define a helpful `toString()` method in all your classes, even if you do not require it as part of the class behavior. Code the `toString()` method so that it represents the state of the object in a fashion that can assist in debugging, typically output the names and values of the main instance variables.

To prepare for the Certification Exam questions, and to use the + operator effectively in your own programs, you should understand the following points.

For a + expression with two operands of primitive numeric type, the result

- Is of a primitive numeric type
- Is at least `int`, because of normal promotions
- Is of a type at least as wide as the wider type of the two operands

- Has a value calculated by promoting the operands to the result type, then performing the addition calculation using that type. This might result in overflow or loss of precision.

For a + expression with any operand that is not of primitive numeric type

- One operand must be a String object, otherwise the expression is illegal.

- If both operands are not String objects, the non-String operand is converted to a String, and the result of the expression is the concatenation of the two.

To convert an operand of some object type to a String, the conversion is performed by invoking the toString() method of that object.

To convert an operand of a primitive type to a String, the conversion is performed by a static method in a container class, such as Integer.toString().

NOTE   If you want to control the formatting of the converted result, you should use the facilities in the java.text package.

Now that you understand arithmetic operators and the concatenation of text using the + operator, you should realize that sometimes, arithmetic does not work as intended—it could result in an error of some kind. The next section discusses what happens under such error conditions.

Arithmetic Error Conditions

We expect arithmetic to produce "sensible" results that reflect the mathematical meaning of the expression being evaluated. However, since the computation is performed on a machine with specific limits on its ability to represent numbers, calculations can sometimes result in errors. You saw, in the section on the multiplication and division operators, that overflow can easily occur if the operands are too large. In overflow, and other exceptional conditions, the following rules apply:

- Integer division by zero, including a modulo (%) operation, results in an ArithmeticException.

- No other arithmetic causes any exception. Instead, the operation proceeds to a result, even though that result might be arithmetically incorrect.

- Floating-point calculations represent out-of-range values using the IEEE 754 infinity, minus infinity, and Not a Number values. Named constants representing these are declared in both the `Float` and `Double` classes.

- Integer calculations, other than division by zero, that cause overflow or similar error, simply leave the final, typically truncated, bit pattern in the result. This bit pattern is derived from the operation and the number representation and might even be of the wrong sign. Because the operations and number representations are platform-independent, so are the result values under error conditions.

These rules describe the effect of error conditions, but there is some additional significance associated with the concept of Not A Number. NoN is used to indicate a calculation that has no result in ordinary arithmetic, such as some calculations involving infinity, or the square root of a negative number.

Comparisons with Not A Number

Some floating-point calculations can return a special result called *Not a Number*. This occurs, for example, as a result of calculating the square root of a negative number. Two Not a Number values are defined in the `java.lang` package (`Float.NaN` and `Double.NaN`) and are considered non-ordinal for comparisons. This means that for *any* value of x, including NaN itself, all of the following comparisons will return `false`:

- `x < Float.NaN`

- `x <= Float.NaN`

- `x == Float.NaN`

- `x > Float.NaN`

- `x >= Float.NaN`

In fact, the test

`Float.Nan != Float.NaN`

and the equivalent with `Double.NaN` return `true`, as you might deduce from the item above indicating that `x == Float.NaN` gives false even if x contains `Float.NaN`.

The most appropriate way to test for a NaN result from a calculation is to use the `Float.isNaN(float)` or `Double.isNaN(double)` static methods provided in the `java.lang` package.

The next section discusses a concept often used for manipulating bit patterns read from I/O ports: the shift operators <<, >>, and >>>.

The Shift Operators: <<, >>, and >>>

Java provides three *shift operators*. Two of these, << and >>, are taken directly from C/C++ but the third, >>>, is new.

Shifting is common in control systems where it can align bits that are read from, or to be written to, I/O ports. It can also provide efficient integer multiplication or division by powers of two. In Java, because the bit-level representation of all types is defined and platform-independent, you can use shifting with confidence.

Fundamentals of Shifting

Shifting is, on the face of it, a simple operation. It involves taking the binary representation of a number and moving the bit pattern left or right. However, the unsigned right-shift operator >>> is a common source of confusion, probably because it does not exist in C and C++.

The shift operators may be applied to arguments of integral types only. In fact, they should generally be applied only to operands of either `int` or `long` type. (See *Arithmetic Promotions of Operands* later in this chapter.) Figure 2.2 illustrates the basic mechanism of shifting.

The diagram in Figure 2.2 shows the fundamental idea of shifting, which involves moving the bits that represent a number to positions either to the left or right of their starting points. This is similar to people standing in line at a store checkout. As one moves forward, the person behind takes their place and so on to the end of the line. This raises two questions:

- What happens to the bits that "fall off" the end? The type of the result will have the same number of bits as the original value, but the result of a shift looks as if it might have more bits than that original.

FIGURE 2.2:

The basic mechanisms of shifting

Original data			192	
in binary	00000000	00000000	00000000	11000000
Shifted left 1 bit	0 00000000	00000000	00000001	1000000?
Shifted right 1 bit	?0000000	00000000	00000000	01100000 0
Shifted left 4 bits	0000 00000000	00000000	00001100	0000????
Original data			−192	
in binary	11111111	11111111	11111111	01000000
Shifted left 1 bit	1 11111111	11111111	11111110	1000000?
Shifted right 1 bit	?1111111	11111111	11111111	00100000 0

- What defines the value of the bits that are shifted in? These are the bits that are marked by question marks in Figure 2.2.

The first question has a simple answer. Bits that move off the end of a representation are discarded.

NOTE   In some languages, especially assembly languages, an additional operation exists, called a *rotate*, which uses these bits to define the value of the bits at the other end of the result. Java, like most high-level languages, does *not* provide a rotate operation.

Shifting Negative Numbers

The second question, regarding the value of the bits that are shifted in, requires more attention. In the case of the left-shift << and the unsigned right-shift >>> operators, the new bits are set to zero. However, in the case of the signed right-shift >> operator, the new bits take the value of the most significant bit before the shift. Figure 2.3 shows this. Notice that where a 1 bit is in the most significant position before the shift (indicating a negative number), 1 bits are introduced to fill the spaces introduced by shifting. Conversely when a 0 bit is in the most significant position before the shift, 0 bits are introduced during the shift.

FIGURE 2.3:

Signed right shift of positive and negative numbers

	192			
Original data				
in binary	00000000	00000000	00000000	11000000
Shifted right 1 bit	00000000	00000000	00000000	01100000
Shifted right 7 bits	00000000	00000000	00000000	00000001

	−192			
Original data				
in binary	11111111	11111111	11111111	01000000
Shifted right 1 bit	11111111	11111111	11111111	10100000
Shifted right 7 bits	11111111	11111111	11111111	11111110

It might seem like an arbitrary and unduly complex rule that governs the bits that are shifted in during a signed right-shift operation, but there is a good reason for the rule. If a binary number is shifted left one position (and provided that none of the bits that move off the ends of a left-shift operation are lost), the effect of the shift is to double the original number. Shifts by more than one bit effectively double and double again, so the result is as if the number had been multiplied by 2, 4, 8, 16, and so on.

If shifting the bit pattern of a number left by one position doubles that number then you might reasonably expect that shifting the pattern right, which apparently puts the bits back where they came from, would halve the number, returning it to its original value. If the right shift results in zero bits being added at the most significant bit positions, then for positive numbers, this division does result. However, if the original number was negative, then the assumption is false.

Notice that with the negative number in two's-complement representation, the most significant bits are ones. In order to preserve the significance of a right shift as a division by two when dealing with negative numbers, we must bring in bits set to one, rather than zero. This is how the behavior of the arithmetic right shift is determined. If a number is positive, its most significant bit is zero and when shifting right, more zero bits are brought in. However, if the number is negative, its most significant bit is one, and more one bits must be propagated in when the shift occurs. This is illustrated in the examples in Figure 2.4.

FIGURE 2.4:

Shifting positive and negative numbers right

			192		
Original data					
in binary	00000000	00000000	00000000	11000000
Shifted right 1 bit = 96 = 192 / 2	00000000	00000000	00000000	01100000
Shifted right 4 bits = 12 = 192 / 16 = 192 / 2^4	00000000	00000000	00000000	00001100

			−192		
Original data					
in binary	11111111	11111111	11111111	01000000
Shifted right 1 bit = −96 = −192 / 2	11111111	11111111	11111111	10100000
Shifted right 4 bits = −12 = −192 / 16 = −192 / 2^4	11111111	11111111	11111111	11110100

WARNING There is a feature of the arithmetic right shift which differs from simple division by two. If you divide −1 by 2, the result will be 0. However, the result of arithmetic shift right of −1 right is −1. You can think of this as the shift operation rounding down, while the division rounds to 0.

We now have two right-shift operators: one that treats the left-hand integer argument as a bit pattern with no special arithmetic significance, and another that attempts to insure that the arithmetic equivalence of shifting right with division by powers of two is maintained.

NOTE Why does Java need a special operator for unsigned shift right, when neither C nor C++ required this? The answer is simple: Both C and C++ provide for unsigned numeric types, but Java does not. If you shift an unsigned value right in either C or C++, you get the behavior associated with the >>> operator in Java. However, this does not work in Java simply because the numeric types (other than char) are signed.

Reduction of the Right-Hand Operand

The right-hand argument of the shift operators is taken to be the number of bits by which the shift should move. However, for shifting to behave properly, this value should be smaller than the number of bits in the result. That is, if the shift is being done as an `int` type, then the right-hand operand should be less than 32, or if the shift is being done as `long`, then the right-hand operand should be less than 64.

In fact, the shift operators do not reject values which exceed these limits. Instead, they calculate a new value by reducing the supplied value modulo the number of bits. This means that if you attempt to shift an `int` value by 33 bits, you will actually shift by 33 % 32—that is, by only one bit. This produces an anomalous result. You would expect that shifting a 32-bit number by 33 bits would produce zero as a result (or possibly –1 in the signed right-shift case). However, because of the reduction of the right-hand operand, this is not the case.

Why Java reduces the right-hand operand to shift operators, or "The sad story of the sleepy processor"

The first reason for reducing the number of bits to shift modulo the number of bits in the left-hand operand is that many CPUs implement the shift operations in this way. Why should CPUs do this?

Some years ago, there was a powerful and imaginatively designed CPU that provided both shift and rotate operations and could shift by any number of bits specified by any of its registers. Since the registers were wide, this was a very large number, and as each bit position shifted took a finite time to complete, the effect was that you could code an instruction that would take minutes to complete.

One of the intended target applications of this particular CPU was in control systems, and one of the most important features of real-time control systems is the worst-case time to respond to an external event, known as the *interrupt latency*. Unfortunately since a single instruction on this CPU was indivisible—so that interrupts could not be serviced until it was complete—execution of a large shift instruction effectively crippled the CPU. The next version of that CPU changed the implementation of shift and rotate so that the number of bits by which to shift or rotate were treated as being limited to the size of the target data item. This restored a sensible interrupt latency. Since then, many other CPUs have adopted reduction of the right-hand operand.

Arithmetic Promotion of Operands

Arithmetic promotion of operands takes place before any binary operator is applied, so that all numeric operands are at least int type. This has an important consequence for the unsigned right-shift operator when applied to values that are narrower than int.

FIGURE 2.5

Unsigned right shift of a byte

Calculation for –64 >>> 2.

Original data (–64 decimal)			11000000
Promote to int gives:	11111111	11111111	11111111	11000000
Shift right unsigned 2 bits gives:	00001111	11111111	11111111	11111100
Truncate to byte gives:				11111100
Expected result was:				00001100

The diagram in Figure 2.5 shows the process by which a byte is shifted right. First the byte is promoted to an int, which is done treating the byte as a signed quantity. Next, the shift occurs, and zero bits are indeed propagated into the top bits of the result, but these bits are not part of the original byte. When the result is cast down to a byte again, the high-order bits of that byte appear to have been created by a signed shift right, rather than an unsigned one. This is why you should generally not use the logical right-shift operator with operands smaller than an int: It is unlikely to produce the result you expected.

There are still a few more operators to cover before we leave this behind. Let's move on to the comparison operators: <, <=, >, >=, ==, and !=. They are commonly used to form conditions, such as in if() statements or in loop control.

The Comparison Operators

Comparison operators all return a boolean result; either the relationship as written is true or it is false. There are three types of comparison: ordinal, object type, and equality. *Ordinal* comparisons test the relative value of numeric operands.

Object-type comparisons determine if the runtime type of an object is of a particular type or a subclass of that particular type. *Equality* comparisons test if two values are the same and may be applied to values of non-numeric types.

Ordinal Comparisons With <, <=, >, and >=

The ordinal comparison operators are

- Less than: <

- Less than or equal to: <=

- Greater than: >

- Greater than or equal to: >=

These are applicable to all numeric types and to `char` and produce a `boolean` result.

So, for example, given these declarations

```
int p = 9;
int q = 65;
int r = -12;
float f = 9.0F;
char c = 'A';
```

the following tests all return true:

```
p < q
f < q
f <= c
c > r
c >=q
```

Notice that arithmetic promotions are applied when these operators are used. This is entirely according to the normal rules discussed in Chapter 4, *Converting and Casting*. For example, although it would be an error to attempt to assign, say, the `float` value 9.0F to the `char` variable c, it is perfectly in order to compare the two. To achieve the result, Java promotes the smaller type to the larger type, hence the `char` value 'A' (represented by the Unicode value 65) is promoted to a float 65.0F. The comparison is then performed on the resulting `float` values.

Although the ordinal comparisons operate satisfactorily on dissimilar numeric types, including char, they are not applicable to any non-numeric types. They cannot take boolean or any class-type operands.

The *instanceof* Operator

The instanceof operator tests the class of an object at run time. The left-hand argument can be any object reference expression, usually a variable or an array element, while the right-hand operand must be a class, interface, or array type. You cannot use a java.lang.Class object or its string name as the right-hand operand.

This code fragment shows an example of how instanceof may be used. Assume that a class hierarchy exists with Person as a base class and Parent as a subclass.

```
1. public class Classroom {
2.    private Hashtable inTheRoom = new Hashtable();
3.    public void enterRoom(Person p) {
4.       inTheRoom.put(p.getName(), p);
5.    }
6.    public Person getParent(String name) {
7.       Object p = inTheRoom.get(name);
8.       if (p instanceof Parent) {
9.          return (Parent)p;
10.      }
11.      else {
12.         return null;
13.      }
14.   }
15. }
```

The method getParent() at lines 6–14 checks to see if the Hashtable contains a parent with the specified name. This is done by first searching the Hashtable for an entry with the given name and then testing to see if the entry that is returned is actually a Parent or not. The instanceof operator returns true if the class of the left-hand argument is the same as, or is some subclass of, the class specified by the right-hand operand.

The right-hand operand may equally well be an interface. In such a case, the test determines if the object at the left-hand argument implements the specified interface.

You can also use the `instanceof` operator to test if a reference refers to an array. Since arrays are themselves objects in Java, this is natural enough, but the test that is performed actually checks two things: First it will check if the object is an array, then it checks if the element type of that array is some subclass of the element type of the right-hand argument. This is a logical extension of the behavior that is shown for simple types and reflects the idea that an array of, say, `Button` objects is an array of `Component` objects, because a `Button` is a `Component`. A test for an array type looks like this:

```
if (x instanceof Component[])
```

Note, however, that you cannot simply test for "any array of any element type," as the syntax. This line is not legal:

```
if (x instanceof [])
```

If the left-hand argument is a `null` value, the `instanceof` test simply returns `false`—it does not cause an exception.

The Equality Comparison Operators: == and *!=*

The operators == and != test for equality and inequality respectively, returning a `boolean` value. For primitive types, the concept of equality is quite straightforward and is subject to promotion rules so that, for example, a `float` value 10.0 is considered equal to a `byte` value of 10. For variables of object type, the "value" is taken as the reference to the object; typically this is the memory address. You should not use these operators to compare the contents of objects, such as strings, because they will return `true` if two references refer to the same object, rather than if the two objects have an equivalent meaning.

To achieve a content or semantic comparison, for example, so that two different `String` objects containing the text "Hello" are considered equal, you must use the `equals()` method rather than the == or != operators.

TIP

To operate appropriately, the equals() method must have been defined for the class of the objects you are comparing. To determine whether it has, check the documentation supplied with the JDK or, for third-party classes, produced by javadoc. This should report that an equals() method is defined for the class and overrides equals() in some superclass. If this is not indicated, then you should assume that the equals() method will not produce a useful content comparison. You also need to know that equals() is defined as accepting an Object argument, but the actual argument must be of the same type as the object upon which the method is invoked—that is for x.equals(y) the test y instanceof x must be true. If this is not the case, then equals() must return false.

The Bitwise Operators: &, ^, and |

The *bitwise operators* &, ^, and | provide bitwise AND, Exclusive-OR (XOR), and OR operations respectively. They are applicable to integral types. Collections of bits are sometimes used to save storage space where several boolean values are needed or to represent the states of a collection of binary inputs from physical devices.

The bitwise operations calculate each bit of their results by comparing the corresponding bits of the two operands on the basis of these three rules:

- For AND operations, 1 AND 1 produces 1. Any other combination produces 0.

- For XOR operations, 1 XOR 0 produces 1, as does 0 XOR 1. (The operation is commutative). Any other combination produces 0.

- For OR operations 0 OR 0 produces 0. Any other combination produces 1.

The names AND, XOR, and OR are intended to be mnemonic for these operations. You get a 1 result from an AND operation if both the first operand *and* the second operand are 1. An XOR gives a 1 result if one or the other operand, but not both (the exclusivity part), is 1. In the OR operation, you get a 1 result if either the first operand *or* the second operand (or both) is 1. These rules are represented in Table 2.3 through Table 2.5.

TABLE 2.3: The AND operation

Op1	Op2	Op 1 AND Op 2
0	0	0
0	1	0
1	0	0
1	1	1

TABLE 2.4: The XOR operation

Op1	Op2	Op1 XOR Op2
0	0	0
0	1	1
1	0	1
1	1	0

TABLE 2.5: The OR operation

Op1	Op2	Op1 OR OP2
0	0	0
0	1	1
1	0	1
1	1	1

Compare the rows of each table with the corresponding rule for the operations listed in the bullets above. You will see that for the AND operation the only situation that leads to a 1 bit as the result is when both operands are 1 bits. For XOR, 1 bits result when one or other but not both of the operands are 1 bits. Finally for the OR operation, the result is generally a 1 bit, *except* where both operands are 0 bits. Now let's see how this works when applied to whole binary numbers, rather than just single bits. The approach can be applied to any size of integer, but we will look at bytes because they serve to illustrate the idea without putting so many digits on the page as to cause confusion. Consider this example:

```
        00110011
        11110000
AND     - - - - - - - -
        00110000
```

Observe that each bit in the result above is calculated solely on the basis of the two bits appearing directly above it in the calculation. The next calculation looks at the least significant bit:

```
        0011001|1|
        1111000|0|
AND     - - - - - - -|-|
        0011000|0|
```

This result bit is calculated as 1 and 0, which gives 0.

For the fourth bit from the left, as shown in the following calculation

```
        001|1|0011
        111|1|0000
AND     - - -|-|- - - -
        001|1|0000
```

This result bit is calculated as 1 AND 1, which gives 1. All the other bits in the result are calculated in the same fashion, using the two corresponding bits and the rules stated above.

Exclusive-or operations are done by a comparable approach, using the appropriate rules for calculating the individual bits, as the following calculations show:

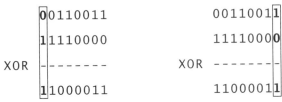

All the highlighted bits are calculated as either 1 XOR 0 or as 0 XOR 1, producing 1 in either case.

```
      0011 0011

      1111 0000

XOR   --- - ----

      110 0 0011
```

In the previous calculation, the result bits are 0 because both operand bits were 1.

```
      00110 0 11

      11110 0 00

XOR   ----- - --

      11000 0 11
```

And above, the 0 operand bits also result in 0 result bits.

The OR operation again takes a similar approach, but with its own rules for calculating the result bits. Consider this example:

```
      0011001 1

      1111000 0

OR    ------- -

      1111001 1
```

Here, the two operand bits are 1 and 0, so the result is 1.

```
      0011 0 011

      1111 0 000

OR    ---- - ---

      0011 0 000
```

While in the calculation above, both operand bits are 0, which is the condition that produces a 0 result bit for the OR operation.

Although programmers usually apply these operators to the bits in integer variables, it is also permitted to apply them to boolean operands.

Boolean operations

The &, ^, and | operators behave in fundamentally the same way when applied to arguments of `boolean`, rather than integral, types. However, instead of calculating the result on a bit-by-bit basis, the `boolean` values are treated as single bits, with `true` corresponding to a 1 bit, and `false` to a 0 bit. The general rules discussed in the previous section may be modified like this when applied to `boolean` values:

- For AND operations, `true` AND `true` produces `true`. Any other combination produces `false`.

- For XOR operations, `true` XOR `false` produces `true`, `false` XOR `true` produces `true`. Other combinations produce `false`.

- For OR operations `false` OR `false` produces `false`. Any other combination produces `true`.

These rules are represented in Table 2.6 through Table 2.8.

TABLE 2.6: The AND operation on boolean values

Op1	Op2	Op1 AND OP2
false	false	false
false	true	false
true	false	false
true	true	true

TABLE 2.7: The XOR operation on boolean values

Op1	Op2	Op1 XOR OP2
false	false	false
false	true	true
true	false	true
true	true	false

TABLE 2.8: The OR operation on boolean values

Op1	Op2	Op1 OR OP2
false	false	false
false	true	true
true	false	true
true	true	true

Again, compare these tables with the rules stated in the bulleted list. Also compare them with Tables 2.3 through 2.5, which describe the same operations on bits. You will see that 1 bits are replaced by true, while 0 bits are replaced by false.

NOTE As with all operations, the two operands must be of compatible types. So, if either operand is of boolean type, both must be. Java does not permit you to cast any type to boolean, instead you must use comparisons or methods that return boolean values.

The next section covers the short-circuit logical operators. These operators implement logical AND and OR operations, but are slightly different in implementation from the operators just discussed.

The Short-Circuit Logical Operators

The short-circuit logical operators && and || provide logical AND and OR operations on boolean types. Note that there is no XOR operation provided. Superficially, this is similar to the & and | operators with the limitation of only being applicable to boolean values and not integral types. However, the && and || operations have a valuable additional feature: the ability to "short circuit" a calculation if the result is definitely known. This feature makes these operators central to a popular null-reference handling idiom in Java programming. They can also improve efficiency.

The main difference between the & and && and between the | and || operators is that the right-hand operand might not be evaluated. We will look at how this happens in the rest of this section. This behavior is based on two mathematical rules that define conditions under which the result of a `boolean` AND or OR operation is entirely determined by one operand without regard for the value of the other:

- For an AND operation, if one operand is `false`, the result is `false`, without regard to the other operand.

- For an OR operation, if one operand is `true`, the result is `true`, without regard to the other operand.

To put it another way, for any `boolean` value X:

- `false` AND X = `false`

- `true` OR X = `true`

Given these rules, if the left-hand operand of a `boolean` AND operation is `false`, then the result is definitely `false` whatever the right-hand operand. It is therefore unnecessary to evaluate the right-hand operand. Similarly, if the left-hand operand of a `boolean` OR operation is `true`, the result is definitely `true` and the right-hand operand need not be evaluated.

Note that although these short cuts do not affect the *result* of the operation, side effects might well be changed. If the evaluation of the right-hand operand involves a side effect, then omitting the evaluation will change the overall meaning of the expression in some way. This behavior distinguishes these operators from the bit-wise operators applied to boolean types. Consider a fragment of code intended to print out a string if that string exists and is longer than 20 characters:

```
1. if (s != null) {
2.   if (s.length() > 20) {
3.     System.out.println(s);
4.   }
5. }
```

However, the same operation can be coded very succinctly like this:

```
1. if ((s != null) && (s.length() > 20)) {
2.   System.out.println(s);
3. }
```

If the `String` reference s is `null`, then calling the `s.length()` method would raise a `NullPointerException`. In both of these examples, however, the situation never arises. In the second example, avoiding execution of the `s.length()` method is a direct consequence of the short-circuit behavior of the && operator. If the test (s != null) returns false (if s is in fact null), then the whole test expression is guaranteed to be false. Where the first operand is false, the && operator does not evaluate the second operand, so in this case the sub-expression (s.length() > 20) is not evaluated.

So, the essential points about the && and || operators are

- They accept boolean operands.
- They only evaluate the right-hand operand if the outcome is not certain based solely on the left-hand operand. This is determined using the identities
  - false AND X = false
  - true OR X = true

The next section discusses the ternary, or conditional operator. Like the short-circuit logical operators, this operator may be less familiar than others, especially to programmers without a background in C or C++.

The Ternary Operator: *?:*

The *ternary* (or *conditional*) operator ?: provides a way to code simple conditions (if/else) into a single expression. The (boolean) expression left of the ? is evaluated. If true, the result of the whole expression is the value of the sub-expression to the left of the colon; otherwise it is the value of the sub-expression to the right of the colon. The sub-expressions on either side of the colon must have the same type.

For example, if a, b, and c are int variables, and x is a boolean, then the statement a = x ? b : c; is directly equivalent to the textually longer version:

```
1. if (x) {
2.    a = b;
3. }
4. else {
5.    a = c;
6. }
```

Of course x, a, b, and c can all be complex expressions if you desire.

Many people do not like the ternary operator, and in some companies its use is prohibited by the local style guide. This operator does keep source code more concise, but in many cases an optimizing compiler will generate equally compact and efficient code from the longer, and arguably more readable, if/else approach. One particularly effective way to abuse the ternary operator is to nest it, producing expressions of the form a = b ? c ? d : e ? f : g : h ? i : j ? k : l; Whatever your feelings, or corporate mandate, you should at least be able to read this operator, as you will find it used by other programmers.

The points you should review for handling operators in an exam question, or to use it properly in a program, are listed below.

In an expression of the form a = x ? b : c;

- The types of the expressions b and c should be compatible and are made identical through conversion.

- The type of the expression x should be boolean.

- The type of the expressions b and c should be assignment compatible with the type of a.

- The value assigned to a will be b if x is true, or will be c if x is false.

Now that we have discussed the ternary operator only one group of operators remains: the assignment operators.

The Assignment Operators

Assignment operators set the value of a variable or expression to a new value. Assignments are supported by a battery of operators. Simple assignment uses =. Besides simple assignment, compound "calculate and assign" is provided by operators like += and *=. These operators take a general form op= where op can be any of the binary non-boolean operators already discussed. In general, for any compatible expressions x and y, the expression x op= y is a shorthand for x = x op y. However, be aware that side effects in the expression x are evaluated exactly once, not twice as the expanded view might suggest. Assignment of object references copies the reference value, not the object body.

TIP

The statement x += 2; involves typing two fewer characters, but is otherwise no more effective than the longer version x = x + 2; and is neither more nor less readable. However, if x is a complex expression, such as target[temp.calculateOffset(1.9F) + depth++].item it is definitely more readable to express incrementing this value by 2 using the += 2 form. This is because these operators define that the exact same thing will be read on the right-hand side as is written to on the left-hand side. So the maintainer does not have to struggle to decide whether the two complex expressions are actually the same, and the original programmer avoids some of the risk of mistyping a copy of the expression.

Assignment has Value

All the operators discussed to this point have produced a value as a result of the operation. The expression 1 + 2, for example, results in a value 3 which can then be used in some further way, perhaps assignment to a variable. The assignment operators in Java are considered to be operators because they have a resulting value. So, given three int variables a, b, and c, the statement a = b = c = 0; is entirely legal. It is executed from right to left, so that first 0 is assigned into the variable c. After it has been executed, the expression c = 0 takes the value that was assigned to the left-hand side—that is zero. Next, the assignment of b takes place, using the value of the expression to the right of the equals sign. This is again zero. Similarly that expression takes the value that was assigned, so finally the variable a is also set to zero.

Chapter Summary

We have covered a lot of material in this chapter, so let's recap the key points.

The Unary Operators

The seven unary operators are ++, --, +, -, !, ~, and (). Their key points are

- The ++ and -- operators increment and decrement expressions. The position of the operator (either prefix or suffix) is significant.

- The + operator has no effect on an expression other than to make it clear that a literal constant is positive. The − operator negates an expression's value.

- The ! operator inverts the value of a `boolean` expression.

- The ~ operator inverts the bit pattern of an integral expression.

- The (`type`) operator is used to persuade the compiler to permit certain assignments which the programmer believes are appropriate, but which break the normal, rigorous rules of the language. Its use is subject to extensive checks at compile time and run time.

The Arithmetic Operators

There are five arithmetic operators, which are

- Multiplication: *

- Division: /

- Modulo: %

- Addition and `String` concatenation: +

- Subtraction: −

The arithmetic operators can be applied to any numeric type. Additionally, the + operator performs text concatenation if either of its operands is a `String` object. Under the conditions where one operand in a + expression is a `String` object, the other is forced to be a `String` object, too. Conversions are performed as necessary which might result in cryptic text but are definitely legal.

Under conditions of arithmetic overflow or similar errors, accuracy is generally lost silently. The only conditions that throw exceptions result from integer division by zero. Floating-point calculations can produce Not A Number or an infinity as their result under error conditions.

The Shift Operators

These are the key points about the shift operators:

- The <<, >>, and >>> operators perform bit shifts of the binary representation of the left operand.

- The operands should be an integral type, either int or long.

- The right-hand operand is reduced modulo x where x depends upon the type of the result of the operation. That type is either int or long, smaller operands being subjected to promotion. If the left-hand operand is assignment compatible with int, then x is 32. If the left-hand operand is a long, then x is 64.

- The << operator shifts left. Zero bits are introduced at the least significant bit position.

- The >> operator performs a signed, or arithmetic, right shift. The result has 0 bits at the most significant positions if the original left-hand operand was positive, and has 1 bits at the most significant positions if the original left-hand operand was negative. The result approximates dividing the left-hand operand by two raised to the power of the right-hand operand.

- The >>> operator performs an unsigned, or logical, right shift. The result has 0 bits at the most significant positions and might not represent a division of the original left operand.

The Bitwise Operators

There are three bitwise operators: &, ^, and |. They are usually named AND, Exclusive-OR (XOR), and OR respectively. For each operator the following points apply:

- In bitwise operations, each result bit is calculated on the basis of the two bits from the same, corresponding position in the operands.

- For the AND operation, a 1 bit results if the first operand bit *and* the second operand bit are both 1.

- For the XOR operation, a 1 bit results only if exactly one operand bit is 1.

- For the OR operation, a 1 bit results if either the first operand bit *or* the second operand bit is 1.

For boolean operations, the arguments and results are treated as single bit values with true represented by 1 and false by 0.

The Assignment Operators

The key points about the assignment operators are

- Simple assignment, using =, assigns the *value* of the right-hand operand to the left-hand operand.

- The *value* of an object is its reference, not its contents.

- The right-hand operand must be a type that is assignment compatible with the left-hand operand. Assignment compatibility and conversions are discussed in detail in Chapter 4, *Converting and Casting*.

- The assignment operators all return a value, so that they can be used within larger expressions. The value returned is the value that was assigned to the left-hand operand.

- The compound assignment operators, of the form op=, when applied in an expression like a op= b; appear to behave like a = a op b; except that the expression a, and any of its side effects, is evaluated only once.

Compound assignment operators exist for all binary non-boolean operators: *=, /=, %=, +=, -=, <<=, >>=, >>>=, &=, ^=, and |=. We have now discussed all the operators that are provided by Java and all that remains are the test questions. Good luck!

Test Yourself

1. After execution of the code fragment below, what are the values of the variables x, a, and b?

```
1. int x, a = 6, b = 7;
2. x = a++ + b++;
```

   A. x = 15, a = 7, b = 8

   B. x = 15, a = 6, b = 7

   C. x = 13, a = 7, b = 8

   D. x = 13, a = 6, b = 7

2. Which of the following expressions are legal? (Choose one or more.)

   A. `int x = 6; x = !x;`

   B. `int x = 6; if (!(x > 3)) {}`

   C. `int x = 6; x = ~x;`

3. Which of the following expressions results in a positive value in x? (Choose one.)

   A. `int x = -1; x = x >>> 5;`

   B. `int x = -1; x = x >>> 32;`

   C. `byte x = -1; x = x >>> 5;`

   D. `int x = -1; x = x >> 5;`

4. Which of the following expressions are legal? (Choose one or more.)

   A. `String x = "Hello"; int y = 9; x += y;`

   B. `String x = "Hello"; int y = 9; if (x == y) {}`

   C. `String x = "Hello"; int y = 9; x = x + y;`

   D. `String x = "Hello"; int y = 9; y = y + x;`

   E. `String x = null;`
      `int y = (x != null) && (x.length() > 0) ? x.length() : 0;`

5. Which of the following code fragments would compile successfully and print "Equal" when run? (Choose one or more.)

   A. `int x = 100; float y = 100.0F;`
      `if (x == y){ System.out.println("Equal");}`

   B. `int x = 100; Integer y = new Integer(100);`
      `if (x == y) { System.out.println("Equal");}`

   C. `Integer x = new Integer(100);`
      `Integer y = new Integer(100);`
      `if (x == y) { System.out.println("Equal");}`

D.
```
String x = new String("100");
String y = new String("100");
if (x == y) { System.out.println("Equal");}
```

E.
```
String x = "100";
String y = "100";
if (x == y) { System.out.println("Equal");}
```

6. What results from running the following code?

```
1. public class Short {
2.   public static void main(String args[]) {
3.     StringBuffer s = new StringBuffer("Hello");
4.     if ((s.length() > 5) &&
5.       (s.append(" there").equals("False")))
6.         ; // do nothing
7.     System.out.println("value is " + s);
8.   }
9. }
```

A. The output: `value is Hello`

B. The output: `value is Hello there`

C. A compiler error at line 4 or 5

D. No output

E. A `NullPointerException`

7. What results from running the following code?

```
1. public class Xor {
2.   public static void main(String args[]) {
3.     byte b = 10; // 00001010 binary
4.     byte c = 15; // 00001111 binary
5.     b = (byte)(b ^ c);
6.     System.out.println("b contains " + b);
7.   }
8. }
```

A. The output: `b contains 10`

B. The output: `b contains 5`

C. The output: `b contains 250`

D. The output: `b contains 245`

8. What results from attempting to compile and run the following code?

```
1. public class Ternary {
2.   public static void main(String args[]) {
3.     int x = 4;
4.     System.out.println("value is " +
5.       ((x > 4) ? 99.99 : 9));
6.   }
7. }
```

A. The output: `value is 99.99`

B. The output: `value is 9`

C. The output: `value is 9.0`

D. A compiler error at line 5

9. What is the output of this code fragment?

```
1. int x = 3; int y = 10;
2. System.out.println(y % x);
```

A. 0

B. 1

C. 2

D. 3

10. What results from the following fragment of code?

```
1. int x = 1;
2. String [] names = { "Fred", "Jim", "Sheila" };
3. names[--x] += ".";
4. for (int i = 0; i < names.length; i++) {
5.   System.out.println(names[i]);
6. }
```

A. The output includes `Fred.` with a trailing period.

B. The output includes `Jim.` with a trailing period.

C. The output includes `Sheila.` with a trailing period.

D. None of the outputs shows a trailing period.

E. An `ArrayIndexOutOfBoundsException` is thrown.

Modifiers

- Access modifiers

- Non-access modifiers

In this chapter you will cover the following Java Certification Exam objectives:

- Declare classes using the modifiers `public`, `abstract`, or `final`.

- Declare variables using the modifiers `private`, `protected`, `public`, `static`, `final`, `native`, or `abstract`.

- State the consequences, in terms of the results of an assignment to a variable, of the qualifiers `static` or `final` being applied to that variable.

- State the effects on scope and accessibility of an instance variable or method of these factors:

  - The calling method is static.

  - The calling method is non-static.

  - The calling method is in the same class as the target.

  - The calling method is in a subclass of the class containing the target.

  - The calling method is in a class which is in the same package as the class containing the target.

  - No special relationship exists between the class of the caller and the class of the target.

The target declaration is qualified by any of `private`, `protected`, `public`, `static`, `final`, or `abstract`.

Modifiers are Java keywords that give the compiler information about the nature of code, data, or classes. Modifiers specify, for example, that a particular feature is static, or final, or transient. (A *feature* is a class, a method, or a variable.) A group of modifiers, called *access modifiers*, dictate which classes are allowed to use a feature. Other modifiers can be used in combination to describe the attributes of a feature.

In this chapter you will learn about all of Java's modifiers as they apply to top-level classes. Inner classes are not discussed here, but are covered in Chapter 6, *Objects and Classes*.

Modifier Overview

The most common modifiers are the access modifiers: `public`, `protected`, and `private`. The access modifiers are covered in the next section. The remaining modifiers do not fall into clear categories. They are

- `final`
- `abstract`
- `static`
- `native`
- `transient`
- `synchronized`
- `volatile`

Each of these modifiers is discussed in its own section.

The Access Modifiers

Access modifiers control which classes may use a feature. A class' features are

- The class itself
- Its class variables
- Its methods and constructors

Note that, with rare exceptions, the only variables that may be controlled by access modifiers are class-level variables. The variables that you declare and use within a class' methods may not have access modifiers. This makes sense; a method variable can only be used within its method.

The access modifiers are

- `public`
- `protected`
- `private`

The only access modifier permitted to non-inner classes is `public`; there is no such thing as a protected or private top-level class.

A feature may have at most one access modifier. If a feature has no access modifier, its access defaults to *friendly*. Be aware that *friendly* is not a Java keyword; it is just the colloquial name that we humans use for the type of access a feature gets if no modifier is specified.

The following declarations are all legal (provided they appear in an appropriate context):

```
class Parser { ... }
public class EightDimensionalComplex  { ... }
private int i;
Graphics offScreenGC;
protected double getChiSquared(){ ... }
private class Horse { ... }
```

The following declarations are illegal:

```
public protected int x;            // At most 1 access modifier allowed
friendly Button getBtn(){ ... }  // "friendly" is not a modifier
```

public

The most generous access modifier is `public`. A public class, variable, or method may be used in any Java program without restriction. An applet (that is, a custom subclass of class `java.applet.Applet`) is declared as a public class so that it may be instantiated by browsers. An application declares its `main()` method to be public so that `main()` may be invoked from any Java runtime environment.

private

The least generous access modifier is `private`. Top level classes may not be declared private. A private variable or method may only be used by an instance of the class that declares the variable or method. As an example of private access, consider the following code:

```
1. class Complex {
2.    private double real, imaginary;
3.
4.    public Complex(double r, double i)  { real = r; imaginary = i; }
5.
6.    public Complex add(Complex c) {
7.       return new Complex(real + c.real, imaginary + c.imaginary);
```

```
 8.    }
 9. }
10.
11.
12. class Client {
13.    void useThem() {
14.       Complex c1 = new Complex(1, 2);
15.       Complex c2 = new Complex(3, 4);
16.       Complex c3 = c1.add(c2);
17.       double d = c3.real;              // Illegal!
18.    }
19. }
```

On line 16, a call is made to c1.add(c2). Object c1 will execute the method, using object c2 as a parameter. In line 7, c1 accesses its own private variables as well as those of c2. There is nothing wrong with this. Declaring real and imaginary to be private means that they may only be accessed by instances of the Complex class, but they may be accessed by any instance of Complex. Thus c1 may access its own real and imaginary variables, as well as the real and imaginary of any other instance of Complex. Access modifiers dictate which *classes*, not which *instances*, may access features.

Line 17 is illegal and will cause a compiler error. The error message says, "Variable real in class Complex not accessible from class Client." The private variable real may only be accessed by an instance of Complex.

Private data can be hidden from the very object that owns the data. If class Complex has a subclass called SubComplex, then every instance of SubComplex will inherit its own real and imaginary variables. Nevertheless, no instance of SubComplex can ever access those variables. Once again, the private features of Complex may only be accessed by an instance of Complex; an instance of a subclass is denied access. Thus, for example, the following code will not compile:

```
 1. class Complex {
 2.    private double real, imaginary;
 3. }
 4.
 5.
 6. class SubComplex extends Complex {
 7.    SubComplex(double r, double i) {
 8.       real = r;              // Trouble!
 9.    }
10. }
```

In the constructor for class SubComplex (on line 8), the variable real is accessed. This line causes a compiler error, with a message that is very similar to the message of the previous example: "Variable real in class Complex not accessible from class SubComplex." The private nature of variable real prevents an instance of SubComplex from accessing one of its own variables!

Friendly

Friendly is the name of the default access of classes, variables, and methods, if you don't specify an access modifier. A class' data and methods may be friendly, as well as the class itself. A class' friendly features are accessible to any class in the same package as the class in question.

Friendly is not a Java keyword; it is simply a name that is given to the access level that results from not specifying an access modifier.

It would seem that friendly access is only of interest to people who are in the business of making packages. This is technically true, but actually everybody is always making packages, even if they aren't aware of it. The result of this behind-the-scenes package-making is a degree of convenience for programmers that deserves investigation.

When you write an application that involves developing several different classes, you probably put keep all your .java sources and all your .class class files in a single working directory. When you execute your code, you do so from that directory. The Java runtime environment considers that all class files in its current working directory constitute a package.

Imagine what happens when you develop several classes in this way and don't bother to provide access modifiers for your classes, data, or methods. These features are neither public, nor private, nor protected. They default to friendly access, which means they are accessible to any other classes in the package. Since Java considers that all the classes in the directory actually make up a package, all your classes get to access one another's features. This makes it easy to develop code quickly without worrying too much about access.

Now imagine what happens if you are deliberately developing your own package. A little extra work is required: You have to put a package statement in your source code, and you have to compile with the -d option. Any features of the package's classes that you do not explicitly mark with an access modifier will be accessible to all the members of the package, which is probably what you want. Fellow package members have a special relationship, and it stands to reason that they should get access not granted to classes outside the package. Classes outside the package may not access the friendly features, because the features are friendly, not public. Classes outside the package may subclass the classes in the package (you do something like this, for example, when you write an applet); however, even the subclasses may not access the friendly features, because the features are friendly, not protected or public. Figure 3.1 illustrates friendly access both within and outside a package.

FIGURE 3.1:

Friendly access

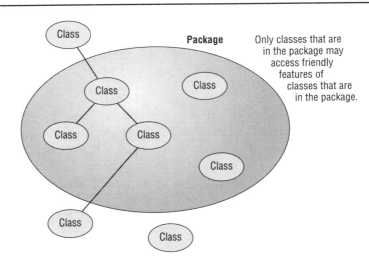

Only classes that are in the package may access friendly features of classes that are in the package.

protected

The name *protected* is a bit misleading. From the sound of it, you might guess that protected access is extremely restrictive—perhaps the next closest thing to private access. In fact, protected features are even more accessible than friendly features.

Only variables, methods, and inner classes and methods may be declared protected. A protected feature of a class is available to all classes in the same package, just like a friendly feature. Moreover, a protected feature of a class is available to all subclasses of the class that owns the protected feature. This access is provided even to subclasses that reside in a different package from the class that owns the protected feature.

As an example of protected access, consider the following source module:

```
1. package sportinggoods;
2. class Ski {
3.    void applyWax() { . . . }
4. }
```

The applyWax() method defaults to friendly access. Now consider the following subclass:

```
1. package sportinggoods;
2. class DownhillSki extends Ski {
3.    void tuneup() {
4.      applyWax();
5.      // other tuneup functionality here
6.    }
7. }
```

The subclass calls the inherited method applyWax(). This is not a problem as long as both the Ski and DownhillSki classes reside in the same package. However, if either class were to be moved to a different package, DownhillSki would no longer have access to the inherited applyWax() method, and compilation would fail. The problem would be fixed by making applyWax() protected on line 3:

```
1. package adifferentpackage;   // Class Ski now in a different package
2. class Ski {
3.    protected void applyWax() { . . . }
4. }
```

Subclasses and Method Privacy

Java specifies that methods may not be overridden to be more private. For example, most applets provide an init() method, which overrides the do-nothing version inherited from the java.applet.Applet superclass. The inherited version is declared public, so declaring the subclass version to be private, protected, or friendly would result in a compiler error. The error message says, "Methods can't be overridden to be more private."

Figure 3.2 shows the legal access types for subclasses. A method with some particular access type may be overridden by a method with a different access type, provided there is a path in the figure from the original type to the new type.

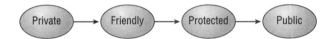

The rules for overriding can be summarized as follows:

- A private method may be overridden by a private, friendly, protected, or public method.

- A friendly method may be overridden by a friendly, protected, or public method.

- A protected method may be overridden by a protected or public method.

- A public method may only be overridden by a public method.

Figure 3.3 shows the illegal access types for subclasses. A method with some particular access type may not be overridden by a method with a different access type, if there is a path in the figure from the original type to the new type.

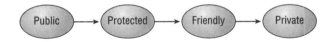

The illegal overriding combinations can be summarized as follows:

- A friendly method may not be overridden by a private method.

- A protected method may not be overridden by a friendly or private method.

- A public method may not be overridden by a protected, friendly, or private method.

Summary of Access Modes

To summarize, Java's access modes are

- `public`: A public feature may be accessed by any class at all.

- `protected`: A protected feature may only be accessed by a subclass of the class that owns the feature, or by a member of the same package as the class that owns the feature.

- friendly: A friendly feature may only be accessed by a class from the same package as the class that owns the feature.

- private: A private feature may only be accessed by the class that owns the feature.

Other Modifiers

The rest of this chapter covers Java's other modifiers: final, abstract, static, native, transient, synchronized, and volatile. (Transient and volatile are not mentioned in the Certification Exam objectives, so they are just touched on briefly in this chapter.)

Java does not care about order of appearance of modifiers. Declaring a class to be public final is no different from declaring it final public. Declaring a method to be protected static has the same effect as declaring it static protected.

Not every modifier can be applied to every kind of feature. Table 3.1, at the end of this chapter, summarizes which modifiers apply to which features.

final

The final modifier applies to classes, methods, and variables. The meaning of final varies from context to context, but the essential idea is the same: Final features may not be changed.

A final class may not be subclassed. For example, the code below will not compile, because the java.lang.Math class is final:

```
class SubMath extends java.lang.Math { }
```

The compiler error says, "Can't subclass final classes."

A final variable may not be modified once it has been assigned a value. In Java, final variables play the same role as consts in C++ and #define'd constants in C. For example, the java.lang.Math class has a final variable, of type double, called PI. Obviously, pi is not the sort of value that should be changed during the execution of a program.

If a final variable is a reference to an object, it is the reference that must stay the same, not the object. This is shown in the code below:

```
1.   class Walrus {
2.     int weight;
3.     Walrus(int w) { weight = w; }
4.   }
5.
6.   class Tester {
7.     final Walrus w1 = new Walrus(1500);
8.     void test() {
9.       w1 = new Walrus(1400);     // Illegal
10.      w1.weight = 1800;          // Legal
11.    }
12. }
```

Here the final variable is w1, declared on line 7. Since it is final, w1 may not receive a new value; line 9 is illegal. However, the data inside w1 is not final, and line 10 is perfectly legal. In other words

- You *may not* change a final object reference variable.

- You *may* change data owned by an object that is referred to by a final object reference variable.

A final method may not be overridden. For example, the following code will not compile:

```
1. class Mammal {
2.   final void getAround() { }
3. }
4.
5. class Dolphin extends Mammal {
6.   void getAround() { }
7. }
```

Dolphins get around in a very different way from most mammals, so it makes sense to try to override the inherited version of getAround(). However, getAround() is final, so the only result is a compiler error at line 6 that says, "Final methods can't be overridden."

abstract

The abstract modifier can be applied to classes and methods. A class that is abstract may not be instantiated (that is, you may not call its constructor).

Abstract classes provide a way to defer implementation to subclasses. Consider the class hierarchy shown in Figure 3.4.

FIGURE 3.4:

A class hierarchy with abstraction

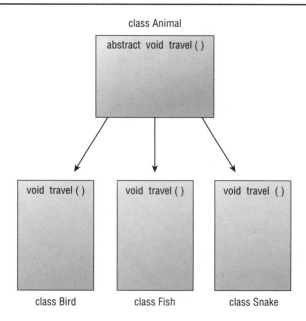

class Animal

abstract void travel ( )

void travel ( )   void travel ( )   void travel ( )

class Bird   class Fish   class Snake

The designer of class Animal has decided that every subclass should have a travel() method. Each subclass has its own unique way of traveling, so it is not possible to provide travel() in the superclass and have each subclass inherit the same parental version. Instead, the Animal superclass declares travel() to be *abstract*. The declaration looks like this:

```
abstract void travel();
```

At the end of the line is a semicolon where you would expect to find curlies containing the body of the method. The method body—its implementation—is deferred to the subclasses. The superclass only provides the method name and signature. Any subclass of Animal must provide an implementation of travel() or declare itself to be abstract. In the latter case, implementation of travel() is deferred yet again, to a subclass of the subclass.

If a class contains one or more abstract methods, the compiler insists that the class must be declared abstract. This is a great convenience to people who will be using the class: They only need to look in one place (the class declaration) to find out if they are allowed to instantiate the class directly or if they have to build a subclass.

In fact, the compiler insists that a class must be declared abstract if any of the following conditions is true:

- The class has one or more abstract methods.

- The class inherits one or more abstract methods (from an abstract parent) for which it does not provide implementations.

- The class declares that it implements an interface but does not provide implementations for every method of that interface.

These three conditions are very similar to one another. In each case, there is a class that is in some sense incomplete. Some part of the class' functionality is missing and must be provided by a subclass.

In a way, `abstract` is the opposite of `final`. A final class, for example, may not be subclassed; an abstract class *must* be subclassed.

static

The `static` modifier can be applied to variables, methods, and even a strange kind of code that is not part of a method. You can think of static features as belonging to a class, rather than being associated with an individual instance of the class.

The following example shows a simple class with a single static variable:

```
1. class Ecstatic {
2.   static int x = 0;
3.   Ecstatic() { x++; }
4. }
```

Variable x is static; this means that there is only one x, no matter many how many instances of class Ecstatic might exist at any particular moment. There might be one Ecstatic, or many, or even none; there is always precisely one x. The four bytes of memory occupied by x are allocated when class Ecstatic is loaded. The initialization to zero (line 2) also happens at class-load time. The static variable is incremented every time the constructor is called, so it is possible to know how many instances have been created.

There are two ways to reference a static variable:

- Via a reference to any instance of the class
- Via the class name

The first method works, but it can result in confusing code and is considered bad form. The following example shows why:

```
1. Ecstatic e1 = new Ecstatic();
2. Ecstatic e2 = new Ecstatic();
3. e1.x = 100;
4. e2.x = 200;
5. reallyImportantVariable = e1.x;
```

If you didn't know that x is static, you might think that reallyImportantVariable gets set to 100 in line 5. In fact, it gets set to 200, because e1.x and e2.x refer to the same (static) variable.

A better way to refer to a static variable is via the class name. The following code is identical to the code above:

```
1. Ecstatic e1 = new Ecstatic();
2. Ecstatic e2 = new Ecstatic();
3. Ecstatic.x = 100;      // Why did I do this?
4. Ecstatic.x = 200;
5. reallyImportantVariable = Ecstatic.x;
```

Now it is clear that line 3 is useless, and the value of reallyImportantVariable gets set to 200 in line 5. Referring to static features via the class name rather than an instance results in source code that more clearly describes what will happen at run time.

Methods, as well as data, can be declared static. Static methods are not allowed to use the non-static features of their class (although they are free to access the class' static data and call its other static methods). Thus static methods are not concerned with individual instances of a class. They may be invoked before even a single instance of the class is constructed. Every Java application is an example, because every application has a main() method that is static:

```
1. class SomeClass {
2.     static int i = 48;
3.     int j = 1;
4.
5.     public static void main(String args[]) {
```

```
6.    i += 100;
7.    // j *= 5;    Lucky for us this line is commented out!
8.  }
9. }
```

When this application is started (that is, when somebody types `java SomeClass` on a command line), no instance of class `SomeClass` exists. At line 6, the `i` that gets incremented is static, so it exists even though there are no instances. Line 7 would result in a compiler error if it were not commented out, because `j` is non-static.

Non-static methods have an implicit variable named `this`, which is a reference to the object executing the method. In non-static code, you can refer to a variable or method without specifying which object's variable or method you mean. The compiler assumes you mean `this`. For example, consider the code below:

```
1. class Xyzzy {
2.   int w;
3.
4.   void bumpW() {
5.     w++;
6.   }
7. }
```

On line 5, the programmer has not specified which object's `w` is to be incremented. The compiler assumes that line 5 is an abbreviation for

```
this.w++;
```

With static methods, there is no `this`. If you try to access it, you will get an error message that says, "Undefined variable: `this`." The concept of "the instance that is executing the current method" does not mean anything, because there is no such instance. Like static variables, static methods are not associated with any individual instance of their class.

If a static method needs to access a non-static variable or call a non-static method, it must specify which instance of its class owns the variable or executes the method. This situation is familiar to anyone who has ever written an application with a GUI:

```
1.  import java.awt.*;
2.
3.  public class MyFrame extends Frame {
4.    MyFrame() {
5.      setSize(300, 300);
```

```
6.    }
7.
8.    public static void main(String args[]) {
9.       MyFrame theFrame = new MyFrame();
10.      theFrame.setVisible(true);
11.   }
12. }
```

In line 9, the static method `main()` constructs an instance of class `MyFrame`. In the next line, that instance is told to execute the (non-static) method `setVisible()`. This technique bridges the gap from static to non-static, and it is frequently seen in applications.

A static method may not be overridden to be non-static. The code below, for example, will not compile:

```
1. class Cattle {
2.   static void foo() {}
3. }
4.
5. class Sheep extends Cattle {
6.   void foo() {}
7. }
```

The compiler flags line 6 with the message, "Static methods can't be overridden." If line 6 were changed to "`static void foo() { }`", then compilation would succeed.

To summarize static methods

- A static method may only access the static data of its class; it may not access non-static data.

- A static method may only call the static methods of its class; it may not call non-static methods.

- A static method has no `this`.

- A static method may not be overridden to be non-static.

Static Initializers

It is legal for a class to contain static code that does not exist within a method body. A class may have a block of initializer code that is simply surrounded by curlies and labeled `static`. For example

```
1.  public class StaticDemo {
2.     static int i=5;
3.
4.     static {
5.        System.out.println("Static code: i = " + i++);
6.     }
7.
8.     public static void main(String args[]) {
9.        System.out.println("main: i = " + i++);
10.    }
11. }
```

Something seems to be missing from line 4. You might expect to see a complete method declaration there: `static void printAndBump()`, for example, instead of just `static`. In fact, line 4 is perfectly valid; it is known as *static initializer* code. The code inside the curlies is executed exactly once, at the time the class is loaded. At class-load time, all static initialization (such as line 2) and all free-floating static code (such as lines 4–6) are executed in order of appearance within the class definition.

Free-floating initializer code should be used with caution, as it can easily lead to obfuscated code. The compiler supports multiple initializer blocks within a class, but there is never a good reason for having more than one such block.

native

The `native` modifier can refer only to methods. Like the `abstract` keyword, `native` indicates that the body of a method is to be found elsewhere. In the case of abstract methods, the body is in a subclass; with native methods, the body lies entirely outside the Java Virtual Machine, in a library.

Native code is written in a non-Java language, typically C or C++, and compiled for a single target machine type. (Thus Java's platform independence is violated.) People who port Java to new platforms implement extensive native code to support GUI components, network communication, and a broad range of other platform-specific functionality. However, it is rare for application and applet programmers to need to write native code.

One technique, however, is of interest in light of the last section's discussion of static code. When a native method is invoked, the library that contains the native code ought to be loaded and available to the Java Virtual Machine; if it is not loaded, there will be a delay. The library is loaded by calling `System.loadLibrary` (`"library_name"`), and to avoid a delay, it is desirable to make this call as early as possible. Often programmers will use the technique shown in the code sample below, which assumes the library name is `MyNativeLib`:

```
1. class NativeExample {
2.    native void doSomethingLocal(int i);
3.
4.    static {
5.      System.loadLibrary("MyNativeLib");
6.    }
7. }
```

Notice the native declaration on line 2, which declares that the code that implements `doSomethingLocal()` resides in a local library. Lines 4–6 are static initializer code, so they are executed at the time that class `NativeExample` is loaded; this insures that the library will be available by the time somebody needs it.

Callers of native methods do not have to know that the method is native. The call is made in exactly the same way as if it were non-native:

```
1. NativeExample natex;
2. natex = new NativeExample();
3. ne.doSomethingLocal(5);
```

Many common methods are native, including all the number-crunching methods of the Math class and the `clone()`, and `notify()` methods of the `Object` class.

transient

The `transient` modifier applies only to variables. A transient variable is not stored as part of its object's persistent state.

Many objects (specifically, those that implement either the `Serializable` or `Externalizable` interfaces) can have their state serialized and written to some destination outside the Java Virtual Machine. This is done by passing the object to the `writeObject()` method of the `ObjectOutputStream` class. If the stream is chained to a File Output Stream, then the object's state is written to a file. If the stream is chained to a socket's Output Stream, then the object's state is written to the network. In both cases the object can be reconstituted by reading it from an Object Input Stream.

There will be times when an object will contain extemely sensitive information. Consider the following class:

```
1. class WealthyCustomer extends Customer implements Serializable {
2.     private float $wealth;
3.     private String accessCode;
4. }
```

Once an object is written to a destination outside the JVM, none of Java's elaborate security mechanisms is in effect. If an instance of this class were to be written to a file or to the Internet, somebody could snoop the access code. Line 3 should be marked with the transient keyword:

```
1. class WealthyCustomer extends Customer implements Serializable {
2.     private float $wealth;
3.     private transient String accessCode;
4. }
```

Now the value of accessCode will not be written out during serialization.

Transient variables may not be final or static.

synchronized

The synchronized modifier is used to control access to critical code in multi-threaded programs. Multithreading is an extensive topic in its own right, and is covered in Chapter 7, *Threads*.

volatile

The last modifier is volatile. It is mentioned here only to make our list complete, as it is not mentioned in the exam objectives and is not yet in common use. Only variables may be volatile; declaring them so indicates that such variables might be modified asynchronously, so the compiler takes special precautions. Volatile variables are of interest in multiprocessor environments.

Modifiers and Features

Not all modifiers can be applied to all features. Top-level classes may not be protected. Methods may not be transient. Static is so general that you can apply it to free-floating blocks of code.

Table 3.1 shows all the possible combinations of features and modifiers. Note that classes here are strictly top-level (that is, not inner) classes. (Inner classes are covered in Chapter 6, *Objects and Classes*.)

TABLE 3.1: All Possible Combinations of Features and Modifiers

Modifier	Class	Variable	Method/Constructor	Free-Floating Block
public	yes	yes	yes	no
protected	no	yes	yes	no
(friendly)*	yes	yes	yes	no
private	no	yes	yes	no
final	yes	yes	yes	no
abstract	yes	yes	yes	no
static	yes	yes	yes	yes
native	no	no	yes	no
transient	no	yes	no	no
synchronized	no	no	yes	no

*friendly is not a modifier; it is just the name of the default if no modifier is specified.

Chapter Summary

Java's access modifiers are

- public

- protected

- private

If a feature does not have an access modifier, its access defaults to "friendly."

Java's other modifiers are

- final

- abstract

- static

- native

- transient

- synchronized

- volatile

Test Yourself

1. Which of the following declarations are illegal? (Choose one or more.)

   A. friendly String s;

   B. transient int i = 41;

   C. public final static native int w();

   D. abstract double d;

   E. abstract final double hyperbolicCosine();

2. Which one of the following statements is true?

A. An abstract class may not have any final methods.

B. A final class may not have any abstract methods.

3. What is the *minimal* modification that will make the code below compile correctly?

```
1. final class Aaa
2. {
3.     int xxx;
4.     void yyy() { xxx = 1; }
5. }
6.
7.
8. class Bbb extends Aaa
9. {
10.     final Aaa finalref = new Aaa();
11.
12.     final void yyy()
13.     {
14.         System.out.println("In method yyy()");
15.         finalref.xxx = 12345;
16.     }
17. }
```

A. On line 1, remove the `final` modifier.

B. On line 10, remove the `final` modifier.

C. Remove line 15.

D. On lines 1 and 10, remove the `final` modifier.

E. The code will compile as is. No modification is needed.

4. Which one of the following statements is true?

A. Transient methods may not be overridden.

B. Transient methods must be overridden.

C. Transient classes may not be serialized.

D. Transient variables must be static.

E. Transient variables are not serialized.

5. Which one statement is true about the application below?

```
1. class StaticStuff
2  {
3.      static int x = 10;
4.
5.      static { x += 5; }
6.
7.      public static void main(String args[])
8.      {
9.          System.out.println("x = " + x);
10.     }
11.
12.     static {x /= 5; }
13. }
```

A. Lines 5 and 12 will not compile, because the method names and return types are missing.

B. Line 12 will not compile, because you can only have one static initializer.

C. The code compiles, and execution produces the output x = 10.

D. The code compiles, and execution produces the output x = 15.

E. The code compiles, and execution produces the output x = 3.

6. Which one statement is true about the code below?

```
1. class HasStatic
2. {
3.      private static int x = 100;
4.
5.      public static void main(String args[])
6.      {
7.          HasStatic hs1 = new HasStatic();
8.          hs1.x++;
9.          HasStatic hs2 = new HasStatic();
10.         hs2.x++;
11.         hs1 = new HasStatic();
12.         hs1.x++;
13.         HasStatic.x++;
14.         System.out.println("x = " + x);
15.     }
16. }
```

A. Line 8 will not compile, because it is a static reference to a private variable.

B. Line 13 will not compile, because it is a static reference to a private variable.

C. The program compiles, and the output is x = 102.

D. The program compiles, and the output is x = 103.

E. The program compiles, and the output is x = 104.

7. Given the code below, and making no other changes, which access modifiers (public, protected, or private) can legally be placed before aMethod() on line 3? If line 3 is left as it is, which keywords can legally be placed before aMethod() on line 8?

```
1. class SuperDuper
2. {
3.     void aMethod() { }
4. }
5.
6. class Sub extends SuperDuper
7. {
8.     void aMethod() { }
9. }
```

8. Which modifier or modifiers should be used to denote a variable that should not be written out as part of its class' persistent state? (Choose the shortest possible answer.)

A. private

B. protected

C. private protected

D. transient

E. private transient

The next two questions concern the following class definition:

```
1. package abcde;
2.
3. public class Bird {
4.    protected static int referenceCount = 0;
5.    public Bird() { referenceCount++; }
6.    protected void fly() { /* Flap wings, etc. */ }
7.    static int getRefCount() { return referenceCount; }
8. }
```

9. Which one statement is true about class Bird above and class Parrot below?

```
1. package abcde;
2.
3. class Parrot extends abcde.Bird {
4.    public void fly() { /* Parrot specific flight code. */ }
5.    public int getRefCount() { return referenceCount; }
6. }
```

A. Compilation of Parrot.java fails at line 4, because method fly() is protected in the superclass and classes Bird and Parrot are in the same package.

B. Compilation of Parrot.java fails at line 4, because method fly() is protected in the superclass and public in the subclass and methods may not be overridden to be more public.

C. Compilation of Parrot.java fails at line 5, because method getRefCount() is static in the superclass and static methods may not be overriden to be non-static.

D. Compilation of Parrot.java succeeds, but a runtime exception is thrown if method fly() is ever called on an instance of class Parrot.

E. Compilation of Parrot.java succeeds, but a runtime exception is thrown if method getRefCount() is ever called on an instance of class Parrot.

10. Which one statement is true about class `Bird` above and class `Nightingale` below?

```
 1. package singers;
 2.
 3. class Nightingale extends abcde.Bird {
 4.   Nightingale() { referenceCount++; }
 5.
 6.   public static void main(String args[]) {
 7.     System.out.print("BEFORE: " + referenceCount);
 8.     Nightingale florence = new Nightingale();
 9.     System.out.println("  AFTER: " + referenceCount);
10.     florence.fly();
11.   }
12. }
```

A. The program will compile and execute. The output will be

Before: 0 After: 2.

B. The program will compile and execute. The output will be

Before: 0 After: 1.

C. Compilation of `Nightingale` will fail at line 4, because statics cannot be overridden.

D. Compilation of `Nightingale` will fail at line 10, because method `fly()` is protected in the superclass.

E. Compilation of `Nightingale` will succeed, but an exception will be thrown at line 10, because method `fly()` is protected in the superclass.

CHAPTER

FOUR

4

Converting and Casting

- Conversion of primitive data types

- Casting of primitive data types

- Conversion of object references

- Casting of object references

In this chapter you will cover the following Java Certification Exam objectives:

- Determine if an assignment is permitted between any two variables, of possibly different types.

- Determine the effect of assignment and modification operations upon variables of any type.

Every Java variable has a type. Primitive data types include `int`, `long`, `double`, and so on. Object reference data types may be classes (such as `Vector` or `Graphics`) or interfaces (such as `LayoutManager` or `Runnable`). There can also be arrays of primitives, objects, or arrays.

This chapter discusses the ways that a data value can change its type. Values can change type either explicitly or implicitly; that is, either they change at your request or at the system's initiative. Java places a lot of importance on type, and successful Java programming requires that you be aware of type changes.

Explicit and Implicit Type Changes

You can *explicitly* change the type of a value by *casting*. To cast an expression to a new type, just prefix the expression with the new type name in parentheses. For example, the following line of code retrieves an element from a vector, casts that element to type `Button`, and assigns the result to a variable called `btn`:

```
Button btn = (Button) (myVector.elementAt(5));
```

Of course, the fifth element of the vector must be capable of being treated as a Button. There are compile-time rules and runtime rules that must be observed. This chapter will familiarize you with those rules.

There are situations in which the system *implicitly* changes the type of an expression without your explicitly performing a cast. For example, suppose you have a variable called `myColor` that refers to an instance of `Color`, and you want to store `myColor` in a vector. You would probably do the following:

```
myVector.addElement(myColor);
```

There is more to this code than meets the eye. The addElement() method of class Vector is declared with a parameter of type Object, not of type Color. As the argument is passed to the method, it undergoes an implicit type change. Such automatic, non-explicit type changing is known as *conversion*. Conversion, like casting, is governed by a number of rules. Unlike the casting rules, all conversion rules are enforced at compile time.

The number of casting and conversion rules is rather large, due to the large number of cases to be considered. (For example, can you cast a char to a double? Can you convert an interface to a final class?) The good news is that most of the rules accord with common sense, and most of the combinations can be generalized into rules of thumb. By the end of this chapter, you will know when you can explicitly cast, and when the system will implicitly convert on your behalf.

Primitives and Conversion

The two broad categories of Java data types are primitives and objects. *Primitive* data types are ints, floats, booleans, and so on. (There are eight primitive data types in all; see Chapter 1, *Language Fundamentals*, for a complete explanation of Java's primitives.) *Object* data types (or more properly, *object reference* data types) are all the hundreds of classes and interfaces of the JDK, plus the infinity of classes and interfaces to be invented by Java programmers.

Both primitive values and object references can be converted and cast, so there are four general cases to consider:

- Conversion of primitives
- Casting of primitives
- Conversion of object references
- Casting of object references

The simplest topic is implicit conversion of primitives (that is, ints, longs, chars, booleans, and so on). All conversion of primitive data types takes place at compile time; this is because all the information needed to determine whether or not the conversion is legal is available at compile time. (This is not the case for object data, as you will see later in this chapter.)

There are three contexts or situations in which conversion of a primitive might occur:

- Assignment
- Method call
- Arithmetic promotion

The following sections deal with each of these contexts in turn.

Primitive Conversion: Assignment

Assignment conversion happens when you assign a value to a variable of a different type from the original value. For example

```
1. int i;
2. double d;
3. i = 10;
4. d = i;    // Assign an int value to a double variable
```

Obviously, d cannot hold an integer value. At the moment the fourth line of code is executed, the integer 10 that is stored in variable i gets converted to the double-precision value 10.0000000000000 (remaining zeros omitted for brevity).

The code above is perfectly legal. Some assignments, on the other hand, are illegal. For example, the following code will not compile:

```
1. double d;
2. short s;
3. d = 1.2345;
4. s = d;    // Assign a double value to a short variable
```

This code will not compile. (The error message says "Incompatible type for =.") The compiler recognizes that trying to cram a double value into a short variable is like trying to pour a quart of coffee into an eight-ounce teacup, as shown in Figure 4.1. It can be done (that is, the value assignment can be done; the coffee thing is impossible), but you have to use an explicit cast, which will be explained in the following section.

FIGURE 4.1:

Illegal conversion of a quart to a cup, with loss of data

The general rules for primitive assignment conversion can be stated as follows:

- A boolean may not be converted to any other type.

- A non-boolean may be converted to another non-boolean type, provided the conversion is a *widening conversion*.

- A non-boolean may not be converted to another non-boolean type, if the conversion would be a *narrowing conversion*.

Widening conversions change a value to a type that accommodates a wider range of values than the original type can accommodate. In most cases, the new type has more bits than the original and can be visualized as being "wider" than the original, as shown in Figure 4.2.

FIGURE 4.2:

Widening conversion

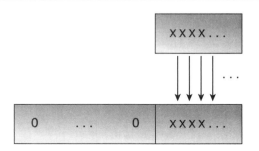

Widening conversions do not lose information about the magnitude of a value. In the first example in this section, an int value was assigned to a double variable. This was legal, because doubles are, so to speak, "wider" than ints, so there is room in a double to accommodate the information in an int. Java's widening conversions are

- From a byte to a short, an int, a long, a float, or a double

- From a short to an int, a long, a float, or a double

- From a char to an int, a long, a float, or a double

- From an int to a long, a float, or a double

- From a long to a float or a double

- From a float to a double

Figure 4.3 illustrates all the widening conversions. The arrows can be taken to mean "can be widened to." To determine whether it is legal to convert from one type to another, find the first type in the figure and see if you can reach the second type by following the arrows.

FIGURE 4.3:

Widening conversions

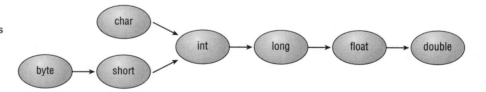

The figure shows, for example, that it is perfectly legal to assign a byte value to a float variable, because you can trace a path from *byte* to *float* by following the arrows (*byte* to *short* to *int* to *long* to *float*). You cannot, on the other hand, trace a path from *long* to *short*, so it is not legal to assign a long value to a short variable.

Figure 4.3 is easy to memorize. The figure consists mostly of the numeric data types in order of size. The only extra piece of information is *char*, but that goes in the only place it could go: a 16-bit char "fits inside" a 32-bit int. (Note that you can't convert a byte to a char or a char to a short, even though it seems reasonable to do so.)

Any conversion between primitive types that is not represented by a path of arrows in Figure 4.3 is a *narrowing conversion*. These conversions lose information about the magnitude of the value being converted, and are not allowed in assignments. It is geometrically impossible to portray the narrowing conversions in a graph like Figure 4.3, but they can be summarized as follows:

- From a byte to a char
- From a short to a byte or a char
- From a char to a byte or a short
- From an int to a byte, a short, or a char
- From a long to a byte, a short, a char, or an int
- From a float to a byte, a short, a char, an int, or a long
- From a double to a byte, a short, a char, an int, a long, or a float

You do not really need to memorize this list. It simply represents all the conversions not shown in Figure 4.3, which is easier to memorize.

Primitive Conversion: Method Call

Another kind of conversion is *method-call conversion*. A method-call conversion happens when you pass a value of one type as an argument to a method that expects a different type. For example, the cos() method of the Math class expects a single argument of type double. Consider the following code:

```
1. float frads;
2. double d;
3. frads = 2.34567f;
4. d = Math.cos(frads);   // Pass float to method that expects double
```

The float value in frads is automatically converted to a double value before it is handed to the cos() method. Just as with assignment conversions, there are strict rules that govern which conversions are allowed and which conversions will be rejected by the compiler. The code below quite reasonably generates a compiler error (assuming there is a vector called myVector):

```
1. double d = 12.0;
2. Object ob = myVector.elementAt(d);
```

The compiler error message says, "Incompatible type for method. Explicit cast needed to convert double to int." This means that the compiler can't convert the double argument to a type that is supported by a version of the elementAt()

method. It turns out that the only version of elementAt() is the version that takes an integer argument. Thus a value may only be passed to elementAt() if that value is an int or can be converted to an int.

Fortunately, the rule that governs which method-call conversions are permitted is the same rule that governs assignment conversions. Widening conversions (as shown in Figure 4.3) are permitted; narrowing conversions are forbidden.

Primitive Conversion: Arithmetic Promotion

The last kind of primitive conversion to consider is *arithmetic promotion*. Arithmetic-promotion conversions happen within arithmetic statements, while the compiler is trying to make sense out of many different possible kinds of operand.

Consider the following fragment:

```
1. short s = 9;
2. int i = 10;
3. float f = 11.1f;
4. double d = 12.2;
5. if (++s * i  >=  f / d)
6.    System.out.println(">>>>");
7. else
8.    System.out.println("<<<<");
```

The code on line 5 multiplies an incremented short by an int; then it divides a float by a double; finally it compares the two results. Behind the scenes, the system is doing extensive type conversion to ensure that the operands can be meaningfully incremented, multiplied, divided, and compared. These conversions are all widening conversions. Thus they are known as *arithmetic-promotion conversions*, because values are "promoted" to wider types.

The rules that govern arithmetic promotion distinguish between unary and binary operators. *Unary* operators operate on a single value. *Binary* operators operate on two values. Figure 4.4 shows Java's unary and binary arithmetic operators.

FIGURE 4.4:

Unary and binary arithmetic operators

Unary operators:	+	−	++	− −		~		
Binary operators:	+	−	*	/	%	>>	>>>	<<
		&	^	|				

For unary operators, two rules apply, depending on the type of the single operand:

- If the operand is a byte, a short, or a char, it is converted to an int.

- Else if the operand is of any other type, it is not converted.

For binary operators, there are four rules, depending on the types of the two operands:

- If one of the operands is a double, the other operand is converted to a double.

- Else if one of the operands is a float, the other operand is converted to a float.

- Else if one of the operands is a long, the other operand is converted to a long.

- Else both operands are converted to ints.

With these rules in mind, it is possible to determine what really happens in the code example given at the beginning of this section:

1. The short s is promoted to an int and then incremented.

2. The result of step 1 (an int) is multiplied by the int i. Since both operands are of the same type, and that type is not narrower than an int, no conversion is necessary. The result of the multiplication is an int.

3. Before dividing float f by double d, f is widened to a double. The division generates a double-precision result.

4. The result of step 2 (an int) is to be compared to the result of step 3 (a double). The int is converted to a double, and the two operands are compared. The result of a comparison is always of type boolean.

Primitives and Casting

So far this chapter has shown that Java is perfectly willing to perform widening conversions on primitives. These conversions are implicit and behind the scenes; you don't need to write any explicit code to make them happen.

Casting means explicitly telling Java to make a conversion. A casting conversion may widen or narrow its argument. To cast, just precede a value with the parenthesized name of the desired type. For example, the following lines of code cast an int to a double:

```
1. int i = 5;
2. double d = (double)i;
```

Of course, the cast is not necessary. The following code, in which the cast has been omitted, would do an assignment conversion on i, with the same result as the example above:

```
1. int i = 5;
2. double d = i;
```

Casts are useful when you want to perform a narrowing conversion. Such conversion will never be performed implicity; you have to program an explicit cast to convince the compiler that what you really want is a narrowing conversion. Narrowing runs the risk of losing information; the cast tells the compiler that you accept the risk.

For example, the following code generates a compiler error:

```
1. short s = 259;
2. byte b = s;    // Compiler error
3. System.out.println("s = " + s + ", b = " + b);
```

The compiler error message for the second line will say (among other things), "Explicit cast needed to convert short to byte." Adding an explicit cast is easy:

```
1. short s = 259;
2. byte b = (byte)s;     // Explicit cast
3. System.out.println("b = " + b);
```

When this code is executed, the number 259 (binary 100000011) must be squeezed into a single byte. This is accomplished by preserving the low-order byte of the value and discarding the rest. The code prints out the (perhaps surprising) message:

```
b = 3
```

The 1 bit in bit position 8 gets discarded, leaving only 3, as shown in Figure 4.5. Narrowing conversions can result in radical value changes; this is why the compiler requires you to cast explicitly. The cast tells the compiler, "Yes, I really want to do it."

FIGURE 4.5:

Casting a short
to a byte

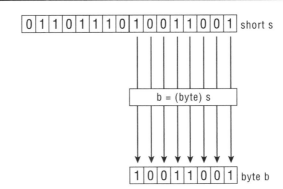

Casting a value to a wider value (as shown in Figure 4.3) is always permitted but never required; if you omit the cast, an implicit conversion will be performed on your behalf. However, explicitly casting can make your code a bit more readable. For example

```
  1. int i = 2;
  2. double radians;
     .        // Hundreds of
     .        // lines of
     .        // code
600. radians = (double)i;
```

The cast in the last line is not required, but it serves as a good reminder to any readers (including yourself) who might have forgotten the type of radians.

There are two simple rules that govern casting of primitive types:

- You can cast any non-boolean type to any other non-boolean type.

- You cannot cast a boolean to any other type; you cannot cast any other type to a boolean.

Note that while casting is ordinarily used when narrowing, it is perfectly legal to cast when widening. The cast is unnecessary, but provides a bit of clarity.

Object Reference Conversion

Object reference values, like primitive values, participate in assignment conversion, method-call conversion, and casting. (There is no arithmetic promotion of object references, since references cannot be arithmetic operands.) Object reference conversion is more complicated than primitive conversion, because there are more possible combinations of old and new types—and more combinations mean more rules.

Reference conversion, like primitive conversion, takes place at compile time, because the compiler has all the information it needs to determine whether or not the conversion is legal. Later you will see that this is not the case for object casting.

The following sections examine object reference assignment, method-call, and casting conversions.

Object Reference Assignment Conversion

Object reference assignment conversion happens when you assign an object reference value to a variable of a different type. There are three general kinds of object reference type:

- A class type, such as `Button` or `FileWriter`
- An interface type, such as `Cloneable` or `LayoutManager`
- An array type, such as `int[][]` or `TextArea[]`

Generally speaking, assignment conversion of a reference looks like this:

```
1. OldType x = new OldType();
2. NewType y = x;    // reference assignment conversion
```

This is the general format of an assignment conversion from an OldType to a NewType. Unfortunately, OldType can be a class, an interface, or an array; NewType can also be a class, an interface, or an array. Thus there are nine (= 3×3) possible combinations to consider. Figure 4.6 shows the rules for all nine cases.

FIGURE 4.6:

The rules for object reference assignment conversion

Converting `Oldtype` to `Newtype`:

	`Oldtype` is a class	`Oldtype` is an interface	`Oldtype` is an array
`Newtype` is a class	`Oldtype` must be a subclass of `Newtype`	`Newtype` must be `Object`	`Newtype` must be `Object`
`Newtype` is an interface	`Oldtype` must implement interface `Newtype`	`Oldtype` must a subinterface of `Newtype`	`Newtype` must be `Cloneable`
`Newtype` is an array	Compiler error	Compiler error	`Oldtype` must be an array of some object reference type that can be converted to whatever `Newtype` is an array of

It would be difficult to memorize the nine rules shown in Figure 4.6. Fortunately, there is a rule of thumb.

Recall that with primitives, conversions were permitted, provided they were widening conversions. The notion of widening does not really apply to references, but there is a similar principle at work. In general, object reference conversion is permitted when the direction of the conversion is "up" the inheritance hierarchy; that is, the old type should inherit from the new type. This rule of thumb does not cover all nine cases, but it is a helpful way to look at things.

The rules for object reference conversion can be stated as follows:

- An interface type may only be converted to an interface type or to `Object`. If the new type is an interface, it must be a superinterface of the old type.

- A class type may be converted to a class type or to an interface type. If converting to a class type, the new type must be a superclass of the old type. If converting to an interface type, the old class must implement the interface.

- An array may be converted to the class `Object`, to the interface `Cloneable`, or to an array. Only an array of object reference types may be converted to an array, and the old element type must be convertible to the new element type.

To illustrate these rules, consider the inheritance hierarchy shown in Figure 4.7 (assume there is an interface called `Squeezable`).

FIGURE 4.7:

A simple class
hierarchy

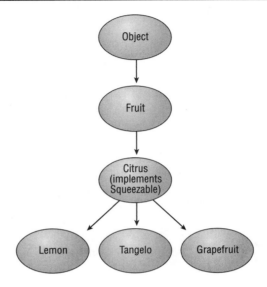

As a first example, consider the following code:

```
1. Tangelo tange = new Tangelo();
2. Citrus cit = tange;
```

This code is fine. A Tangelo is being converted to a Citrus. The new type is a superclass of the old type, so the conversion is allowed. Converting in the other direction ("down" the hierarchy tree) is not allowed:

```
1. Citrus cit = new Citrus();
2. Tangelo tange = cit;
```

This code will result in a compiler error.

What happens when one of the types is an interface?

```
1. Grapefruit g = new Grapefruit();
2. Squeezable squee = g;    // No problem
3. Grapefruit g2 = squee;  // Error
```

The second line ("No problem") changes a class type (Grapefruit) to an interface type. This is correct, provided Grapefruit really implements Squeezable. A glance at Figure 4.7 shows that this is indeed the case, because Grapefruit inherits from Citrus, which implements Squeezable. The third line is an error, because an interface can never be implicitly converted to any reference type other than Object.

Finally, consider an example with arrays:

```
1. Fruit fruits[];
2. Lemon lemons[];
3. Citrus citruses[] = new Citrus[10];
4. for (int i=0; i<10; i++) {
5.   citruses[i] = new Citrus();
6. }
7. fruits = citruses;    // No problem
8. lemons = citruses;    // Error
```

Line 7 converts an array of Citrus to an array of Fruit. This is fine, because Fruit is a superclass of Citrus. Line 8 converts in the other direction and fails, because Lemon is not a superclass of Citrus.

Object Method-Call Conversion

Fortunately, the rules for method-call conversion of object reference values are the same as the rules described above for assignment conversion of objects. The general rule of thumb is that converting to a superclass is permitted and converting to a subclass is not permitted. The specific, formal rules were given in a bulleted list in the previous section and are shown again here:

- An interface type may only be converted to an interface type or to Object. If the new type is an interface, it must be a superinterface of the old type.

- A class type may be converted to a class type or to an interface type. If converting to a class, the new type must be a superclass of the old type. If converting an an interface type, the old class must implement the interface.

- An array may be converted to the class Object, to the interface Cloneable, or to an array. Only an array of object reference types may be converted to an array, and the old element type must be convertible to the new element type.

To see how the rules make sense in the context of method calls, consider the extremely useful Vector class. You can store anything you like in a Vector (anything non-primitive, that is) by calling the method `addElement(Object ob)`. For example, the code below stores a tangelo in a vector:

```
1. Vector myVec = new Vector();
2. Tangelo tange = new Tangelo();
3. myVec.addElement(myTange);
```

The `myTange` argument will automatically be converted to type Object. The automatic conversion means that the people who wrote the Vector class didn't have to write a separate method for every possible type of object that anyone might conceivably want to store in a vector. This is fortunate: The Tangelo class was developed two years after the invention of the Vector, so the developer of the Vector class could not possibly have written specific Tangelo-handling code. An object of any class (and even an array of any type) can be passed into the single `addElement (Object ob)` method.

Object Reference Casting

Object reference casting is like primitive casting: By using a cast, you convince the compiler to let you do a conversion that otherwise might not be allowed.

Any kind of conversion that is allowed for assignments or method calls is allowed for explicit casting. For example, the following code is legal:

```
1. Lemon lem = new Lemon();
2. Citrus cit = (Citrus)lem;
```

The cast is legal, but not needed; if you leave it out, the compiler will do an implicit assignment conversion. The power of casting appears when you explicitly cast to a type that is not allowed by the rules of implicit conversion.

To understand how object casting works, it is important to understand the difference between objects and object reference variables. Every object (well, nearly every object; there are some obscure cases) is constructed via the new operator. The argument to new determines for all time the true class of the object. For example, if an object is constructed by calling new `Color(222, 0, 255)`, then throughout that object's lifetime its class will be `Color`.

Java programs do not deal directly with objects. They deal with *references* to objects. For example, consider the following code:

```
Color purple = new Color(222, 0, 255);
```

The variable `purple` is not an object; it is a reference to an object. The object itself lives in memory somewhere in the Java Virtual Machine. The variable `purple` contains something similar to the address of the object. This address is known as a *reference* to the object. The difference between a reference and an object is illustrated in Figure 4.8. References are stored in variables, and variables have types that are specified by the programmer at compile time. Object reference variable types can be classes (such as `Graphics` or `FileWriter`), interfaces (such as `Runnable` or `LayoutManager`), or arrays (such as `int[][]` or `Vector[]`).

FIGURE 4.8:

Reference and object

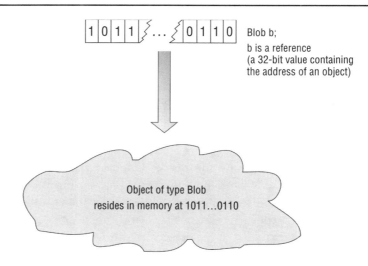

While an object's class is unchanging, it may be referenced by variables of many different types. For example, consider a stack. It is constructed by calling new `Stack()`, so its class really is Stack. Yet at various moments during the lifetime of this object, it may be referenced by variables of type Stack (of course), or of type Vector (because Stack inherits from Vector), or of type Object (because everything inherits from Object). It may even be referenced by variables of type Serializable, which is an interface, because the Stack class implements the Serializable interface. This situation is shown in Figure 4.9.

FIGURE 4.9:

Many variable types, one class

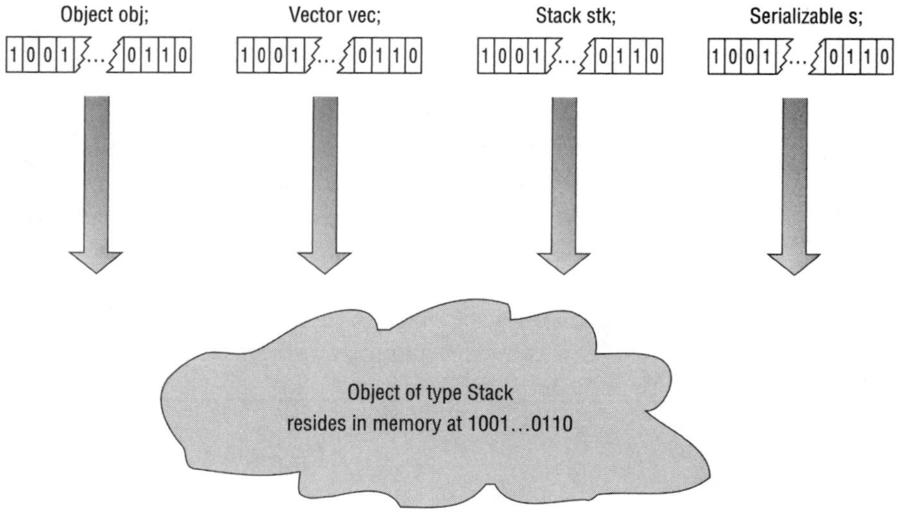

The type of a reference variable is obvious at compile time. However, the class of an object referenced by such a variable cannot be known until run time. This lack of knowledge is not a shortcoming of Java technology; it results from a fundamental principle of computer science. The distinction between compile-time knowledge and runtime knowledge was not relevant to our discussion of conversions; however, the difference becomes important with reference value casting. The rules for casting are a bit broader than those for conversion. Some of these rules concern reference type and can be enforced by the compiler at compile time; other rules concern object class and can only be enforced during execution.

There is no escaping the fact that there are quite a few rules governing object casting. The good news is that most of the rules cover obscure cases. You might as well start by seeing the big picture in all its complicated glory, but after this glimpse you will be presented with a few simple ideas that will see you through most common situations.

For object reference casting, there are not three but *four* possibilities for both the old type and the new type. Each type can be a non-final class, a final class, an interface, or an array. The first round of rule enforcement happens at compile time. The compile-time rules are summarized in the imposing Figure 4.10.

FIGURE 4.10:

Compile-time rules for object reference casting

	`Oldtype` is a non-final class	`Oldtype` is a final class	`Oldtype` is an interface	`Oldtype` is an array
`Newtype` is a non-final class	`Oldtype` must extend `Newtype`, or vice versa	`Oldtype` must extend `Newtype`	Always OK	`Oldtype` must be `Object`
`Newtype` is a final class	`Newtype` must extend `Oldtype`	`Oldtype` and `Newtype` must be the same class	`Newtype` must implement interface `Oldtype`	Compiler error
`Newtype` is an interface	Always OK	`Oldtype` must implement interface `Newtype`	Always OK	Compiler error
`Newtype` is an array	`Newtype` must be `Object`	Compiler error	Compiler error	`Oldtype` must be an array of some type that can be cast to whatever `Newtype` is an array of.

`Newtype` nt; `Oldtype` ot; nt = (newtype)ot;

Assuming that a desired cast survives compilation, a second check must occur at run time. The second check determines whether the class of the object being cast is compatible with the new type. Here *compatible* means that the class can be converted according to the conversion rules discussed in the previous two sections.

What a baffling collection of rules! For sanity's sake, bear in mind that only a few of the situations covered by these rules are commonly encountered in real life. (For instance, final classes are relatively rare.) A few rules of thumb and some examples should help to clarify things.

First, to simplify dealing with the compile-time rules, bear in mind the following facts about casting from `Oldtype` to `Newtype`:

- When both `Oldtype` and `Newtype` are classes, one class must be a subclass of the other.

- When both `Oldtype` and `Newtype` are arrays, both arrays must contain reference types (not primitives), and it must be legal to cast an element of `Oldtype` to an element of `Newtype`.

- You can always cast between an interface and a non-final object.

As for the runtime rule, remember that the conversion to Newtype must actually be possible. The following rules of thumb cover the most common cases:

- If Newtype is a class, the class of the expression being converted must be Newtype or must inherit from Newtype.

- If Newtype is an interface, the class of the expression being converted must implement Newtype.

It is definitely time for some examples! Look once again at the Fruit/Citrus hierarchy that you saw earlier in this chapter.

FIGURE 4.11:

Fruit hierarchy (reprise)

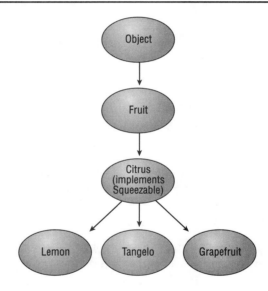

First, consider the following code:

```
1. Grapefruit g, g1;
2. Citrus c;
3. Tangelo t;
4. g = new Grapefruit();   // Class is Grapefruit
5. c = g;                   // Legal assignment conversion, no cast needed
6. g1 = (Grapefruit)c;     // Legal cast
7. t = (Tangelo)c;         // Illegal cast (throws an exception)
```

This code has four references but only one object. The object's class is Grapefruit, because it is Grapefruit's constructor that gets called on line 4. The assignment c = g on line 5 is a perfectly legal assignment conversion ("up" the inheritance hierarchy), so no explicit cast is required. In lines 6 and 7, the Citrus is cast to a Grapefruit and to a Tangelo. Recall that for casting between class types, one of the two classes (it doesn't matter which one) must be a subclass of the other. The first cast is from a Citrus to its subclass Grapefruit; the second cast is from a Citrus to its subclass Tangelo. Thus both casts are legal—at compile time. The compiler cannot determine the class of the object referenced by c, so it accepts both casts and lets fate determine the outcome at run time.

When the code is executed, eventually the Java Virtual Machine attempts to execute line 6: g1 = (Grapefruit)c; The class of c is determined to be Grapefruit, and there is no objection to converting a Grapefruit to a Grapefruit.

Line 7 attempts (at run time) to cast c to type Tangelo. The class of c is still Grapefruit, and a Grapefruit cannot be cast to a Tangelo. In order for the cast to be legal, the class of c would have to be Tangelo itself or some subclass of Tangelo. Since this is not the case, a runtime exception (java.lang.ClassCastException) is thrown.

Now take an example where an object is cast to an interface type. Begin by considering the following code fragment:

```
1. Grapefruit g, g1;
2. Squeezable s;
3. g = new Grapefruit();
4. s = g;              // Convert Grapefruit to Squeezable (Ok)
5. g1 = s;             // Convert Squeezable to Grapefruit (Compile error)
```

This code will not compile. Line 5 attempts to convert an interface (Squeezable) to a class (Grapefruit). It doesn't matter that Grapefruit implements Squeezable. Implicitly converting an interface to a class is never allowed; it is one of those cases where you have to use an explicit cast to tell the compiler that you really know what you're doing. With the cast, line 5 becomes

```
5. g1 = (Grapefruit)s;
```

Adding the cast makes the compiler happy. At run time, the Java Virtual Machine checks whether the class of s (which is Grapefruit) can be converted to Citrus. It can be, so the cast is allowed.

For a final example, involving arrays, look at the code below:

```
1. Grapefruit g[];
2. Squeezable s[];
3. Citrus c[];
4. g = new Grapefruit[500];
5. s = g;              // Convert Grapefruit array to Squeezable array (Ok)
6. c = (Citrus[])s;  // Cast Squeezable array to Citrus array (Ok)
```

Line 6 casts an array of Squeezables (s) to an array of Citruses (c). An array cast is legal if casting the array element types is legal (and if the element types are references, not primitives). In this example, the question is whether or not a Squeezable (the element type of array s) can be cast to a Citrus (the element type of the cast array). The previous example showed that this is a legal cast.

Chapter Summary

Primitive values and object references are very different kinds of data. Both can be converted (implicitly) or cast (explicitly). Primitive type changes are caused by

- Assignment conversion

- Method-call conversion

- Arithmetic-promotion conversion

- Explicit casting

Primitives may only be converted if the conversion widens the data. Primitives may be narrowed by casting, as long as neither the old nor the new type is boolean.

Object references may be converted or cast; the rules that govern these activities are extensive, as there are many combinations of cases to be covered. In general, going "up" the inheritance tree may be accomplished implicitly through conversion; going "down" the tree requires explicit casting. Object reference type changes are caused by

- Assignment conversion

- Method-call conversion

- Explicit casting

Test Yourself

1. Which of the following statements is correct? (Choose one.)

    A. Only primitives are converted automatically; to change the type of an object reference, you have to do a cast.

    B. Only object references are converted automatically; to change the type of a primitive, you have to do a cast.

    C. Arithmetic promotion of object references requires explicit casting.

    D. Both primitives and object references can be both converted and cast.

    E. Casting of numeric types may require a runtime check.

2. Which one line in the following code will not compile?

    ```
    1. byte b = 5;
    2. char c = '5';
    3. short s = 55;
    4. int i = 555;
    5. float f = 555.5f;
    6. b = s;
    7. i = c;
    8. if (f > b)
    9.    f = i;
    ```

3. Will the following code compile?

    ```
    1. byte b = 2;
    2. byte b1 = 3;
    3. b = b * b1;
    ```

4. In the code below, what are the possible types for variable `result`? (Choose the most complete true answer.)

    ```
    1. byte b = 11;
    2. short s = 13;
    3. result = b * ++s;
    ```

    A. byte, short, int, long, float, double

    B. boolean, byte, short, char, int, long, float, double

    C. byte, short, char, int, long, float, double

    D. byte, short, char

    E. int, long, float, double

5. Consider the following class:

```
1.   class Cruncher {
2.     void crunch(int i)    {System.out.println("int version");}
3.     void crunch(String s) {System.out.println("String version");}
4.
5.     public static void main(String args[]) {
6.       Cruncher crun = new Cruncher();
7.       char ch = 'p';
8.       crun.crunch(ch);
9.     }
10.  }
```

Which of the statements below is true? (Choose one.)

    A. Line 3 will not compile, because void methods cannot be overridden.

    B. Line 8 will not compile, because there is no version of `crunch()` that takes a char argument.

    C. The code will compile but will throw an exception at line 8.

    D. The code will compile and produce the following output:

```
int version
```

    E. The code will compile and produce the following output:

```
String version
```

6. Which of the statements below is true? (Choose one.)

    A. Object references can be converted in assignments but not in method calls.

    B. Object references can be converted in method calls but not in assignments.

    C. Object references can be converted in both method calls and assignments, but the rules governing these conversions are very different.

    D. Object references can be converted in both method calls and assignments, and the rules governing these conversions are identical.

    E. Object references can never be converted.

7. Consider the following code:

```
1. Object ob = new Object();
2. String stringarr[] = new String[50];
3. Float floater = new Float(3.14f);
4.
5. ob = stringarr;
6. ob = stringarr[5];
7. floater = ob;
8. ob = floater;
```

Which line above will not compile?

Questions 8–10 refer to the class hierarchy shown in Figure 4.12.

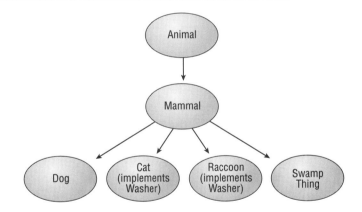

8. Consider the following code:

```
1. Dog        rover, fido;
2. Animal     anim;
3.
4. rover = new Dog();
5. anim = rover;
6. fido = (Dog)anim;
```

Which of the statements below is true? (Choose one.)

A. Line 5 will not compile.

B. Line 6 will not compile.

C. The code will compile but will throw an exception at line 6.

D. The code will compile and run.

E. The code will compile and run, but the cast in line 6 is not required and can be eliminated.

9. Consider the following code:

```
1. Cat sunflower;
2. Washer wawa;
3. SwampThing pogo;
4.
5. sunflower = new Cat();
6. wawa = sunflower;
7. pogo = (SwampThing)wawa;
```

Which of the statements below is true? (Choose one.)

A. Line 6 will not compile; an explicit cast is required to convert a Cat to a Washer.

B. Line 7 will not compile, because you cannot cast an interface to a class.

C. The code will compile and run, but the cast in line 7 is not required and can be eliminated.

D. The code will compile but will throw an exception at line 7, because runtime conversion from an interface to a class is not permitted.

E. The code will compile but will throw an exception at line 7, because the runtime class of wawa cannot be converted to type SwampThing.

10. Consider the following code:

```
1. Raccoon rocky;
2. SwampThing pogo;
3. Washer w;
4.
5. rocky = new Raccoon();
6. w = rocky;
7. pogo = w;
```

Which of the following statements is true? (Choose one.)

A. Line 6 will not compile; an explicit cast is required to convert a Raccoon to a Washer.

B. Line 7 will not compile; an explicit cast is required to convert a Washer to a SwampThing.

C. The code will compile and run.

D. The code will compile but will throw an exception at line 7, because runtime conversion from an interface to a class is not permitted.

E. The code will compile but will throw an exception at line 7, because the runtime class of w cannot be converted to type SwampThing.

Flow Control and Exceptions

- Loop constructs

- Conditional constructs

- Catching exceptions

- Throwing exceptions

- Checked exceptions

In this chapter, you will cover the following Java Certification Exam objectives:

- Write nested conditional code using the if, else and switch constructs.

- Identify the legal expression types for the argument of if() and switch().

- Write nested loops to iterate blocks within specific values in loop counter variables.

- Demonstrate the use of both the labeled and unlabeled versions of the break and continue keywords to modify normal loop behavior.

- Demonstrate the flow of control that occurs in try, catch(), and finally constructions under conditions of normal execution, caught exception, and uncaught exception.

- Write code that correctly uses the throws clause in a method declaration where that method contains code that might throw exceptions.

- State what exceptions may legitimately be thrown from an overriding method in a subclass, based on the declaration of the overridden super-class method.

- Write code to create and throw a specified exception.

Flow control is a fundamental facility of almost any programming language. Sequence, iteration, and selection are the major elements of flow control, and Java provides these in forms that are familiar to C and C++ programmers. Additionally, Java provides for exception handling.

Sequence is provided simply by the specification that within a single block of code, execution starts at the top and proceeds towards the bottom. Iteration is catered for by three styles of loop: These are the for(), while(), and do constructions. Selection occurs when either the if()/else() or switch() construct is used.

Java's complement omits one common element of flow control. This is this idea of a goto statement. When Java was being designed, the team responsible did some analysis of a large body of existing code and determined that there were two situations where the use of goto was appropriate in new code. These occasions were breaking out of nested loops and handling of exception conditions or errors. So, the designers left out goto and, in its place, provided alternative constructions to handle these particular conditions. The break and continue statements that control the execution of loops were extended to handle nested loops, and formalized exception handling was introduced, using ideas similar to those of C++.

This chapter discusses the flow-control facilities of Java. We will look closely at the exception mechanism, since this is an area that commonly causes some confusion. But first, we will discuss the loop mechanisms.

The Loop Constructs

Java provides three loop constructions. Taken from C and C++, these are the `while()`, do, and `for()` constructs. Each provides the facility for repeating the execution of a block of code until some condition occurs. We will discuss the `while()` loop, which is perhaps the most simple, first.

The *while()* Loop

The general form of the `while()` loop is

```
1. while (boolean_condition)
2.     repeated_statement
```

In such a construct, the element `boolean_condition` can be any expression that returns a `boolean` result. Notice that this differs from C and C++, where a variety of types may be used: In Java you can *only* use a `boolean` expression. Typically, you might use a comparison of some kind, such as x > 5.

The `repeated_statement` will be executed again and again until the `boolean_condition` becomes `false`. If the condition never becomes `false`, then the loop will repeat forever. In practice, this really means that the loop will repeat until the program is stopped or the machine is turned off.

You will often need a loop that executes not just a single statement as its body, but a sequence of statements. In fact a block, surrounded by braces, is treated as a single statement, so you will commonly see a `while()` loop of this form:

```
1. while (boolean_condition) {
2.     do_something..
3.     do_some_more..
4. }
```

Notice the pairing of the curly braces ({ and }). These make the statements within them appear to be a single statement from the loop's point of view.

NOTE

The exact position of the opening curly brace that marks a block of code is a matter of near-religious contention. Some programmers put it at the end of a line, as in the examples in this book. Others put it on a line by itself. Provided it is otherwise placed in the correct sequence, it does not matter how many space, tab, and newline characters are placed before or after the opening curly brace. However, this positioning is not relevant to syntactic correctness. You should be aware, however, that the style used in presenting the exam questions, as well as that used for the code in the developer-level exam, is the style shown here, where the opening brace is placed at the end of the line.

TIP

A second point of style relates to the redundant use of braces. If only one statement is subordinate to a `while()` condition or other construction, then you can omit the braces. However, it is often a good idea to use these braces anyway, because doing so can avoid the introduction of bugs if you subsequently add statements intended to be subordinate to the loop.

Observe that if the `boolean_condition` is already `false` when the loop is first encountered, then the body of the loop will never be executed. This relates to the main distinguishing feature of the do loop, which we will discuss next.

The *do* Loop

The general form of the do loop is

```
1. do
2.   repeated_statement
3. while (boolean_condition);
```

This is similar to the `while()` loop just discussed, and as before, it is common to have a loop body consisting of multiple statements. Under such conditions, you can use a block:

```
1. do {
2.   do_something
3.   do_more
4. } while (boolean_condition);
```

Again, repetition of the loop is terminated when the `boolean_condition` becomes `false`. The significant difference is that this loop always executes the body of the loop at least once, since the test is performed at the end of the body.

In general, the `do` loop is probably less frequently used than the `while()` loop, but the third loop format is perhaps the most common. The third form is the `for()` loop, which we will discuss next.

The *for()* Loop

A common requirement in programming is to perform a loop so that a single variable is incremented over a range of values between two limits. This is frequently provided for by a loop that uses the keyword `for`. Java's `while()` loop can achieve this effect, but it is most commonly achieved using the `for()` loop. However, as with C and C++, the `for()` loop is more general than simply providing for iteration over a sequence of values.

The general form of the `for()` loop is

```
1. for (init_statement ; boolean_condition ; iter_expression)
2.     loop_body
```

Again, a block can be used like this:

```
1. for (init_statement ; boolean_condition ; iter_expression) {
2.     do_something
3.     do_more
4. }
```

The keys to this loop are in the three parts contained in the brackets following the `for` keyword:

- The `init_statement` is executed immediately before the loop itself is started. It is often used to set up starting conditions. You will see shortly that it can also contain variable declarations.

- The `boolean_condition` is treated exactly the same as in the `while()` loop. The body of the loop will be executed repeatedly until the condition ceases to be true. As with the `while()` loop, it is possible that the body of a `for()` loop might never be executed. This occurs if the condition is already `false` at the start of the loop.

- The `iter_expression` (short for "iteration expression") is executed immediately after the body of the loop, just before the test is performed again.
  Com-monly, this is used to increment a loop counter.

If you have already declared an `int` variable x, you can code a simple sequence
counting loop like this:

```
1. for (x = 0; x < 10; x++) {
2.    System.out.println("value is " + x);
3. }
```

This would result in 10 lines of output starting with

```
value is 0
```

and ending with

```
value is 9
```

In fact, because `for()` loops commonly need a counting variable, you are
allowed to declare variables in the `init_statement` part. The scope of such a
variable is restricted to the statement or block following the `for()` statement and
the `for()` part itself. This protects loop counter variables from interfering with
each other and prevents leftover loop count values from accidental re-use. This
results in code like this:

```
1. for (int x = 0; x < 10; x++) {
2.    System.out.println("value is " + x);
3. }
```

It might be useful to look at the equivalent of this code implemented using a
`while()` loop:

```
1. {
2.    int x = 0;
3.    while (x < 10) {
4.       System.out.println("value is " + x);
5.       x++;
6.    }
7. }
```

This version reinforces a couple of points. First, the scope of the variable x,
declared in the `init_statement` part of the `for()` loop, is restricted to the loop
and its control parts (that is, the `init_statement`, `boolean_condition`, and `iter
_expression`). Second, the `iter_expression` is executed after the rest of the loop
body, effectively before control comes back to the test condition.

The *for()* Loop and the Comma Separator

The for() loop allows the use of the comma separator in a special way. The init_statement and iter_expression parts described previously can actually contain a sequence of expressions rather than just a single one. If you want such a sequence, you should separate those expressions, not with a semicolon (which would be mistaken as the separator between the three parts of the for() loop control structure) but with a comma. This behavior is borrowed from C and C++ where the comma is an operator, but in Java the comma serves only as a special case separator for conditions where the semicolon would be unsuitable. This example demonstrates:

```
1. int i, j;
2. for (j = 3, k = 6; j + k < 20; j++, k +=2) {
3.   System.out.println("j is " + j + " k is " + k);
4. }
```

Note that while you can use the comma to separate several expressions, you cannot mix expressions with variable declarations. So this would be illegal:

```
1. int i;
2. for (i = 7, int j = 0; i < 10; j++) { } // illegal !
```

We have now discussed the three loop constructions in their basic forms. The next section looks at more advanced flow control in loops, specifically the use of the break and continue statements.

The *break* and *continue* Statements in Loops

Sometimes you need to abandon execution of the body of a loop, or perhaps a number of nested loops. The Java development team recognized this situation as a legitimate use for a goto statement. Java provides two statements, break and continue, which can be used instead of goto to achieve this effect.

Using *continue*

Suppose you have a loop which is processing an array of items that contain two String references. The first String is always non-null, but the second might not be present. To process this, you might decide that you want, in pseudocode, something along these lines:

```
for each element of the array
  process the first String
```

```
     if the second String exists
       process the second String
     endif
   endfor
```

You will recognize that this can be coded easily by using an if block to control processing of the second String. However, you can also use the continue statement like this:

```
1. for (int i = 0; i < array.length; i++) {
2.    // Process first string
3.    if (array[i].secondString == null) {
4.      continue;
5.    }
6.    // process second string
7. }
```

In this case, the example is sufficiently simple that you probably do not see any advantage over using the if() condition to control the execution of the second part. If the second String processing was long, and perhaps heavily indented in its own right, you might find that the use of continue was slightly simpler visually.

The real strength of continue is that it is able to skip out of multiple levels of loop. Suppose our example, instead of being two String objects, had two arrays of char values. Now we will need to nest our loops. Consider this sample:

```
1. mainLoop: for (int i = 0; i < array.length; i++) {
2.    // Process first array
3.    for (int j = 0; j < array[i].secondArray.length; j++) {
4.      if (array[i].secondArray[j] == '\u0000') {
5.        continue mainLoop;
6.      }
7.    }
8. }
```

Notice particularly the label mainLoop which has been applied to the for() on line 1. The fact that this is a label is indicated by the trailing colon. You can apply labels of this form to the opening loop statements: do, while(), or for().

Here, when the processing of the second array comes across a zero value it abandons the whole processing not just for the second array, but for the current object in the main array. This is equivalent to jumping to the statement i++ in the first for() statement.

You might still think that this is not really any advantage over using if() statements, but imagine that further processing was done between lines 6 and 7 and that finding the zero character in the array was required to avoid that further processing, too. To achieve that without continue, you would have to set a flag in the inner loop and use that to abandon the outer loop processing. It can be done, but it is rather messier.

Using *break*

The break statement, when applied to a loop, is somewhat similar to the continue statement. However, instead of prematurely completing the current iteration of a loop, break causes the entire loop to be abandoned. Consider this example:

```
1. for (int j = 0; j < array.length; j++) {
2.   if (array[j] == null) {
3.     break; //break out of inner loop
4.   }
5.   // process array[j]
6. }
```

In this case, instead of simply skipping some processing for array[j] and proceeding directly to processing array[j+1], this version quits the entire inner loop as soon as a null element is found.

You can also use labels on break statements, and as before, you must place a matching label on one of the three loop statements of an enclosing loop. The break and continue statements provide a convenient way to make parts of a loop conditional, especially when used in their labeled formats.

The next section discusses the if()/else and switch() constructions, which provide the normal means of implementing conditional code.

The Selection Statements

Java provides a choice of two selection constructs. These are the if()/else and switch() mechanisms. You can easily write simple conditional code or a choice of two execution paths based on the value of a boolean expression using if()/else. If you need more complex choices between multiple execution paths, and if an appropriate argument is available to control the choice, then you can use switch(); otherwise you can use either nests or sequences of if()/else.

The *if()/else* Construct

The if()/else construct takes a boolean argument as the basis of its choice. Often you will use a comparison expression to provide this argument, for example:

```
1. if (x > 5)
2.   System.out.println("x is more than 5");
```

This sample executes line 2 provided the test (x > 5) in line 1 returns true. Often you will require more than one line of code to be conditional upon the result of the test, and you can achieve this using a block, just as with the loops discussed earlier.

Additionally, you can use an else part to give code that is executed under the conditions that the test returns false. For example

```
1. if (x > 5) {
2.   System.out.println("x is more than 5");
3. }
4. else {
5.   System.out.println("x is not more than 5");
6. }
```

Beyond this, you can use if()/else in a nested fashion, refining conditions to more specific, or narrower, tests at each point.

The if()/else construction makes a test between only two possible paths of execution, although you can create nests or sequences to select between a greater range of possibilities. The next section discusses the switch() construction, which allows a single value to select between multiple possible execution paths.

The *switch()* Construct

If you need to make a choice between multiple alternative execution paths, and the choice can be based upon an int value, you can use the switch() construct. Consider this example:

```
1. switch (x) {
2.   case 1:
3.     System.out.println("Got a 1");
4.     break;
```

```
5.    case 2:
6.    case 3:
7.      System.out.println("Got 2 or 3");
8.      break;
9.    default:
10.     System.out.println("Got something other then 1, 2, or 3");
11.     break;
12. }
```

Note that you cannot determine by inspection that the variable x must be either byte, short, char, or int. It must not be long, either of the floating point types, boolean, or an object reference.

The comparison of values following case labels with the value of the expression supplied as an argument to switch() determines the execution path. The arguments to case labels must be constants, or at least a constant expression that can be fully evaluated at compile time. You cannot use a variable or expression involving variables.

Each case label takes only a single argument, but when execution jumps to one of these labels, it continues downward until it reaches a break statement. This occurs even if it passes another case label or the default label. So in the example shown above, if x has the value 2, execution goes through lines 1, 5, 6, 7, 8, and continues beyond line 12. This requirement for break to indicate the completion of the case part is important. More often than not, you do not want to omit the break, as you do not want execution to "fall through." However, to achieve the effect shown in the example, where more than one particular value of x causes execution of the same block of code, you use multiple case labels with only a single break.

The default statement is comparable to the else part of an if()/else construction. Execution jumps to the default statement if none of the explicit case values matches the argument provided to switch(). Although the default statement is shown at the end of the switch() block in the example (and this is both a conventional and reasonably logical place to put it), there is no rule that requires this placement.

Now that we have examined the constructions that provide for iteration and selection under normal program control, we will look at the flow of control under exception conditions—that is, conditions when some runtime problem has arisen.

Exceptions

Sometimes when a program is executing, something occurs that is not quite normal from the point of view of the goal at hand. For example, a user might enter an invalid filename, or a file might contain corrupted data, a network link can fail, or there could be a bug in the program that causes it to try to make an illegal memory access, such as referring to an element beyond the end of an array.

Circumstances of this type are called *exception* conditions in Java. If you take no steps to deal with an exception, execution jumps to the end of the current method. The exception then appears in the caller of that method, and execution jumps to the end of the calling method. This continues until execution reaches the "top" of the affected thread, at which point the thread dies.

The process of an exception "appearing" either from the immediate cause of the trouble, or because a method call is abandoned and passes the exception up to its caller, is called *throwing* an exception in Java. You will hear other terms used, particularly an exception being *raised*.

Exceptions are actually objects, and a subtree of the class hierarchy is dedicated to describing them. All exceptions are subclasses of a class called `java.lang.Throwable`.

Flow of Control in Exception Conditions

Using *try{} catch() {}*

To intercept, and thereby control, an exception, you use a `try/catch/finally` construction. You place lines of code that are part of the normal processing sequence in a `try` block. You then put code that attempts to deal with an exception that might arise during execution of the `try` block in a `catch` block. If there are multiple exception classes that might arise in the `try` block, then several `catch` blocks are allowed to handle them. Code that must be executed no matter what happens can be placed in a `finally` block. Let's take a moment to consider an example:

```
1. int x = (int)(Math.random() * 5);
2. int y = (int)(Math.random() * 10);
3. int [] z = new int[5];
```

```
 4. try {
 5.   System.out.println("y/x gives " + (y/x));
 6.   System.out.println("y is " + y + " z[y] is " + z[y]);
 7. }
 8. catch (ArithmeticException e) {
 9.   System.out.println("Arithmetic problem " + e);
10. }
11. catch (ArrayIndexOutOfBoundsException e) {
12.   System.out.println("Subscript problem " + e);
13. }
```

In this example, there is a possibility of an exception at line 5 and at line 6. Line 5 has the potential to cause a division by 0, which in integer arithmetic results in an ArithmeticException being thrown. Line 6 will sometimes throw an ArrayIndexOutOfBoundsException.

If the value of x happens to be 0, then line 5 will result in the construction of an instance of the ArithmeticException class which is then thrown. Execution continues at line 8, where the variable e takes on the reference to the newly created exception. At line 9, the message printed includes a description of the problem which comes directly from the exception itself. A similar flow occurs if line 5 executes without a problem but the value of y is 5 or greater, causing an out-of-range subscript in line 6. In that case, execution jumps directly to line 11.

In either of these cases, where an exception is thrown in a try block and is caught by a matching catch block, the exception is considered to have been handled: Execution continues after the last catch block as if nothing had happened. If, however, there is no catch block that names either the class of exception that has been thrown or a class of exception that is a parent class of the one that has been thrown, then the exception is considered to be unhandled. In such conditions, execution generally leaves the method directly, just as if no try had been used.

Table 5.1 summarizes the flow of execution that occurs in the exception handling scenarios discussed up to this point. You should not rely on this table for exam preparation, because it is only describes the story so far. You will find a more complete study reference in the summary at the end of this chapter.

TABLE 5.1: Outline of flow in simple exception conditions

Exception	try {}	Matching catch() {}	Behavior
No			Normal Flow
Yes	No		Method terminates
Yes	Yes	No	Method terminates
Yes	Yes	Yes	Terminate try {} block Execute body of matching catch block Continue normal flow after catch blocks

Using *finally*

The generalized exception handling code has one more part to it than you saw in the last example. This is the finally block. If you put a finally block after a try and its associated catch blocks, then the code in that finally block will definitely be executed whatever the circumstances—well, nearly definitely. If an exception arises with a matching catch block, then the finally block is executed after the catch block. If no exception arises, the finally block is executed after the try block. If an exception arises for which there is no appropriate catch block, then the finally block is executed after the try block.

The circumstances that can prevent execution of the code in a finally block are

- The death of the thread
- The use of System.exit()
- Turning off the power to the CPU
- An exception arising in the finally block itself

Notice that an exception in the finally block behaves exactly like any other exception; it can be handled via a try/catch. If no catch is found, then control jumps out of the method from the point at which the exception is raised, perhaps leaving the finally block incompletely executed.

Catching Multiple Exceptions

When you define a catch block, that block will catch exceptions of the class specified, including any exceptions that are subclasses of the one specified. In this way, you can handle categories of exceptions in a single catch block. If you specify one exception class in one particular catch block, and a parent class of that exception in another catch block, you can handle the more specific exceptions—those of the subclass—separately from others of the same general parent class. Under such conditions these rules apply:

- A more specific catch block must precede a more general one in the source. Failure to meet this ordering requirement causes a compiler error.

- Only one catch block, that is the first applicable one, will be executed.

Now let's look at the overall framework for try, multiple catch blocks, and finally:

```
1. try {
2.   // statements….
3.   // some are safe, some might throw an exception
4. }
5. catch (SpecificException e) {
6.   // do something, perhaps try to recover
7. }
8. catch (OtherException e) {
9.   // handling for OtherException
10. }
11. catch (GeneralException e) {
12.   // handling for GeneralException
13. }
14. finally {
15.   // code that must be executed under
16.   // successful or unsuccessful conditions.
17. }
18. // more lines of method code…
```

In this example, GeneralException is a parent class of SpecificException. Several scenarios can arise under these conditions:

- No exceptions occur.

- A SpecificException occurs.

- A GeneralException occurs.

- An entirely different exception occurs, which we will call an UnknownException.

If no exceptions occur, execution completes the try block, lines 1, 2, 3, and 4 and then proceeds to the finally block, lines 14, 15, 16, and 17. The rest of the method, line 18 onward, is then executed.

If a SpecificException occurs, execution abandons the try block at the point the exception is raised and jumps into the SpecificException catch block. Typically this might result in lines 1 and 2, then 5, 6, and 7 being executed. After the catch block, the finally block and the rest of the method are executed, lines 14–17 and line 18 onward.

If a GeneralException that is not a SpecificException occurs, then execution proceeds out of the try block, into the GeneralException catch block at lines 11, 12, and 13. After that catch block, execution proceeds to the finally block and the rest of the method, just as in the last example.

If an UnknownException occurs, execution proceeds out of the try block directly to the finally block. After the finally block is completed, the rest of the method is abandoned. This is an uncaught exception; it will appear in the caller just as if there had never been any try block in the first place.

Now that we have discussed what happens when an exception is thrown, let's proceed to how exceptions are thrown and the rules that relate to methods that might throw exceptions.

Throwing Exceptions

The last section discussed how exceptions modify the flow of execution in a Java program. We will now continue by examining how exceptions are issued in the first place, and how you can write methods that use exceptions to report difficulties.

The *throw* Statement

Throwing an exception, in its most basic form, is simple. You need to do two things. First, you create an instance of an object that is a subclass of java.lang.Throwable. Next you use the throw keyword to actually throw the exception. These two are normally combined into a single statement like this:

```
throw new IOException("File not found");
```

There is an important reason why the throw statement and the construction of the exception are normally combined. The exception builds information about the point at which it was created, and that information is shown in the stack trace when the exception is reported. It is convenient if the line reported as the origin of the exception is the same line as the throw statement, so it is a good idea to combine the two parts, and throw new xxx() becomes the norm.

The *throws* Statement

You have just seen how easy it is to generate and throw an exception; however, the overall picture is more complex. First, as a general rule, Java requires that any method that might throw an exception must declare the fact. In a way, this is a form of enforced documentation, but you will see that there is a little more to it than just that.

If you write a method that might throw an exception (and this includes unhandled exceptions that are generated by other methods called from your method), then you must declare the possibility using a throws statement. For example, the (incomplete) method shown here can throw a MalformedURLException or an EOFException.

```
1. public void doSomeIO(String targetUrl)
2. throws MalformedURLException, EOFException {
3.    // the URL constructor can throw MalformedURLException
4.    URL url = new URL(targetUrl);
5.    // open the url and read from it...
6.    // set flag 'completed' when IO is completed satisfactorily
7.    //....
8.    // so if we get here with completed == false, we got
9.    // unexpected end of file.
10.   if (!completed) {
11.      throw new EOFException("Invalid file contents");
12.   }
13. }
```

Line 11 demonstrates the use of the throw statement—it is usual for a throw statement to be conditional in some way; otherwise the method has no way to complete successfully. Line 2 shows the use of the throws statement. In this case, there are two distinct exceptions listed that the method might throw under different failure conditions. The exceptions are given as a comma-separated list.

The section *Catching Multiple Exceptions,* earlier in this chapter, explained that the class hierarchy of exceptions is significant in `catch` blocks. The hierarchy is also significant in the `throws` statement. In this example, line 2 could be shortened to `throws IOException`. This is because both `MalformedURLException` and `EOFException` are subclasses of `IOException`.

Checked Exceptions

So far we have discussed throwing exceptions and declaring methods that might throw exceptions. We have said that any method that throws an exception should use the `throws` statement to declare the fact. The whole truth is slightly subtler than that.

The class hierarchy that exists under the class `java.lang.Throwable` is divided into three parts. One part contains the errors, which are `java.lang.Error` and all subclasses. Another part is called the runtime exceptions, which are `java.lang.RuntimeException`, and all the subclasses of that. The third part contains the checked exceptions, which are all subclasses of `java.lang.Exception` (except for `java.lang.RuntimeException` and its subclasses). Figure 5.1 shows this diagramatically.

FIGURE 5.1:

Categories of exceptions

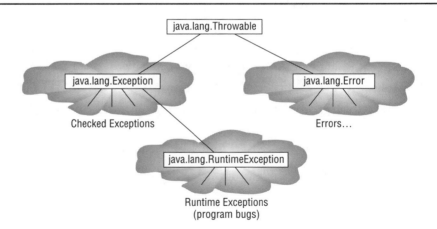

You might well ask why the hierarchy is divided up and what these various names mean.

The *checked exceptions* describe problems that can arise in a correct program, typically difficulties with the environment such as user mistakes or I/O problems. For example, attempting to open a socket to a machine that is not responding can fail if the remote machine does not exist or is not providing the requested service. Neither of these problems indicates a programming error; it's more likely to be a problem with the machine name (the user mistyped it) or with the remote machine (perhaps it is incorrectly configured). Because these conditions can arise at any time, in a commercial-grade program you must write code to handle and recover from them. In fact, the Java compiler checks that you have indeed stated what is to be done when they arise, and it is because of this checking that they are called checked exceptions.

Runtime exceptions describe program bugs. You could use a runtime exception as deliberate flow control, but it would be an odd way to design code and rather poor style. Runtime exceptions generally arise from things like out-of-bounds array accesses, and normally these would be avoided by a correct program. Because runtime exceptions should never arise in a correct program, you are not required to handle them. After all, it would only clutter your program if you had to write code that your design states should never be executed.

NOTE

An approach to program design and implementation that is highly effective in producing robust and reliable code is known as programming by contract. Briefly, this approach requires clearly defined responsibilities for methods and the callers of those methods. For example, a square-root method could require that it must be called only with a non-negative argument. If called with a negative argument, the method would react by throwing an exception, since the contract between it and its caller has been broken. This approach simplifies code, since methods only attempt to handle properly formulated calls. It also brings bugs out into the open as quickly as possible, thereby insuring they get fixed. You should use runtime exceptions to implement this approach, as it is clearly inappropriate for the caller to have to check for programming errors; the programmer should fix them.

Errors generally describe problems that are sufficiently unusual, and sufficiently difficult to recover from, that you are not required to handle them. They might reflect a program bug, but more commonly they reflect environmental problems, such as running out of memory. As with runtime exceptions, Java does not require that you state how these are to be handled.

Checking Checked Exceptions

We have stated that of the three categories of exceptions, the checked exceptions make certain demands of the programmer: You are obliged to state how the exception is to be handled. In fact you have two choices. You can put a try block around the code that might throw the exception and provide a corresponding catch block that will apply to the exception in question. This handles the exception so it effectively goes away. Alternatively, you might decide that if this exception occurs, your method cannot proceed and should be abandoned. In this case, you do not need to provide the try/catch construction, but you must instead make sure that the method declaration includes a throws part that informs potential callers that the exception might arise. Notice that by insisting that the method be declared in this way, the responsibility for handling the exception is explicitly passed to the caller of the method, which must then make the same choice—whether to declare or handle the exception. The following example demonstrates this choice:

```
1. public class DeclareOrHandle {
2.   // this method makes no attempt to recover from the
3.   // exception, rather it declares that it might throw
4.   // it and uses no try block
5.   public void declare(String s) throws IOException {
6.     URL u = new URL(s); // might throw an IOException
7.     // do things with the URL object u...
8.   }
9.
10.   // this method handles the exception that might arise
11.   // when it calls the method declare(). Because of this,
12.   // it does not throw any exceptions and so does not use
13.   // any throws declaration
14.   public void handle(String s) {
15.     boolean success = false;
16.     while (!success) {
17.         try {
18.       declare(s);  // might throw an IOException
19.       success = true;  // execute this if declare() succeeded
20.     }
21.     catch (IOException e) {
22.       // Advise user that String s is somehow unusable
23.       // ask for a new one
24.     }
25.   } // end of while loop, exits when success is true.
26. }
```

Notice that the method `declare()` does not attempt to handle the exception that might arise during construction of the URL object. Instead, the `declare()` method states that it might throw the exception. By contrast, the `handle()` method uses a `try/catch` construction to insure that control remains inside the `handle()` method itself until it becomes possible to recover from the problem.

We have now discussed the handling of exceptions and the constructions that allow you to throw exceptions of your own. Before we have finished with exceptions, we must consider a rule relating to overriding methods and exceptions. The next section discusses this rule.

Exceptions and Overriding

When you extend a class and override a method, Java insists that the new method cannot be declared as throwing checked exceptions of classes other than those that were declared by the original method. Consider these examples (assume they are declared in separate source files; the line numbers are simply for reference):

```
1. public class BaseClass {
2.   public void method() throws IOException {
3.   }
4. }
5.
6. public class LegalOne extends BaseClass {
7.   public void method() throws IOException {
8.   }
9. }
10.
11. public class LegalTwo extends BaseClass {
12.   public void method() {
13.   }
14. }
15.
16. public class LegalThree extends BaseClass {
17.   public void method()
18.   throws EOFException, MalformedURLException {
19.   }
20. }
21.
```

```
22. public class IllegalOne extends BaseClass {
23.   public void method()
24.   throws IOException, IllegalAccessException {
25.   }
26. }
27.
28.
29. public class IllegalTwo extends BaseClass {
30.   public void method()
31.   throws Exception {
32.   }
33. }
```

Notice that the original method() in BaseClass is declared as throwing IOException. This allows it, and any overriding method defined in a subclass, to throw an IOException or any object that is a subclass of IOException. Overriding methods may not, however, throw any checked exceptions that are not subclasses of IOException.

Given these rules, you will see that line 7 in LegalOne is correct, since method() is declared exactly the same way as the original that it overrides. Similarly, line 18 in LegalThree is correct, since both EOFException and MalformedURLException are subclasses of IOException—so this adheres to the rule that nothing may be thrown that is not a subclass of the exceptions already declared. Line 12 in LegalTwo is correct, since it throws no exceptions and therefore cannot throw any exceptions that are not subclasses of IOException.

The methods at lines 23 and 30 are not permissible, since both of them throw checked exceptions that are not subclasses of IOException. In IllegalOne, IllegalAccessException is a superclass of IOException; in IllegalTwo, Exception itself is a superclass of IOException. Both IllegalAccessException and Exception are checked exceptions, so the methods that attempt to throw them are illegal as overriding methods of method() in BaseClass.

The point of this rule relates to the use of base class variables as references to objects of subclass type. Chapter 4, *Converting and Casting*, explains that you can declare a variable of a class X, and then use that variable to refer to any object that is of class X or any subclass of X.

Imagine that in the examples just described, you had declared a variable myBaseObject of class BaseClass; you can use it to refer to objects of any of the classes LegalOne, LegalTwo and LegalThree. (You couldn't use it to refer to objects of class IllegalOne or IllegalTwo, since those objects cannot be created in the first place: Their code won't compile.) The compiler imposes checks on how you call myBaseObject.method(). Those checks insure that for each call, you have either enclosed the call in a try block and provided a corresponding catch block, or you have declared that the calling method itself might throw an IOException. Now suppose that at run time the variable myBaseObject was used to refer to an object of class IllegalOne. Under these conditions, the compiler would still believe that the only exceptions that must be dealt with are of class IOException. This is because it believes that myBaseObject refers to an object of class BaseClass. The compiler would therefore not insist that you provide a try/catch construct that catches the IllegalAccessException, nor that you declare the calling method as throwing that exception. This means that if the class IllegalOne were permitted, then overriding methods would be able to bypass the enforced checks for checked exceptions.

NOTE

> Because an overriding method cannot throw more exceptions than were declared for the original method, it is important to consider the likely needs of subclasses whenever you define a class. For example, the InputStream class cannot, of itself, actually throw any exceptions, since it doesn't interact with real devices that could fail. However, it is used as the base class for a whole hierarchy of classes that do interact with physical devices: FileInputStream and so forth. It is important that the read() methods of those subclasses be able to throw exceptions, so the corresponding read() methods in the InputStream class itself must be declared as throwing IOException.

We have now looked at all the aspects of exception handling that you will need to prepare for the Certification Exam and to make effective use of exceptions in your programs. The next section summarizes all the key points of flow control and exceptions.

Chapter Summary

Loop Constructs

- Three loop constructs are provided: `while()`, do, and `for()`.

- Each loop statement is controlled by an expression that must be of `boolean` type.

- In both `while()` and `for()`, the test occurs at the "top" of the loop, so the body might not be executed at all.

- In do, the test occurs at the end of the loop so the body of the loop definitely executes at least once.

- The `for()` loop takes three elements in its brackets. The first is executed once only, before the loop starts. Typically you might use it for initializing the loop or for declaring a loop counter variable. The second is the loop control test. The third is executed at the end of the loop body, just prior to performing the test.

- The first element in the brackets of a `for()` construction can declare a variable. In that case, the scope of the variable is restricted to the control parts in the brackets, and the following statement. The following statement is often a block in its own right, in which case the variable remains in scope throughout that block.

- The `continue` statement causes the current iteration of the loop to be abandoned. Flow restarts at the bottom of the loop. For `while()` and do, this means the test is executed next. For the `for()` loop, the third statement in the brackets is executed, followed by the test.

- The `break` statement abandons the loop altogether; the test is not performed on the way out.

- Both `break` and `continue` can take a label which causes them to skip out of multiple levels of nested loop. The matching label must be placed at the head of a loop and is indicated by using an identifier followed by a colon (:).

Selection Statements

- The if() statement takes a boolean argument.

- The else part is optional after if().

- The switch() statement takes an argument that is assignment compatible to int (that is, one of byte, short, char, or int).

- The argument to case must be a constant or constant expression that can be calculated at compile time.

- The case label takes only a single argument. To create a list of values that lead to the same point, use multiple case statements and allow execution to "fall through."

- The default label may be used in a switch() construction to pick up execution where none of the explicit cases match.

Flow in Exception Handling

- An exception causes a jump to the end of the enclosing try block even if the exception occurs within a method called from the try block, in which case the called method is abandoned.

- If any of the catch blocks associated with the try block just terminated specifies an exception class which is the same as, or a parent class of, the exception that was thrown, then execution proceeds to the first such catch block. The exception is now considered handled. If no appropriate catch block is found, the exception is considered unhandled.

- Regardless of whether or not an exception occurred, or whether or not it was handled, execution proceeds next to the finally block associated with the try block, if such a finally block exists.

- If there was no exception, or if the exception was handled, execution continues after the finally block.

- If the exception was unhandled, the process repeats, looking for the next enclosing try block. If the search for a try block reaches the top of the method call hierarchy (that is, the point at which the thread was created), then the thread is killed and a message and stack trace is dumped to System.err.

Exception Throwing

- To throw an exception, use the construction throw new XXXException();

- Any object that is of class java.lang.Exception, or any subclass of java .lang.Exception except subclasses of java.lang.RuntimeException, is a checked exception.

- In any method that contains lines that might throw a checked exception, you must either handle the exception using a try/catch construct, or declare that the method throws the exception using a throws construct in the declaration of the method.

- An overriding method may not throw a checked exception unless the overridden method also throws that exception or a superclass of that exception.

Test Yourself

1. Consider the following code:

```
1. for (int i = 0; i < 2; i++) {
2.    for (int j = 0; j < 3; j++) {
3.       if (i == j) {
4.          continue;
5.       }
6.       System.out.println("i = " + i + " j = " + j);
7.    }
8. }
```

Which lines would be part of the output?

A. i = 0 j = 0

B. i = 0 j = 1

C. i = 0 j = 2

D. i = 1 j = 0

E. i = 1 j = 1

F. i = 1 j = 2

2. Consider the following code:

```
1. outer: for (int i = 0; i < 2; i++) {
2.   for (int j = 0; j < 3; j++) {
3.     if (i == j) {
4.       continue outer;
5.     }
6.     System.out.println("i = " + i + " j = " + j);
7.   }
8. }
```

Which lines would be part of the output?

A. i = 0 j = 0

B. i = 0 j = 1

C. i = 0 j = 2

D. i = 1 j = 0

E. i = 1 j = 1

F. i = 1 j = 2

3. Which of the following are legal loop constructions? (Choose one or more.)

A. `while (int i < 7) { i++; System.out.println("i is " + i); }`

B. `int i = 3; while (i) { System.out.println("i is " + i); }`

C.
```
1. int j = 0; for (int k = 0; j + k != 10; j++, k++) {
2.   System.out.println("j is " + j + " k is " + k);
3. }
```

D.
```
1. int j = 0;
2. do {
3.   System.out.println("j is " + j++);
4.   if (j == 3) { continue loop; }
5. } while (j < 10);
```

4. What would be the output from this code fragment?

```
1. int x = 0, y = 4, z = 5;
2. if (x > 2) {
3.    if (y < 5) {
4.       System.out.println("message one");
5.    }
6.    else {
7.       System.out.println("message two");
8.    }
9. }
10. else if (z > 5) {
11.    System.out.println("message three");
12. }
13. else {
14.    System.out.println("message four");
15. }
```

A. message one

B. message two

C. message three

D. message four

5. Which statement is true about the following code fragment?

```
1. int j = 2;
2. switch (j) {
3.    case 2:
4.       System.out.println("value is two");
5.    case 2 + 1:
6.       System.out.println("value is three");
7.       break;
8.    default:
9.       System.out.println("value is " + j);
10.       break;
11. }
```

A. The code is illegal because of the expression at line 5.

B. The acceptable types for the variable j, as the argument to the switch() construct, could be any of byte, short, int, or long.

C. The output would be only the text value is two.

    D. The output would be the text value is two followed by the text value is three.

    E. The output would be the text value is two, followed by the text value is three, followed by the text value is 2.

6. Consider the following class hierarchy and code fragments:

```
java.lang.Exception
          \
    java.io.IOException
       /            \
java.io.StreamCorruptedException    java.net.MalformedURLException
```

```
1. try {
2.    URL u = new URL(s); // assume s is a previously defined String
3.    Object o = in.readObject(); // in is a valid ObjectInputStream
4.    System.out.println("Success");
5. }
6. catch (MalformedURLException e) {
7.    System.out.println("Bad URL");
8. }
9. catch (StreamCorruptedException e) {
10.    System.out.println("Bad file contents");
11. }
12. catch (Exception e) {
13.    System.out.println("General exception");
14. }
15. finally {
16.    System.out.println("doing finally part");
17. }
18. System.out.println("Carrying on");
```

What lines are output if the method at line 2 throws a MalformedURLException?

    A. Success

    B. Bad URL

    C. Bad file contents

D. General exception

E. doing finally part

F. Carrying on

7. Consider the following class hierarchy and code fragments:

java.lang.Exception

\

java.io.IOException

/ \

java.io.StreamCorruptedException   java.net.MalformedURLException

```
1. try {
2.    URL u = new URL(s); // assume s is a previously defined String
3.    Object o = in.readObject(); // in is a valid ObjectInputStream
4.    System.out.println("Success");
5. }
6. catch (MalformedURLException e) {
7.    System.out.println("Bad URL");
8. }
9. catch (StreamCorruptedException e) {
10.    System.out.println("Bad file contents");
11. }
12. catch (Exception e) {
13.    System.out.println("General exception");
14. }
15. finally {
16.    System.out.println("doing finally part");
17. }
18. System.out.println("Carrying on");
```

What lines are output if the methods at lines 2 and 3 complete successfully without throwing any exceptions?

A. Success

B. Bad URL

C. Bad file contents

D. General exception

E. doing finally part

F. Carrying on

8. Consider the following class hierarchy and code fragments:

```
                java.lang.Throwable

             /                    \

   java.lang.Error          java.lang.Exception

        /                            \

java.lang.OutOfMemoryError     java.io.IOException

                              /              \

   java.io.StreamCorruptedException   java.net.MalformedURLException
```

```
1. try {
2.   URL u = new URL(s); // assume s is a previously defined String
3.   Object o = in.readObject(); // in is a valid ObjectInputStream
4.   System.out.println("Success");
5. }
6. catch (MalformedURLException e) {
7.   System.out.println("Bad URL");
8. }
9. catch (StreamCorruptedException e) {
10.   System.out.println("Bad file contents");
11. }
12. catch (Exception e) {
13.   System.out.println("General exception");
14. }
15. finally {
16.   System.out.println("doing finally part");
17. }
18. System.out.println("Carrying on");
```

What lines are output if the method at line 3 throws an OutOfMemoryError?

A. Success

B. Bad URL

C. Bad file contents

D. General exception

E. doing finally part

F. Carrying on

9. Which *one* of the following fragments shows the *most* appropriate way to throw an exception? Assume that any undeclared variables have been appropriately declared elsewhere and are in scope and have meaningful values.

A.
```
1. Exception e = new IOException("File not found");
2. if (!f.exists()) { // f is a File object
3.    throw e;
4. }
```

B.
```
1. if (!f.exists()) { // f is a File object
2.    throw new IOException("File " + f.getName() + " not found");
3. }
```

C.
```
1. if (!f.exists()) {
2.    throw IOException;
3. }
```

D.
```
1. if (!f.exists()) {
2.    throw "File not found";
3. }
```

E.
```
1. if (!f.exists()) { // f is a File object
2.    throw new IOException();
3. }
```

10. Given that the method dodgy() might throw a java.io.IOException, java.lang.RuntimeException, or java.net.MalformedURLException (which is a subclass of java.io.IOException), which of the following classes and sets of classes are legal? (Choose one or more.)

A.
```
1. public class aClass {
2.    public void aMethod() {
3.       dodgy();
4.    }
5. }
```

B.
```
1. public class aClass {
2.    public void aMethod() throws java.io.Exception {
3.      dodgy();
4.    }
5. }
```

C.
```
1. public class aClass {
2.    public void aMethod() throws java.lang.RuntimeException {
3.      dodgy();
4.    }
5. }
```

D.
```
 1. public class aClass {
 2.    public void aMethod() {
 3.      try {
 4.        dodgy();
 5.      }
 6.      catch (IOException e) {
 7.        e.printStackTrace();
 8.      }
 9.    }
10. }
```

E.
```
 1. public class aClass {
 2.    public void aMethod() throws java.net.MalformedURLException {
 3.      try { dodgy(); }
 4.      catch (IOException e) { /*  ignore it */ }
 5.    }
 6. }
 7.
 8. public class anotherClass extends aClass {
 9.    public void aMethod() throws java.io.IOException {
10.      super.aMethod();
11.    }
12. }
```

CHAPTER

SIX

Objects and Classes

- Overloading and overriding

- Virtual method invocation

- Accessing parent class code

- Inner classes

- Variable access from inner classes

In this chapter, you will cover the following Java Certification Exam objectives:

- Write classes that implement object-oriented relationships using the clauses "is a" and "has a."

- Distinguish between overloaded and overridden methods.

- State the legal return types for an overloading method given the original method declaration.

- State the legal return types for an overriding method given the original method declaration.

- Describe the effect of invoking overridden methods in base and derived classes.

- Write code for any method that invokes the parental method, using `super`.

- Write constructor bodies using `this()` and `super()` to access overloaded or parent class constructors.

- Define a non-static inner class in a class or method scope.

- Define, in method scope, an anonymous inner class that implements a specified interface.

- Write code in a non-static method of the outer class to construct an instance of the inner class.

- Write code to construct an instance of an inner class where either no `this` object exists or the current `this` object is not an instance of the outer class.

- State which variables and methods in enclosing scopes are accessible from methods of the inner class.

This chapter discusses the object-oriented features of Java. Good coding in Java requires a sound understanding of the object-oriented paradigm, and this in turn requires a good grasp of the language features that implement objects and classes. The many benefits of object orientation have been the subject of considerable public debate, but for most programmers these benefits have not been realized. In most cases, the reason the promise has not been fulfilled is simply that programmers have not been writing objects. Instead, many C++ programmers have been writing a hybrid form of C with a mixture of procedural and object-oriented code. Unfortunately, such an approach has given rise, not to some of the benefits of OO, but instead to all the disadvantages of both styles.

Implementing Object-Oriented Relationships

This section is not intended to discuss object-oriented design; rather it considers the implementation of classes for which you have been given a basic description.

There are two clauses that are commonly used when describing a class in plain English. These are "is a" and "has a." As a working simplification, these are used to describe the superclass and member variables respectively. For example, consider this description:

"A home is a house which has a family and a pet."

This description would give rise to the outline of a Java class in this form:

```
1. public class Home extends House {
2.    Family inhabitants;
3.    Pet thePet;
4. }
```

Notice the direct correspondence between the "is a" clause and the extends clause. In this example, there is also a direct correspondence between the items listed after "has a" and the member variables. Such a correspondence is representative in simple examples and in a test situation; however, you should be aware that in real examples there are other ways that you can provide a class with attributes. Probably the most important of these alternatives is the approach taken by Java Beans, which is to supply accessor and mutator methods that operate on private data members.

Overloading and Overriding

As you construct classes and add methods to them, there are circumstances when you will want to re-use the same name for a method. There are two ways that you can do this with Java. Re-using the same method name with different arguments and perhaps a different return type is known as *overloading*. Using the same method name with identical arguments and return type is known as *overriding*.

A method name can be re-used anywhere, as long as certain conditions are met:

- In an unrelated class, no special conditions apply and the two methods are not considered related in any way.

- In the class that defines the original method, or a subclass of that class, the method name can be re-used if the argument list differs in terms of the type of at least one argument. This is overloading. It is important to realize that a difference in return type alone is not sufficient to constitute an overload and is illegal.

- In a strict subclass of the class that defines the original method, the method name can be re-used with identical argument types and order and with identical return type. This is overriding. In this case, additional restrictions apply to the accessibility of, and exceptions that may be thrown by, the method.

NOTE

In general, a class is considered to be a subclass of itself. That is, if classes A, B, and C are defined so that C extends B, and B extends A, then the subclasses of A are A, B, and C. The term *strict subclass* is used to describe the subclasses excluding the class itself. So the strict subclasses of A are only B and C.

Now let's take a look at these ideas in detail. First, we will consider overloading method names.

Overloading Method Names

In Java a method is uniquely identified by the combination of its fully qualified class name, method name, and the exact sequence of its argument types. Overloading is the re-use of a method name in the one class or subclass for a *different* method. This is not related to object orientation, although there is a purely coincidental correlation that shows that object-oriented languages are more likely to support overloading. Notice that overloading is essentially a trick with names, hence this section's title is *Overloading Method Names* rather than *Overloading Methods*. The following are all different methods:

```
1. public void aMethod(String s) { }
2. public void aMethod() { }
3. public void aMethod(int i, String s) { }
4. public void aMethod(String s, int i) { }
```

These methods all have identical return types and names, but their argument lists are different either in the types of the arguments that they take or in the order. Only the argument types are considered, not their names, hence a method

```
public void aMethod(int j, String name) { }
```

would *not* be distinguished from the method defined in line 3 above.

What is Overloading For?

Why is overloading useful? There are times when you will be creating several methods that perform closely related functions under different conditions. For example, imagine methods that calculate the area of a triangle. One such method might take the Cartesian coordinates of the three vertices, another might take the polar coordinates. A third method might take the lengths of all three sides, while a fourth might take three angles and the length of one side. These would all be performing the same essential function, and so it is entirely proper to use the same name for the methods. In languages that do not permit overloading, you would have to think up four different method names, such as areaOfTriangleByCoordinate (Point p, Point q, Point r), areaOfTriangleByPolarCoordinates(PolarPoint p, PolarPoint q, PolarPoint r), and so forth.

Overloading is really nothing new. Almost every language that has a type system has used overloading in a way, although most have not allowed the programmer free use of it. Consider the arithmetic operators +, -, *, and /. In most languages these can be used with integer or floating-point operands. The actual implementation of, say, multiplication for integer and floating-point operands generally involves completely different code, and yet the compiler permits the same symbol to be used. Because the operand types are different, the compiler can decide which version of the operation should be used. This is known as operator overloading and is the same principle as method overloading.

So it is quite useful, for thinking up method names and for improving program readability, to be able to use one method name for several related methods requiring different implementations. However, you should restrict your use of overloaded method names to situations where the methods really are performing the same basic function with different data sets. Methods that perform different jobs should have different names.

One last point to consider is the return type of an overloaded method. The language treats methods with overloaded names as totally different methods, and as such they *can* have different return types (you will see shortly that overriding methods do not have this freedom). However, if two methods are performing the same job with different data sets, shouldn't they produce the same result type? Generally this is true, and you should expect overloaded methods to be defined with the same result types. There is one particular condition, however, under which it is clearly sensible to define different return types for overloaded methods. This is the situation where the return type is derived from the argument type and is exactly parallel with the arithmetic operators discussed earlier. If you define three methods called addUp() which take two arguments, both int, both float, or both double, then it is entirely reasonable for the method to return int, float or double in line with its arguments.

Invoking Overloaded Methods

When you write multiple methods that perform the same basic function with different arguments, you often find that it would be useful to call one of these methods as support for another version. Consider a method printRightJustified() that is to be provided in versions that take a String or an int value. The version that takes an int could most easily be coded so that it converts the int to a String and then calls the version that operates on String objects.

You can do this easily. Remember that the compiler decides which method to call simply by looking at the argument list and that the various overloaded methods are in fact unrelated. All you have to do is write the method call exactly as normal—the compiler will do the rest. Consider this example:

```
1. public class RightJustify {
2.    private static final String padding =
3.       "                                                                " +
4.       "                                                                "; // 80 spaces
5.    public static void print(String s, int w) {
6.       System.out.print(padding.substring(0, w - s.length()));
7.       System.out.print(s);
8.    }
9.    public static void print(int i, int w) {
10.      print("" + i, w);
11.   }
12. }
```

At line 10 the int argument is converted to a String object by adding it to an empty String. The method call at this same line is then seen by the compiler as a call to a method called print() that takes a String as the first argument, which results in selection of the method at line 5.

To summarize, these are the key points about overloading methods:

- The identity of a method is determined by the combination of its fully qualified class, name, and the type, order, and count of arguments in the argument list.

- Two or more methods in the same class (including perhaps methods inherited from a superclass) with the same name but different argument lists are called overloaded.

- Methods with overloaded names are effectively independent methods— using the same name is really just a convenience to the programmer. Return type, accessibility, and exception lists may vary freely.

- Overloaded methods may call one another simply by providing a normal method call with an appropriately formed argument list.

Now that we have considered overloading thoroughly, let's look at overriding.

Method Overriding

You have just seen that overloading is essentially a trick with names, effectively treating the argument list as part of the method identification. Overriding is somewhat more subtle, relating directly to subclassing and hence to the object-oriented nature of a language.

When you extend one class to produce a new one, you inherit and have access to all the non-private methods of the original class. Sometimes, however, you might need to modify the behavior of one of these methods to suit your new class. In this case, you actually want to redefine the method, and this is the essential purpose of overriding.

There are a number of key distinctions between overloading and overriding:

- Overloaded methods supplement each other; an overriding method (largely) replaces the method it overrides.

- Overloaded methods can exist, in any number, in the same class. Each method in a parent class can be overridden at most once in any one subclass.

- Overloaded methods must have *different* argument lists; overriding methods must have argument lists of *identical* type and order (otherwise they are simply treated as overloaded methods).

- The return type of an overloaded method may be chosen freely; the return type of an overriding method must be *identical* to that of the method it overrides.

What is Overriding For?

Overloading allows multiple implementations of the same essential functionality to use the same name. Overriding, on the other hand, modifies the implementation of a particular piece of behavior for a subclass.

Consider a class that describes a rectangle. Imaginatively, we'll call it Rectangle. We're talking about an abstract rectangle here, so there is no visual representation associated with it. This class has a method called setSize(), which is used to set width and height values. In the Rectangle class itself, the implementation of the setSize() method simply sets the value of the private width and height variables for later use. Now imagine we create a DisplayedRectangle class which is a subclass of the original Rectangle. Now, when the setSize() method is called, we need to arrange a new behavior. Specifically, the width and height variables must be changed, but also the visual representation must be redrawn. This is achieved by overriding.

If you define a method that has exactly the same name and exactly the same argument types as a method in a parent class, then you are overriding the method. Under these conditions, the method must also have the identical return type to that of the method it overrides. Consider this example:

```
1. class Rectangle {
2.    int x, y, w, h;
3.
4.    public void setSize(int w, int h) {
5.       this.w = w; this.h = h;
6.    }
7. }
8. class DisplayedRectangle extends Rectangle {
9.    public void setSize(int w, int h) {
10.      this.w = w; this.h = h;
11.      redisplay(); // implementation
12.   }
13.   public void redisplay() {
14.      // implementation not shown
15.   }
16. }
```

```
17.
18. public class TestRectangle {
19.    public static void main(String args[]) {
20.       Rectangle [] recs = new Rectangle[4];
21.       recs[0] = new Rectangle();
22.       recs[1] = new DisplayedRectangle();
23.       recs[2] = new DisplayedRectangle();
24.       recs[3] = new Rectangle();
25.       for (int r=0; r<4; r++) {
26.          int i = ((int)(Math.random() * 4));
27.          int w = ((int)(Math.random() * 400));
28.          int h = ((int)(Math.random() * 200));
29.          recs[r].setSize(w, h);
30.       }
31.    }
32. }
```

Clearly this example is incomplete, since no code exists to cause the display of the DisplayedRectangle objects, but it is complete enough for us to discuss.

At line 20 you will see the array recs is created as an array of Rectangle objects, yet at lines 21–24 the array is used to hold not only two instances of Rectangle but also two instances of DisplayedRectangle. Subsequently, when the setSize() method is called, it will be important that the code that is executed should be the code associated with the actual object referred to by the array element, rather than always being the code of the Rectangle class. This is actually exactly what Java does, and this is the essential point of overriding methods. It is as if you ask an object to perform certain behavior and that object makes its own interpretation of that request. This is a point that C++ programmers should take particular note of, as it differs significantly from the default behavior of overriding methods in that language.

In order for any particular method to override another correctly, there are a number of requirements that must be met. Some of these have been mentioned before in comparison with overloading, but all are listed here for completeness:

- The method name and the type and order of arguments must be identical to those of a method in a parent class. If this is the case, then the method is an attempt to override the corresponding parent class method and the remaining points listed here must be adhered to, or a compiler error arises. If these criteria are not met, then the method is not an attempt to override and the following rules are irrelevant.

- The return type must be identical.

- The accessibility must not be more restricted than the original method.

- The method must not throw checked exceptions of classes which are not possible for the original method.

The first two points have been covered, but the last two are new. The accessibility of an overriding method must not be less than that of the method it overrides simply because it is considered to be the replacement method in conditions like those of the rectangles example earlier. So, imagine that the `setSize()` method of `DisplayedRectangle` was inaccessible from the `main()` method of the `TestRectangle` class. The calls to `recs[1].setSize()` and `recs[2].setSize()` would be illegal, but the compiler would be unable to determine this, since it only knows that the elements of the array are `Rectangle` objects. If you like, you can consider that the `extends` keyword literally requires that the subclass be an extension of the parent class: If methods could be removed from the class, or made less accessible, then the subclass would not be a simple extension, but would potentially be a reduction. Under those conditions, the idea of treating `DisplayedRectangle` objects as being `Rectangle` objects when used as method arguments or elements of a collection would be severely flawed.

A similar logic gives rise to the final rule relating to checked exceptions. Checked exceptions are those that the compiler insures are handled in the source you write. As with accessibility, it must be possible for the compiler to make correct use of a variable of the parent class even if that variable really refers to an object of a derived class. For checked exceptions, this means that an overriding method must not be able to throw exceptions that would not be thrown by the original method. Chapter 5, *Flow Control and Exceptions*, discusses checked exceptions and this rule in more detail.

Late Binding or Virtual Method Invocation

It is interesting to consider the mechanisms by which this magic is achieved. Normally when a compiler for a non-object-oriented language comes across a method (or function or procedure) invocation, it determines exactly what target code should be called and builds machine language to represent that call. In an object-oriented language, this is not possible, since the proper code to invoke is determined based upon the class of the object being used to make the call, not the type of the variable. Instead, code is generated that will allow the decision to be made at run time. This delayed decision-making is variously referred to as *late binding* (binding is one term for the job a linker does when it glues various bits of machine code together to make an executable program file) or *virtual method invocation*.

In Java, because the Virtual Machine has been designed from the start to support an object-oriented programming system, there are machine-level instructions for making method calls, so that the compiler only needs to prepare the argument list and produce one method invocation instruction; the job of identifying and calling the proper target code is performed by the Virtual Machine.

If the Virtual Machine is to be able to decide what actual code should be invoked by a particular method call, it must be able to determine the class of the object upon which the call is based. Again, the Virtual Machine design has supported this from the beginning. Unlike traditional languages or runtime environments, every time the Java system allocates memory, it marks that memory with the type of the data that it has been allocated to hold. This means that given any object, and without regard to the type associated with the reference variable acting as a handle to that object, the runtime system can determine the real class of that object by inspection. This is the basis of the `instanceof` operator, which allows you to program a test to determine the actual class of an object at run time. The `instanceof` operator is described in Chapter 2, *Operators and Assignments*.

Invoking Overridden Methods

When we discussed overloading methods you saw how to invoke one version of a method from another. It is also useful to be able to invoke an overridden method from the method that overrides it. Consider that when you write an overriding method, that method entirely replaces the original method, but sometimes you only wish to add a little extra behavior and want to retain all the original behavior. This can be achieved, although it requires a small trick of syntax to perform. Look at this example:

```
1. class Rectangle {
2.    private int x, y, w, h;
3.    public String toString() {
4.      return "x = " + x + ", y = " + y +
5.         ", w = " + w + ", h = " + h;
6.    }
7. }
8. class DecoratedRectangle extends Rectangle {
9.    private int borderWidth;
```

```
10.    public String toString() {
11.       return super.toString() + ", borderWidth = " + borderWidth;
12.    }
13. }
```

At line 11 the overriding method in the DecoratedRectangle class uses the parental toString() method to perform the greater part of its work. Note that since the variables x, y, w, and h in the Rectangle class are marked as private, it would have been impossible for the overriding method in DecoratedRectangle to achieve its work directly.

A call of the form super.xxx() always invokes the behavior that would have been used if the current overloading method had not been defined. It does not matter if the parental method is defined in the immediate superclass, or in some ancestor class farther up the hierarchy, super invokes the version of this method that is "next up the tree." Be aware that you cannot bypass a level in the hierarchy. That is, if three classes, A, B, and C, all define a method m(), and they are all part of a hierarchy—so that B extends A, and C extends B—then the method m() in class C *cannot* directly invoke the method m() in class A.

To summarize, these are the key points about overriding methods:

- A method which has an identical name, and identical number, types, and order of arguments as a method in a parent class is an overriding method.

- Each parent class method may be overridden at most once in any one subclass. (That is, you cannot have two identical methods in the same class.)

- Overriding methods must return exactly the same type as the method they override.

- An overriding method must not be less accessible than the method it overrides.

- An overriding method must not throw any checked exceptions that are not declared for the overridden method.

- An overridden method is completely replaced by the overriding method unless the overridden method is deliberately invoked from within the subclass.

- An overridden method can be invoked from within the subclass using the construction super.xxx() where xxx() is the method name. Methods that are overridden more than once (by chains of subclasses) are not directly accessible.

There is quite a lot to think about in overriding methods, so you might like to have a break before you move on to the next topic: constructors.

Constructors and Subclassing

Inheritance generally makes the code and data that are defined in a parent class available for use in a subclass. This is subject to accessibility so that, for example, private items in the parent class are not directly accessible in the methods of the subclass, even though they exist. In fact, constructors are not inherited in the normal way but must be defined in the class itself.

When you write code to construct an instance of any particular class, you write code of the form new MyClass(arg, list);. In these conditions there must be a constructor defined for MyClass, and that constructor must take arguments of the types (or some superclass) of the variables arg and list. In the case of a constructor, it is not sufficient for this to have been defined in the parent class; rather, a constructor is generally available for a class only if it is explicitly defined in that class. The exception to this is the default constructor. The default constructor takes no arguments and is created by the compiler if no other constructors are defined for the class. Notice the default constructor is not inherited: It is created for you by the compiler if, and only if, you do not provide *any* other constructors in the source of the particular class.

Often you will define a constructor that takes arguments and will want to use those arguments to control the construction of the parent part of the object. You can pass control to a constructor in the parent class by using the keyword super(). To control the particular constructor that is used, you simply provide the appropriate arguments. Consider this example:

```
1. class Base {
2.   public Base(String s) {
3.     // initialize this object using s
4.   }
5.   public Base(int i) {
6.     // initialize this object using i
7.   }
8. }
9.
10. class Derived extends Base {
```

```
11.   public Derived(String s) {
12.      super(s); // pass control to Base constructor at line 2
13.   }
14.   public Derived(int i) {
15.      super(i); // pass control to Base constructor at line 5
16.   }
17. }
```

The code at lines 12 and 15 demonstrate the use of super() to control the construction of the parent class part of an object. The definitions of the constructors at lines 11 and 14 select an appropriate way to build the parental part of themselves by invoking super() with an argument list that matches one of the constructors for the parent class. It is important to know that the superclass constructor must be called before any reference is made to any part of this object. This rule is imposed to guarantee that nothing is ever used in an uninitialized state. Generally the rule means that if super() is to appear at all in a constructor, then it must be the first statement.

Although the example shows the invocation of parental constructors with argument lists that match those of the original constructor, this is not a requirement. It would be perfectly acceptable, for example, if line 15 had read:

```
15.      super("Value is " + i);
```

This would have caused control to be passed to the constructor at line 2, which takes a String argument, rather than the one at line 5.

Overloading Constructors

Although you have just seen that constructors are not inherited in the same way as methods, the overloading mechanisms apply quite normally. In fact, the example discussing the use of super() to control the invocation of parental constructors showed overloaded constructors. You saw earlier how you could invoke one method from another that overloads its name, simply by calling the method with an appropriate parameter list. There are also times when it would be useful to invoke one constructor from another. Imagine you have a constructor that takes five arguments and does considerable processing to initialize the object. You wish to provide another constructor that takes only two arguments and sets the remaining three to default values. It would be nice to avoid re-coding the body of the first constructor, and instead simply set up the default values and pass control to the first constructor. This is possible but requires a small trick of syntax to achieve.

Usually you would invoke a method by using its name followed by an argument list in parentheses, and you would invoke a constructor by using the keyword new, followed by the name of the class, followed again by an argument list in parentheses. This might lead you to try to use the new ClassName(args) construction to invoke another constructor of your own class. Unfortunately, although this is legal syntax, it results in an entirely separate object being created. The approach Java takes is to provide another meaning for the keyword this. Look at this example:

```
1. public class AnyClass {
2.   public AnyClass(int a, String b, float c, Date d) {
3.     // complex processing to initialize based on arguments
4.   }
5.   public AnyClass(int a) {
6.     this(a, "default", 0.0F, new Date());
7.   }
8. }
```

The constructor at line 5 takes a single argument and uses that, along with three other default values, to call the constructor at line 2. The call itself is made using the this() construction at line 6. As with super(), this() must be positioned as the first statement of the constructor.

We have said that any use of either super() or this() in a constructor must be placed at the first line. Clearly you cannot put both on the first line. In fact, this is not a problem. If you write a constructor that has neither a call to super(...) nor a call to this(...), then the compiler automatically inserts a call to the parent class constructor with no arguments. If an explicit call to another constructor is made using this(...), then the superclass constructor is not called until the other constructor runs. It is permitted for that other constructor to start with a call to either this(...) or super(...) if desired. Java insists that the object is initialized from the top of the class hierarchy downward; that is why the call to super(...) or this(...) must occur at the start of a constructor.

Let's summarize the key points about constructors before we move on to inner classes:

- Constructors are not inherited in the same way as normal methods. You can only create an object if a constructor with an argument list that matches the one your new call provides is defined in the class itself.

- If you define no constructors at all in a class, then the compiler provides a default that takes no arguments. If you define even a single constructor, this default is not provided.

- It is common to provide multiple overloaded constructors: that is, constructors with different argument lists. One constructor can call another using the syntax this(arguments...).

- A constructor delays running its body until the parent parts of the class have been initialized. This commonly happens because of an implicit call to super() added by the compiler. You can provide your own call to super(arguments...) to control the way the parent parts are initialized. If you do this, it must be the first statement of the constructor.

- A constructor can use overloaded constructor versions to support its work. These are invoked using the syntax this(arguments...) and if supplied, this call must be the first statement of the constructor. In such conditions, the initialization of the parent class is performed in the overloaded constructor.

Inner Classes

The material we have looked at so far has been part of Java since its earliest versions. Inner classes, however, are a new feature added with the release of JDK 1.1. Inner classes, which are sometimes called nested classes in other languages, can give your programs additional clarity and make them more concise.

Fundamentally, an *inner class* is the same as any other class, but is declared inside (that is, between the opening and closing curly braces of) some other class. The complexity of inner classes relates to scope and access, particularly access to variables in enclosing scopes. Before we consider these matters, let's look at the basic construction of an inner class, which is really quite simple. Consider this example:

```
1. public class OuterOne {
2.    int x;
3.    public class InnerOne {
4.       int y;
```

```
5.      public void innerMethod() {
6.          System.out.println("y is " + y);
7.      }
8.  }
9.  public void outerMethod() {
10.     System.out.println("x is " + x);
11. }
12. // other methods...
13. }
```

In this example, there is no obvious benefit in having declared the class called InnerOne as an inner class; so far we are only interested in the basic syntax. When an inner class is declared like this, the enclosing class name becomes part of the fully qualified name of the inner class. In this case, the two classes' full names are OuterOne and OuterOne.InnerOne. This format is reminiscent of a class called InnerOne declared in a package called OuterOne. This point of view is not entirely inappropriate, since an inner class belongs to its enclosing class in a fashion similar to the way a class belongs to a package. It is illegal for a package and a class to have the same name, so there can be no ambiguity.

TIP

Although the dotted representation of inner class names works for the declaration of the type of an identifier, it does not reflect the real name of the class. If you try to load this class using the Class.forName() method, the call will fail. On the disk, and from the point of view of the Class class and class loaders, the name of the class is actually OuterOne$InnerOne. The dollar-separated name is also used if you print out the class name by using the methods getClass().getName() on an instance of the inner class. You probably recall that classes are located in directories that reflect their package names. The dollar ($) separated convention is adopted for inner class names to insure that there is no ambiguity on the disk between inner classes and package members and also to reduce conflicts with filing systems that treat the dot character as special, perhaps limiting the number of characters that can follow it.

Although for the purpose of naming there is some organizational benefit in being able to define a class inside another class, this is not the end of the story. Objects that are instances of the inner class generally retain the ability to access the members of the outer class. This is discussed in the next section.

The Enclosing *this* Reference and Construction of Inner Classes

When an instance of an inner class is created, there must normally be a preexisting instance of the outer class acting as context. This instance of the outer class will be accessible from the inner object. Consider this example, which is expanded from the earlier one:

```
1.  public class OuterOne {
2.    int x;
3.    public class InnerOne {
4.      int y;
5.      public void innerMethod() {
6.        System.out.println("enclosing x is " + x);
7.        System.out.println("y is " + y);
8.      }
9.    }
10.   public void outerMethod() {
11.     System.out.println("x is " + x);
12.   }
13.   public void makeInner() {
14.     InnerOne anInner = new InnerOne();
15.     anInner.innerMethod();
16.   }
17.   // other methods...
18. }
```

You will see two changes in this code when you compare it to the earlier version. First, at line 6, innerMethod() now outputs not just the value of y, which is defined in InnerOne, but also the value of x which is defined in OuterOne. The second change is that in lines 13–16, there is code that creates an instance of the InnerOne class and invokes innerMethod() upon it.

The accessibility of the members of the enclosing class is crucial and very useful. It is possible because the inner class actually has a hidden reference to the outer class instance that was the current context when the inner class object was created. In effect, it insures that the inner class and the outer class belong together, rather than the inner instance being just another member of the outer instance.

Sometimes you might want to create an instance of an inner class from a static method, or in some other situation where there is no this object available. The situation arises in a main() method or if you need to create the inner class from a method of some object of an unrelated class. You can achieve this by using the `new` operator as though it were a member method of the outer class. Of course you still must have an instance of the outer class. The following code, which is a `main()` method in isolation, could be added to the code seen so far to produce a complete example:

```
1. public static void main(String args[]) {
2.   OuterOne.InnerOne i = new OuterOne().new InnerOne();
3.   i.innerMethod();
4. }
```

From the point of view of the inner class instance, this use of two `new` statements on the same line is a compacted way of doing this:

```
1. public static void main(String args[]) {
2.   OuterOne o = new OuterOne();
3.   OuterOne.InnerOne i = o.new InnerOne();
4.   i.innerMethod();
5. }
```

If you attempt to use the `new` operation to construct an instance of an inner class without a prefixing reference to an instance of the outer class, then the implied prefix `this.` is assumed. This behavior is identical to that which you find with ordinary member accesses and method invocations. As with member access and method invocation, it is important that the `this` reference be valid when you try to use it. Inside a `static` method there is no `this` reference, which is why you must take special efforts in these conditions.

Static Inner Classes

Java's inner class mechanisms allow an inner class to be marked `static`. When applied to a variable, `static` means that the variable is associated with the class, rather than with any particular instance of the class. When applied to an inner class, the meaning is similar. Specifically, a `static` inner class does *not* have any reference to an enclosing instance. Because of this, methods of a `static` inner class cannot access instance variables of the enclosing class; those methods can, however, access `static` variables of the enclosing class. This is similar to the rules that apply to `static` methods in ordinary classes. As you would expect, you can create an instance of a `static` inner class without the need for a current instance of the enclosing class.

The net result is that a `static` inner class is really just a top-level class with a modified naming scheme. In fact, you can use `static` inner classes as an extension to packaging.

Not only can you declare a class inside another class, but you can also declare a class inside a method of another class. We will discuss this next.

Classes Defined Inside Methods

So far you have seen classes defined inside other classes, but Java also allows you to define a class inside a method. This is superficially similar to what you have already seen, but in this case there are two particular aspects to be considered. First, an object created from an inner class within a method can have some access to the variables of the enclosing method. Second, it is possible to create an anonymous class, literally a class with no specified name, and this can be very eloquent when working with event listeners.

The rule that governs access to the variables of an enclosing method is simple. Any variable, either a local variable or a formal parameter, can be accessed by methods within an inner class, provided that variable is marked `final`. A `final` variable is effectively a constant, so this is perhaps quite a severe restriction, but the point is simply this: An object created inside a method is likely to outlive the method invocation. Since local variables and method arguments are conventionally destroyed when their method exits, these variables would be invalid for access by inner class methods after the enclosing method exits. By allowing access only to `final` variables, it becomes possible to copy the values of those variables into the object itself, thereby extending their lifetime. The other possible approaches to this problem would be writing to two copies of the same data every time it got changed or putting method local variables onto the heap instead of the stack. Either of these approaches would significantly degrade performance.

Let's look at an example:

```
1. public class MOuter {
2.   public static void main(String args[]) {
3.     MOuter that = new MOuter();
4.     that.go((int)(Math.random() * 100),
5.       (int)(Math.random() * 100));
6.   }
7.
8.   public void go(int x, final int y) {
```

```
9.      int a = x + y;
10.     final int b = x - y;
11.     class MInner {
12.       public void method() {
13. //        System.out.println("x is " + x); //Illegal!
14.          System.out.println("y is " + y);
15. //        System.out.println("a is " + a); //Illegal!
16.          System.out.println("b is " + b);
17.       }
18.     }
19.
20.     MInner that = new MInner();
21.     that.method();
22.   }
23. }
```

In this example, the class MInner is defined in lines 11–18. Within it, method() has access to the member variables of the enclosing class (as with the previous examples) but also to the final variables of method() itself. Lines 13 and 15 are illegal, because they attempt to refer to non-final variables in method(): If these were included in the source proper, they would cause compiler errors.

Anonymous Classes

Some classes that you define inside a method do not need a name. A class defined in this way without a name is called an *anonymous class*. Clearly you cannot use new in the usual way to create an instance of a class if you do not know its name. In fact, anonymous classes are defined in the place they are constructed:

```
1. public void aMethod() {
2.   theButton.addActionListener(
3.     new ActionListener() {
4.       public void actionPerformed(ActionEvent e) {
5.         System.out.println("The action has occurred");
6.       }
7.     }
8.   );
9. }
```

In this fragment, theButton at line 2 is a Button object. Notice that the action listener attached to the button is defined in lines 3–7. The entire declaration forms the argument to the addActionListener() method call at line 2; the closing parenthesis that completes this method call is on line 8.

At line 3, the `new` call is followed immediately by the start of the class definition; the class has no name but is referred to simply using an interface name. The effect of this syntax is to state that you are defining a class and you do not want to think up a name for that class. Further, the class implements the specified interface without using the `implements` keyword.

An anonymous class gives you a convenient way to avoid having to think up trivial names for classes, but the facility should be used with care. Clearly, you cannot instantiate objects of this class anywhere except in the code shown. Further, anonymous classes should be small. If the class has methods other than those of a simple, well-known interface such as an AWT event listener, it probably should not be anonymous. Similarly, if the class has methods containing more than one or two lines of straightforward code, it probably should not be anonymous. The point here is that if you do not give the class a name, you have only the "self-documenting" nature of the code itself to explain what it is for. If in fact the code is not simple enough to be genuinely self-documenting, then you probably should give it a descriptive name.

These are the points you need to understand about anonymous inner classes to succeed in the Certification Exam:

- The class is instantiated and declared in the same place.

- The declaration and instantiation takes the form

      new Xxxx () { //body }

  where Xxxx is an interface name.

- An anonymous class cannot have a constructor. Since you do not specify a name for the class, you cannot use that name to specify a constructor.

Additional Features of Anonymous Inner Classes

The Certification Exam objectives only discuss anonymous inner classes that implement specific interfaces. There are some additional points that relate to anonymous inner classes that extend specific parent classes. You might find these points useful, even though they do not relate to the exam.

- An anonymous class can be a subclass of another explicit class, or it can implement a single explicit interface. An anonymous class cannot be both an explicit subclass and implement an interface. Note that extending `Object` is implicit where an interface is implemented.

- If an anonymous class extends an existing class, rather than implementing an interface, then arguments for the superclass constructor may be placed in the argument part of the new expression, like this:

```
new Button("Press Me") { // define some modification of Button }
```

Note that for anonymous classes that implement interfaces the parent class is java.lang.Object. The constructor for java.lang.Object takes no arguments, so it is impossible to use any arguments in the new part for these classes.

Chapter Summary

We have covered a lot of material in this chapter, but all of it is important. Let's look again at the key points.

Implementing Object-Oriented Relationships

- The "is a" relationship is implemented by inheritance, using the Java keyword extends.

- The "has a" relationship is implemented by providing the class with member variables.

Overloading and Overriding

- A method can have the same name as another method in the same class, providing it forms either a valid overload or override.

- A valid overload differs in the number or type of its arguments. Differences in argument names are not significant. A different return type is permitted, but it is not sufficient by itself to distinguish an overloading method.

- Methods that overload a name are different methods and can coexist in a single class.

- Both overloaded and overloading methods are accessed simply by providing the correct argument types for the method call.

- A valid override has identical argument types and order, identical return type, and is not less accessible than the original method. The overriding method must not throw any checked exceptions that were not declared for the original method.

- Overriding methods completely replace the original method unless the derived class makes specific reference to that original method using the `super.xxx()` construction.

- An overriding method cannot be defined in the same class as the method it overrides; rather, it must be defined in a subclass.

- The `super.xxx()` mechanism gives access to an overridden method from within the subclass that defines the overriding method.

- Overridden methods are not accessible outside the overriding class. Virtual method invocation otherwise insures that the behavior associated with the object class (not with the variable type) will be the behavior that occurs.

Constructors and Subclassing

- Constructors are not inherited into subclasses; you must define each form of constructor that you require.

- A class that has no constructors defined in the source is given exactly one constructor. This is the default constructor; it takes no arguments and is of `public` accessibility.

- A constructor can call upon other constructors in its class to help with its work. The `this()` construction does this. If you use the `this()` mechanism, it must occur at the start of the constructor.

- A constructor can call the constructor of the parent class explicitly by using the `super()` mechanism. If you use the `super()` mechanism, it must occur at the start of the constructor.

Inner Classes

- A class can be declared in any scope. Classes defined in other classes, including those defined in methods, are called inner classes.

- An inner class can have any accessibility, including `private`.

- Classes defined in methods can be anonymous, in which case they must be instantiated at the same point they are defined.

- Inner classes, unless `static`, have an implicit reference to the enclosing instance. The enclosing instance must be provided to the new call that constructs the inner class. In many cases, inner classes are constructed inside instance methods of the enclosing class, in which case `this.new` is implied by new.

- Inner classes, unless `static`, have access to the variables of the enclosing class instance. Additionally, inner classes defined in method scope have read access to `final` variables of the enclosing method.

- Anonymous inner classes may implement interfaces or extend other classes.

- Anonymous inner classes cannot have any explicit constructors.

That's it for classes. This summary includes a great deal of information condensed into terminology, so be sure to review the sections of this chapter if you are unsure about any point. Otherwise, you're ready to move on to the test questions. Good luck!

Test Yourself

1. Consider this class:

```
1. public class Test1 {
2.    public float aMethod(float a, float b) {
3.    }
4.
5. }
```

Which of the following methods would be legal if added (individually) at line 4?

A. `public int aMethod(int a, int b) { }`

B. `public float aMethod(float a, float b) { }`

C. `public float aMethod(float a, float b, int c) throws Exception { }`

    D. `public float aMethod(float c, float d) { }`

    E. `private float aMethod(int a, int b, int c) { }`

2. Consider these classes, defined in separate source files:

```
1. public class Test1 {
2.   public float aMethod(float a, float b) throws IOException {
3.   }
4. }
```

```
1. public class Test2 extends Test1 {
2.
3. }
```

Which of the following methods would be legal (individually) at line 2 in class Test2?

    A. `float aMethod(float a, float b) { }`

    B. `public int aMethod(int a, int b) throws Exception { }`

    C. `public float aMethod(float a, float b) throws Exception { }`

    D. `public float aMethod(float p, float q) { }`

3. You have been given a design document for a veterinary registration system for implementation in Java. It states:

> "A pet has an owner, a registration date, and a vaccination-due date. A cat is a pet that has a flag indicating if it has been neutered, and a textual description of its markings."

Given that the pet class has already been defined, which of the following fields would be appropriate for inclusion in the cat class as members?

    A. `Pet thePet;`

    B. `Date registered;`

    C. `Date vaccinationDue;`

    D. `Cat theCat;`

    E. `boolean neutered;`

    F. `String markings;`

4. You have been given a design document for a veterinary registration system for implementation in Java. It states:

> "A pet has an owner, a registration date, and a vaccination-due date. A cat is a pet that has a flag indicating if it has been neutered, and a textual description of its markings."

Given that the pet class has already been defined and you expect the Cat class to be used freely throughout the application, how would you make the opening declaration of the Cat class, up to but not including the first opening brace? Use only these words and spaces: boolean, Cat, class, Date, extends, Object, Owner, Pet, private, protected, public, String.

5. Consider the following classes, declared in separate source files:

```
1. public class Base {
2.    public void method(int i) {
3.       System.out.println("Value is " + i);
4.    }
5. }
```

```
1. public class Sub extends Base {
2.    public void method(int j) {
3.       System.out.println("This value is " + j);
4.    }
5.    public void method(String s) {
6.       System.out.println("I was passed " + s);
7.    }
8.    public static void main(String args[]) {
9.       Base b1 = new Base();
10.      Base b2 = new Sub();
11.      b1.method(5);
12.      b2.method(6);
13.    }
14. }
```

What output results when the main method of the class Sub is run?

A. Value is 5
   Value is 6

B. This value is 5
   This value is 6

    C. Value is 5
       This value is 6

    D. This value is 5
       Value is 6

    E. I was passed 5
       I was passed 6

6. Consider the following class definition:

```
1. public class Test extends Base {
2.    public Test(int j) {
3.    }
4.    public Test(int j, int k) {
5.       super(j, k);
6.    }
7. }
```

Which of the following are legitimate calls to construct instances of the Test class?

    A. Test t = new Test();

    B. Test t = new Test(1);

    C. Test t = new Test(1, 2);

    D. Test t = new Test(1, 2, 3);

    E. Test t = (new Base()).new Test(1);

7. Consider the following class definition:

```
1. public class Test extends Base {
2.    public Test(int j) {
3.    }
4.    public Test(int j, int k) {
5.       super(j, k);
6.    }
7. }
```

Which of the following forms of constructor must exist explicitly in the definition of the Base class?

A. `Base() { }`

B. `Base(int j) { }`

C. `Base(int j, int k) { }`

D. `Base(int j, int k, int l) { }`

8. Which of the following statements are true? (Choose one or more.)

   A. An inner class may be declared `private`.

   B. An inner class may be declared `static`.

   C. An inner class defined in a method should always be anonymous.

   D. An inner class defined in a method can access all the method local variables.

   E. Construction of an inner class may require an instance of the outer class.

9. Consider the following definitions:

```
1. public class Outer {
2.    public int a = 1;
3.    private int b = 2;
4.    public void method(final int c) {
5.       int d = 3;
6.       public class Inner {
7.          private void iMethod(int e) {
8.
9.          }
10.      }
11.   }
12. }
```

Which variables may be referenced correctly at line 8?

   A. a

   B. b

   C. c

   D. d

   E. e

10. Which of the following statements are true? (Choose one or more.)

A. Given that `Inner` is a non-static class declared inside a public class `Outer`, and appropriate constructor forms are defined, an instance of `Inner` may be constructed like this:

```
(new Outer()).new Inner()
```

B. If an anonymous inner class inside the class `Outer` is defined to implement the interface `ActionListener`, it may be constructed like this:

```
(new Outer()).new ActionListener()
```

C. Given that `Inner` is a non-static class declared inside a public class `Outer` and appropriate constructor forms are defined, an instance of `Inner` may be constructed in a static method like this:

```
new Inner()
```

D. An anonymous class instance that implements the interface `MyInterface` may be constructed and returned from a method like this:

```
1. return new MyInterface(int x) {
2.     int x;
3.     public MyInterface(int x) {
4.       this.x = x;
5.     }
6. };
```

CHAPTER

S E V E N

Threads

- The run() method

- Subclassing Thread and implementing Runnable

- Thread priorities

- Thread management

In this chapter you will cover the following Java Certification Exam objectives:

- Write code to create a new thread of execution, using both the Runnable interface and the Thread class.

- State the requirements for a concrete class that is declared to implement the java.lang.Runnable interface.

- Name the method that provides the starting point for execution of a thread.

- Write code to start the execution of a thread.

- State and recognize conditions that might prevent a thread from executing.

- Write code to use the synchronized keyword to require a thread of execution to obtain an object lock prior to proceeding.

- Define the behavior of a thread which invokes the wait() method of an object and the effect of that method on the object lock flag.

- Define the behavior of a thread which invokes the notify() or notifyAll() methods of an object and the effect of the method on the object lock flag.

- Define the interaction between threads executing the wait(), notify(), or notifyAll() methods, and the object lock flag.

Threads are Java's way of making a single Java Virtual Machine look like many machines, all running at the same time. This effect, of course, is an illusion: There is only one JVM, but it switches among its various projects so often that there seem to be many machines.

Java provides you with a number of tools for creating and managing threads. It is important to know about Java's thread support, because Java is fundamentally multi-threaded. There are system threads that work behind the scenes on your behalf, listening for user input and managing garbage collection. The best way to cooperate with these facilities is to understand what threads really are. Moreover, when you know how to create and manage your own threads, you can write very powerful and useful code.

The Certification objectives reflect the importance of threads and suggest that you are familiar with Java's thread support.

Thread Fundamentals

Java's thread support resides in three places:

- The `java.lang.Thread` class
- Certain parts of the `java.lang.Object` class
- Certain functionality of the Java language and runtime environment

Most (but definitely not all) support resides in the `Thread` class. In Java, every thread corresponds to an instance of the `Thread` class. These objects can be in various states: at any moment, at most one object is executing per CPU, while others might be waiting for resources, or waiting for a chance to execute, or sleeping, or dead.

In order to really understand threads, you need to be able to answer a few questions:

- When a thread executes, what code does it execute?
- What states can a thread be in?
- How does a thread change its state?

The next few sections will look at each of these questions in turn.

What a Thread Executes

To make a thread execute, you call its `start()` method. This registers the thread with a piece of code called the *thread scheduler.* The scheduler determines which thread gets to run. Note that calling your thread's `start()` method doesn't immediately cause the thread to run; it just makes it *eligible* to run. The thread must still contend for CPU time with all the other threads. At some point in the future (hopefully), the thread scheduler will permit your thread to execute.

At some point in its lifetime, a thread will execute; that is, it gets exclusive use of the virtual CPU. From time to time the thread may step out of the CPU and enter some non-executing state for a while. In this section, you can ignore for the moment the question of how the thread got into the CPU and how it deals with state changes. The question at hand is: When the thread gets to execute, what does it execute?

The simple answer is that it executes a method called run(). But which object's run() method? You have two choices:

- The thread can execute its own run() method.

- The thread can execute the run() method of some other object.

If you want the thread to execute its own run() method, you need to subclass the Thread class and give your subclass a run(). This method must be public, with a void return type. For example

```
1. public class CounterThread extends Thread {
2.   public void run() {
3.     for (int i=1; i<=10; i++) {
4.       System.out.println("Counting: " + i);
5.     }
6.   }
7. }
```

Notice that the return type of run() is void and there are no arguments. This exact signature is mandatory.

This run() method just prints out the numbers from 1 to 10. To do this in a thread, you first construct an instance of CounterThread, and then invoke its start() method:

```
1. CounterThread ct = new CounterThread();
2. ct.start();       // start(), not run()
```

What you *don't* do is call run() directly; that would just count to 10 in the current thread. Instead, you call start(), which class CounterThread inherits from its parent class, Thread. The start() method registers the thread (that is, ct) with the thread scheduler; eventually the thread will execute, and at that time its run() method will be called.

If you want your thread to execute the run() method of some other object, you still need to construct an instance of the Thread class. The only difference is that when you call the Thread constructor, you have to specify which object owns the run() method that you want. To do this, you invoke an alternate form of the Thread constructor:

```
public Thread(Runnable target)
```

The Runnable interface describes a single method:

```
public void run();
```

Thus you can pass any object you want into the constructor, provided it implements the Runnable interface (so that it really does have a run() method for the thread scheduler to invoke).

Having constructed an instance of Thread, you proceed as before: You invoke the start() method. As before, this registers the thread with the scheduler, and eventually the run() method of the target will be called.

For example, the following class has a run() method that counts down from 10 to 1:

```
1. public class DownCounter implements Runnable {
2.    public void run() {
3.       for (int i=10; i>=1; i-) {
4.          System.out.println("Counting Down: " + i);
5.       }
6.    }
7. }
```

This class does *not* extend Thread. However, it has a run() method, and it declares that it implements the Runnable interface. Thus any instance of the DownCounter class is eligible to be passed into the alternative constructor for Thread:

```
1. DownCounter dc = new DownCounter();
2. Thread t = new Thread(dc);
3. t.start();
```

This section has presented two strategies for constructing threads. The only difference between these two strategies is the location of the run() method. The second strategy is clearly a bit more complicated. There is a good reason why you might choose to make the extra effort. The run() method is allowed to access the private data, and call the private methods, of whatever class you put it in. Putting run() in a subclass of Thread may mean that the method cannot get to features it needs (or cannot get to those features in a clean, reasonable manner). When you choose which class to put run() in, you should base your choice on good object-oriented design principles.

To summarize, there are two approaches to specifying which run() method will be executed by a thread:

- Subclass Thread. Put run() in the subclass.

- Write a class that implements Runnable. Pass an instance of that class into your call to the Thread constructor.

When Execution Ends

When the run() method returns, the thread has finished its task and is considered *dead*. There is no way out of this state. Once a thread is dead, it may not be started again; if you want the thread's task to be performed again, you have to construct and start a new thread instance. The dead thread continues to exist; it is an object like any other object, and you can still access its data and call its methods. You just can't make it run again. In other words

- You *can't* restart a dead thread.

- You *can* call the methods of a dead thread.

You can kill a thread prematurely by calling its stop() method. The thread will enter the Dead state, just as if it had completed run().

Thread States

When you call start() on a thread, the thread does not run immediately. It goes into a "ready-to-run" state and stays there until the scheduler moves it to the "running" state. Then the run() method is called. In the course of executing run(), the thread may temporarily give up the CPU and enter some other state for a while. It is important to be aware of the possible states a thread might be in and of the triggers that can cause a state change.

The thread states are

- Running: the state that all threads aspire to

- Various waiting states: Waiting, Sleeping, Suspended, Blocked

- Ready: not waiting for anything except the CPU

- Dead: all done

Figure 7.1 shows the non-dead states. Notice that the figure does not show the Dead state.

At the top of Figure 7.1 is the Running state. At the bottom is the Ready state. In between are the various not-ready states. A thread in one of these intermediate states is waiting for something to happen; when that something eventually happens, the thread moves to the Ready state, and eventually (hopefully) the thread scheduler will permit it to run again.

FIGURE 7.1:

Living thread states

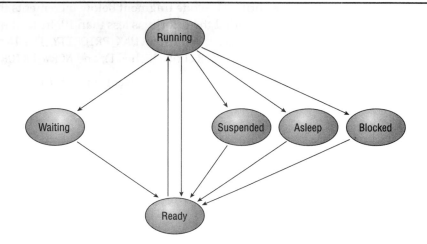

The arrows between the bubbles in Figure 7.1 represent state transitions, and the direction of the arrows tell you what triggers the transitions. Notice that only the thread scheduler can move a ready thread into the CPU.

Later in this chapter, you will examine in detail the various waiting states. For now, the important thing to observe in Figure 7.1 is the general flow: A running thread enters a waiting state for some reason; later, whatever the thread was waiting for comes to pass, and the thread enters the Ready state; later still, the scheduler grants the CPU to the thread.

Thread Priorities

Every thread has a priority. The priority is an integer from 1 to 10; threads with higher priority get preference over threads with lower priority. The priority is considered by the thread scheduler, when it decides which ready thread should execute. The scheduler generally chooses the highest-priority waiting thread. If there is more than one waiting thread, the scheduler chooses one of them. There is no guarantee that the thread chosen will be the one that has been waiting the longest.

The default priority is 5, but all newly created threads have their priority set to that of the creating thread. To set a thread's priority, call the setPriority() method, passing in the desired new priority. The getPriority() method returns a thread's priority. The code fragment below increments the priority of thread theThread, provided the priority is less than 10. Instead of hardcoding the value 10, the fragment uses the constant MAX_PRIORITY. The Thread class also defines constants for MIN_PRIORITY (which is 1), and NORM_PRIORITY (which is 5).

```
1. int oldPriority = theThread.getPriority();
2. int newPriority = Math.min(oldPriority+1, Thread.MAX_PRIORITY);
3. theThread.setPriority(newPriority);
```

WARNING   The specifics of how thread priorities affect scheduling are platform-dependent. The Java specification states that threads must have priorities, but it does not dictate precisely what the scheduler should do about priorities. This vagueness is a problem: Algorithms that rely on manipulating thread priorities are unpredictable.

Controlling Threads

Thread control is the art of moving threads from state to state. You control threads by triggering state transitions. This section examines the various pathways out of the Running state. These pathways are

- Yielding

- Suspending and then resuming

- Sleeping and then waking up

- Blocking and then continuing

- Waiting and then being notified

Yielding

A thread can voluntarily move out of the virtual CPU by *yielding*. A call to the yield() method causes the currently executing thread to move to the Ready state. The state transition is shown in Figure 7.2.

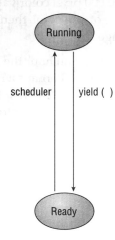

A thread that has yielded goes into the Ready state. There are two possible scenarios. If any other threads are in the Ready state, then the thread that just yielded may have to wait a while before it gets to execute again. However, if there are no other waiting threads, then the thread that just yielded will get to continue executing immediately.

The `yield()` method is a static method of the `Thread` class. It always causes the currently executing thread to yield.

Yielding allows a time-consuming thread to permit other threads to execute. For example, consider an applet that computes a 300×300 pixel image using a ray-tracing algorithm. The applet might have a "Compute" button and an "Interrupt" button. The action event handler for the "Compute" button would create and start a separate thread, which would call a `traceRays()` method. A first cut at this method might look like this:

```
1. private void traceRays() {
2.   for (int j=0; j<300; j++) {
3.     for (int i=0; i<300; i++) {
4.       computeOnePixel(i, j);
5.     }
6.   }
7. }
```

There are 90,000 pixel color values to compute. If it takes 0.1 second to compute the color value of one pixel, then it will take two-and-a-half hours to compute the complete image.

Suppose after half an hour the user looks at the partial image and realizes that something is wrong. (Perhaps a red light source really should have been blue.) The user will then click the "Interrupt" button, since there is no sense in continuing to compute the useless image. Unfortunately, the thread that handles GUI input may not get a chance to execute until the thread that is executing traceRays() gives up the CPU. Thus the "Interrupt" button will not have any effect for another two hours.

The correct approach is to have the ray-tracing thread periodically yield and run at a slightly lower priority than the input-listening thread. If there is no pending input, the ray-tracing thread will be in the Ready state for only a moment; if it does not have to contend with any other threads, it will be moved back immediately into the Running state. If, on the other hand, there is input to be processed, the input-listening thread will get to execute, since it has a higher priority than the ray-tracing thread. (This assumes that the underlying platform implements priorities in a reasonable way.)

The ray-tracing thread can have its priority set like this:

```
rayTraceThread.setPriority(Thread.NORM_PRIORITY-1);
```

The traceRays() method listed above can yield after each pixel value is computed, after line 4. The revised version looks like this:

```
1. private void traceRays() {
2.   for (int j=0; j<300; j++) {
3.     for (int i=0; i<300; i++) {
4.       computeOnePixel(i, j);
5.       Thread.yield();
6.     }
7.   }
8. }
```

Suspending

A thread that receives a suspend() method call enters the *Suspended* state and stays there until it receives a resume() method call or is stopped. Figure 7.3 shows the state transitions. Unlike the yield() method, suspend() and resume() are non-static.

FIGURE 7.3:

The Suspended state

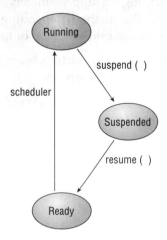

A thread can be suspended by itself or by another thread. A thread can only be resumed by a different thread, of course, since the suspended thread does not run. For example, the class listed below will be disappointing:

```
1. public class BadResume extends Thread {
2.    public void run() {
3.       // Do some stuff.
4.       suspend();
5.       resume();    // TROUBLE!
6.       // Do some more stuff.
7.    }
8. }
```

When this thread executes line 4, it becomes suspended. Since it is no longer in the Running state, line 5 will never get called. An instance of BadResume that gets as far as line 4 will have to be resumed by some other thread.

NOTE   A resume() call on a thread that is not suspended will have no effect.

Sleeping

A *Sleeping* thread passes time without doing anything and without using the CPU. A call to the sleep() method requests the currently executing thread to cease executing for (approximately) a specified amount of time. There are two ways to call this method, depending on whether you want to specify the sleep period to millisecond precision or to nanosecond precision:

- `public static void sleep(long milliseconds) throws InterruptedException`

- `public static void sleep(long milliseconds, int nanoseconds) throws InterruptedException`

NOTE

Note that `sleep()`, like `yield()`, is static. Both methods operate on the currently executing thread.

The state diagram for sleeping is shown in Figure 7.4. Notice that when the thread has finished sleeping, it does not continue execution. As you would expect, it enters the Ready state and will only execute when the thread scheduler allows it to do so.

The `Thread` class has a method called `interrupt()`. A sleeping thread that receives an `interrupt()` call moves immediately into the Ready state; when it gets to run, it will execute its `InterruptedException` handler.

FIGURE 7.4:

The Sleeping state

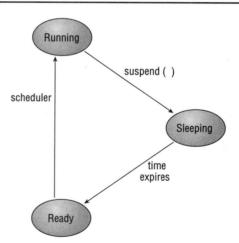

Blocking

Many methods that perform input or output have to wait for some occurrence in the outside world before they can proceed; this behavior is known as *blocking*. A good example is reading from a socket:

```
1. try {
2.    Socket sock = new Socket("magnesium", 5505);
3.    InputStream istr = sock.getInputStream();
4.    int b = istr.read();
5. }
6. catch (IOException ex) {
7.    // Handle the exception
8. }
```

If you aren't familiar with Java's socket and stream functionality don't worry; it's all covered in Chapter 14, *Input and Output*. The discussion here is not complicated.

It looks like line 4 reads a byte from an input stream that is connected to port 5505 on a machine called "magnesium." Actually, line 4 *tries* to read a byte. If a byte is available (that is, if magnesium has previously written a byte), then line 4 can return immediately and execution can continue. If magnesium has not yet written anything, however, the read() call has to wait. If magnesium is busy doing other things and takes half an hour to get around to writing a byte, then the read() call has to wait for half an hour.

Clearly, it would be a serious problem if the thread executing the read() call on line 4 remained in the Running state for the entire half hour. Nothing else could get done. In general, if a method needs to wait an indeterminable amount of time until some I/O occurrence takes place, then a thread executing that method should graciously step out of the Running state. All Java I/O methods behave this way. A thread that has graciously stepped out in this fashion is said to be *blocked*. Figure 7.5 shows the transitions of the Blocked state.

A thread can also become blocked if it fails to acquire the lock for a monitor. Locks and monitors are explained in detail later in this chapter, beginning in the section *Monitors, wait(), and notify()*.

The Blocked state

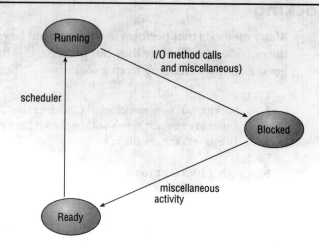

Waiting

Figure 7.6 (which is just a rerun of Figure 7.1) shows all the thread state transitions. The intermediate states on the right-hand side of the figure (Suspended, Sleeping, and Blocked) have been discussed in previous sections. The Waiting state is drawn all alone on the left-hand side of the figure to emphasize that it is very different from the other intermediate states.

FIGURE 7.6:

Thread states (reprise)

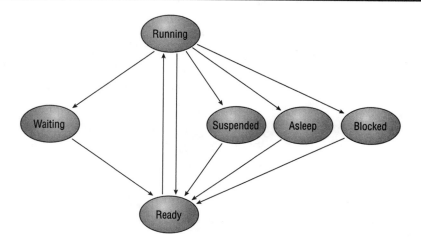

The wait() method puts an executing thread into the *Waiting* state, and the notify() and notifyAll() methods put waiting threads into the Ready state. However, these methods are very different from suspend(), resume(), and yield(). For one thing, they are implemented in the Object class, not in Thread. For another, they may only be called in synchronized code. The Waiting state, and the associated issues and subtleties, are discussed in the final several sections of this chapter. But first, there is one more topic to look at concerning thread control.

Scheduling Implementations

Historically, two approaches have emerged for implementing thread schedulers:

- Preemptive scheduling
- Time-sliced or round robin scheduling

So far, the facilities described in this chapter have been preemptive. In preemptive scheduling, there are only two ways for a thread to leave the Running state without explicitly calling a thread-scheduling method such as wait() or suspend():

- It can cease to be ready to execute (by calling a blocking I/O method, for example).
- It can get *preempted* by a higher-priority thread which becomes ready to execute.

With time slicing, a thread is only allowed to execute for a limited amount of time. It is then moved to the Ready state, where it must contend with all the other ready threads. Time slicing insures against the possibility of a single high-priority thread getting into the Running state and never getting out, preventing all other threads from doing their jobs. Unfortunately, time slicing creates a non-deterministic system; at any moment you can't be certain which thread is executing or for how long it will continue to execute.

NOTE   It is natural to ask which implementation Java uses. The answer is that it depends on the platform; the Java specification gives implementations a lot of leeway. Solaris machines are preemptive. Macintoshes are time-sliced. Windows platforms were originally preemptive, but changed to time-sliced with the 1.0.2 release of the JDK.

Monitors, *wait()*, and *notify()*

A *monitor* is an object that can block and revive threads. The concept is simple, but it takes a bit of work to understand what monitors are good for and how to use them effectively.

The reason for having monitors is that sometimes a thread cannot perform its job until an object reaches a certain state. For example, consider a class that handles requests to write to standard output:

```
1. class Mailbox {
2.    public boolean     request;
3.    public String      message;
4. }
```

The intention of this class is that a client can set `message` to some value, then set `request` to `true`:

```
1. myMailbox.message = "Hello everybody.";
2. myMailbox.request = true;
```

There must be a thread that checks `request`; on finding it `true`, the thread should write `message` to `System.out`, and then set `request` to `false`. (Setting `request` to `false` indicates that the mailbox object is ready to handle another request.) It is tempting to implement this thread like this:

```
1. public class Consumer extends Thread {
2.    private Mailbox myMailbox;
3.
4.    public Consumer(Mailbox box) {
5.       this.myMailbox = box;
6.    }
7.
8.    public void run() {
9.      while (true) {
10.        if (myMailbox.request) {
11.          System.out.println(myMailbox.message);
12.          myMailbox.request = false;
13.        }
14.
15.        try {
16.          sleep(50);
17.        }
```

```
18.          catch (InterruptedException e) { }
19.      }
20.  }
```

The consumer thread loops forever, checking for requests every 50 milliseconds. If there is a request (line 10), the consumer writes the message to standard output (line 11), and then sets `request` to `false` to show that it is ready for more requests.

The `Consumer` class may look fine at first glance, but it has two serious problems:

- The `Consumer` class accesses data internal to the `Mailbox` class, introducing the possibility of corruption. On a time-sliced system, the consumer thread could just possibly be interrupted between lines 10 and 11. The interrupting thread could just possibly be a client that sets `message` to its own message (ignoring the convention of checking `request` to see if the handler is available). The consumer thread would send the wrong message.

- The choice of 50 milliseconds for the delay can never be ideal. Sometimes 50 milliseconds will be too long, and clients will receive slow service; Sometimes 50 milliseconds will be too frequent, and cycles will be wasted. A thread that wants to send a message has a similar dilemma if it finds the `request` flag set: The thread should back off for a while, but for how long?

Ideally, these problems would be solved by making some modifications to the `Mailbox` class:

- The mailbox should be able to protect its data from irresponsible clients.

- If the mailbox is not available—that is, if the `request` flag is already set—then a client consumer should not have to guess how long to wait before checking the flag again. The handler should tell the client when the time is right.

Java's monitor support addresses these issues by providing the following resources:

- A lock for each object

- The `synchronized` keyword for accessing an object's lock

- The `wait()`, `notify()`, and `notifyAll()` methods, which allow the object to control client threads

The sections below describe locks, synchronized code, and the `wait()`, `notify()`, and `notifyAll()` methods, and show how these can be used to make thread code more robust.

The Object Lock and Synchronization

Every object has a *lock*. At any moment, that lock is controlled by at most one single thread. The lock controls access to the object's synchronized code. A thread that wants to execute an object's synchronized code must first attempt to acquire that object's lock. If the lock is available—that is, if it is not already controlled by another thread—then all is well. If the lock is under another thread's control, then the attempting thread goes into the Blocked state and only becomes ready when the lock becomes available. When a thread that owns a lock passes out of the synchronized code, the thread automatically gives up the lock. All this lock-checking and state-changing is done behind the scenes; the only explicit programming you need to do is to declare code to be synchronized.

There are two ways to mark code as synchronized:

- Synchronize an entire method, by putting the synchronized modifier in the method's declaration. To execute the method, a thread must acquire the lock of the object that owns the method.

- Synchronize a subset of a method, by surrounding the desired lines of code with curly brackets ({ }), and inserting the synchronized(someObject) expression before the opening curly. This technique allows you to synchronize the block on the lock of any object at all, not necessarily the object that owns the code.

The first technique is by far the more common; synchronizing on any object other than the object that owns the synchronized code can be extremely dangerous. The Certification Exam requires you to know how to apply the second technique, but the exam does not make you think through complicated scenarios of synchronizing on external objects. The second technique is discussed at the very end of this chapter.

Synchronization makes it easy to clean up some of the problems with the Mailbox class:

```
1. class Mailbox {
2.    private boolean   request;
3.    private String    message;
4.
5.    public synchronized void storeMessage(String message) {
6.      request = true;
7.      this.message = message;
8.    }
```

```
9.
10.    public synchronized String retrieveMessage() {
11.       request = false;
12.       return message;
13.    }
14. }
```

Now the `request` flag and the message string are private, so they can only be modified via the public methods of the class. Since `storeMessage()` and `retrieveMessage()` are synchronized, there is no danger of a message-producing thread corrupting the flag and spoiling things for a message-consuming thread, or vice versa.

The `Mailbox` class is now safe from its clients, but the clients still have problems. A message-producing client should only call `storeMessage()` when the request flag is `false`; a message-consuming client should only call `retrieveMessage()` when the request flag is `true`. In the `Consumer` class of the previous section, the consuming thread's main loop polled the request flag every 50 milliseconds. (Presumably a message-producing thread would do something similar.) Now the request flag is private, so you must find another way.

It is possible to come up with any number of clever ways for the client threads to poll the mailbox, but the whole approach is backwards. The mailbox becomes available or unavailable based on changes of its own state. The mailbox should be in charge of the progress of the clients. Java's `wait()` and `notify()` methods provide the necessary controls, as you will see in the next section.

wait() and *notify()*

The `wait()` and `notify()` methods provide a way for a shared object to pause a thread when it becomes unavailable to that thread, and to allow the thread to continue when appropriate. The threads themselves never have to check the state of the shared object.

An object that controls its client threads in this manner is known as a *monitor*. In strict Java terminology, a monitor is any object that has some synchronized code. To be really useful, most monitors make use of `wait()` and `notify()` methods. So the `Mailbox` class is already a monitor; it just is not quite useful yet.

Figure 7.7 shows the state transitions of `wait()` and `notify()`.

FIGURE 7.7:

The Waiting state

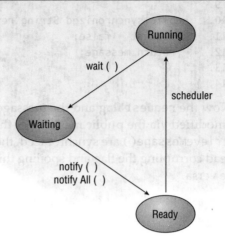

Both `wait()` and `notify()` must be called in synchronized code. A thread that calls `wait()` releases the virtual CPU; at the same time, it releases the lock. It enters a pool of waiting threads, which is managed by the object whose `wait()` method got called. Every object has such a pool. The code below shows how the `Mailbox` class' `retrieveMessage()` method could be modified to begin taking advantage of calling `wait()`.

```
1. public synchronized String retrieveMessage() {
2.   while (request == false) {
3.     try {
4.       wait();
5.     } catch (InterruptedException e) { }
6.   }
7.   request = false;
8.   return message;
9. }
```

Now consider what happens when a message-consuming thread calls this method. The call might look like this:

```
myMailbox.retrieveMessage();
```

When a message-consuming thread calls this method, the thread must first acquire the lock for `myMailbox`. Acquiring the lock could happen immediately, or it could incur a delay if some other thread is executing any of the synchronized code of myMailbox. One way or another, eventually the consumer thread has the lock and begins to execute at line 2. The code first checks the request flag. If the flag is not set, then myMailbox has no message for the thread to retrieve. In this case the wait() method is called at line 4 (it can throw an InterruptedException, so the try/catch code is required, and the while will re-test the condition). When line 4 executes, the consumer thread ceases execution; it also releases the lock for myMailbox and enters the pool of waiting threads managed by myMailbox.

The consumer thread has been successfully prevented from corrupting the myMailbox monitor. Unfortunately, it is stuck in the monitor's pool of waiting threads. When the monitor changes to a state where it can provide the consumer with something to do, then something will have to be done to get the consumer out of the Waiting state. This is done by calling notify() when the monitor's request flag becomes true, which only happens in the storeMessage() method. The revised storeMessage() looks like this:

```
1. public synchronized void storeMessage(String message) {
2.    this.message = message;
3.    request = true;
4.    notify();
5. }
```

On line 4, the code calls notify() just after changing the monitor's state. What notify() does is to select one of the threads in the monitor's waiting pool and move it to the Ready state.

Now imagine a complete scenario. A consumer thread calls retrieveMessage() on a mailbox that has no message. It acquires the lock and begins executing the method. It sees that the request flag is false, so it calls wait() and joins the mailbox's waiting pool. (In this simple example, there are no other threads in the pool.) Since the consumer has called wait(), it has given up the lock. Later, a message-producing thread calls storeMessage() on the same mailbox. It acquires the lock, stores its message in the monitor's instance variable, and sets the request flag to true. The producer then calls notify(). At this moment there is only one thread in the monitor's waiting pool: the consumer. So the consumer gets moved out of the waiting pool and into the Ready state. Now the producer returns from retrieveMessage(); since the producer has exited from synchronized code, it gives up the monitor's lock. Later the patient consumer gets a chance to execute. It must re-acquire the lock; once this happens, it checks the request flag and (finally!) sees that there is a message available for consumption. The consumer returns the message; upon return it automatically releases the lock.

To briefly summarize this scenario: A consumer tried to consume something, but there was nothing to consume, so the consumer waited. Later a producer produced something. At that point there was something for the consumer to consume, so the consumer was notified; once the producer was done with the monitor, the consumer consumed a message.

This example protected the consumer against the possibility that the monitor might be empty; the protection was implemented with a wait() call in retrieveMessage() and a notify() call in storeMessage(). A similar precaution must be taken in case a producer thread wants to produce into a monitor that already contains a message. To be robust, storeMessage() needs to call wait(), and retrieveMessage() needs to call notify(). The complete Mailbox class looks like this:

```
1. class Mailbox {
2.    private boolean   request;
3.    private String    message;
4.
5.    public synchronized void storeMessage(String message) {
6.      while(request == true) {  // No room for another message
7.        try {
8.          wait();
9.        } catch (InterruptedException e) { }
10.     }
11.     request = true;
12.     this.message = message;
13.     notify();
14.   }
15.
16.   public synchronized String retrieveMessage() {
17.     while(request == false) {  // No message to retrieve
18.       try {
19.         wait();
20.       } catch (InterruptedException e) { }
21.     }
22.     request = false;
23.     notify();
24.     return message;
25.   }
26. }
```

NOTE   By synchronizing code and judiciously calling `wait()` and `notify()`, monitors such as the `Mailbox` class can insure the proper interaction of client threads and protect shared data from corruption.

Here are the main points to remember about `wait()`:

- The calling thread gives up the CPU.

- The calling thread gives up the lock.

- The calling thread goes into the monitor's waiting pool.

Here are the main points to remember about `notify()`:

- One thread gets moved out of the monitor's waiting pool and into the Ready state.

- The thread that was notified must re-acquire the monitor's lock before it can proceed.

Beyond the Pure Model

The mailbox example of the previous few sections has been a very simple example of a situation involving one producer and one consumer. In real life things are not always so simple. You might have a monitor that has several methods that do not purely produce or purely consume. All you can say in general about such methods is that they cannot proceed unless the monitor is in a certain state, and they themselves can change the monitor's state in ways that could be of interest to the other methods.

The `notify()` method is not precise: You cannot specify which thread is to be notified. In a mixed-up scenario such as the one described above, a thread might alter the monitor's state in a way that is useless to the thread that gets notified. In such a case, the monitor's methods should take two precautions:

- Always check the monitor's state in a `while` loop rather than an `if` statement.

- After changing the monitor's state, call `notifyAll()` rather than `notify()`.

The first precaution means that you should *not* do the following:

```
1. public synchronized void mixedUpMethod() {
2.    if (i<16  ||  f>4.3f  ||  message.equals("UH-OH") {
3.      try { wait(); } catch (InterruptedException e) { }
4.    }
5.
6.    // Proceed in a way that changes state, and then...
7.    notify();
8. }
```

The danger is that sometimes a thread might execute the test on line 2, then notice that i is (for example) 234, and have to wait. Later another thread might change the monitor's state by setting i to -23444, and then call notify(). If the original thread is the one that gets notified, it will pick up where it left off, even though the monitor is not in a state where it is ready for mixedUpMethod().

The solution is to change mixedUpMethod() as follows:

```
1. public synchronized void mixedUpMethod() {
2.    while (i<16  ||  f>4.3f  ||  message.equals("UH-OH") {
3.      try { wait(); } catch (InterruptedException e) { }
4.    }
5.
6.    // Proceed in a way that changes state, and then...
7.    notifyAll();
8. }
```

The monitor's other synchronized methods should be modified in a similar manner.

Now when a waiting thread gets notified, it does not assume that the monitor's state is acceptable. It checks again, in the loop check on line 2. If the state is still not conducive, the thread waits again.

On line 8, having made its own modifications to the monitor's state, the code calls notifyAll(); this call is like notify(), but it moves *every* thread in the monitor's waiting pool to the Ready state. Presumably every thread's wait() call happened in a loop like the one on lines 2–4, so every thread will once again check the monitor's state and either wait or proceed.

Using a `while` loop to check the monitor's state is a good idea even if you are coding a pure model of one producer and one consumer. After all, you can never be sure that somebody won't try to add an extra producer or an extra consumer.

Strange Ways to Synchronize

There are two ways to synchronize code that have not been explained yet. They are hardly common and generally should not be used without a very compelling reason. The two approaches are

- Synchronizing on the lock of a different object

- Synchronizing on the lock of a class

It was briefly mentioned in an earlier section (*The Object Lock and Synchronization*) that you can synchronize on the lock of any object. Suppose, for example, that you have the following class, which is admittedly a bit contrived:

```
1. class StrangeSync {
2.   Rectangle rect = new Rectangle(11, 13, 1100, 1300);
3.   void doit() {
4.     int x = 504;
5.     int y = x / 3;
6.     rect.width -= x;
7.     rect.height -= y;
8.   }
9. }
```

If you add the `synchronized` keyword at line 3, then a thread that wants to execute the `doit()` method of some instance of `StrangeSync` must first acquire the lock for that instance. That may be exactly what you want; perhaps you only want to synchronize lines 7 and 8, and perhaps you want a thread attempting to execute those lines to synchronize on the lock of `rect`. The way to do this is shown below:

```
1. class StrangeSync {
2.   Rectangle rect = new Rectangle(11, 13, 1100, 1300);
3.   void doit() {
4.     int x = 504;
5.     int y = x / 3;
6.     synchronized(rect) {
```

```
 7.        rect.width -= x;
 8.        rect.height -= y;
 9.      }
10.    }
11. }
```

The code above synchronizes on the lock of some arbitrary object (specified in parentheses after the synchronized keyword on line 6), rather than synchronizing on the lock of the current object. Also, the code above synchronizes just two lines, rather than an entire method.

It is difficult to find a good reason for synchronizing on an arbitrary object. However, synchronizing only a subset of a method can be useful; sometimes you want to hold the lock as briefly as possible, so that other threads can get their turn as soon as possible. The Java compiler insists that when you synchronize a portion of a method (rather than the entire method), you have to specify an object in parentheses after the synchronized keyword. If you put this in the parentheses, then the goal is achieved: You have synchronized a portion of a method, with the lock using the object that owns the method.

So your options are

- To synchronize an entire method, using the lock of the object that owns the method. To do this, put the synchronized keyword in the method's declaration.

- To synchronize part of a method, using the lock of an arbitrary object. To do this, put curly brackets around the code to be synchronized, preceded by synchronized(theArbitraryObject).

- To synchronize part of a method, using the lock of the object that owns the method. To do this, put curly brackets around the code to be synchronized, preceded by synchronized(this).

TIP

Classes, as well as objects, have locks. A class lock is used for synchronizing the static methods of a class. The Certification objectives do not reflect a great emphasis on class locks.

Chapter Summary

A Java thread scheduler can be preemptive or time-sliced, depending on the design of the JVM. No matter which design is used, a thread becomes eligible for execution ("Ready") when its `start()` method is invoked. When a thread begins execution, the scheduler calls the `run()` method of the thread's target (if there is a target) or the `run()` method of the thread itself (if there is no target).

In the course of execution, a thread can become ineligible for execution for a number or reasons: A thread can suspend, or sleep, or block, or wait. In due time (one hopes!) conditions will change so that the thread once more becomes eligible for execution; then the thread enters the Ready state and eventually can execute.

When a thread returns from its `run()` method, it enters the Dead state and cannot be restarted.

You might find the following bulleted lists a useful summary of Java's threads.

Scheduler implementations:

- Preemptive
- Time-sliced

Constructing a thread:

- `new Thread()`: no target; thread's own `run()` method is executed
- `new Thread(Runnable target)`: target's `run()` method is executed

Non-runnable thread states:

- Suspended: caused by `suspend()`, waits for `resume()`
- Sleeping: caused by `sleep()`, waits for timeout
- Blocked: caused by various I/O calls or by failing to get a monitor's lock, waits for I/O or for the monitor's lock
- Waiting: caused by `wait()`, waits for `notify()` or `notifyAll()`
- Dead: caused by `stop()` or returning from `run()`, no way out

Test Yourself

1. Which one statement below is true concerning the following code?

```
1. class Greebo extends java.util.Vector implements Runnable {
2.    public void run(String message) {
3.       System.out.println("in run() method: " + message);
4.    }
5. }
6.
7. class GreeboTest {
8.    public static void main(String args[]) {
9.       Greebo g = new Greebo();
10.      Thread t = new Thread(g);
11.      t.start();
12.   }
13. }
```

   A. There will be a compiler error, because class Greebo does not implement the Runnable interface.

   B. There will be a compiler error at line 11, because you cannot pass a parameter to the constructor of a Thread.

   C. The code will compile correctly but will crash with an exception at line 11.

   D. The code will compile correctly but will crash with an exception at line 12.

   E. The code will compile correctly and will execute without throwing any exceptions.

2. Which one statement below is always true about the following application?

```
1. class HiPri extends Thread {
2.    HiPri() {
3.       setPriority(10);
4.    }
5.
6.    public void run() {
7.       System.out.println("Another thread starting up.");
8.       while (true) { }
9.    }
```

```
10.
11.    public static void main(String args[]) {
12.        HiPri hp1 = new HiPri();
13.        HiPri hp2 = new HiPri();
14.        HiPri hp3 = new HiPri();
15.        hp1.start();
16.        hp2.start();
17.        hp3.start();
18.    }
19. }
```

A. When the application is run, thread hp1 will execute; threads hp2 and hp3 will never get the CPU.

B. When the application is run, all three threads (hp1, hp2, and hp3) will get to execute, taking time-sliced turns in the CPU.

C. Either A or B will be true, depending on the underlying platform.

3. True or False: A thread wants to make a second thread ineligible for execution. To do this, the first thread can call the yield() method on the second thread.

4. True or False: A thread wants to make a second thread ineligible for execution. To do this, the first thread can call the suspend() method on the second thread.

5. A thread's run() method includes the following lines:

```
1. try {
2.    sleep(100);
3. } catch (InterruptedException e) { }
```

Assuming the thread is not interrupted, which one of the following statements is correct?

A. The code will not compile, because exceptions may not be caught in a thread's run() method.

B. At line 2, the thread will stop running. Execution will resume in at most 100 milliseconds.

C. At line 2, the thread will stop running. It will resume running in exactly 100 milliseconds.

D. At line 2, the thread will stop running. It will resume running some time after 100 milliseconds have elapsed.

6. A monitor called mon has 10 threads in its waiting pool; all these waiting threads have the same priority. One of the threads is thr1. How can you notify thr1 so that it alone moves from the Waiting state to the Ready state?

A. Execute notify(thr1); from within synchronized code of mon.

B. Execute mon.notify(thr1); from synchronized code of any object.

C. Execute thr1.notify(); from synchronized code of any object.

D. Execute thr1.notify(); from any code (synchronized or not) of any object.

E. You cannot specify which thread will get notified.

7. Which one statement below is true concerning the following application?

```
1. class TestThread extends Thread {
2.    public void run() {
3.      System.out.println("Starting");
4.      suspend();
5.      resume();
6.      System.out.println("Done");
7.    }
8.
9.    public static void main(String args[]) {
10.     TestThread tt = new TestThread();
11.     tt.start();
12.   }
13. }
```

A. Compilation will fail at line 4, because suspend() must be called in synchronized code.

B. Compilation will fail at line 5, because resume() must be called in synchronized code.

C. Compilation will succeed. On execution, nothing will be printed out.

D. Compilation will succeed. On execution, only one line of output (Starting) will be printed out.

    E. Compilation will succeed. On execution, both lines of output (`Starting` and `Done`) will be printed out.

8. Which one statement below is true concerning the following application?

```
1. class TestThread2 extends Thread {
2.    public void run() {
3.       System.out.println("Starting");
4.       yield();
5.       resume();
6.       System.out.println("Done");
7.    }
8.
9.    public static void main(String args[]) {
10.      TestThread2 tt = new TestThread2();
11.      tt.start();
12.   }
13. }
```

    A. Compilation will fail at line 4, because `yield()` must be called in synchronized code.

    B. Compilation will fail at line 5, because `resume()` must be called in synchronized code.

    C. Compilation will succeed. On execution, nothing will be printed out.

    D. Compilation will succeed. On execution, only one line of output (`Starting`) will be printed out.

    E. Compilation will succeed. On execution, both lines of output (`Starting` and `Done`) will be printed out.

9. If you attempt to compile and execute the application listed below, will it ever print out the message In xxx?

```
1. class TestThread3 extends Thread {
2.    public void run() {
3.       System.out.println("Running");
4.       System.out.println("Done");
5.    }
6.
7.    private void xxx() {
8.       System.out.println("In xxx");
```

```
9.  }
10.
11.  public static void main(String args[]) {
12.    TestThread3 ttt = new TestThread3();
13.       ttt.xxx();
14.       ttt.start();
12.  }
13. }
```

10. True or False: A Java monitor must either extend Thread or implement Runnable.

CHAPTER

EIGHT

The *java.lang* Package

- The Object class

- The Math class

- The wrapper classes

- The String class

- The StringBuffer class

In this chapter you will cover the following Certification Exam objectives:

- Write code to demonstrate the use of the methods of the `java.lang.Math` class in an expression: `abs()`, `ceil()`, `floor()`, `max()`, `min()`, `random()`, `round()`, `sin()`, `cos()`, `tan()`, `sqrt()`.

- Write code to demonstrate the use of the following methods of the `java.lang.String` class: `length()`, `toUpperCase()`, `to LowerCase()`, `equals()`, `equalsIgnoreCase()`, `charAt()`, `concat()`, `indexOf()`, `lastIndexOf()`, `substring()`, `toString()`, `trim()`.

- State all operators that are legal in String expressions.

- Recognize the implications of the immutability rule of the `String` class.

The `java.lang` package contains classes that are central to the operation of the Java language and environment. Very little can be done without the `String` class, for example, and the `Object` class is completely indispensable. The Java compiler automatically imports all the classes in the package into every source file.

This chapter examines some of the most important classes of the `java.lang` package:

- `Object`
- `Math`
- The wrapper classes
- `String`
- `StringBuffer`

The *Object* Class

The `Object` class is the ultimate ancestor of all Java classes. If a class does not contain the `extends` keyword in its declaration, the compiler builds a class that extends directly from `Object`.

All the methods of `Object` are inherited by every class. Three of these methods (`wait()`, `notify()`, and `notifyAll()`) support thread control; they are discussed in detail in Chapter 7, *Threads*. Two other methods, `equals()` and `toString()`, provide little functionality on their own. The intention is that programmers who develop re-usable classes can override `equals()` and `toString()` in order to provide class-specific useful functionality.

The signature of `equals()` is

```
public boolean equals(Object object)
```

The method is supposed to provide "deep" comparison, in contrast to the "shallow" comparison provided by the `==` operator. To see the difference between the two types of comparison, consider the `java.util.Date` class, which represents a moment in time. Suppose you have two references of type `Date`: d1 and d2. One way to compare these two is with the following line of code:

```
if (d1 == d2)
```

The comparison will be true if the reference in d1 is equal to the reference in d2: that is, if both variables contain identical patterns. Of course, this is only the case when both variables refer to the same object.

Sometimes you want a different kind of comparison. Sometimes you don't care whether or not d1 and d2 refer to the same `Date` object. Sometimes you *know* they are different objects; what you care about is whether or not the two objects represent the same moment in time. In this case you don't want the shallow reference-level comparison of `==`; you need to look deeply into the objects themselves. The way to do it is with the `equals()` method:

```
if (d1.equals(d2))
```

The version of `equals()` provided by the `Object` class is not very useful; in fact, it just does an `==` comparison. All classes should override `equals()` so that it performs a useful comparison. That is just what most of the standard Java classes do: They compare the relevant instance variables of two objects.

The purpose of the `toString()` method is to provide a string representation of an object's state. This is especially useful for debugging.

The `toString()` method is similar to `equals()` in the sense that the version provided by the `Object` class is not especially useful. (It just prints out the object's class name, followed by a hash code.) Many JDK classes override `toString()` to provide more useful information. Java's string concatenation facility makes use of this method, as you will see later in this chapter, in the *String Concatenation* section.

The *Math* Class

Java's Math class contains a collection of methods, and two constants, that support mathematical computation. The class is final, so you cannot extend it. The constructor is private, so you cannot create an instance. Fortunately, the methods and constants are static, so they can be accessed through the class name without having to construct a Math object. (See Chapter 3, *Modifiers*, for an explanation of Java's modifiers, including final, static, and private.)

The two constants of the Math class are

- Math.PI
- Math.E

They are declared to be public, static, final, and double.

The methods of the Math class cover a broad range of mathematical functionality, including trigonometry, logarithms and exponentiation, and rounding. The intensive number-crunching methods are generally native, to take advantage of any math acceleration hardware that might be present on the underlying machine.

The Certification Exam requires you to know about the following methods of the Math class:

- int abs(int i): returns the absolute value of i
- long abs(long l): returns the absolute value of l
- float abs(float f): returns the absolute value of f
- double abs(double d): returns the absolute value of d
- double ceil(double d): returns as a double the smallest integer that is not less than d
- double floor(double d): returns as a double the largest integer that is not greater than d
- int max(int i1, int i2): returns the greater of i1 and i2
- long max(long l1, long l2): returns the greater of l1 and l2
- float max(float f1, float f2): returns the greater of f1 and f2
- double max(double d1, double d2): returns the greater of d1 and d2
- int min(int i1, int i2): returns the smaller of i1 and i2

- `long min(long l1, long l2)`: returns the smaller of l1 and l2
- `float min(float f1, float f2)`: returns the smaller of f1 and f2
- `double min(double d1, double d2)`: returns the smaller of d1 and d2
- `double random()`: returns a random number between 0.0 and 1.0
- `int round(float f)`: returns the closest int to f
- `long round(double f)`: returns the closest long to d
- `double sin(double d)`: returns the sine of d
- `double cos(double d)`: returns the cosine of d
- `double tan(double d)`: returns the tangent of d
- `double sqrt(double d)`: returns the square root of d

The Wrapper Classes

Each Java primitive data type has a corresponding *wrapper class*. A wrapper class is simply a class that encapsulates a single, immutable value. For example, the `Integer` class wraps up an `int` value, and the `Float` class wraps up a `float` value. The wrapper class names do not perfectly match the corresponding primitive data type names. Table 8.1 lists the primitives and wrappers.

TABLE 8.1: Primitives and Wrappers

Primitive Data Type	Wrapper Class
boolean	Boolean
byte	Byte
char	Character
short	Short
int	Integer
long	Long
float	Float
double	Double

All the wrapper classes can be constructed by passing the value to be wrapped into the appropriate constructor. The code fragment below shows how to construct an instance of each wrapper type:

```
1. boolean primitiveBoolean = true;
2. Boolean     wrappedBoolean = new Boolean(primitiveBoolean);
3.
4. byte           primitiveByte = 41;
5. Byte         wrappedByte = new Byte(primitiveByte);
6.
7. char           primitiveChar = 'M';
8. Character    wrappedChar = new Character(primitiveChar);
9.
10. short          primitiveShort = 31313;
11. Short        wrappedShort = new Short(primitiveShort);
12.
13. int            primitiveInt = 12345678;
14. Integer      wrappedInt = new Integer(primitiveInt);
15.
16. long           primitiveLong = 12345678987654321;
17. Long         wrappedLong = new Long(primitiveLong);
18.
19. float          primitiveFloat = 1.11f;
20. Float        wrappedFloat = new Float(primitiveFloat);
21.
22. double   primitiveDouble = 1.11111111;
23. Double       wrappedDouble = new Double(primitiveDouble);
```

There is another way to construct any of these classes, with the exception of `Character`. You can pass into the constructor a string that represents the value to be wrapped. Most of these constructors throw `NumberFormatException`, because there is always the possibility that the string will not represent a valid value. Only `Boolean` does not throw this exception: the constructor accepts any `String` input, and wraps a `true` value if the string (ignoring case) is `"true"`. The code fragment below shows how to construct wrappers from strings:

```
1. Boolean wrappedBoolean = new Boolean("True");
2.   try {
3.      Byte wrappedByte = new Byte("41");
4.      Short wrappedShort = new Short("31313");
5.      Integer wrappedInt = new Integer("12345678");
6.      Long wrappedLong = new Long("12345678987654321");
```

```
7.        Float wrappedFloat = new Float("1.11f");
8.        Double wrappedDouble = new Double("1.11111111");
9.      }
10.    catch (NumberFormatException e) {
11.        System.out.println("Bad Number Format");
12.    }
```

The values wrapped inside two wrappers of the same type can be checked for equality by using the `equals()` method discussed in the previous section. For example, the code fragment below checks two instances of `Double`:

```
1.  Double d1 = new Double(1.01055);
2.  Double d2 = new Double("1.11348");
3.  if (d1.equals(d2)) {
4.    // Do something.
5.  }
```

After a value has been wrapped, it may eventually be necessary to extract it. For an instance of `Boolean`, you can call `booleanValue()`. For an instance of `Character`, you can call `charValue()`. The other six classes extend from the abstract superclass `Number`, which provides methods to retrieve the wrapped value as a byte, a short, an int, a long, a float, or a double. In other words, the value of any wrapped number can be retrieved as any numeric type. The retrieval methods are

- `public byte byteValue()`

- `public short shortValue()`

- `public int byteValue()`

- `public long longValue()`

- `public float floatValue()`

- `public double doubleValue()`

The wrapper classes are useful whenever it would be convenient to treat a piece of primitive data as if it were an object. A good example is the `Vector` class, which is a dynamically growing collection of objects of arbitrary type. The method for adding an object to a vector is

```
public void addElement(Object ob)
```

Using this method, you can add any object of any type to a vector; you can even add an array (you saw why in Chapter 4, *Converting and Casting*). You cannot, however, add an int, a long, or any other primitive to a vector. There are no special methods for doing so, and addElement(Object ob) will not work because there is no automatic conversion from a primitive to an object. Thus the code below will not compile:

```
1. Vector vec = new Vector();
2. boolean boo = false;
3. vec.addElement(boo);      // Illegal
```

The solution is to wrap the boolean primitive, as shown below:

```
1. Vector vec = new Vector();
2. boolean boo = false;
3. Boolean wrapper = new Boolean(boo);
4. vec.addElement(wrapper); // Legal
```

The wrapper classes are useful in another way: they provide a variety of utility methods, most of which are static. For example, the Character.isDigit(char ch) static method returns a boolean that tells whether or not the character represents a base-10 digit. All the wrapper classes except Character have a static method called valueOf(String s), which parses a string and constructs and returns a wrapper instance of the same type as the class whose method was called. So, for example, Long.valueOf("23L") constructs and returns an instance of the Long class that wraps the value 23.

To summarize the major facts about the primitive wrapper classes

- Every primitive type has a corresponding wrapper class type.

- All wrapper types can be constructed from primitives; all except Character can also be constructed from strings.

- Wrapped values can be tested for equality with the equals() method.

- Wrapped values can be extracted with various XXXvalue() methods. All six numeric wrapper types support all six numeric XXXvalue() methods.

- Wrapper classes provide various utility methods, including the static valueOf() method; ch parses an input string.

Strings

Java uses the `String` and `StringBuffer` classes to encapsulate strings of characters. As you saw in Chapter 1, *Language Fundamentals*, Java uses 16-bit Unicode characters in order to support a broader range of international alphabets than would be possible with traditional 8-bit characters. Both strings and string buffers contain collections of 16-bit Unicode characters. The next several sections examine these two classes, as well as Java's string concatenation feature.

The *String* Class

The `String` class represents an immutable string: Once an instance is created, the string it contains cannot be changed. There are numerous forms of constructor, allowing you to build an instance out of an array of bytes or chars, a subset of an array of bytes or chars, another string, or a string buffer. Many of these constructors give you the option of specifying a character encoding, specified as a string; however, the Certification Exam does not require you to know the details of character encodings.

Probably the most common string constructor simply takes another string as its input. This is useful when you want to specify a literal value for the new string:

```
String s1 = new String("immutable");
```

An even easier abbreviation could be

```
String s1 = "immutable";
```

It is important to be aware of what happens when you use a string literal ("immutable" in both examples). Every string literal is represented internally by an instance of `String`. Every Java program has a pool of such strings that have been created to represent literals. Usually, when a line of code containing a literal is executed, the system constructs an appropriate instance of `String` and adds it to the pool. However, if the same string already appeared as a literal elsewhere in the program, then it is already represented in the pool. The system does not create a new instance; instead, it uses the existing instance from the pool. This saves on memory and can do no harm: Since strings are immutable, there is no way that a piece of code can harm another piece of code by modifying a shared string.

Earlier in this chapter, you saw how the `equals()` method can be used to provide a deep equality check of two objects. With strings, the `equals()` method does what you would expect: It checks the two contained collections of characters. The code below shows how this is done:

```
1. String s1 = "Compare me";
2. String s2 = "Compare me";
3. if (s1.equals(s2)) {
4.    // whatever
5. }
```

Not surprisingly, the test at line 3 succeeds. Given what you know about how string literals work, you can see that if line 3 is modified to use the == comparison, as shown below, the test still succeeds:

```
1. String s1 = "Compare me";
2. String s2 = "Compare me";
3. if (s1 == s2)) {
4.    // whatever
5. }
```

The new test passes because s2 refers to the string in the pool that was created in line 1. Figure 8.1 shows this graphically.

FIGURE 8.1:

Identical literals

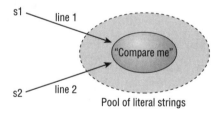

You can also construct a string by explicitly calling the constructor as shown below; however, this may cause the system to work harder than you want it to.

```
String s2 = new String("Constructed");
```

When this line is executed, the first thing that happens is the processing of the literal in parentheses at the end of the line. Like any other literal, it must be represented in the pool, and if it is not already represented, then a new instance of String will be constructed and added to the pool. Then the right-hand side of the = is executed: An instance of String is constructed, copying from the string in the literal pool. (This latest string object does not reside in the literal pool, so the system does not care that it is a duplicate of a string in the pool.) Finally, a reference to the new string is assigned to s2. Figure 8.2 shows the chain of events.

FIGURE 8.2:

Explicitly calling the String constructor

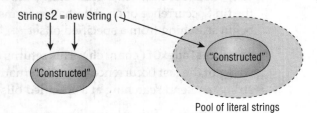

Figure 8.2 shows that explicitly calling new String() results in the construction of two objects, one in the literal pool and the other in the program's space.

There are several convenient methods in the String class. A number of these methods perform a transformation on a string. For example, toUpper() converts all the characters of a string to upper case. It is important to remember that the original string is not modified. That would be impossible, since strings are immutable. What really happens is that a new string is constructed and returned.

The methods below represent a partial list of the methods of the String class. There are more methods than those listed here, and some of those listed here have alternative forms that take different inputs. This list includes all the methods that you are required to know for the Certification Exam, plus a few additional useful ones:

- char charAt(int index): This returns the indexed character of a string, where the index of the initial character is 0.

- String concat(String addThis): This returns a new string consisting of the old string followed by addThis.

- int compareTo(String otherString): This performs a lexical comparison; returns an int that is less than 0 if the current string is less than otherString, equal to 0 if the strings are identical, and greater than 0 if the current string is greater than otherString.

- boolean endsWith(String suffix): This returns true if the current string ends with suffix, otherwise returns false.

- boolean equals(Object ob): This returns true if ob instanceof String, and the string encapsulated by ob matches the string encapsulated by the executing object.

- `boolean equalsIgnoreCase(String s)`: This is like `equals()`, but the argument is a `String`, and the comparison ignores case.

- `int indexOf(char ch)`: This returns the index within the current string of the first occurrence of `ch`. Alternative forms return the index of a string, and begin searching from a specified offset.

- `int lastIndexOf(char ch)`: This returns the index within the current string of the last occurrence of `ch`. Alternative forms return the index of a string, and end searching at a specified offset from the end of the string.

- `int length()`: This returns the number of characters in the current string.

- `replace(char oldChar, char newChar)`: This returns a new string, generated by replacing every occurrence of `oldChar` with `newChar`.

- `boolean startsWith(String prefix)`: This returns `true` if the current string begins with `suffix`, otherwise returns `false`.

- `String substring(int startIndex)`: This returns the substring, beginning at `startIndex`, of the current string and extending to the end of the current string. An alternate form specifies starting and ending offsets.

- `String toLowerCase()`: This converts the executing object to lower case and returns a new string.

- `String toString()`: This returns the executing object.

- `String toUpperCase()`: This converts the executing object to upper case and returns a new string.

- `String trim()`: This returns the string that results from removing whitespace characters from the beginning and ending of the current string.

The code below shows how to use two of these methods to "modify" a string. The original string is `" 5 + 4 = 20"`. The code first strips off the leading blank space, then converts the addition sign to a multiplication sign.

```
1. String s = " 5 + 4 = 20";
2. s = s.trim();                // "5 + 4 = 20"
3. s = s.replace('+', 'x');     // "5 x 4 = 20"
```

After line 3, s refers to a string whose appearance is shown in the line 3 comment. Of course, the modification has not taken place within the original string. Both the `trim()` call in line 2 and the `replace()` call of line 3 construct and return new strings; the address of each new string in turn gets assigned to the reference variable s. Figure 8.3 shows this sequence graphically.

FIGURE 8.3:

Trimming and replacing

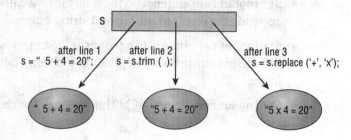

Figure 8.3 shows that the original string only seems to be modified. It is actually replaced, because strings are immutable. The next section discusses a class that represents a mutable string: the StringBuffer class.

The *StringBuffer* Class

An instance of Java's StringBuffer class represents a string that can be dynamically modified.

The most commonly used constructor takes a string as input. You can also construct an empty string buffer (probably with the intention of adding characters to it later). An empty string buffer can optionally have its initial capacity specified at construction time. The three constructors are

- StringBuffer(): This constructs an empty string buffer.

- StringBuffer(int capacity): This constructs an empty string buffer with the specified initial capacity.

- StringBuffer(String initialString): This constructs a string buffer that initially contains the specified string.

A string buffer has a *capacity*, which is the maximum-length string it can represent without needing to allocate more memory. A string buffer can grow without bounds, so usually you do not have to worry about capacity.

The list below presents some of the methods that modify the contents of a string buffer. All of them return the string buffer itself.

- StringBuffer append(String str): This appends str to the current string buffer. Alternative forms support appending primitives and character arrays; these are converted to strings before appending.

- `StringBuffer append(Object obj)`: This calls `toString()` on `obj` and appends the result to the current string buffer

- `StringBuffer insert(int offset, String str)`: This inserts `str` into the current string buffer at position `offset`. There are numerous alternative forms.

- `StringBuffer reverse()`: This reverses the characters of the current string buffer.

- `StringBuffer setCharAt(int offset, char newchar)`: This replaces the character at position `offset` with `newchar`.

- `StringBuffer setLength(int newLength)`: This sets the length of the string buffer to `newLength`. If `newLength` is less than the current length, the string is truncated. If `newLength` is greater than the current length, the string is padded with null characters.

The code below shows the effect of using several of these methods in combination.

```
1. StringBuffer sbuf = new StringBuffer("12345");
2. sbuf.reverse();              // "54321"
3. sbuf.insert(3, "aaa");       // "543aaa21"
4. sbuf.append("zzz");          // "543aaa21zzz"
```

The method calls above actually modify the string buffer they operate on (unlike the `String` class example of the previous section). Figure 8.4 graphically shows what this code does.

FIGURE 8.4:

Modifying a StringBuffer

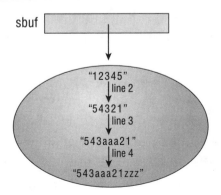

238

One last string buffer method that bears mentioning is `toString()`. You saw earlier in this chapter that every class has one of these methods. Not surprisingly, the string buffer's version just returns the encapsulated string, as an instance of class `String`. You will see in the next section that this method plays a crucial role in string concatenation.

> **NOTE**
>
> Both the `String` and `StringBuffer` classes have `equals()` methods that compare two encapsulated strings. Neither version can be used for mixed comparison: You can compare a string to a string, or a string buffer to a string buffer, but you cannot compare a string to a string buffer. Such a method call would always return `false`, even if the two strings were identical.

String Concatenation the Easy Way

The `concat()` method of the `String` class and the `append()` method of the `StringBuffer` class glue two strings together. An easier way to concatenate strings is to use Java's overloaded + operator. String concatenation is the only situation in which Java supports operator overloading.

String concatenation is useful for debugging print statements. For example, to print the value of a double called `radius`, all you have to do is this:

```
System.out.println("radius = " + radius);
```

This technique also works for object data types. For example, to print the value of a `Dimension` called `dimension`, all you have to do is

```
System.out.println("dimension = " + dimension);
```

It is important to understand how the technique works. At compile time, if either operand of an addition (that is, if what appears on either side of a + sign) is a string, then the compiler recognizes that it is in a *string context*. In a string context, the + sign is interpreted as calling for string concatenation, rather than arithmetic addition.

A string context is simply an arbitrary run of additions, where one of the operands is a string. For example, if variable `aaa` is a string, then the following partial line of code is a string context, regardless of the types of the other operands:

```
aaa + bbb + ccc
```

The Java compiler treats the code above as if it were the following:

```
new StringBuffer().append(aaa).append(bbb).append(ccc).toString();
```

If any of the variables (aaa, bbb, or ccc) is a primitive, the append() method computes an appropriate string representation. For an object variable, the append() method uses the string returned from calling toString() on the object. The conversion begins with an empty string buffer, then appends each element in turn to the string buffer, and finally calls toString() to convert the string buffer to a string.

The code below implements a class with its own toString() method.

```
1. class Abc {
2.    private int a;
3.    private int b;
4.    private int c;
5.
6.    Abc(int a, int b, int c) {
7.        this.a = a;
8.        this.b = b;
9.        this.c = c;
10.   }
11.
12.   public String toString() {
13.       return "a = " + a + ", b = " + b + ", c = " + c;
14.   }
15. }
```

Now the toString() method (lines 12–14) can be used by any code that wants to take advantage of string concatenation. For example

```
Abc theAbc = new Abc(11, 13, 48);
System.out.println("Here it is: " + theAbc);
```

The output is

```
Here it is: a = 11, b = 13, c = 48
```

To summarize, the sequence of events for a string context is

1. An empty string buffer is constructed.

2. Each argument in turn is concatenated to the string buffer, using the append() method.

3. The string buffer is converted to a string with a call to toString().

Chapter Summary

The java.lang package contains classes that are indispensable to Java's operation, so all the classes of the package are automatically imported into all source files. Some of the most important classes in the package are

- Object
- Math
- The wrapper classes
- String
- StringBuffer

In a string context, addition operands are appended in turn to a string buffer, which is then converted to a string; primitive operands are converted to strings, and objects are converted by having their toString() methods invoked.

Test Yourself

1. Given a string constructed by calling s = new String("xyzzy"), which of the calls listed below modify the string? (Choose all that apply.)

   A. s.append("aaa");

   B. s.trim();

   C. s.substring(3);

   D. s.replace('z', 'a');

   E. s.concat(s);

2. Which one statement is true about the code below?

```
1. String s1 = "abc" + "def";
2. String s2 = newString(S1);
3. if (s1 == s2)
4.    System.out.println("== succeeded");
5. if (s1.equals(s2))
6.    System.out.println(".equals() succeeded");
```

A. Lines 4 and 6 both execute.

B. Line 4 executes, and line 6 does not.

C. Line 6 executes, and line 4 does not.

D. Neither line 4 nor line 6 executes.

3. Suppose you want to write a class that offers static methods to compute hyperbolic trigonometric functions. You decide to subclass `java.lang.Math` and provide the new functionality as a set of static methods. Which one statement below is true about this strategy?

A. The strategy works.

B. The strategy works, provided the new methods are public.

C. The strategy works, provided the new methods are not private.

D. The strategy fails, because you cannot subclass `java.lang.Math`.

E. The strategy fails, because you cannot add static methods to a subclass.

4. Which one statement is true about the code fragment below?

```
1. import java.lang.Math;
2. Math myMath = new Math();
3. System.out.println("cosine of 0.123 = " + myMath.cos(0.123));
```

A. Compilation fails at line 2.

B. Compilation fails at line 3.

C. Compilation succeeds, although the import on line 1 is not necessary. During execution, an exception is thrown at line 3.

D. Compilation succeeds. The import on line 1 is necessary. During execution, an exception is thrown at line 3.

E. Compilation succeeds, and no exception is thrown during execution.

5. Which one statement is true about the code fragment below?

```
1. String s = "abcde";
2. StringBuffer s1 = new StringBuffer("abcde");
3. if (s.equals(s1))
4.     s1 = null;
5. if (s1.equals(s))
6.     s = null;
```

A. Compilation fails at line 1, because the `String` constructor must be called explicitly.

B. Compilation fails at line 3, because s and s1 have different types.

C. Compilation succeeds. During execution, an exception is thrown at line 3.

D. Compilation succeeds. During execution, an exception is thrown at line 5.

E. Compilation succeeds. No exception is thrown during execution.

6. Does the code fragment below compile successfully? If so, is line 2 executed?

```
1. if ("Hedgehog".startsWith("Hedge"))
2.    System.out.println("Line 2");
```

7. True or False: In the code fragment below, after execution of line 1, sbuf references an instance of the `StringBuffer` class. After execution of line 2, sbuf still references the same instance.

```
1. StringBuffer sbuf = new StringBuffer("abcde");
2. sbuf.insert(3, "xyz");
```

8. True or False: In the code fragment below, after execution of line 1, sbuf references an instance of the `StringBuffer` class. After execution of line 2, sbuf still references the same instance.

```
1. StringBuffer sbuf = new StringBuffer("abcde");
2. sbuf.append("xyz");
```

9. True or False: In the code fragment below, line 4 is executed.

```
1. String s1 = "xyz";
2. String s2 = "xyz";
3. if (s1 == s2)
4.    System.out.println("Line 4");
```

10. True or False: In the code fragment below, line 4 is executed.

```
1. String s1 = "xyz";
2. String s2 = new String(s1);
3. if (s1 == s2)
4.    System.out.println("Line 4");
```

CHAPTER
NINE

Components

- Components in general

- Visual components

- Container components

- Menu components

In this chapter you will cover the following Java Certification Exam objectives:

- Write code to demonstrate the use of the following methods of the `java.awt.Component` class: `setVisible(boolean)`, `setEnabled(boolean)`, `getSize()`, `setForeground()`, and `setBackground()`.

- Construct a `java.awt.TextArea` or `java.awt.List` that prefers to display a specified number of lines.

- Construct a `java.awt.TextArea` or `java.awt.TextField` that prefers to display a specified number of columns.

- State the significance of a "column" where one of the text components is using a proportional (variable) pitch font or a fixed pitch font.

Components are Java's building blocks for creating graphical user interfaces. Some component types, such as buttons and scroll bars, are used directly for GUI control. Other kinds of components (those that inherit from the abstract `Container` class) provide spatial organization.

GUIs are an important part of any program. Java's Abstract Windowing Toolkit (AWT) provides extensive functionality. These features are the subject of this and subsequent chapters. This chapter introduces components. Chapter 10, *Layout Managers*, discusses how to organize GUI components in two-dimensional space. Chapter 14, *Input and Output*, looks at how to respond to user input.

Components in General

Java's components are implemented by the many subclasses of the `java.awt.Component` and `java.awt.MenuComponent` superclasses. There are 19 non-superclass components in all, and you should know the basics of all the component classes. One way to organize this fairly large number of classes is to divide them into categories:

- Visual components
- Container components
- Menu components

These category names are not official Java terminology, but they serve to organize a fairly large number of component classes. This chapter discusses 16 classes: 11 visual components, four containers, and four menu components.

There are several methods that are implemented by all the visual and container components, by virtue of inheritance from java.awt.Component. (The menu components extend from java.awt.MenuComponent, so they do not inherit the same superclass functionality.) These methods are discussed below.

getSize()

The getSize() method returns the size of a component. The return type is Dimension, which has public data members height and width.

setForeground() and setBackground()

The setForeground() and setBackground() methods set the foreground and background colors of a component. Each method takes a single argument, which is an instance of java.awt.Color. Chapter 12 discusses how to use the Color class.

Generally the foreground color of a component is used for rendering text, and the background color is used for rendering the non-textual area of the component. Thus a label with blue as its foreground color and black as its background color will show up as blue text on a black background.

WARNING The last paragraph describes how things are supposed to be, but some components on some platforms resist having their colors changed.

If you do not explicitly set a component's foreground or background color, the component uses the foreground and background color of its immediate container. Thus if you have an applet whose foreground color is white and whose background color is red, and you add a button to the applet without calling setForeground() or setBackground() on the button, then the button's label will be white on red.

setFont()

The setFont() method determines the font that a component will use for rendering any text that it needs to display. The method takes a single argument, which is an instance of java.awt.Font. Chapter 12 discusses how to use the Font class.

If you do not explicitly set a component's font, the component uses the font of its container, in the same way that the container's foreground and background colors are used if you do not explicitly call setForeground() or setBackground(). Thus if you have an applet whose font is 48-point bold Serif, and you add a check box to the applet without calling setFont() on the check box, you will get a check box whose label appears in 48-point bold Serif.

setEnabled()

The setEnabled() method takes a single argument of type boolean. If this argument is true, then the component has its normal appearance. If the argument is false, then the component is grayed out and does not respond to user input. This method replaces the 1.0 methods enable() and disable(), which are deprecated.

setSize() and setBounds()

These methods set a component's geometry—or rather, they *attempt* to set geometry. They replace the deprecated 1.0 methods resize() and reshape(). The setSize() method takes two int arguments: width and height; an overloaded form takes a single dimension. The setBounds() method takes four int arguments: x, y, width, and height; an overloaded form takes a single rectangle.

If you have tried calling these methods, you know that it is usually futile. Chapter 10, *Layout Managers*, explains that the size and position that you attempt to give a component is overruled by a layout manager. In fact, these two methods exist mostly for the use of layout managers. The major exception to this rule is the Frame class, which is not under the thumb of a layout manager and is perfectly willing to have you set its size or bounds. This is explained below in the *Frame* section.

setVisible()

This method takes a boolean argument that dictates whether or not the component is to be seen on the screen. This is another method that only works for frames, unless you learn some techniques that are beyond the scope of this book or the

Certification Exam. Again, this method is explained in detail in the *Frame* section later in this chapter.

The Visual Components

The visual components are the ones that users can actually see and interact with. The 11 visual components are

- Button
- Canvas
- Checkbox
- Choice
- FileDialog
- Label
- List
- ScrollPane
- Scrollbar
- TextArea
- TextField

To use one of these components in a GUI, you first create an instance by calling the appropriate constructor. Then you add the component to a container. Adding a component to a container is decidedly non-trivial; in fact, this topic merits an entire chapter (Chapter 10, *Layout Managers*). For the sake of this chapter, you will be asked to take it on faith that the components shown in the screen shots below have all been added to their containing applets in straightforward ways.

The next 11 sections show you how to construct each of the visual components. Of course to really learn how to use components, you also have to know how to position them (see Chapter 10) and how to receive event notification from them (see Chapter 11).

NOTE Not all forms of the constructors are given; the intention here is not to provide you with an exhaustive list (you can always refer to the API pages for that), but to expose you to what you will need to know for the Certification Exam.

All the screen shots in this chapter were taken from a Windows 95 platform. Component appearance varies from machine to machine. All the applets were assigned a 24-point italic Serif font; most of the components were not sent `setFont()` method calls, so they inherited this font.

Button

The `Button` class, of course, implements a push button. The button shown in Figure 9.1 was constructed with the following line of code:

```
new Button("Apply");
```

This constructor takes a string parameter that specifies the text of the button's label.

FIGURE 9.1:

A button

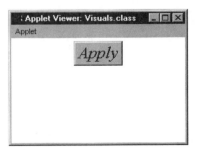

When a button is pushed, it sends an Action event. Action events, and indeed the entire 1.1 event model, are explained in detail in Chapter 11.

Canvas

A canvas is a component that has no default appearance or behavior. You can subclass `Canvas` to create custom drawing regions, work areas, components, and so on. Canvases receive input events from the mouse and the keyboard; it is up to the programmer to transform those inputs into a meaningful look and feel.

The default size (or, more properly, the *preferred size*, as you will see in Chapter 10) of a canvas is uselessly small. One way to deal with this problem is to use a layout manager that will resize the canvas. Another way is to call `setSize()` on the canvas yourself; canvases are a rare case where this will actually work. Figure 9.2 shows a canvas that was created with the following code:

```
1. Canvas canv = new Canvas();
2. canv.setBackground(Color.black);
3. canv.setSize(100, 50);
```

FIGURE 9.2:

A canvas

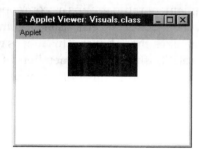

Canvases send Mouse, MouseMotion, and Key events, as explained in Chapter 11.

Checkbox

A check box is a two-state button. The two states are `true` (checked) and `false` (not checked). The two basic forms of the `Checkbox` constructor are

```
Checkbox(String label)
```

```
Checkbox(String label, boolean initialState)
```

If you do not specify an initial state, the default is `false`. Two methods support reading and setting the state of a check box:

- `boolean getState()`

- `void setState(boolean state)`

Figure 9.3 shows a check box in the true state.

FIGURE 9.3:

A check box

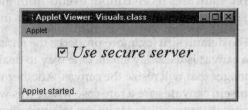

Check boxes can be grouped together into check-box groups, which have radio behavior. With radio behavior, only one member of a check-box group can be true at any time; selecting a new member changes the state of the previously selected member to false. Many window systems (Motif and NextStep, for example) implement radio groups as components in their own right. In Java, the `java .awt .CheckboxGroup` class is *not* a component; it is simply a non-visible class that organizes check boxes. This means that Java imposes no restrictions on the spatial relationships among members of a check-box group. If you wanted to, you could put one member of a group in the upper-left corner of a frame, another member in the lower-right corner, and a third member in a different frame altogether. Of course, the result would hardly be useful.

To use a check-box group, you first create an instance of `CheckboxGroup`, and then pass the instance as a parameter to the `Checkbox` constructor. The code below adds three check boxes to a group called `cbg`. The result is shown in Figure 9.4.

```
1. CheckboxGroup cbg = new CheckboxGroup();
2. p.add(new Checkbox("Cinnamon", false, cbg));
3. p.add(new Checkbox("Nutmeg", false, cbg));
4. p.add(new Checkbox("Allspice", true, cbg));
```

FIGURE 9.4:

Check boxes with radio behavior

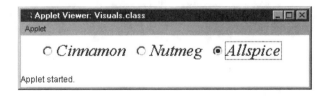

Two methods of the `CheckboxGroup` class support reading and setting the currently selected member of the group:

- `Checkbox getSelectedCheckbox()`

- void setSelectedCheckbox(Checkbox newSelection)

Check boxes send Item events when they are selected, as explained in Chapter 11.

Choice

A choice is a pull-down list, as shown in Figure 9.5. This figure shows two choices, both of which present the same options. The choice on the left is in its normal state; the choice on the right has been mouse-clicked.

To create a choice, first call the constructor, and then populate the choice by repeatedly calling addItem(). The code fragment below shows how to create one of the choices shown in Figure 9.5.

```
1. Choice ch1 = new Choice();
2. ch1.addItem("Alligators");
3. ch1.addItem("Crocodiles");
4. ch1.addItem("Gila Monsters");
5. ch1.addItem("Dragons");
```

Choices, like check boxes, send Item events when they are selected. Item events are explained in Chapter 11.

FIGURE 9.5:

Two choices

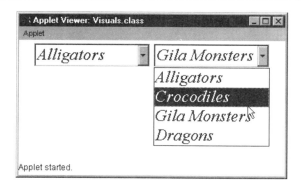

FileDialog

The FileDialog class represents a file open or file save dialog. The appearance of these dialogs varies greatly from platform to platform. A file dialog is modal; this means that input from the dialog's parent frame will be directed exclusively to the dialog, as long as the dialog remains visible on the screen. The dialog is automatically removed when the user specifies a file or clicks the Cancel button.

The most useful `FileDialog` constructor has the following form:

- `FileDialog(Frame parent, String title, int mode)`

The dialog's parent is the frame over which the dialog will appear. The title string appears in the dialog's title bar (on most platforms). The mode should be either `FileDialog.LOAD` or `FileDialog.SAVE`.

After the user has specified a file, the name of the file or its directory can be retrieved with the following methods:

- `String getFile()`

- `String getDirectory()`

The code fragment below constructs a file dialog, and displays it above frame `f`. After the user has specified a file, the file name is retrieved and displayed.

```
1. FileDialog fidi =
2.    new FileDialog(f, "Choose!", FileDialog.LOAD);
3. fidi.setVisible(true);
4. System.out.println(fidi.getFile());
```

Label

The simplest AWT component is the label. Labels do not respond to user input, and they do not send out any events.

There are three ways to construct a label:

- `Label()`

- `Label(String text)`

- `Label(String text, int alignment)`

The default alignment for labels is to the left. To set the alignment, use the third form of the constructor and pass in one of the following:

- `Label.LEFT`

- `Label.CENTER`

- `Label.RIGHT`

Two methods support reading and setting the text of a label:

- `String getText()`
- `void setText(String newText)`

> **NOTE**
>
> If you use the no-arguments version of the label constructor, you will undoubtedly want to `setText()` at some point.

Figure 9.6 shows a label that was created with the following call:

```
new Label("I'm a label, Mabel");
```

FIGURE 9.6:

A label

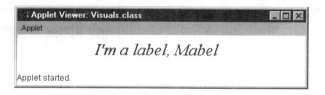

List

A list is a collection of text items, arranged vertically. If a list contains more items than it can display, it acquires a vertical scroll bar. There are three forms of constructor:

- `List()`
- `List(int nVisibleRows)`
- `List(int nVisibleRows, boolean multiSelectOk)`

The number of visible rows (parameter `nVisibleRows`) dictates the height of a list. The first version of the constructor does not specify a number of visible rows, so presumably the height of such list will be dictated by a layout manager. (If this does not make sense yet, it will become clear after you read Chapter 10).

If the version of the third constructor is used and `multiSelectOk` is `true`, then the list supports multiple selection. If multiple selection is not enabled, then selecting a new item causes the old selected item to be deselected.

The code listed below creates the list shown in Figure 9.7:

```
1. List list = new List(4, true);
2. list.addItem("Augustus");
3. list.addItem("Tiberius");
4. list.addItem("Caligula");
5. list.addItem("Claudius");
6. list.addItem("Nero");
7. list.addItem("Otho");
8. list.addItem("Galba");
```

The list has seven items but only four visible rows, so a scroll bar is automatically provided to give access to the bottom three items. Multiple selection is enabled, as shown in the figure: Both barbarian (non-Roman) emperors are selected.

FIGURE 9.7:

A scrolled list with multiple selection

The List class provides a large number of support methods. A partial list of these methods appears below. The methods are intended to give you a feel for how the List class operates.

- void addItem(String text): adds an item to the bottom of the list

- void addItem(String text, int index): inserts an item at the specified index

- String getItem(int index): returns the item with the specified index

- int getItemCount(): returns the number of items in the list

- int getRows(): returns the number of visible lines in the list

- int getSelectedIndex(): returns the index of the currently selected item (the list should be in single-selection mode)

- `int[] getSelectedIndexes()`: returns an array containing the index of every currently selected item (the list should be in multiple-selection mode)

- `String getSelectedItem()`: returns a string that reflects the currently selected item (the list should be in single-selection mode)

- `String[]getSelectedItems()`: returns an array containing a string for every currently selected item (the list should be in multiple-selection mode)

Selecting an item in a list causes the list to send an Item event; double-clicking an item sends an Action event.

ScrollPane

The `ScrollPane` is an extremely useful class that was introduced in 1.1. A scroll pane can contain a single component, which may be taller or wider than the scroll pane itself. If the contained component is larger than the scroll pane, then the default behavior of the scroll pane is to acquire horizontal and/or vertical scroll bars as needed.

There are two constructors for this class:

- `ScrollPane()`: constructs a scroll pane with default scroll bar behavior

- `ScrollPane(int scrollbarPolicy)`: constructs a scroll pane with the specified scroll bar behavior

If you use the second form of the constructor, then `scrollbarPolicy` should be one of

- `ScrollPane.SCROLLBARS_AS_NEEDED`

- `ScrollPane.SCROLLBARS_ALWAYS`

- `ScrollPane.SCROLLBARS_NEVER`

The code listed below creates a scroll pane with default (as-needed) scroll bar behavior. The scroll pane contains a very large button, so the scroll bars will definitely be needed.

```
1. ScrollPane spane = new ScrollPane();
2. Button reallyBigButton =
3.    new Button("What big teeth you have, Grandmother");
4. reallyBigButton.setFont(new Font("Serif", Font.ITALIC, 80));
5. spane.add(reallyBigButton);
```

Figure 9.8 shows the resulting scroll pane.

Scroll panes send Mouse and MouseMotion events.

Scrollbar

The scroll bar component that adjusts lists and scroll panes is available as a component in its own right. There are three constructors:

- `Scrollbar()`: constructs a vertical scroll bar
- `Scrollbar(int orientation)`: constructs a scroll bar with the specified orientation
- `Scrollbar(int orientation, int initialValue, int sliderSize, int minValue, int maxValue)`: constructs a scroll bar with the specified parameters

For constructors that take an orientation parameter, this value should be one of

- `Scrollbar.HORIZONTAL`
- `Scrollbar.VERTICAL`

In the third form of the constructor, the `sliderSize` parameter is a bit confusing. The Java terminology for the piece of the scroll bar that slides is the *slider*, which in itself is confusing because in some window systems the entire component is called a slider. The `sliderSize` parameter controls the size of the slider, but not in pixel units. The units of `sliderSize` parameter are the units defined by the spread between the minimum and maximum value of the scroll bar.

For example, consider a horizontal scroll bar whose minimum value is 600 and maximum value is 700. The spread covered by the scroll bar is the difference between these two numbers, or 100. A sliderSize value of 50 would represent half the spread, and the slider would be half the width of the scroll bar. A sliderSize value of 10 would represent half the spread, and the slider would be one-tenth the width of the scroll bar.

If the scroll bar's minimum and maximum were 1400 and 1500, the spread would still be 100; a sliderSize value of 50 would still represent half the spread, and the slider would still be half the width of the scroll bar. A sliderSize value of 10 would still result in a slider one-tenth the width of the scroll bar.

The line of code below creates a horizontal scroll bar with a range from 600 to 700. The initial value is 625. The slider size is 25 out of a range of 700 – 600 = 100, so the slider should be one-fourth the width of the scroll bar. Figure 9.8 shows that this is indeed the case. The scroll bar is shown in Figure 9.9.

```
Scrollbar sbar = new Scrollbar(Scrollbar.HORIZONTAL, 625, 25, 600, 700);
```

Scroll bars generate Adjustment events, as explained in Chapter 11.

FIGURE 9.9:

A horizontal scroll bar

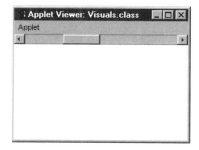

TextField and TextArea

The TextField and TextArea classes implement one-dimensional and two-dimensional components for text input, display, and editing. Both classes extend from the TextComponent superclass, as shown in Figure 9.10.

FIGURE 9.10:

Inheritance of TextField
and TextArea

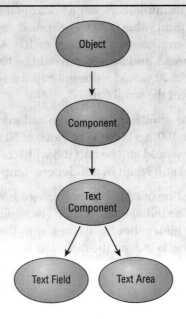

Both classes have a variety of constructors, which offer the option of specifying or not specifying an initial string or a size. That constructors that do not specify size are for use with layout managers that will enforce a size.

The constructors for `TextField` are listed below:

- `TextField()`: constructs an empty text field

- `TextField(int nCols)`: constructs an empty text field with the specified number of columns

- `TextField(String text)`: constructs a text field whose initial content is `text`

- `TextField(String text, int nCols)`: constructs a text field whose initial content is `text`, with the specified number of columns

The constructors for `TextArea` are listed below:

- `TextArea()`: constructs an empty text area

- `TextArea(int nRows, int nCols)`: constructs an empty text area with the specified number of rows and columns

- `TextArea(String text)`: constructs a text area whose initial content is `text`

- `TextArea(String text, int nRows, int nCols)`: constructs a text area whose initial content is `text`, with the specified number of rows and columns

- `TextArea(String text, int nRows, int nCols, int scrollbarPolicy)`: same as above, but the scroll bar placement policy is determined by the last parameter, which should be one of

  - `TextArea.SCROLLBARS_BOTH`

  - `TextArea.SCROLLBARS_NONE`

  - `TextArea.SCROLLBARS_HORIZONTAL_ONLY`

  - `TextArea.SCROLLBARS_VERTICAL_ONLY`

For both classes, there are some surprising issues to the number-of-columns parameter.

First, the number of columns is a measure of width in terms of columns of text, *as rendered in a particular font.* A 25-column text area with a tiny font will be very narrow, while a 5-column text area with a huge font will be extremely wide.

Next, there is the problem of proportional fonts. For a fixed-width font, it is obvious what the column width should be. For a proportional font, the column width is taken to be the average of all the font's character widths.

A final issue is the question of what happens when a user types beyond the rightmost character column in one of these components. In both cases, the visible text scrolls to the left. The insertion point remains in place, at the rightmost column. The component now contains more text than it can display, so scrolling is required. Text areas support scroll bars. Text fields can be scrolled by using the ← and → keys.

Both classes inherit some functionality from their common superclass, `TextComponent`. These methods include

- `String getSelectedText()`: returns the currently selected text

- `String getText()`: returns the text contents of the component

- `void setEditable(boolean editable)`: if `editable` is `true`, permits the user to edit the component

- `void setText(String text)`: sets the text contents of the component

A common experience among beginning AWT programmers who need, for example, to retrieve the contents of a text field, is to look for some promising name among the methods listed on the API page for TextField. There is nothing promising to be found there, and suddenly text fields seem useless. The problem, of course, is inheritance: The desired methods are available, but they are inherited from TextComponent and documented on a different page. If you know that a class must implement a certain method (because you have heard that it does, or because you remember using the method long ago, or because the class would otherwise be useless), don't give up if you don't find what you want on the class' API page. Use the superclass links near the top of the page to check from inherited methods.

The code below creates three text fields. Each is five columns wide, but they all use different fonts. (The fonts are all 24 points, so differences will be subtle).

```
1. TextField tf1 = new TextField(5);
2. tf1.setFont(new Font("Serif", Font.PLAIN, 24));
3. tf1.setText("12345");
4. TextField tf2 = new TextField(5);
5. tf2.setFont(new Font("SansSerif", Font.PLAIN, 24));
6. tf2.setText("12345");
7. TextField tf3 = new TextField(5);
8. tf3.setFont(new Font("Monospaced", Font.PLAIN, 24));
9. tf3.setText("12345");
```

Figure 9.11 shows the text fields. Surprisingly, only four characters appear in each field (although the dot near the right of the first field looks suspiciously like the truncated tail of the "5"). This is not a bug. The fields really are five columns wide, but some of the space is taken up by leading and inter-character whitespace.

FIGURE 9.11:

Three text fields

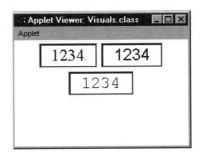

The code below implements three text areas, each with six rows and five columns. Again, each component has a different family of 24-point font. (The font name appears in the first row of each component.) The first two fonts are proportional, so a lot more *i*'s than *w*'s can fit into a row. Again, the components really do have five columns, but whitespace reduces the number of visible characters.

```
1. TextArea ta1 = new TextArea(6, 5);
2. ta1.setFont(new Font("Serif", Font.PLAIN, 24));
3. ta1.setText("Serif\n12345\nabcde\niiiiiiiiiii\nWWWWW");
4. TextArea ta2 = new TextArea(6, 5);
5. ta2.setFont(new Font("SansSerif", Font.PLAIN, 24));
6. ta2.setText("Sans\n12345\nabcde\niiiiiiiiiii\nWWWWW");
7. TextArea ta3 = new TextArea(6, 5);
8. ta3.setFont(new Font("Monospaced", Font.PLAIN, 24));
9. ta3.setText("Mono\n12345\nabcde\niiiiiiiiiii\nWWWWW");
```

Figure 9.12 shows the resulting text areas.

FIGURE 9.12:

Three text areas

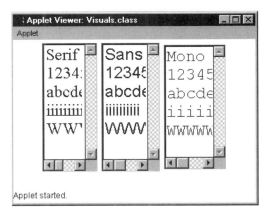

Both text fields and text areas generate Text events. Additionally, text fields generate Action events on receipt of an Enter keystroke.

The Container Components

The four non-superclass container component classes are

- `Applet`
- `Frame`

- Panel
- Dialog

Technically, ScrollPane is also a container, because it inherits from the Container superclass, but it does not present the issues that the other three do.

Figure 9.13 shows the inheritance hierarchy of these classes.

Containers are components capable of holding other components within their boundaries. Every screen shot so far in this chapter has shown an applet acting as a container for the component being illustrated. Adding components to containers requires interacting with layout managers; this entire topic is covered in depth in Chapter 10, *Layout Managers*. The next three sections are brief, because deferring the discussion of containment leaves very little to say about containers!

FIGURE 9.13:

Inheritance of Applet, Frame, and Panel

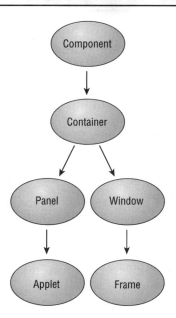

Applet

Applets will be covered in Chapter 13, *Applets and HTML*. The only issue that needs attention here is the problem of resizing. Applets, by virtue of inheriting from Component, have setSize() and setBounds() methods. Applets only exist in browsers. Changing the size of an applet is permitted or forbidden by the applet's browser, and during the development cycle you cannot know which brand of browser will be running your applet. The easiest browser for development is the applet viewer, which allows resizing of applets. It is common for an applet to have a temporary `setSize()` call in its `init()` method, because this provides an easy way to play with different sizes. If you use this technique, remember to delete the `setSize()` call before final delivery, and set the size in your HTML tag.

Frame

A frame is an independent window, decorated by the underlying window system and capable of being moved around on the screen independent of other GUI windows. Any application that requires a GUI must use one or more frames to contain the desired components.

There are only two forms of the `Frame` constructor:

- `Frame()`: constructs a frame with an empty title bar
- `Frame(String title)`: constructs a frame with the specified title

When a frame is constructed, it has no size and is not displayed on the screen. To give a frame a size, call one of the inherited methods `setSize()` or `setBounds()`. (If you call `setBounds()`, the x and y parameters tell the frame where it will appear on the screen.) Once a frame has been given a size, you can display it by calling `setVisible(true)`.

To remove an unwanted frame from the screen, you can call `setVisible(false)`. This does not destroy the frame or damage it in any way; you can always display it again by calling `setVisible(true)`.

When you are finished with a frame, you need to recycle its non-memory resources. (Memory will be harvested by the garbage collector.) Non-memory resources are system-dependent; suffice it to say that it takes a lot to connect a Java GUI to an underlying window system. On a UNIX/Motif platform, for example, a frame's non-memory resources would include at least one file descriptor and X window.

To release the non-memory resources of a frame, just call its `dispose()` method. The code below builds and displays a 500×350 frame; 30 seconds later the frame is removed from the screen and disposed.

```
1. // Construct and display
2. Frame f = new Frame("This is a frame");
3. f.setBounds(10, 10, 500, 350);
4. f.setVisible(true);
5.
6. // Delay
7. try {
8.   Thread.sleep(30*1000);
9. } catch (InterruptedException e) { }
10.
11. // Remove and dispose
12. f.setVisible(false);
13. f.dispose();
```

WARNING If an applet attempts to display a frame, the applet's browser confers with the local security manager. Most browsers have security managers that impose a restriction on frames. Display of the frame is permitted, but the frame unexpectedly contains a label that marks the frame as "untrusted." The rationale is that the frame might have been displayed by an applet which was loaded from the Internet, so any sensitive information entered into the frame's components might possibly be transmitted to parties of dubious moral fiber.

Panel

Applets and frames serve as top-level or outermost GUI components. Panels provide an intermediate level of spatial organization for GUIs. You are free to add all the components of a GUI directly into an applet or a frame, but you can provide additional levels of grouping by adding components to panels and adding panels to a top-level applet or frame. This process is recursive: The components that you add to panels can themselves be panels, and so on, to whatever depth of containment you like. Getting components to go exactly where you want them within a panel is the subject of the oft-mentioned Chapter 10, *Layout Managers*.

Dialog

A dialog is a pop-up window that accepts user input. Dialogs may optionally be made modal. The Dialog class is the superclass of the FileDialog class. The default layout manager for this class is border layout.

The Menu Components

Java supports two kinds of menu: pull-down and pop-up. The Certification Exam does not cover pop-up menus.

Pull-down menus are accessed via a menu bar, which may contain multiple menus. Menu bars may only appear in frames. (Therefore pull-down menus also may only appear in frames.)

To create a frame with a menu bar containing a pull-down menu, you need to go through the following steps:

1. Create a menu bar and attach it to the frame.

2. Create and populate the menu.

3. Attach the menu to the menu bar.

To create a menu bar, just construct an instance of the MenuBar class. To attach it to a frame, pass it into the frame's setMenuBar() method.

To create a menu, just construct an instance of the Menu class. The most common constructor takes a string which is the menu's label; this label appears on the menu bar. There are four kinds of element that can be mixed and matched to populate a menu:

- Menu items

- Check-box menu items

- Separators

- Menus

A menu item is an ordinary textual component available on a menu. The basic constructor for the MenuItem class is

```
MenuItem(String text)
```

where text is the label of the menu item. A menu item is very much like a button that happens to live in a menu. Like buttons, menu items generate Action events.

A check-box menu item looks like a menu item with a check box to the left of its label. When a check-box menu item is selected, the check box changes its state. The basic constructor for the CheckboxMenuItem class is

```
CheckboxMenuItem(String text)
```

where text is the label of the item. A check-box menu item is very much like a check box that happens to live in a menu; you can read and set an item's state by calling getState() and setState() just as you would with a plain check box. Check-box menu items generate Item events.

A separator is just a horizontal mark used for visually dividing a menu into sections. To add a separator to a menu, call the menu's addSeparator() method.

When you add a menu to another menu, the first menu's label appears in the second menu, with a pull-right icon. Pulling the mouse to the right causes the submenu to appear.

After a menu is fully populated, you attach it to a menu bar by calling the menu bar's add() method. If you want the menu to appear in the Help menu position to the right of all other menus, call instead the setHelpMenu() method.

The code below creates and displays a frame with a menu bar and two menus. The first menu contains one of each kind of menu constituent (menu item, check-box menu item, separator, and submenu). The second menu is a Help menu and just contains two menu items.

```
1. Frame          frame;
2. MenuBar        bar;
3. Menu           fileMenu, subMenu, helpMenu;
4.
5. // Create frame and install menu bar.
6. frame = new Frame("Menu demo");
7. frame.setSize(400, 300);
8. bar = new MenuBar();
9. frame.setMenuBar(bar);
10.
11. // Create submenu.
12. subMenu = new Menu("Pull me");
13. subMenu.add(new MenuItem("Sub-This"));
14. subMenu.add(new MenuItem("Sub-That"));
15.
16. // Create and add file menu.
17. fileMenu = new Menu("File");
18. fileMenu.add(new MenuItem("New"));
19. fileMenu.add(new MenuItem("Open"));
20. fileMenu.addSeparator();
```

```
21. fileMenu.add(new CheckboxMenuItem("Print Preview Mode"));
22. fileMenu.add(subMenu);
23. bar.add(fileMenu);
24.
25. // Create help menu.
26. helpMenu = new Menu("Help");
27. helpMenu.add(new MenuItem("Contents ..."));
28. helpMenu.add(new MenuItem("About this program ..."));
29. bar.setHelpMenu(helpMenu);
30.
31. // Now that the frame is completely built, display it.
32. frame.setVisible(true);
```

Figure 9.14 shows the frame with the File menu and the submenu visible.

FIGURE 9.14:

Frame with file menu and submenu

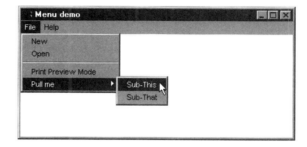

Figure 9.15 shows the frame with the Help menu visible.

FIGURE 9.15:

Frame with help menu

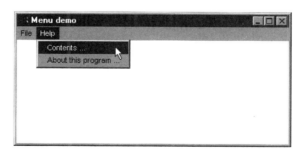

Chapter Summary

This chapter has introduced three categories of components:

- Visual components
- Container components
- Menu components

Visual components are the components that the user interacts with. Container components contain other components. Menu components support menus in frames.

Test Yourself

1. A text field is constructed and then given a foreground color of white and a 64-point bold serif font. The text field is then added to an applet which has a foreground color of red, background color of blue, and 7-point plain sans-serif font. Which one statement below is true about the text field?

   A. Foreground color is black, background color is white, font is 64-point bold serif.

   B. Foreground color is red, background color is blue, font is 64-point bold serif.

   C. Foreground color is red, background color is blue, font is 7-point bold serif.

   D. Foreground color is white, background color is blue, font is 7-point bold serif.

   E. Foreground color is white, background color is blue, font is 64-point bold serif.

2. You have a check box in a panel; the panel is in an applet. The applet contains no other components. Using `setFont()`, you give the applet a 100-point font, and you give the panel a 6-point font. Which statement or statements below are correct?

   A. The check box uses a 12-point font.

   B. The check box uses a 6-point font.

    C. The check box uses a 100-point font.

    D. The check box uses the applet's font, because you can't set a font on a panel.

    E. The check box uses the panel's font, because you did not explicitly set a font for the check box.

3. You have a check box in a panel; the panel is in an applet. The applet contains no other components. Using `setFont()`, you give the applet a 100-point font. Which statement or statements below are correct?

    A. The check box uses a 12-point font.

    B. The check box uses a 6-point font.

    C. The check box uses a 100-point font.

    D. The check box uses the applet's font.

    E. The check box uses the panel's font, because you did not explicitly set a font for the check box.

4. You want to construct a text area that is 80 character-widths wide and 10 character-heights tall. What code do you use?

    A. `new TextArea(80, 10)`

    B. `new TextArea(10, 80)`

5. You construct a list by calling `new List(10, false)`. Which statement or statements below are correct? (Assume that layout managers do not modify the list in any way.)

    A. The list has 10 items.

    B. The list supports multiple selection.

    C. The list has 10 visible items.

    D. The list does not support multiple selection.

    E. The list will acquire a vertical scroll bar if needed.

6. A text field has a variable-width font. It is constructed by calling new `TextField("iiiii")`. What happens if you change the contents of the text field to `"wwwww"`? (Bear in mind that *i* is one of the narrowest characters, and *w* is one of the widest.)

   A. The text field becomes wider.

   B. The text field becomes narrower.

   C. The text field stays the same width; to see the entire contents you will have to scroll by using the ← and → keys.

   D. The text field stays the same width; to see the entire contents you will have to scroll by using the text field's horizontal scroll bar.

7. Which of the following may a menu contain? (Choose all that apply.)

   A. A separator

   B. A check box

   C. A menu

   D. A button

   E. A panel

8. Which of the following may contain a menu bar? (Choose all that apply.)

   A. A panel

   B. A frame

   C. An applet

   D. A menu bar

   E. A menu

9. Your application constructs a frame by calling `Frame f = new Frame();` but when you run the code, the frame does not appear on the screen. What code will make the frame appear? (Choose one.)

   A. `f.setSize(300, 200);`

   B. `f.setFont(new Font("SansSerif", Font.BOLD, 24));`

   C. `f.setForeground(Color.white);`

    D. `f.setVisible(true);`

    E. `f.setSize(300, 200); f.setVisible(true);`

10. True or False: The `CheckboxGroup` class is a subclass of the `Component` class.

10

Layout Managers

- Layout manager theory

- Containers

- Layout policies: Flow, Grid, and Border layout managers

In this chapter you will cover the following Java Certification Exam objectives:

- Demonstrate the use of the methods add(Component) and add(String, Component) of the java.awt.Container class, and recognize which classes in the java.awt package are valid arguments to these methods.

- Distinguish between AWT classes which are directly responsible for determining component layout and those which are responsible for implementing that layout.

- Write code to change the layout scheme associated with an AWT container.

- Use BorderLayout, FlowLayout, and GridLayout to achieve required dynamic resizing behavior of a component.

Java's layout manager approach to Graphical User Interfaces is a novelty. Many GUI systems encourage GUI programmers to think in terms of precise specification of the size and location of interface components. Java changes all that. The Abstract Windowing Toolkit (AWT) provides a handful of layout managers, each of which implements its own layout policy. In Java, you create a GUI by choosing one or more layout managers and letting them take care of the details.

When you started working with layout managers, you probably had two impressions:

- You no longer bore the burden of specifying the exact position and dimensions of each component.

- You no longer had the power to specify the exact position and dimensions of each component.

Some people enjoy working with layout managers and others resent them. They are here to stay, so the job at hand is to master this feature of the language. Acquiring this competence requires three things:

- An understanding of why Java has you use layout managers

- An understanding of the layout policies of the more basic layout managers

- Some practice

The next section explains why Java uses layout managers. Then, after some intervening theory about how layout managers work, the last three sections of this chapter describe Java's three simplest layout managers: Flow Layout, Grid Layout, and Border Layout. As for the practice, once you successfully work through the questions in *Test Yourself* at the end of the chapter and move through the relevant material in the simulated tester on the CD, you should be in good shape. The polish is up to you.

Why Java Uses Layout Managers

There are two reasons why Java's AWT uses layout managers. The first reason is a bit theoretical, and you may or may not find yourself convinced by it. The second reason is thoroughly practical.

The theory lies in the position that precise layout (that is, specification in pixels of each component's size and position) is a repetitious and often-performed task; therefore, according to the principles of object-oriented programming, layout functionality ought to be encapsulated into one or more classes to automate the task. Certainly the layout managers eliminate a lot of development tedium. Many programmers dislike the idea of layout managers at first, but come to appreciate them more and more as tedious chores are eliminated.

The practical reason for having layout managers stems from Java's platform independence. Java components borrow their behavior from the window system of the underlying hardware on which the Java Virtual Machine is running. Thus on a Macintosh, an AWT button looks like any other Mac button; on a Motif platform, a Java button looks like any other Motif button, and so on. The problem here is that buttons and other components have different sizes when instantiated on different platforms.

For example, consider the button that is constructed by the following line of code:

```
Button b = new Button("OK");
```

On a Windows 95 machine, this button will be 32 pixels wide by 21 pixels high. On a Motif platform, the button will still be 32 pixels wide, but it will be 22 pixels high, even though it uses the same font. The difference seems small until you consider the effect such a difference would have on a column of many buttons. Other components can also vary in size from platform to platform. If Java encouraged precise pixel-level sizing and positioning, there would be a lot of Java GUIs that looked exquisite on their platform of origin—and terrible on other hosts.

> **NOTE**   There is no guarantee that fonts with identical names will truly be 100 per-
> cent identical from platform to platform; there could be minute differ-
> ences. Therefore, Java cannot even guarantee that two *strings* drawn with
> the same text and font will display at the same size across platforms.
> Similarly, there is no way to achieve size consistency among components,
> which have to deal with font differences and with decoration differences.

Java deals with this dilemma by delegating precision layout work to layout managers. The rest of this chapter investigates what layout managers are and explores the three most common managers.

Layout Manager Theory

There are five layout manager classes in the AWT toolkit. You might expect that there would be a common abstract superclass, called something like `LayoutManager`, from which these five layout managers would inherit common functionality. In fact, there is a `java.awt.LayoutManager`, but it is an interface, not a class, because the layout managers are so different from one another that they have nothing in common except a handful of method names. (There is also a `java.awt.LayoutManager2` interface, which the GridBag, Border, and Card layout managers implement. The Certification Exam does not cover the GridBag and Card layout managers.)

Layout managers work in partnership with containers. In order to understand layout managers, it is important to understand what a container is and what happens when a component gets inserted into a container. The next two sections explore these topics; the information is not directly addressed by the Certification Exam, but some relevant theory at this point will make it much easier to understand the material that is required for the exam.

Containers and Components

Containers are Java components that can contain other components. There is a `java.awt.Container` class which, like `java.awt.Button` and `java.awt.Choice`, inherits from the `java.awt.Component` superclass. This inheritance relationship is shown in Figure 10.1.

FIGURE 10.1:

Inheritance of
java.awt.Container

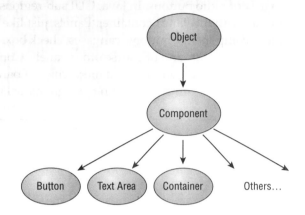

The `Container` class is abstract; its most commonly used concrete subclasses are `Applet`, `Frame`, and `Panel`, as shown in Figure 10.2. (Note that `Applet` is a subclass of `Panel`.)

FIGURE 10.2:

Common subclasses of
java.awt.Container

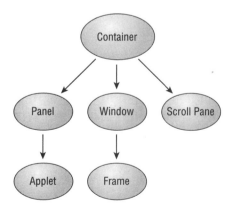

Java GUIs reside in applets or in frames. For simple applets, you just put your components in your applet; for simple applications, you just put your components in your frame. (In both cases, you might wonder how the components end up where they do; layout managers are lurking in the background, taking care of details.) For more complicated GUIs, it is convenient to divide the applet or frame into smaller regions. These regions might constitute, for example, a toolbar or a matrix of radio buttons. In Java, GUI sub-regions are implemented most commonly with the Panel container. Panels, just like applets and frames, can contain other components: buttons, canvases, check boxes, scroll bars, scroll panes, text areas, text fields, and of course other panels. Complicated GUIs sometimes have very complicated containment hierarchies of panels within panels within panels within panels, and so on, down through many layers of containment.

NOTE
In Java, the term *hierarchy* is ambiguous. When discussing classes, *hierarchy* refers to the hierarchy of inheritance from superclass to subclass. When discussing GUIs, *hierarchy* refers to the containment hierarchy of applets or frames, which contain panels containing panels containing panels.

The GUI in Figure 10.3 is a moderate-size frame for specifying a color. You can see at a glance that the panel contains labels, scroll bars, text fields, and buttons. You have probably guessed that the frame also contains some panels, even though they cannot be seen. In fact, the frame contains five panels. Each of the six containers (the five panels, plus the frame itself) has its own layout manager: There are four instances of Grid layout managers, one Flow layout manager, and one Border layout manager. Don't worry if you're not yet familiar with any of these managers—they will all be discussed shortly.

FIGURE 10.3:

A GUI with several levels of containment

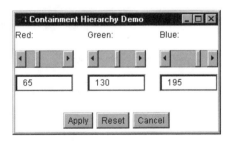

Figure 10.4 schematically shows the frame's containment hierarchy. A Java GUI programmer must master the art of transforming a proposed GUI into a workable and efficient containment hierarchy. This is a skill that comes with experience,

once the fundamentals are understood. The Java Certification Exam does not require you to develop any complicated containments, but it does require you to understand the fundamentals.

FIGURE 10.4:

Containment hierarchy

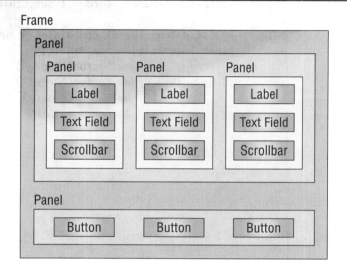

The code that implements the color chooser is listed below:

```
1. import  java.awt.*;
2.
3. public class Hier extends Frame {
4.   Hier() {
5.     super("Containment Hierarchy Demo");
6.     setBounds (20, 20, 300, 180);
7.     setLayout(new BorderLayout(0, 25));
8.
9.     // Build upper panel with 3 horizontal "strips".
10.    String strings[] = {"Red:", "Green:", "Blue:"};
11.    Panel bigUpperPanel = new Panel();
12.    bigUpperPanel.setLayout(new GridLayout(1, 3, 20, 0));
13.    for (int i=0; i<3; i++) {
14.      // Add strips. Each strip is a panel within bigUpperPanel.
15.      Panel levelPanel = new Panel();
16.      levelPanel.setLayout(new GridLayout(3, 1, 0, 10));
17.      levelPanel.add(new Label(strings[i]));
18.      levelPanel.add(new Scrollbar(Scrollbar.HORIZONTAL, i,
```

```
19.                                     10, 0, 255));
20.         levelPanel.add(new TextField("0"));
21.         bigUpperPanel.add(levelPanel);
22.      }
23.      add(bigUpperPanel, BorderLayout.CENTER);
24.
25.      // Build lower panel containing 3 buttons.
26.      Panel lowerPanel = new Panel();
27.      lowerPanel.add(new Button("Apply"));
28.      lowerPanel.add(new Button("Reset"));
29.      lowerPanel.add(new Button("Cancel"));
30.      add(lowerPanel, BorderLayout.SOUTH);
31.   }
32. }
```

As you can see from the listing, there is no code anywhere that specifies exactly where the labels, scroll bars, text fields, buttons, or panels should go. Instead, there are a number of calls (lines 7, 12, and 16) to layout manager constructors. In those same lines, the new layout managers are set as the managers for the corresponding containers. The lower panel constructed in line 26 uses its default layout manager, so it is not necessary to give it a new one.

NOTE

A component inside a container receives certain properties from the container. For example, if a component is not explicitly assigned a font, it uses the same font that its container uses. The same principle holds true for foreground and background color. Layout managers, however, are different. A panel's default layout manager is *always* Flow. An applet's default layout manager is also always Flow. A frame's default layout manager is always Border.

After each panel is constructed and assigned an appropriate layout manager, the panel is populated with the components it is to contain. For example, the lower panel, constructed in line 26, is populated with buttons in lines 27, 28, and 29. Finally, the now-populated panel is added to the container that is to hold it (line 30).

The add() method call in line 30 does not specify which object is to execute the call. That is, the form of the call is add(params), and not someObject.add(params).

In Java, every non-static method call is executed by some object; if you don't specify one, Java assumes that you intended the method to be executed by this. So line 30 is executed by the instance of Hier, which is the outermost container in the hierarchy. Line 23, which adds the big upper panel, is similar: No executing object is specified in the add()call, so the panel is added to this.

In lines 17–20, and also in lines 27–29, a container is specified to execute the add() call. In those lines, components are added to intermediate containers.

Each panel in the sample code is built in four steps:

1. Construct the panel.
2. Give the panel a layout manager.
3. Populate the panel.
4. Add the panel to its own container.

When a container is constructed (Step 1), it is given a default layout manager. For panels, the default is a flow layout manager, and Step 2 can be skipped if this is the desired manager. In Step 3, populating the panel involves constructing components and adding them to the panel; if any of these components is itself a panel, Steps 1–4 must be recursed.

A container confers with its layout manager to determine where components will be placed and (optionally) how they will be resized. If the container subsequently gets resized, the layout manager again lays out the container's components (probably with different results, since it has a different area to work with). This "conference" between the container and the layout manager is the subject of the next section.

Component Size and Position

Components know where they are and how big they are. That is to say, the java.awt.Component class has instance variables called x, y, width, and height. The x and y variables specify the position of the component's upper-left corner (as measured from the upper-left corner of the container that contains the component), and width and height are in pixels. Figure 10.5 illustrates the x, y, width, and height of a text field inside a panel inside an applet.

FIGURE 10.5:

Position and size

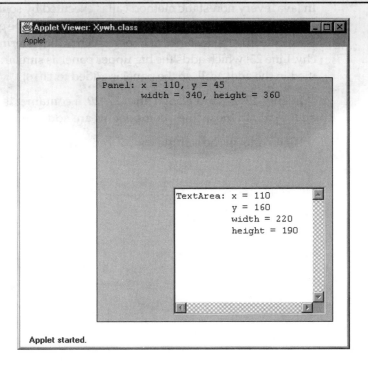

A component's position and size can be changed by calling the component's setBounds() method. (In releases of the JDK before 1.1, the method was called reshape(); this has been deprecated in favor of setBounds().) It seems reasonable to expect that the following code, which calls setBounds() on a button, would create an applet with a fairly big button:

```
1. import java.awt.Button;
2. import java.applet.Applet;
3.
4. public class AppletWithBigButton extends Applet {
5.    public void init() {
6.       Button b = new Button("I'm enormous!");
7.       b.setBounds(3, 3, 333, 333);  // Should make button really big
8.       add(b);
9.    }
10. }
```

If you have tried something like this, you know that the result is disappointing. A screen shot appears in Figure 10.6.

FIGURE 10.6:

A disappointing button

It seems that line 7 should force the button to be 333 pixels wide by 333 pixels tall. In fact, the button is just the size it would be if line 7 were omitted or commented out.

Line 7 has no effect because after it executes, the button is added to the applet (line 8). Eventually (after a fairly complicated sequence of events), the applet calls on its layout manager to enforce its layout policy on the button. The layout manager decides where and how big the button should be; in this case, the layout manager wants the button to be just large enough to accommodate its label. When this size has been calculated, the layout manager calls setBounds() on the button, clobbering the work you did in line 7.

In general, it is futile to call setBounds() on a component, because layout managers always get the last word; that is, their call to setBounds() happens after yours. There are ways to defeat this functionality, but they tend to be complicated, difficult to maintain, and not in the spirit of Java. Java's AWT toolkit wants you to let the layout managers do the layout work. Java impels you to use layout managers, and the Certification Exam expects you to know the layout policies of the more basic managers. These policies are covered in the next several sections.

Layout Policies

Every Java component has a *preferred size*. The preferred size expresses how big the component would like to be, barring conflict with a layout manager. Preferred size is generally the smallest size necessary to render the component in a visually meaningful way. For example, a button's preferred size is the size of its label text, plus a little border of empty space around the text, plus the shadowed decorations that mark the boundary of the button. Thus a button's preferred size is "just big enough."

Preferred size is platform-dependent, since component boundary decorations vary from system to system.

When a layout manager lays out its container's child components, it has to balance two considerations: the layout policy and each component's preferred size. First priority goes to enforcing layout policy. If honoring a component's preferred size would mean violating the layout policy, then the layout manager overrules the component's preferred size.

Understanding a layout manager means understanding where it will place a component, and also how it will treat a component's preferred size. The next several sections discuss some of the some of the simpler layout managers: FlowLayout, GridLayout, and BorderLayout. These are the three managers that you must know for the Certification Exam.

The Flow Layout Manager

The *Flow layout manager* arranges components in horizontal rows. It is the default manager type for panels and applets, so it is usually the first layout manager that programmers encounter. It is a common experience for new Java developers to add a few components to an applet and wonder how they came to be arranged so neatly. The following code is a good example:

```
1. import java.awt.*;
2. import java.applet.Applet;
```

```
3.
4. public class NeatRow extends Applet {
5.    public void init() {
6.       Label label = new Label("Name:");
7.       add(label);
8.       TextField textfield = new TextField("Beowulf");
9.       add(textfield);
10.      Button button = new Button("OK");
11.      add(button);
12.    }
13. }
```

The resulting applet is shown in Figure 10.7.

FIGURE 10.7:

Simple applet using
Flow layout manager

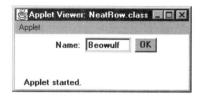

If the same three components appear in a narrower applet, as shown in Figure 10.8, there is not enough space for all three to fit in a single row. The Flow layout manager fits as many components as possible into the top row, and spills the remainder into a second row. The components always appear, left to right, in the order in which they were added to their container.

FIGURE 10.8:

A narrower applet
using Flow layout
manager

If the applet is thinner still, as in Figure 10.9, then the Flow layout manager creates still another row.

FIGURE 10.9:

A very narrow applet
using Flow layout
manager

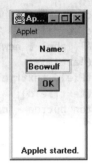

Within every row, the components are evenly spaced, and the cluster of components is centered. The direction of the clustering can be controlled by passing a parameter to the FlowLayout constructor. The possible values are FlowLayout .LEFT, FlowLayout.CENTER, and FlowLayout.RIGHT. The applet listed below explicitly constructs a Flow layout manager to right-justify three buttons:

```
1. import java.awt.*;
2. import java.applet.Applet;
3.
4. public class FlowRight extends Applet {
5.   public void init() {
6.     setLayout(new FlowLayout(FlowLayout.RIGHT));
7.     for (int i=0; i<4; i++) {
8.       add(new Button("Button #" + i));
9.     }
10.   }
11. }
```

Figure 10.10 shows the resulting applet with a wide window.

FIGURE 10.10:

A right-justifying Flow
layout manager

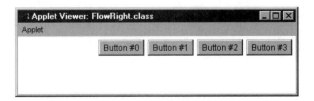

Figure 10.11 uses the same layout manager and components as Figure 10.10, but the applet is narrower.

FIGURE 10.11:

A narrow right-justifying Flow layout manager

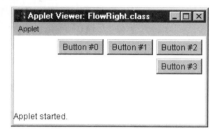

By default, the Flow layout manager leaves a gap of five pixels between components in both the horizontal and vertical directions. This default can be changed by calling an overloaded version of the `FlowLayout` constructor, passing in the desired horizontal and vertical gaps. All layout managers have this capability. Gaps are not covered in the Certification Exam, but they are certainly good to know about. A small gap modification can greatly improve a GUI's appearance. In the sample program in this chapter's *Containers and Components* section, gaps were used in lines 12 and 16.

The Grid Layout Manager

The Flow layout manager always honors a component's preferred size. The *Grid layout manager* takes the opposite extreme: It always *ignores* a component's preferred size.

The Grid layout manager subdivides its territory into a matrix of rows and columns. The number of rows and number of columns are specified as parameters to the manager's constructor:

```
GridLayout(int nRows, int Ncolumns)
```

The code listed below uses a Grid layout manager to divide an applet into 5 rows and 3 columns, and then puts a button in each grid cell:

```
1. import java.awt.*;
2. import java.applet.Applet;
3.
```

```
4. public class ThreeByFive extends Applet {
5.   public void init() {
6.     setLayout(new GridLayout(5, 3));
7.     for (int row=0; row<5; row++) {
8.       add(new Label("Label " + row));
9.       add(new Button("Button " + row));
10.      add(new TextField("TextField " + row));
11.    }
12.  }
13. }
```

Note that the constructor in line 6 yields five rows and three columns, not the other way around. After so many years of programming with Cartesian coordinates, it is probably second nature for most programmers to specify horizontal sorts of information before the comma, and vertical sorts of information after the comma. The GridLayout constructor uses "row-major" notation, which is sometimes confusing for humans.

As you can see in Figure 10.12, every component in the applet is exactly the same size. Components appear in the order in which they were added, from left to right, row by row.

FIGURE 10.12:

Grid layout

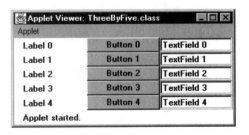

If the same components are to be laid out in a taller, narrower applet, then every component is proportionally taller and narrower, as shown in Figure 10.13.

Grid layout managers behave strangely when you have them manage very few components (that is, significantly fewer than the number of rows times the number of columns) or very many components (that is, more than the number of rows times the number of columns).

FIGURE 10.13:

Tall, narrow Grid layout

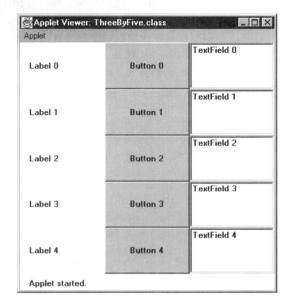

The Border Layout Manager

The *Border layout manager* is the default manager for frames, so sooner or later application programmers are certain to come to grips with it. It enforces a much less intuitive layout policy than either the Flow or Grid managers.

The Flow layout manager always honors a component's preferred size; the Grid layout manager never does. The Border layout manager does something in between.

The Border layout manager divides its territory into five regions. The names of these regions are *North*, *South*, *East*, *West*, and *Center*. Each region may contain a single component (but no region is *required* to contain a component).

The component at North gets positioned at the top of the container, and the component at South gets positioned at the bottom. The layout manager honors the preferred height of the North and South components, and forces them to be exactly as wide as the container.

The North and South regions are useful for toolbars, status lines, and any other controls that ought to be as wide as possible, but no higher than necessary. Figure 10.14 shows an applet that uses a Border layout manager to position a toolbar at North and a status line at South. The font of the status line is set large to illustrate that the height of each of these regions is dictated by the preferred height of the component in the region. (For simplicity, the toolbar is just a panel containing a few buttons.)

FIGURE 10.14:

Border layout for toolbar and status line

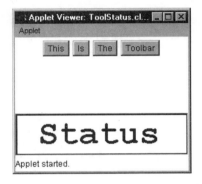

Figure 10.15 shows what happens if the same code is used to lay out a larger applet. Notice that the toolbar is still at the top, and the status line is still at the bottom. The toolbar and the status line are as tall as they were in Figure 10.14, and they are automatically as wide as the applet itself.

FIGURE 10.15:

Larger Border layout for toolbar and status line

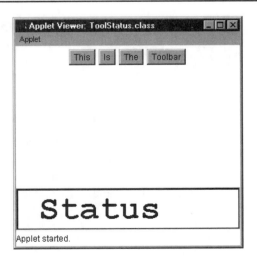

The code that produced these screen shots appears below:

```
1. import java.awt.*;
2. import java.applet.Applet;
3.
4. public class ToolStatus extends Applet {
5.    public void init() {
6.       setLayout(new BorderLayout());
7.
8.       // Build, populate, and add toolbar.
9.       Panel toolbar = new Panel();
10.      toolbar.add(new Button("This"));
11.      toolbar.add(new Button("Is"));
12.      toolbar.add(new Button("The"));
13.      toolbar.add(new Button("Toolbar"));
14.      add(toolbar, BorderLayout.NORTH);
15.
16.      // Add status line.
17.      TextField status = new TextField("Status line.");
18.      status.setFont(new Font("Courier", Font.BOLD, 48));
19.      add(status, BorderLayout.SOUTH);
20.    }
21. }
```

Notice that in lines 14 and 19, an overloaded form of the **add()** method is used. The border layout is not affected by the order in which you add components. Instead, you must specify which of the five regions will receive the component you are adding. The overloaded version of **add()** takes two parameters: first the component being added, and second an Object. Proper use of the Border layout manager requires that the second parameter be a String that specifies the name of the region; the valid values for this String are

- "North"
- "South"
- "East"
- "West"
- "Center"

The string must be spelled exactly as in shown above. The `BorderLayout` class has defined constants that you can use instead of the strings (the constants are defined to be the strings themselves). It is a good idea to use the defined constants rather than the strings, because if you misspell the name of a constant, the compiler will let you know. (On the other hand, if you use a misspelled String literal, a runtime exception will be thrown.) The five constants are

- `BorderLayout.NORTH`
- `BorderLayout.SOUTH`
- `BorderLayout.EAST`
- `BorderLayout.WEST`
- `BorderLayout.CENTER`

The East and West regions are the opposite of North and South: In East and West, a component gets to be its preferred width but has its height constrained. Here a component extends vertically up to the bottom of the North component (if there is one) or to the top of the container (if there is no North component). A component extends down to the top of the South component (if there is one) or to the bottom of the container (if there is no South component). Figures 10.16 through 10.19 show applets that use a Border layout manager to lay out two scroll bars, one at East and one at West. In Figure 10.16, there are no components at North or South to contend with.

FIGURE 10.16:

East and West

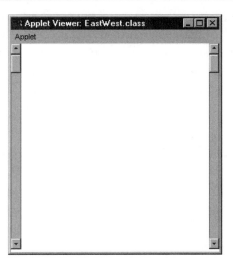

In Figure 10.17, there is a label at North.

FIGURE 10.17:

East and West, with
North

In Figure 10.18, there is a label at South. The label has white text on black background so that you can see exactly where the South region is.

FIGURE 10.18:

East and West, with
South

In Figure 10.19 there are labels at both North and South. The labels have white text on black background so that you can see exactly where the North and South regions are.

East and West, with
both North and South

The code that generated these four applets is listed below—there is only one program. The code, as shown, generates Figure 10.19 (both North and South); lines 19 and 24 were judiciously commented out to generate the other figures:

```
1. import java.awt.*;
2. import java.applet.Applet;
3.
4. public class EastWest extends Applet {
5.   public void init() {
6.     setLayout(new BorderLayout());
7.
8.     // Scrollbars at East and West.
9.     Scrollbar sbRight = new Scrollbar(Scrollbar.VERTICAL);
10.    add(sbRight, BorderLayout.EAST);
11.    Scrollbar sbLeft = new Scrollbar(Scrollbar.VERTICAL);
12.    add(sbLeft, BorderLayout.WEST);
13.
```

```
14.      // Labels at North and South.
15.      Label labelTop = new Label("This is North");
16.      labelTop.setFont(new Font("TimesRoman", Font.ITALIC, 36));
17.      labelTop.setForeground(Color.white);
18.      labelTop.setBackground(Color.black);
19.      add(labelTop, BorderLayout.NORTH);
20.      Label labelBottom = new Label("This is South");
21.      labelBottom.setFont(new Font("Courier", Font.BOLD, 18));
22.      labelBottom.setForeground(Color.white);
23.      labelBottom.setBackground(Color.black);
24.      add(labelBottom, BorderLayout.SOUTH);
25.   }
26. }
```

The fifth region that a Border layout manager controls is called *Center*. Center is simply the part of a container that remains after North, South, East, and West have been allocated. Figure 10.20 shows an applet with buttons at North, South, East, and West, and a panel at Center. The panel is the white region.

FIGURE 10.20:

Center

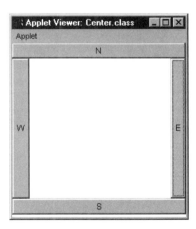

The code that generated Figure 10.20 is listed below:

```
1. import java.awt.*;
2. import java.applet.Applet;
3.
```

```
 4. public class Center extends Applet {
 5.   public void init() {
 6.     setLayout(new BorderLayout());
 7.     add(new Button("N"), BorderLayout.NORTH);
 8.     add(new Button("S"), BorderLayout.SOUTH);
 9.     add(new Button("E"), BorderLayout.EAST);
10.     add(new Button("W"), BorderLayout.WEST);
11.     Panel p = new Panel();
12.     p.setBackground(Color.white);
13.     add(p, BorderLayout.CENTER);
14.   }
15. }
```

In line 13, the white panel is added to the Center region. When adding a component to Center, it is legal to omit the second parameter to the add( ) call; the Border layout manager will assume that you meant Center. However, it is easier for other people to understand your code if you explicitly specify the region, as in line 13 above.

Figures 10.21 and 10.22 show what happens to the Center region in the absence of various regions. The applets are generated by commenting out line 7 (for Figure 10.21) and lines 8–10 (for Figure 10.22). The figures show that Center (the white panel) is simply the area that is left over after space has been given to the other regions.

FIGURE 10.21:

Center, no North

FIGURE 10.22:

Center, no South, East, or West

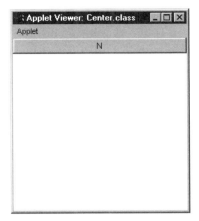

Other Layout Options

The Certification Exam only requires you to know about the Flow, Grid, and Border layout managers. However, it is useful to know a little bit about the other options. If you are in a situation where Flow, Grid, and Border will not create the layout you need, your choices are

- To use a GridBag layout manager

- To use a Card layout manager

- To use no layout manager

- To create your own layout manager

GridBag is by far the most complicated layout manager. It divides its container into an array of cells, but (unlike the cells of a Grid layout manager) different cell rows can have different heights, and different cell columns can have different widths. A component can occupy a single cell, or it can span a number of cells. A GridBag layout manager requires a lot of information to know where to put a component. A helper class called `GridBagConstraints` is used to hold all the layout position information. When you add a component, you use the `add(Component, Object)` version of the `add()` method, passing an instance of `GridBagConstraints` as the `Object` parameter.

The Card layout manager lays out its components in time rather than in space. At any moment, a container using a Card layout manager is displaying one or another of its components; all the other components are unseen. A method call to the layout manager can tell it to display a different component. All the components (which are usually panels) are resized to occupy the entire container. The result is similar to a tabbed panel without the tabs.

You always have the option of using no layout manager at all. To do this, just call

```
myContainer.setLayout(null);
```

If a container has no layout manager, it honors each component's x, y, width, and height values. Thus you can call setBounds() on a component, add it to a container which has no layout manager, and have the component end up where you expect it to be. This is certainly tempting, but hopefully the first part of this chapter has convinced you that layout managers are simple and efficient to work with. Moreover, if your container resides in a larger container (a frame, for example) that gets resized, your layout may need to be redone to save components from being overlaid or clipped away. People who set a container's layout manager to null find that they have to write code to detect when the container resizes, and more code to do the right thing when resizing occurs. This ends up being more complicated than creating your own layout manager.

It is beyond the scope of this book to show you how to concoct your own layout manager, but for simple layout policies it is not especially difficult to do so. The advantage of creating a custom layout manager over setting a container's layout manager to null is that you no longer have to write code to detect resizing of the container; you just have to write code to implement the layout policy, and the system will make the right calls at the right time. Writing your own layout manager class involves implementing the LayoutManager interface (or possibly the LayoutManager2 interface). For a good reference with examples on how to do this, see *Java 1.1 Developer's Handbook* (Sybex, 1997).

Improving Your Chances

More than any other Java-related topic, layout managers require you to use your ability to visualize in two dimensions. When you take the Certification Exam, you will be given the perfect tool to support two-dimensional thinking: a blank sheet of scratch paper. This is the only thing you will be allowed to bring into your test cubicle (and you will have to give it back when you leave).

Aside from layout manager problems, it is difficult to imagine what the scratch paper is good for. Consider drawing a picture of *every* layout manager problem, whether or not it feels like you need one. You won't run out of paper. Your picture might not convince you to choose a different answer than you would otherwise, but if this trick helps you get the right answer to even one extra layout manager problem, then it has done its job.

Test Yourself

1. A Java program creates a check box using the code listed below. The program is run on two different platforms. Which of the statements following the code are true? (Choose one or more.)

   ```
   1. Checkbox cb = new Checkbox("Autosave");
   2. Font f = new Font("Courier", Font.PLAIN, 14);
   3. cb.setFont(f);
   ```

   A. The check box will be the same size on both platforms, because Courier is a standard Java font.

   B. The check box will be the same size on both platforms, because Courier is a fixed-width font.

   C. The check box will be the same size on both platforms, provided both platforms have identical 14-point plain Courier fonts.

   D. The check box will be the same size on both platforms, provided both platforms have identical check-box decorations.

   E. There is no way to guarantee that the buttons will be the same size on both platforms.

2. What is the result of attempting to compile and execute the following application?

   ```
   1. import java.awt.*;
   2.
   3. public class Q2 extends Frame {
   4.   Q2() {
   5.     setSize(300, 300);
   6.     Button b = new Button("Apply");
   ```

```
7.        add(b);
8.    }
9.
10.   public static void main(String args[]) {
11.      Q2 that = new Q2();
12.      that.setVisible(true);
13.   }
14. }
```

A. There is a compiler error at line 11, because the constructor on line 4 is not public.

B. The program compiles but crashes with an exception at line 7, because the frame has no layout manager.

C. The program displays an empty frame.

D. The program displays the button, using the default font for the button label. The button is just large enough to encompass its label.

E. The program displays the button, using the default font for the button label. The button occupies the entire frame.

3. What is the result of compiling and running the following application?

```
1. import java.awt.*;
2.
3. public class Q3 extends Frame {
4.    Q3() {
5.       // Use Grid layout manager.
6.       setSize(300, 300);
7.       setLayout(new GridLayout(1, 2));
8.
9.       // Build and add 1st panel.
10.      Panel p1 = new Panel();
11.      p1.setLayout(new FlowLayout(FlowLayout.RIGHT));
12.      p1.add(new Button("Hello"));
13.      add(p1);
14.
15.      // Build and add 2nd panel.
16.      Panel p2 = new Panel();
17.      p2.setLayout(new FlowLayout(FlowLayout.LEFT));
18.      p2.add(new Button("Goodbye"));
```

```
19.      add(p2);
20.    }
21.
22.    public static void main(String args[]) {
23.      Q3 that = new Q3();
24.      that.setVisible(true);
25.    }
26. }
```

A. The program crashes with an exception at line 7, because the frame's default layout manager cannot be overridden.

B. The program crashes with an exception at line 7, because a Grid layout manager must have at least two rows and two columns.

C. The program displays two buttons, which are just large enough to encompass their labels. The buttons appear at the top of the frame. The "Hello" button is just to the left of the vertical midline of the frame; the "Goodbye" button is just to the right of the vertical midline of the frame.

D. The program displays two large buttons. The "Hello" button occupies the entire left half of the frame, and the "Goodbye" button occupies the entire right half of the frame.

E. The program displays two buttons, which are just wide enough to encompass their labels. The buttons are as tall as the frame. The "Hello" button is just to the left of the vertical midline of the frame; the "Goodbye" button is just to the right of the vertical midline of the frame.

4. What is the result of compiling and running the following application?

```
1. import java.awt.*;
2.
3. public class Q4 extends Frame {
4.   Q4() {
5.     // Use Grid layout manager.
6.     setSize(300, 300);
7.     setLayout(new GridLayout(3, 1));
8.
9.     // Build and add 1st panel.
10.    Panel p1 = new Panel();
11.    p1.setLayout(new BorderLayout());
```

```
12.        p1.add(new Button("Alpha"), BorderLayout.NORTH);
13.        add(p1);
14.
15.        // Build and add 2nd panel.
16.        Panel p2 = new Panel();
17.        p2.setLayout(new BorderLayout());
18.        p2.add(new Button("Beta"), BorderLayout.CENTER);
19.        add(p2);
20.
21.        // Build and add 3rd panel.
22.        Panel p3 = new Panel();
23.        p3.setLayout(new BorderLayout());
24.        p3.add(new Button("Gamma"), BorderLayout.SOUTH);
25.        add(p3);
26.    }
27.
28.    public static void main(String args[]) {
29.        Q4 that = new Q4();
30.        that.setVisible(true);
31.    }
32. }
```

A. Each button is as wide as the frame and is just tall enough to encompass its label. The "Alpha" button is at the top of the frame. The "Beta" button is in the middle. The "Gamma" button is at the bottom.

B. Each button is as wide as the frame. The "Alpha" button is at the top of the frame and is just tall enough to encompass its label. The "Beta" button is in the middle of the frame; its height is approximately ⅓ the height of the frame. The "Gamma" button is at the bottom of the frame and is just tall enough to encompass its label.

C. Each button is just wide enough and just tall enough to encompass its label. All three buttons are centered horizontally. The "Alpha" button is at the top of the frame. The "Beta" button is in the middle. The "Gamma" button is at the bottom.

D. Each button is just wide enough to encompass its label. All three buttons are centered horizontally. The "Alpha" button is at the top of the frame and is just tall enough to encompass its label. The "Beta" button is in the middle of the frame; its height is approximately ⅓ the height of the frame. The "Gamma" button is at the bottom of the frame and is just tall enough to encompass its label.

    E.   Each button is as tall as the frame and is just wide enough to encompass its label. The "Alpha" button is at the left of the frame. The "Beta" button is in the middle. The "Gamma" button is at the right.

5. You would like to compile and execute the following code. After the frame appears on the screen (assuming you get that far), you would like to resize the frame to be approximately twice its original width and approximately twice its original height. Which of the statements following the code is correct? (Choose one.)

```
1. import java.awt.*;
2.
3. public class Q5 extends Frame {
4.    Q5() {
5.       setSize(300, 300);
6.       setFont(new Font("Helvetica", Font.BOLD, 36));
7.       Button b = new Button("Abracadabra");
8.       add(b, BorderLayout.SOUTH);
9.    }
10.
11.   public static void main(String args[]) {
12.      Q5 that = new Q5();
13.      that.setVisible(true);
14.   }
15. }
```

    A. Compilation fails at line 8, because the frame has not been given a layout manager.

    B. Before resizing, the button appears at the top of the frame and is as wide as the frame. After resizing, the button retains its original width and is still at the top of the frame.

    C. Before resizing, the button appears at the bottom of the frame and is as wide as the frame. After resizing, the button retains its original width and is the same distance from the top of the frame as it was before resizing.

    D. Before resizing, the button appears at the bottom of the frame and is as wide as the frame. After resizing, the button is as wide as the frame's new width and is still at the bottom of the frame.

E. Before resizing, the button appears at the bottom of the frame and is as wide as the frame. After resizing, the button retains its original width and is about twice as tall as it used to be. It is still at the bottom of the frame.

6. The following code builds a GUI with a single button. Which one statement is true about the button's size?

```
1. import java.awt.*;
2.
3. public class Q6 extends Frame {
4.    Q6() {
5.      setSize(500, 500);
6.      setLayout(new FlowLayout());
7.
8.      Button b = new Button("Where am I?");
9.      Panel p1 = new Panel();
10.     p1.setLayout(new FlowLayout(FlowLayout.LEFT));
11.     Panel p2 = new Panel();
12.     p2.setLayout(new BorderLayout());
13.     Panel p3 = new Panel();
14.     p3.setLayout(new GridLayout(3, 2));
15.
16.     p1.add(b);
17.     p2.add(p1, BorderLayout.NORTH);
18.     p3.add(p2);
19.     add(p3);
20.   }
21.
22.   public static void main(String args[]) {
23.     Q6 that = new Q6();
24.     that.setVisible(true);
25.   }
26. }
```

A. The button is just wide enough and tall enough to encompass its label.

B. The button is just wide enough to encompass its label; its height is the entire height of the frame.

C. The button is just tall enough to encompass its label; its width is the entire width of the frame.

     D. The button is just wide enough to encompass its label, and its height is approximately half the frame's height.

     E. The button's height is approximately half the frame's height. Its width is approximately half the frame's width.

7. An application has a frame that uses a Border layout manager. Why is it probably not a good idea to put a vertical scroll bar at North in the frame?

     A. The scroll bar's height would be its preferred height, which is not likely to be high enough.

     B. The scroll bar's width would be the entire width of the frame, which would be much wider than necessary.

     C. Both A and B.

     D. Neither A nor B. There is no problem with the layout as described.

8. What is the default layout manager for an applet? for a frame? for a panel?

9. True or False: If a frame uses a Grid layout manager and does not contain any panels, then all the components within the frame are the same width and height.

10. True of False: If a frame uses its default layout manager and does not contain any panels, then all the components within the frame are the same width and height.

11. True or False: With a Border layout manager, the component at Center gets all the space that is left over, after the components at North and South have been considered.

12. True or False: With a Grid layout manager, the preferred width of each component is honored, while height is dictated; if there are too many components to fit in a single row, additional rows are created.

Events

- Event delegation

- Explicit enabling

- Adapters

In this chapter you will cover the following Java Certification Exam objectives:

- Write a non-abstract class that implements a specified Listener interface, given the interface definition.

- Select methods from the classes in the `java.awt.event` package that identify the affected component, mouse position, nature, and time of the event.

- Demonstrate correct use of the `addXXXListener()` methods in the `Component`, `TextArea`, and `TextField` classes.

- For any listener in the `java.awt.event` package, state the argument type and return type of a specified listener method, given the name of the interface that declares the method and the name of the method itself.

Java's original "outward rippling" event model proved to have some shortcomings. A new "event delegation" model was introduced in release 1.1 of the JDK. Both models are supported in 1.1, but eventually the old model will disappear. For now, all methods that support the old event model are deprecated in 1.1.

The two models are mutually incompatible. A Java program that uses both models is likely to fail, with events being lost or incorrectly processed.

This chapter reviews the new model in detail.

Motivation for the New Model

Certain flaws in the original event model became apparent after Java had been in the world long enough for large programs to be developed.

The major problem was that an event could only be handled by the component that originated the event or by one of the containers that contained the originating component. This restriction violated one of the fundamental principles of object-oriented programming: Functionality should reside in the most appropriate class. Often the most appropriate class for handling an event is not a member of the originating component's containment hierarchy.

Another drawback of the original model was that a large number of CPU cycles were wasted on uninteresting events. Any event in which a program had no interest would ripple all the way through the containment hierarchy before eventually being discarded. The original event model provided no way to disable processing of irrelevant events.

In the new delegation event model, a component may be told which object or objects should be notified when the component generates a particular kind of event. If a component is not interested in an event type, then events of that type will not be propagated.

The delegation model is based on four concepts:

- Event classes
- Event listeners
- Explicit event enabling
- Adapters

This chapter explains each of these concepts in turn.

The Event Class Hierarchy

The 1.1 event-delegation model defines a large number of new event classes. The hierarchy of event classes is shown in Figure 11.1. Most of the event classes reside in the `java.awt.event` package.

FIGURE 11.1:

Event class hierarchy

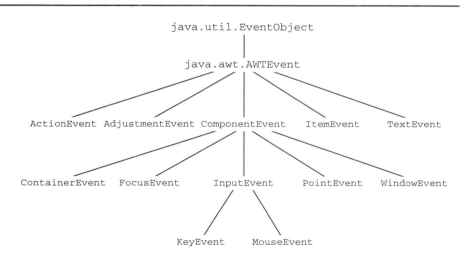

All classes belong to `java.awt.event` package unless otherwise noted.

The topmost superclass of all the new event classes is `java.util.EventObject`. It is a very general class, with only one method of interest:

- `Object getSource()`: returns the object that originated the event

One subclass of `EventObject` is `java.awt.AWTEvent`, which is the superclass of all the delegation model event classes. Again, there is only one method of interest:

- `int getID()`: returns the ID of the event

An event's ID is an int that specifies the exact nature of the event. For example, an instance of the `MouseEvent` class can represent one of seven occurrences: a click, a drag, an entrance, an exit, a move, a press, or a release. Each of these possibilities is represented by an int: `MouseEvent.MOUSE_CLICKED`, `MouseEvent.MOUSE_DRAGGED`, and so on.

The subclasses of `java.awt.AWTEvent` represent the various event types that can be generated by the various AWT components. These event types are

- `ActionEvent`: generated by activation of components
- `AdjustmentEvent`: generated by adjustment of adjustable components such as scroll bars
- `ContainerEvent`: generated when components are added to or removed from a container
- `FocusEvent`: generated when a component receives input focus
- `ItemEvent`: generated when an item is selected from a list, choice, or check box
- `KeyEvent`: generated by keyboard activity
- `MouseEvent`: generated by mouse activity
- `PaintEvent`: generated when a component is painted
- `MouseEvent`: generated when a text component is modified
- `WindowEvent`: generated by window activity (such as iconifying or de-iconifying)

NOTE   The `InputEvent` class has a `getWhen()` method that returns the time when the event took place; the return type is `long`. The `MouseEvent` class has `getX()` and `getY()` methods that return the position of the mouse within the originating component at the time the event took place; the return types are both `int`.

There are two ways to handle the events listed above. The first way is to delegate event handling to a listener object. The second way is to explicitly enable the originating component to handle its own events. These two strategies are discussed in the next two sections.

Event Listeners

An *event listener* is an object to which a component has delegated the task of handling a particular kind of event. When the component experiences input, an event of the appropriate type is constructed; the event is then passed as the parameter to a method call on the listener. A listener must implement the interface that contains the event-handling method.

For example, consider a button in an applet. When the button is clicked, an action event is to be sent to an instance of class MyActionListener. The code for MyActionListener is as follows:

```
1. class MyActionListener implements ActionListener {
2.   public void actionPerformed(ActionEvent ae) {
3.     System.out.println("Action performed.");
4.   }
5. }
```

The class implements the ActionListener interface, thus guaranteeing the presence of an actionPerformed() method. The applet code looks like this:

```
1. public class ListenerTest extends Applet {
2.   public void init() {
3.     Button btn = new Button("OK");
4.     MyActionListener listener = new MyActionListener();
5.     btn.addActionListener(listener);
6.     add(btn);
7.   }
8. }
```

On line 4, an instance of MyActionListener is created. On line 5, this instance is set as one of the button's action listeners. The code follows a standard formula for giving an action listener to a component; the formula can be summarized as follows:

1. Create a listener class that implements the ActionListener interface.

2. Construct the component.

3. Construct an instance of the listener class.

4. Call addActionListener() on the component, passing in the listener object.

In all, there are 11 listener types, each represented by an interface. Table 11.1 lists the listener interfaces, along with the interface methods and the addXXXListener() methods.

TABLE 11.1: Listener interfaces

Interface	Interface Methods	Add Method
ActionListener	actionPerformed(ActionEvent)	addActionListener()
AdjustmentListener	adjustmentValueChanged (AdjustmentEvent)	addAdjustmentListener()
ComponentListener	componentHidden(ComponentEvent) componentMoved(ComponentEvent) componentResized (ComponentEvent) componentShown (ComponentEvent)	addComponentListener()
ContainerListener	componentAdded(ContainerEvent) componentRemoved(ContainerEvent)	addContainerListener()
FocusListener	focusGained(FocusEvent) focusLost(FocusEvent)	addFocusListener()
ItemListener	itemStateChanged(ItemEvent)	addItemListener()
KeyListener	keyPressed(KeyEvent) keyReleased(KeyEvent) keyTyped(KeyEvent)	addKeyListener()
MouseListener	mouseClicked(MouseEvent) mouseEntered(MouseEvent) mouseExited(MouseEvent) mousePressed(MouseEvent) mouseReleased(MouseEvent)	addMouseListener()
MouseMotionListener	mouseDragged(MouseEvent) mouseMoved(MouseEvent)	addMouseMotionListener()
TextListener	textValueChanged(TextEvent)	addTextListener()
WindowListener	windowActivated(WindowEvent) windowClosed(WindowEvent) windowClosing(WindowEvent) windowDeactivated(WindowEvent) windowDeiconified(WindowEvent) windowIconified(WindowEvent) windowOpened(WindowEvent)	addWindowListener()

NOTE A component may have multiple listeners for any event type. There is no guarantee that listeners will be notified in the order in which they were added. There is also no guarantee that all listener notification will occur in the same thread; thus listeners must take precautions against corrupting shared data.

An event listener may be removed from a component's list of listeners by calling a removeXXXListener() method, passing in the listener to be removed. For example, the code below removes action listener al from button btn:

```
btn.removeActionListener(al);
```

The techniques described in this section represent the standard way to handle events in the 1.1 delegation model. Event delegation is sufficient in most situations; however, there are times when it is preferable for a component to handle its own events, rather than delegating its events to listeners. The next section describes how to make a component handle its own events.

Explicit Event Enabling

There is an alternative to delegating a component's events. It is possible to subclass the component and override the method that receives events and dispatches them to listeners. For example, components that originate action events have a method called processActionEvent(ActionEvent), which dispatches its action event to each action listener. The following code implements a subclass of Button which overrides processActionEvent():

```
1. class MyBtn extends Button  {
2.    public MyBtn(String label) {
3.      super(label);
4.      enableEvents(AWTEvent.ACTION_EVENT_MASK);
5.    }
6.
7.    public void processActionEvent(ActionEvent ae) {
8.      System.out.println("Processing an action event.");
9.      super.processActionEvent(ae);
10.   }
11. }
```

On line 4, the constructor calls enableEvents(), passing in a constant that enables processing of action events. The AWTEvent class defines 11 constants that can be used to enable processing of events; these constants are listed in Table 11.2. (Event processing is automatically enabled when event listeners are added, so if you restrict yourself to the listener model, you never have to call enableEvents().)

Line 7 is the beginning of the subclass' version of the processActionEvent() method. Notice the call on line 9 to the superclass' version. This call is necessary because the superclass' version is responsible for calling actionPerformed() on the button's action listeners; without line 9, action listeners would be ignored.

Of course, you can always make a component subclass handle its own events by making the subclass an event listener of itself, as shown in the listing below:

```
1.  class MyBtn extends Button implements ActionListener {
2.    public MyBtn(String label) {
3.      super(label);
4.      addActionListener(this);
5.    }
6.
7.    public void actionPerformed(ActionEvent ae) {
8.      // Handle the event here.
9.    }
10. }
```

The only difference between this strategy and the enableEvents() strategy is the order in which event handlers are invoked. When you explicitly call enable Events(), the component's processActionEvent() method will be called before any action listeners are notified. When the component sub-subclass is its own event listener, there is no guarantee as to order of notification.

Each of the 11 listener types has a corresponding XXX_EVENT_MASK constant defined in the AWTEvent class, and corresponding processXXXEvent() methods. Table 11.2 lists the mask constants and the processing methods.

TABLE 11.2: Event masks

Mask	Method
AWTEvent.ACTION_EVENT_MASK	processActionEvent()
AWTEvent.ADJUSTMENT_EVENT_MASK	processAdjustmentEvent()
AWTEvent.COMPONENT_EVENT_MASK	processComponentEvent()

TABLE 11.2 CONTINUED: Event masks

Mask	Method
AWTEvent.CONTAINER_EVENT_MASK	processContainerEvent()
AWTEvent.FOCUS_EVENT_MASK	processFocusEvent()
AWTEvent.ITEM_EVENT_MASK	processItemEvent()
AWTEvent.KEY_EVENT_MASK	processKeyEvent()
AWTEvent.MOUSE_EVENT_MASK	processMouseEvent()
AWTEvent.MOUSE_MOTION_EVENT_MASK	processMouseMotionEvent()
AWTEvent.TEXT_EVENT_MASK	processTextEvent()
AWTEvent.WINDOW_EVENT_MASK	processWindowEvent()

The strategy of explicitly enabling events for a component can be summarized as follows:

1. Create a subclass of the component.

2. In the subclass constructor, call enableEvents(AWTEvent.XXX_EVENT_MASK).

3. Provide the subclass with a processXXXEvent() method; this method should call the superclass' version before returning.

Adapters

If you look at Table 11.1, which lists the methods of the 11 event listener interfaces, you will see that several of the interfaces have only a single method, while others have several methods. The largest interface, WindowListener, has seven methods.

Suppose you want to catch iconified events on a frame. You might try to create the following class:

```
1. class MyIkeListener implements WindowListener {
2.    public void windowIconified(WindowEvent we) {
3.       // Process the event.
4.    }
5. }
```

Unfortunately, this class will not compile. The `WindowListener` interface defines seven methods, and class `MyIkeListener` needs to implement the other six before the compiler will be satisfied.

Typing in the remaining methods and giving them empty bodies is tedious. The `java.awt.event` package provides seven *adapter* classes, one for each listener interface that defines more than just a single method. An adapter is simply a class that implements an interface by providing do-nothing methods. For example, the `WindowAdapter` class implements the `WindowListener` interface with seven do-nothing methods. Our example can be modified to take advantage of this adapter:

```
1. class MyIkeListener extends WindowAdapter {
2.   public void windowIconified(WindowEvent we) {
3.     // Process the event.
4.   }
5. }
```

Table 11.3 lists all the adapter classes, along with the event-listener interfaces that they implement.

TABLE 11.3: Adapters

Adapter Class	Listener Interface
ComponentAdapter	ComponentListener
ContainerAdapter	ContainerListener
FocusAdapter	FocusListener
KeyAdapter	KeyListener
MouseAdapter	MouseListener
MouseMotionAdapter	MouseMotionListener
WindowAdapter	WindowListener

Chapter Summary

The event-delegation model allows you to designate any object as a listener for a component's events. A component may have multiple listeners for any event type. All listeners must implement the appropriate interface. If the interface defines more than one method, the listener may extend the appropriate adapter class.

A component subclass may handle its own events by calling `enableEvents()`, passing in an event mask. With this strategy, a `processXXXEvent()` method is called before any listeners are notified.

Test Yourself

1. True or False: The delegation event model, introduced in release 1.1 of the JDK, is fully compatible with the 1.0 event model.

2. Which statement or statements are true about the code listed below?

```
1. public class MyTextArea extends TextArea {
2.   public MyTextArea(int nrows, int ncols) {
3.     enableEvents(AWTEvent.TEXT_EVENT_MASK);
4.   }
5.
6.   public void processTextEvent(TextEvent te) {
7.     System.out.println("Processing a text event.");
8.   }
9. }
```

   A. The source code must appear in a file called `MyTextArea.java`.

   B. Between lines 2 and 3, a call should be made to `super(nrows, ncols)` so that the new component will have the correct size.

   C. At line 6, the return type of `processTextEvent()` should be declared `boolean`, not `void`.

   D. Between lines 7 and 8, the following code should appear: `return true;`.

   E. Between lines 7 and 8, the following code should appear: `super.ProcessTextEvent(te);`.

3. Which statement or statements are true about the code listed below?

```
1. public class MyFrame extends Frame {
2.   public MyFrame(String title) {
3.     super(title);
4.     enableEvents(AWTEvent.WINDOW_EVENT_MASK);
5.   }
6.
7.   public void processWindowEvent(WindowEvent we) {
8.     System.out.println("Processing a window event.");
9.   }
10. }
```

A. Adding a window listener to an instance of MyFrame will result in a compiler error.

B. Adding a window listener to an instance of MyFrame will result in the throwing of an exception at run time.

C. Adding a window listener to an instance of MyFrame will result in code that compiles cleanly and executes without throwing an exception.

D. A window listener added to an instance of MyFrame will never receive notification of window events.

4. Which statement or statements are true about the code fragment listed below? (Assume that classes F1 and F2 both implement the FocusListener interface.)

```
1. TextField tf = new TextField("Not a trick question");
2. FocusListener flis1 = new F1();
3. FocusListener flis2 = new F2();
4. tf.addFocusListener(flis1);
5. tf.addFocusListener(flis2);
```

A. Lines 2 and 3 generate compiler errors.

B. Line 5 throws an exception at run time.

C. The code compiles cleanly and executes without throwing an exception.

5. Which statement or statements are true about the code fragment listed below? (Assume that classes F1 and F2 both implement the FocusListener interface.)

```
1. TextField tf = new TextField("Not a trick question");
2. FocusListener flis1 = new F1();
3. FocusListener flis2 = new F2();
4. tf.addFocusListener(flis1);
5. tf.addFocusListener(flis2);
6. tf.removeFocusListener(flis1);
```

A. Lines 2 and 3 generate compiler errors.

B. Line 6 generates a compiler error.

C. Line 5 throws an exception at run time.

D. Line 6 throws an exception at run time.

E. The code compiles cleanly and executes without throwing an exception.

6. Which statement or statements are true about the code fragment listed below?

```
1. class MyListener extends MouseAdapter implements MouseListener
{
2.   public void mouseEntered(MouseEvent mev) {
3.     System.out.println("Mouse entered.");
4.   }
5. }
```

A. The code compiles without error and defines a class that could be used as a mouse listener.

B. The code will not compile correctly, because the class does not provide all the methods of the MouseListener interface.

C. The code compiles without error. The words implements Mouse Listener can be removed from line 1 without affecting the code's behavior in any way.

D. The code compiles without error. During execution, an exception will be thrown if a component uses this class as a mouse listener and receives a mouse exited event.

7. Which statement or statements are true about the code fragment listed below? (Hint: The ActionListener and ItemListener interfaces each define a single method.)

```
1. class MyListener implements ActionListener, ItemListener {
2.   public void actionPerformed(ActionEvent ae) {
3.     System.out.println("Action.");
4.   }
5.
6.   public void itemStateChanged(ItemEvent ie) {
7.     System.out.println("Item");
8.   }
9. }
```

A. The code compiles without error and defines a class that could be used as an action listener or as an item listener.

B. The code generates a compiler error on line 1.

C. The code generates a compiler error on line 6.

8. Which statement or statements are true about the code fragment listed below?

```
1. class MyListener extends MouseAdapter, KeyAdapter {
2.   public void mouseClicked(MouseEvent mev) {
3.     System.out.println("Mouse clicked.");
4.   }
5.
6.   public void keyPressed(keyEventEvent kev) {
7.     System.out.println("KeyPressed.");
8.   }
9. }
```

A. The code compiles without error and defines a class that could be used as a mouse listener or as a key listener.

B. The code generates a compiler error on line 1.

C. The code generates a compiler error on line 6.

9. True or False: A component subclass that has executed `enableEvents()` to enable processing of a certain kind of event cannot also use an adapter as a listener for the same kind of event.

10. Assume that the class `AcLis` implements the `ActionListener` interface. The code fragment below constructs a button and gives it four action listeners. When the button is pressed, which action listener is the first to get its `actionPerformed()` method invoked?

```
 1. Button btn = new Button("Hello");
 2. AcLis a1 = new AcLis();
 3. AcLis a2 = new AcLis();
 4. AcLis a3 = new AcLis();
 5. AcLis a4 = new AcLis();
 6. btn.addActionListener(a1);
 7. btn.addActionListener(a2);
 8. btn.addActionListener(a3);
 9. btn.addActionListener(a4);
10. btn.removeActionListener(a2);
11. btn.removeActionListener(a3);
12. btn.addActionListener(a3);
13. btn.addActionListener(a2);
```

A. a1 gets its `actionPerformed()` method invoked first.

B. a2 gets its `actionPerformed()` method invoked first.

C. a3 gets its `actionPerformed()` method invoked first.

D. a4 gets its `actionPerformed()` method invoked first.

E. It is impossible to know which listener will be first.

CHAPTER

TWELVE

Painting

- The paint() method and the graphics context

- The GUI thread and the repaint() method

- Spontaneous painting

- Painting to images

In this chapter you will cover the following Java Certification Exam objectives:

- Identify the sequence of Component methods involved in redrawing areas of an AWT GUI under exposure and programmed redraw conditions.

- Distinguish between methods invoked by the user thread and those normally invoked by an AWT thread.

- Write code to implement the paint() method of a java.awt.Component.

- Identify the following as methods of the Graphics class: drawString(), drawLine(), drawRect(), drawImage(), drawPolygon(), drawArc(), fillRect(), fillPolygon(), fillArc().

- Write code to obtain a suitable Graphics object from an image.

- Distinguish between situations that require the use of an Image object from those that require the use of a Graphics object.

Chapter 9, *Components*, discussed the various components of the AWT toolkit. Many types of component (buttons and scroll bars, for example) have their appearance dictated by the underlying window system. Other component types, notably applets, frames, panels, and canvases, have no intrinsic appearance. If you use any of these classes and want your component to look at all useful, you will have to provide the code that implements the component's appearance.

Java's painting mechanism provides the way for you to render your components. The mechanism is robust, and if you use it correctly you can create good, scaleable, re-usable code. The best approach is to understand how Java's painting really works. The fundamental concepts of painting are

- The paint() method and the graphics context

- The GUI thread and the repaint() method

- Spontaneous painting

- Painting to images

This chapter will take you through the steps necessary to understand these concepts and how to apply them.

The *paint()* Method and the Graphics Context

Most programmers encounter the paint() method in the early chapters of an introductory Java book. The applet listed below is a simple example of this method:

```
1. import java.applet.Applet;
2. import java.awt.*;
3.
4. public class SimplePaint extends Applet {
5.    public void paint(Graphics g) {
6.       g.setColor(Color.black);
7.       g.fillRect(0, 0, 300, 300);
8.       g.setColor(Color.white);
9.       g.fillOval(30, 30, 50, 50);
10.    }
11. }
```

Figure 12.1 shows a screen shot of this applet.

FIGURE 12.1:

A very simple
painting applet

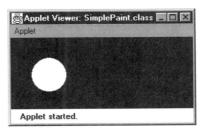

One interesting point about this applet is that no calls are made to the paint() method. The method is simply *provided*. The environment seems to do a good job of calling paint() at the right moment. Exactly when the environment chooses to call paint() is the subject of *Spontaneous Painting*, later in this chapter. For now, the topic at hand is the paint() method itself.

Painting on a component is accomplished by making calls to a *graphics context*, which is an instance of the Graphics class. A graphics context knows how to render onto a single target. The three media a graphics context can render onto are

- Components

- Images

- Printers

Most of this chapter discusses graphics contexts that render onto components; at the end of the chapter is a section that discusses how to render onto an image.

Any kind of component can be associated with a graphics context. The association is permanent; a context cannot be reassigned to a new component. Although you can use graphics contexts to paint onto any kind of component, it is unusual to do so with components that already have an appearance. Buttons, choices, check boxes, labels, scroll bars, text fields, and text areas do not often require programmer-level rendering. Most often, these components just use the version of `paint()` that they inherit from the `Component` superclass. This version does nothing; the components are rendered by the underlying window system. However, there are four classes of "blank" component that have no default appearance and will show up as empty rectangles unless they are subclassed and given `paint()` methods. These four component classes are

- `Applet`

- `Canvas`

- `Frame`

- `Panel`

If you look at line 5 of the applet code sample earlier in this section, you will see that a graphics context is passed into the `paint()` method. When you subclass a component class and give the subclass its own `paint()` method, the environment calls that method at appropriate times, passing in an appropriate instance of `Graphics`.

The four major operations provided by the `Graphics` class are

- Selecting a color

- Selecting a font

- Drawing and filling

- Clipping

Selecting a Color

Colors are selected by calling the `setColor()` method. The argument is an instance of the `Color` class. There are 13 pre-defined colors, accessible as static final variables of the Color class. (The variables are themselves instances of the Color class, which makes some people uneasy, but Java has no trouble with such things.) The predefined colors are

- `Color.red`
- `Color.yellow`
- `Color.blue`
- `Color.green`
- `Color.orange`
- `Color.magenta`
- `Color.cyan`
- `Color.pink`
- `Color.lightGray`
- `Color.darkGray`
- `Color.gray`
- `Color.white`
- `Color.black`

If you want a color that is not on this list, you can construct your own. There are several versions of the Color constructor; the simplest is

```
Color(int redLevel, int greenLevel, int blueLevel)
```

The three parameters are intensity levels for the primary colors, with a range of 0–255. The code fragment below lists the first part of a paint() method that sets the color of its graphics context to pale green:

```
1. public void paint(Graphics g) {
2. Color c = new Color(170, 255, 170);
3. g.setColor(c);
       . . .
```

After line 3 above, all graphics will be painted in pale green, until the next g.setColor() call. Calling g.setColor() does not change the color of anything that has already been drawn; it only affects *subsequent* operations.

Selecting a Font

Setting the font of a graphics context is like setting the color: Subsequent string-drawing operations will use the new font, while previously drawn strings are not affected.

Before you can set a font, you have to create one. The constructor for the Font class looks like this:

```
Font(String fontname, int style, int size)
```

The first parameter is the name of the font. Font availability is platform-dependent. You can get a list of available font names, returned as an array of strings, by calling the getFontList() method on your toolkit; an example follows:

```
String fontnames[] = Toolkit.getDefaultToolkit().getFontList()
```

There are three font names that you can always count on, no matter what platform you are running on:

- "Serif"
- "SansSerif"
- "Monospaced"

On releases of the JDK before 1.1, these were called, respectively, "TimesRoman", "Helvetica", and "Courier".

The style parameter of the Font constructor should be one of the following three ints:

- Font.PLAIN
- Font.BOLD
- Font.ITALIC

The code fragment below sets the font of graphics context gc to 24-point bold sans serif:

```
1. Font f = new Font("SansSerif", Font.BOLD, 24);
2.  gc.setFont(f);
```

You can specify a bold italic font by passing Font.BOLD+Font.ITALIC as the style parameter to the Font constructor.

Drawing and Filling

All the rendering methods of the Graphics class specify pixel coordinate positions for the shapes they render. Every component has its own coordinate space, with the origin in the component's upper-left corner, x increasing to the right, and y increasing downward. Figure 12.2 shows the component coordinate system.

FIGURE 12.2:

The component
coordinate system

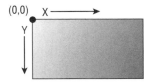

Graphics contexts do not have an extensive repertoire of painting methods. (Sophisticated rendering is handled by non-core APIs such as 2D, 3D, and Animation.) The ones to know about are

- drawLine()
- drawRect() and fillRect()
- drawOval() and fillOval()
- drawArc() and fillArc()
- drawPolygon() and fillPolygon()
- drawPolyline()
- drawString()

These methods are covered in detail in the next several sections.

drawLine()

The drawLine() method draws a line from point (x0, y0) to point (x1, y1). The method's signature is

```
public void drawLine(int x0, int y0, int x1, int y1);
```

Figure 12.3 shows a simple applet whose paint() method makes the following call:

```
g.drawLine(20, 120, 100, 50);
```

FIGURE 12.3:

drawLine()

drawRect() and *fillRect()*

The drawRect() and fillRect() methods respectively draw and fill rectangles. The methods' signatures are

```
public void drawRect(int x, int y, int width, int height);
public void fillRect(int x, int y, int width, int height);
```

The x and y parameters are the coordinates of the upper-left corner of the rectangle. Notice that the last two parameters are width and height—not the coordinates of the opposite corner. Width and height must be positive numbers, or nothing will be drawn. (This is true of all graphics-context methods that take a width and a height).

Figure 12.4 shows a simple applet whose paint() method makes the following call:

```
g.drawRect(20, 20, 100, 80);
```

FIGURE 12.4:

drawRect()

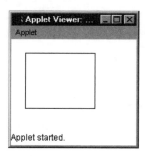

Figure 12.5 shows a simple applet whose `paint()` method makes the following call:

```
g. fillRect(20, 20, 100, 80);
```

FIGURE 12.5:

fillRect()

drawOval() and *fillOval()*

The `drawOval()` and `fillOval()` methods respectively draw and fill ovals. An oval is specified by a rectangular bounding box. The oval lies inside the bounding box and is tangent to each of the box's sides at the midpoint, as shown in Figure 12.6. To draw a circle, use a square bounding box.

FIGURE 12.6:

Bounding box for an oval

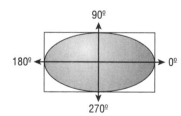

The two oval-drawing methods require you to specify a bounding box in exactly the same way that you specified a rectangle in the `drawRect()` and `fillRect()` methods:

```
public void drawOval(int x, int y, int width, int height);
public void fillOval(int x, int y, int width, int height);
```

Here x and y are the coordinates of the upper-left corner of the bounding box, and `width` and `height` are the width and height of the box.

Figure 12.7 shows a simple applet whose paint() method makes the following call:

```
g.drawOval(10, 10, 150, 100);
```

FIGURE 12.7:

drawOval()

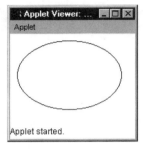

Figure 12.8 shows an applet whose paint() method calls

```
g. fillOval(10, 10, 150, 100);
```

FIGURE 12.8:

fillOval()

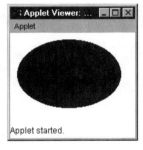

drawArc() and *fillArc()*

An *arc* is a segment of an oval. To specify an arc, you first specify the oval's bounding box, just as you do with drawOval() and fillOval(). You also need to specify the starting and ending points of the arc, which you do by specifying a starting angle and the angle swept out by the arc. Angles are measured in degrees. For the starting angle, 0 degrees is to the right, 90 degrees is upward, and so on, increasing counterclockwise.

A filled arc is the region bounded by the arc itself and the two radii from the center of the oval to the endpoints of the arc.

The method signatures are

```
public void drawArc(int x, int y, int width, int height,
                    int startDegrees, int arcDegrees);
public void fillArc(int x, int y, int width, int height,
                    int startDegrees, int arcDegrees);
```

Figure 12.9 shows an applet whose `paint()` method calls

```
g. drawArc(10, 10, 150, 100, 45, 180);
```

FIGURE 12.9:

drawArc()

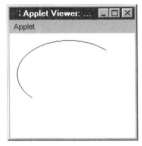

Figure 12.10 shows an applet whose `paint()` method calls

```
g. fillArc(10, 10, 150, 100, 45, 180);
```

FIGURE 12.10:

fillArc()

drawPolygon and *fillPolygon*

A *polygon* is a closed figure with an arbitrary number of vertices. The vertices are passed to the drawPolygon() and fillPolygon() methods as two int arrays. The first array contains the x coordinates of the vertices; the second array contains the y coordinates. A third parameter specifies the number of vertices. The method signatures are

```
public void drawPolygon(int xs[], int ys[], int numPoints);
public void fillPolygon(int xs[], int ys[], int numPoints);
```

Figure 12.11 shows an applet whose paint() method calls

```
1. int polyXs[] = {20, 150, 150};
2. int polyYs[] = {20, 20,  120};
3. g.drawPolygon(polyXs, polyYs, 3);
```

FIGURE 12.11:

drawPolygon()

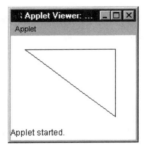

Figure 12.12 shows an applet whose paint() method calls

```
1. int polyXs[] = {20, 150, 150};
2. int polyYs[] = {20, 20,  120};
3. g.fillPolygon(polyXs, polyYs, 3);
```

FIGURE 12.12:

fillPolygon()

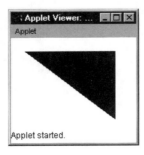

drawPolyline()

A *polyline* is similar to a polygon, but it is open rather than closed: There is no line segment connecting the last vertex to the first. The parameters to drawPolyline() are the same as those to drawPolygon(): a pair of int arrays representing vertices, and an int that tells how many vertices there are. There is no fillPolyline() method, since fillPolygon() achieves the same result.

The signature for drawPolyline() is

```
public void drawPolyline(int xs[], int ys[], int numPoints);
```

Figure 12.13 shows an applet whose paint() method calls

```
1. int polyXs[] = {20, 150, 150};
2. int polyYs[] = {20,  20,  120};
3. g.drawPolyline (polyXs, polyYs, 3);
```

FIGURE 12.13:

drawPolyline()

drawString()

The drawString() method paints a string of text. The signature is

```
public  void drawString(String s, int x, int y);
```

The x and y parameters specify the left edge of the baseline of the string. Characters with descenders (g, j, p, q, and y in most fonts) extend below the baseline.

By default, a graphics context uses the font of the associated component. However, you can set a different font by calling the graphics context's setFont() method, as you saw in the section *Selecting a Font*.

Figure 12.14 shows an applet whose `paint()` method calls

```
1. Font font = new Font("Serif", Font.PLAIN, 24);
2. g.setFont(font);
3. g.drawString("juggle quickly", 20, 50);
4. g.setColor(Color.darkGray);
5. g.drawLine(20, 50, 150, 50);
```

The string in line 3 contains five descender characters. Lines 4 and 5 draw the baseline, so you can see it in relation to the rendered string.

FIGURE 12.14:

drawString()

drawImage()

An *image* is an off-screen representation of a rectangular collection of pixel values. Java's image support is complicated, and a complete description would go well beyond the scope of this book. The last section of this chapter, *Images*, discusses what you need to know about creating and manipulating images.

For now, assume that you have somehow obtained an image (that is, an instance of class `java.awt.Image`) that you want to render to the screen using a certain graphics context. The way to do this is to call the graphics context's `drawImage()` method, which has the following signature:

```
void drawImage(Image im, int x, int y, ImageObserver observer);
```

There are other versions of the method, but this is the most common form. Obviously, im is the image to be rendered, and x and y are the coordinates within the destination component of the upper-left corner of the image. The image observer must be an object that implements the `ImageObserver` interface.

NOTE

Image observers are part of Java's complicated image-support system; the point to remember is that your image observer can always be the component into which you are rendering the image. For a complete discussion of images, please refer to the *Java 1.1 Developer's Handbook* (Sybex, 1997).

Clipping

Most calls that programmers make on graphics contexts involve color selection or drawing and filling. A less common operation is *clipping*. Clipping is simply restricting the region that a graphics context can modify.

Every graphics context—that is, every instance of the Graphics class—has a *clip region*, which defines all or part of the associated component. When you call one of the drawXXX() or fillXXX() methods of the Graphics class, only those pixels that lie within the graphics context's clip region are modified. The default clip region for a graphics context is the entire associated component. There are methods that retrieve and modify a clip region.

NOTE

In releases of the JDK up to and including 1.1.1, clip regions are rectangular. Release 1.2 is likely to support clip regions of arbitrary shape.

In a moment you will see an example of clipping, but to set things up, consider the following paint() method:

```
1. public void paint(Graphics g) {
2.   for (int i=10; i<500; i+=20)
3.     for (int j=10; j<500; j+=20)
4.       g.fillOval(i, j, 15, 15);
5. }
```

This method draws a polka-dot pattern. Consider what happens when this is the paint() method of an applet that is 300 pixels wide by 300 pixels high. Because the loop counters go all the way up to 500, the method attempts to draw outside the bounds of the applet. This is not a problem, because the graphics context by default has a clip region that coincides with the applet itself. Figure 12.15 shows the applet.

FIGURE 12.15:

Applet with default clipping

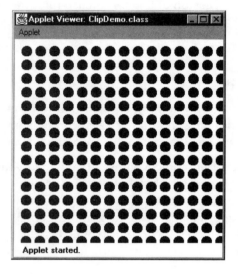

To set a rectangular clip region for a graphics context, you can call the setClip (x, y, width, height) method, passing in four ints that describe the position and size of the desired clip rectangle. For example, the code above could be modified as follows:

```
1. public void paint(Graphics g) {
2.   g.setClip(100, 100, 100, 100);
3.   for (int i=10; i<500; i+=20)
4.     for (int j=10; j<500; j+=20)
5.       g.fillOval(i, j, 15, 15);
6. }
```

Now painting is clipped to a 100×100 rectangle in the center of the 300×300 applet, as Figure 12.16 shows.

FIGURE 12.16:

Applet with default
clipping

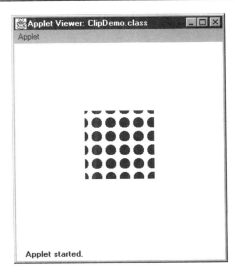

Clipping is good to know about in its own right. Clipping also comes into play when the environment needs to repair exposed portions of a component, as described in *Spontaneous Painting,* later in this chapter.

Painting a Contained Component

If an applet or a frame contains components that have their own `paint()` methods, then all the `paint()` methods will be called by the environment when necessary. For example, if a frame contains a panel and a canvas, then at certain times the environment will call the frame's `paint()`, the panel's `paint()`, and the canvas' `paint()`.

The code listed below implements a frame that contains a panel and a canvas. The frame uses a Grid layout manager with three rows and one column. The panel is added to the frame first, so it appears in the top third of the frame. The canvas is added second, so it appears in the middle third. Since there is no component in the last grid cell, what you see in the bottom third of the frame is the frame itself (that is, you see whatever the frame itself draws in its own `paint()` method).

The panel draws concentric ovals. The canvas draws concentric rectangles. The frame draws text.

```
1.  import java.awt.*;
2.
3.  public class ThingsInFrame extends Frame {
4.    public ThingsInFrame() {
5.      super("Panel and Canvas in a Frame");
6.      setSize(350, 500);
7.      setLayout(new GridLayout(3, 1));
8.      add(new RectsPanel());
9.      add(new OvalsCanvas());
10.   }
11.
12.   public static void main(String args[]) {
13.     ThingsInFrame tif = new ThingsInFrame();
14.     tif.setVisible(true);
15.   }
16.
17.   public void paint(Graphics g) {
18.   Rectangle bounds = getBounds();
19.     int y = 12;
20.     while (y < bounds.height) {
21.       g.drawString("frame frame frame frame frame frame", 60, y);
22.       y += 12;
23.     }
24.   }
25. }
26.
27.
28.
29. class RectsPanel extends Panel {
30.   public RectsPanel() {
31.     setBackground(Color.lightGray);
32.   }
33.
34.   public void paint(Graphics g) {
35.     Rectangle bounds = getBounds();
```

```
36.      int x = 0;
37.      int y = 0;
38.      int w = bounds.width - 1;
39.      int h = bounds.height - 1;
40.      for (int i=0; i<10; i++) {
41.         g.drawRect(x, y, w, h);
42.         x += 10;
43.         y += 10;
44.         w -= 20;
45.         h -= 20;
46.      }
47.   }
48. }
49.
50.
51. class OvalsCanvas extends Canvas {
52.    public OvalsCanvas() {
53.       setForeground(Color.white);
54.       setBackground(Color.darkGray);
55.    }
56.
57.    public void paint(Graphics g) {
58.       Rectangle bounds = getBounds();
59.       int x = 0;
60.       int y = 0;
61.       int w = bounds.width - 1;
62.       int h = bounds.height - 1;
63.       for (int i=0; i<10; i++) {
64.          g.drawOval(x, y, w, h);
65.          x += 10;
66.          y += 10;
67.          w -= 20;
68.          h -= 20;
69.       }
70.    }
71. }
```

Figure 12.17 shows the frame.

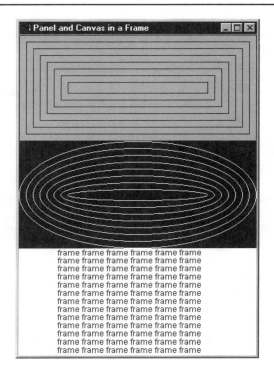

FIGURE 12.17:

A frame with contained components

On line 31, the constructor for RectsPanel called setBackground(). On lines 53 and 54, the constructor for OvalsCanvas called both setBackground() and setForeground(). The screen shot in Figure 12.15 shows that the foreground and background colors seem to have taken effect without any effort on the part of the paint() methods. The environment is not only making paint() calls at the right times; it is also doing the right thing with the foreground and background colors.

The next several sections discuss what the environment is really up to. But first, to summarize what you have learned so far about the paint() method and the graphics context:

- A graphics context is dedicated to a single component.

- To paint on a component, you call the graphics context's drawXXX() and fillXXX() methods.

- To change the color of graphics operations, you call the graphics context's setColor() method.

The GUI thread and the *repaint()* method

In Chapter 7, *Threads*, you reviewed Java's facilities for creating and controlling threads. The runtime environment creates and controls its own threads that operate behind the scenes, and one of these threads is responsible for GUI management.

This *GUI thread* is the environment's tool for accepting user input events and (more importantly for this chapter) for calling the paint() method of components that need painting.

Calls to paint() are not all generated by the environment. Java programs can of course make their own calls, either directly (which is not recommended) or indirectly (via the repaint() method). The next two sections cover the two ways that paint() calls can be generated:

- Spontaneous painting, initiated by the environment

- Programmer-initiated painting

Spontaneous Painting

Spontaneous Painting is not an official Java term, but it gets the point across. Some painting happens all by itself, with no impetus from the program. For example, as every introductory Java book explains, when a browser starts up an applet, shortly after the init() method completes, a call is made to the paint() method. Also, when part or all of a browser or a frame is covered by another window and then becomes exposed, a call is made to the paint() method.

It is the GUI thread that makes these calls to paint(). Every applet, and every application that has a GUI, has a GUI thread. The GUI thread spontaneously calls paint() under four circumstances, two of which are only applicable for applets:

- After exposure

- After de-iconification

- Shortly after init() returns (applets only)

- When a browser returns to a previously displayed page containing an applet, provided the applet is at least partially visible

When the GUI thread calls paint(), it must supply a graphics context, since the paint() method's input parameter is an instance of the Graphics class. An earlier section (*Clipping*) discussed the fact that every graphics context has a clip region. The GUI thread makes sure that the graphics contexts that get passed to `paint()` have their clip regions appropriately set. Most often, the default clip region is appropriate. (Recall that the default clip region is the entire component.) However, when a component is exposed, the clip region is set to be just that portion of the component that requires repair. If only a small piece of the component was exposed, then the clip region insures that no time is wasted on drawing pixels that are already the correct color.

The *repaint()* method

There are times when the program, not the environment, should initiate painting. This usually happens in response to input events.

Suppose you have an applet that wants to draw a red dot at the point of the most recent mouse click. The remainder of the applet should be yellow. Assume that the applet is handling its own mouse-motion events. Your event handler might look like this:

```
1. public void mouseClicked(MouseEvent e) {
2.    Graphics g = getGraphics();              // Obtain graphics context
3.    g.setColor(Color.yellow);                // Yellow background
4.    g.fillRect(0, 0, getSize().width, getSize().height);
5.    g.setColor(Color.red);                   // Red dot
6.    g.fillOval(e.getX()-10, e.getY()-10, 20, 20);
7. }
```

There are two reasons why this approach is far from optimal.

First, if the applet ever gets covered and exposed, the GUI thread will call `paint()`. Unfortunately, `paint()` does not know about the red circle that was drawn in `mouseClicked()`, so the red circle will not be repaired. It is a good rule of thumb to do *all* drawing operations in `paint()`, or in methods called from `paint()`, so that the GUI thread will be able to repair exposure damage. The GUI thread expects `paint()` to be able to correctly reconstruct the screen at any arbitrary moment.

The way to give the GUI thread what it expects is to remove all drawing code from event handlers. Event handlers such as `mouseClicked()` above should store state information in instance variables, and then cause a call to `paint()`. The `paint()` method should use the values of the instance variables as instructions on what to draw. In our example, `mouseClicked()` should be modified as shown below, assuming that the class has instance variables `mouseX` and `mouseY`:

```
1. public void mouseClicked(MouseEvent e) {
2.    mouseX = e.getX();
3.    mouseY = e.getY();
4.    Graphics g = getGraphics();
5.    paint(g);
6. }
```

The `paint()` method should be as follows:

```
1. public void paint(Graphics g) {
2.    g.setColor(Color. yellow);          // Yellow background
3.    g.fillRect(0, 0, getSize().width, getSize().height);
4.    g.setColor(Color.red);              // Red dot
5.    g.fillOval(mouseX-10, mouseY-10, 20, 20);
6. }
```

Much better! Now if a dot gets covered and exposed, the damage will be repaired automatically. There remains, however, a second problem, and it is a bit subtler than the spontaneous painting issue.

The program can be simplified a bit. There is a method of the Component class called `update()`, which clears the component to its background color and then calls `paint()`. The input parameter to `update()` is a graphics context. The applet's `init()` method could set the background color to yellow:

```
setBackground(Color.yellow);
```

Now the event handler should call `update()` rather than `paint()`, and `update()`only needs to draw the red dot:

```
 1. public void mouseClicked(MouseEvent e) {
 2.    mouseX = e.getX();
 3.    mouseY = e.getY();
 4.    Graphics g = getGraphics();
 5.    update(g);
 6. }
 7.
 8. public void paint(Graphics g) {
 9.    g.setColor(Color.red);
10.    g.fillOval(mouseX-10, mouseY-10, 20, 20);
11. }
```

This code works just fine as it is. It is a simple program that only cares about mouse-click events. In the real world, programs often need to track many different kinds of events: action events, adjustment events, key events, focus events, mouse events, mouse-motion events, and so on. It may be that every event requires painting the screen anew.

Consider what happens if a large number of events of different types are generated in rapid succession. (This is not unusual; moving or dragging the mouse can create a lot of mouse-moved and mouse-dragged events in very short order.) Time after time, an event will be generated, event handlers will modify instance variables, and paint() will modify the screen, only to have the cycle repeat and repeat. Most of the screen-drawing operations will instantly get clobbered by other screen-drawing operations triggered by more recent events. Many compute cycles will be wasted. The more compute-intensive the paint() method is, the worse the situation becomes. If the user can generate events faster than paint() can handle them, then the program will fall farther and farther behind.

It would be ideal if the event handlers could just modify the instance variables and have paint() run from time to time, often enough that the screen stays up to date, but not so often that compute cycles are wasted. This is where the repaint() method comes in.

The repaint() method *schedules* a call to the update() method. All this means is that a request flag is set in the GUI thread. Every 100 milliseconds (on most platforms), the GUI thread checks the flag. If the flag is set, the GUI thread calls update() and clears the flag. No matter how many requests are made during any 100-millisecond period, only a single call is made to update(). The example code can be modified one last time, as shown below:

```
1. public void mouseClicked(MouseEvent e) {
2.    mouseX = e.getX();
3.    mouseY = e.getY();
4.    repaint();
5. }
6.
7. public void paint(Graphics g) {
8.    g.setColor(Color.red);
9.    g.fillOval(mouseX-10, mouseY-10, 20, 20);
10. }
```

The repaint() call at line 4 has replaced the calls to getGraphics() and update(). Now even if the world's fastest kangaroo hops up and down on the mouse at 50 khops per second, there will still be only 10 calls to `paint()` per second, and the system cannot possibly fall behind.

The code above shows the preferred approach to handling events that cause the screen to be changed: Event handlers store information in instance variables and then call `repaint()`, and `paint()` draws the screen according to the information in the instance variables. The two benefits of this approach are

- The screen is correctly repaired when the environment spontaneously calls `paint()`.

- The Virtual Machine never gets overwhelmed by events.

If you want to accumulate dots, rather than have each dot cleared away when a new one is to be drawn, you can always override `update()` so that it does not clear. All `update()` needs to do in this case is call `paint()`, as shown below:

```
1. public void update(Graphics g) {
2.    paint(g);
3. }
```

This is a standard technique.

Images

Images are off-screen representations of rectangular pixel patterns. There are three things you can do with images:

- Create them

- Modify them

- Draw them to the screen or to other images

There are two ways to create an image. You can create an empty one, or you can create one that is initialized from a `.gif` or a `.jpeg` file.

To create an empty image, call the `createImage()` method of the `Component` class and pass in the desired width and height. For example, the following line creates an image called `im1` that is 400 pixels wide and 250 pixels high; it might appear in the `init()` method of an applet:

```
Image im1 = createImage(400, 250);
```

An image can be created based on the information in a `.gif` or a `.jpeg` file. The `Applet` and `Toolkit` classes both have a method called `getImage()`, which has two common forms:

```
getImage(URL fileURL)
getImage(URL dirURL, String path)
```

The first form takes an URL that references the desired image file. The second form takes an URL that references a directory and the path of the desired image file, relative to that directory. The code fragment below shows an applet's `init()` method; it loads an image from a file that resides in the same server directory as the page that contains the applet:

```
1. public void init() {
2.    Image im = getImage(getDocumentBase(), "thePicture.gif");
3. }
```

If you load an image from a file, you may want to modify it; you will definitely want to modify any image that you create via `createImage()`. Fortunately, images have graphics contexts. All you need to do is obtain a graphics context for the image you wish to modify and make the calls that were discussed earlier in this chapter in *Drawing and Filling*. To obtain a graphics context, just call `getGraphics()`. The code below implements an applet whose `init()` method creates an image and then obtains a graphics context in order to draw a blue circle on a yellow background. The applet's `paint()` method renders the image onto the screen using the `drawImage()` method, which is documented earlier in this chapter.

```
1. import java.applet.Applet;
2. import java.awt.*;
3.
4. public class PaintImage extends Applet {
5.    Image im;
6.
7.    public void init() {
8.       im = createImage(300, 200);
9.       Graphics imgc = im.getGraphics();
10.      imgc.setColor(Color.yellow);
11.      imgc.fillRect(0, 0, 300, 200);
12.      imgc.setColor(Color.blue);
13.      imgc.fillOval(50, 50, 100, 100);
14.   }
15.
```

```
16.    public void paint(Graphics g) {
17.      g.drawImage(im, 25, 80, this);
18.    }
19. }
```

Notice that in lines 9–13, imgc is a graphics context that draws to the off-screen image im. In lines 16–17, g is a graphics context that draws to the applet's screen.

Chapter Summary

The paint() method provides a graphics context for drawing. The functionality of the graphics context (class Graphics) includes

- Selecting a color
- Selecting a font
- Drawing and filling
- Clipping

Calls to paint() can be generated spontaneously by the system, under four circumstances:

- After exposure
- After de-iconification
- Shortly after init() returns (applets only)
- When a browser returns to a previously displayed page containing an applet (applets only)

In all cases, the clip region of the graphics context will be set appropriately.

Event handlers that need to modify the screen can store state information in instance variables, and then call repaint(). This method schedules a call to update(), which clears the component to its background color and then calls paint().

Images can be created from scratch or loaded from external files. An image can be modified by using a graphics context.

Test Yourself

1. How would you set the color of a graphics context called **g** to cyan?

   A. `g.setColor(Color.cyan);`

   B. `g.setCurrentColor(cyan);`

   C. `g.setColor("Color.cyan");`

   D. `g.setColor("cyan");`

   E. `g.setColor(new Color(cyan));`

2. The code below draws a line. What color is the line?

   ```
   1. g.setColor(Color.red.green.yellow.red.cyan);
   2. g.drawLine(0, 0, 100, 100);
   ```

   A. Red

   B. Green

   C. Yellow

   D. Cyan

   E. Black

3. What does the following code draw?

   ```
   1. g.setColor(Color.black);
   2. g.drawLine(10, 10, 10, 50);
   3. g.setColor(Color.red);
   4. g.drawRect(100, 100, 150, 150);
   ```

   A. A red vertical line that is 40 pixels long and a red square with sides of 150 pixels

   B. A black vertical line that is 40 pixels long and a red square with sides of 150 pixels

   C. A black vertical line that is 50 pixels long and a red square with sides of 150 pixels

   D. A red vertical line that is 50 pixels long and a red square with sides of 150 pixels

E. A black vertical line that is 40 pixels long and a red square with sides of 100 pixels

---

FIGURE 12.18:

Question 4

A)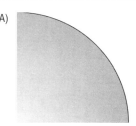

B)

4. Figure 12.18 shows two shapes. Which shape (A or B) is drawn by the following line of code?

```
g.fillArc(10, 10, 100, 100, 0, 90);
```

5. Which of the statements below are true? (Choose one or more.)

   A. A polyline is always filled.

   B. A polyline cannot be filled.

   C. A polygon is always filled.

   D. A polygon is always closed.

   E. A polygon may be filled or not filled.

6. True or False: When the GUI thread calls `paint()` in order to repair exposure damage, the `paint()` method must determine what was damaged and set its clip region appropriately.

7. Your `mouseDragged()` event handler and your `paint()` method look like this:

```
1. public void mouseDragged(MouseEvent e) {
2.    mouseX = e.getX();
3.    mouseY = e.getY();
4.    repaint();
5. }
6.
7. public void paint(Graphics g) {
8.    g.setColor(Color.cyan);
9.    g.drawLine(mouseX, mouseY, mouseX+10, mouseY+10);
10. }
```

You want to modify your code so that the cyan lines accumulate on the screen, rather than getting erased every time `repaint()` calls `update()`. What is the simplest way to proceed?

A. On line 4, replace `repaint()` with `paint()`.

B. On line 4, replace `repaint()` with `update()`.

C. After line 7, add this: `super.update(g);`

D. Add the following method:

`public void update(Graphics g) {paint(g);}`

8. What code would you use to construct a 24-point bold serif font?

A. `new Font(Font.SERIF, 24, Font.BOLD);`

B. `new Font("Serif", 24, "Bold");`

C. `new Font("Bold", 24, Font.SERIF);`

D. `new Font("Serif", Font.BOLD, 24);`

E. `new Font(Font.SERIF, "Bold", 24);`

9. What does the following `paint()` method draw?

```
1. public void paint(Graphics g) {
2.    g.drawString("question #9", 10, 0);
3. }
```

A. The string "question #9", with its top-left corner at 10, 0

B. A little squiggle coming down from the top of the component, a little way in from the left edge

10. What does the following `paint()` method draw?

```
1. public void paint(Graphics g) {
2.   g.drawOval(100, 100, 44);
3. }
```

    A. A circle at (100, 100), with radius of 44

    B. A circle at (100, 44) with radius of 100

    C. A circle at (100, 44) with radius of 44

    D. The code does not compile.

CHAPTER
THIRTEEN

13

Applets and HTML

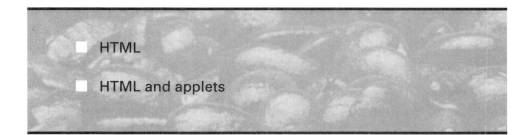

- HTML
- HTML and applets

In this chapter you will cover the following Java Certification Exam objectives:

- Construct an HTML <APPLET> tag to embed an applet in a Web page.

- Control the width and height of an applet by means of the <APPLET> tag.

- Supply named parameter values by means of the <APPLET> tag.

- Write code in an applet that reads the value of a named parameter specified in the <APPLET> tag.

The `java.applet.Applet` class extends from `java.awt.Component` and `java.awt.Container`. Thus every applet inherits all the component functionality discussed in Chapter 9, *Components*, as well as the container and layout functionality discussed in Chapter 10, *Layout Managers*.

An *applet* is a container component that resides on an HTML page within a browser. This chapter discusses the relationship between HTML and the `Applet` class.

HTML

HTML (*HyperText Markup Language*) is a page-description language. HTML supports text, graphics, and other resources, along with the instructions for presenting these elements in a browser. HTML focuses on multimedia presentation and delivering applications that can run on the client's processor.

Tags in HTML indicate instructions. A browser can read any HTML tag that its interpreter has been programmed to recognize; there is, of course, a lot of industry effort dedicated to creating a standard HTML convention that HTML authors can expect to work regardless of the browser a user is using.

Java-enabled browsers extend the obvious advantages of screen-based presentation by supporting applets that run on the client's processor. For example, you have probably done something like the following:

```
1. <APPLET CODE=Clock2.class WIDTH=170 HEIGHT=150>
2. </APPLET>
```

This is sufficient when testing with an appletviewer, but to insure workability with all browsers, your minimum HTML text should include a few other items. A more robust version of the code above might be

```
 1. <HTML> [Tim]
 2. <HEAD>
 3. <TITLE>Our Applet</TITLE>
 4. </HEAD><BODY>
 5. <H1>
 6. Here's the applet that will change the way we all view time.</H1><BR>
 7. <APPLET CODE=Clock2.class WIDTH=170 HEIGHT=150>
 8. </APPLET>
 9. </BODY>
10. </HTML> [Tim]
```

NOTE   <APPLET> tags must appear between the <BODY> and </BODY> tags.

HTML and Applets

If you can produce the code above, you can toss an applet into any Web page. However, this code is limited:

- The Clock2.class file must reside in the same directory on the same server as the Web page itself.

- No data is passed from the page to the applet.

To make the most of <APPLET> tags—and to get the best possible test score— you need to know all the functionality available within the tag. Here is a synopsis of the tag (optional values are bracketed):

```
<APPLET
   CODE= class file (file or URL)
   HEIGHT= pixels
   WIDTH= pixels
 [ CODEBASE= URL directory ]
 [ ALT= alternate text message ]
 [ ARCHIVE= names of JAR files]
 [ ALIGN= alignment ]
```

```
      [ NAME= name for other applets on page ]
      [ HSPACE= pixel ]
      [ VSPACE= pixel ]

   >
      [ <PARAM NAME=identifier VALUE=value> ]
      [ <PARAM NAME=identifier VALUE=value> ]
                        .
                        .
                        .
      [ alternate HTML ]
   </APPLET>
```

The CODE, WIDTH, and HEIGHT tags are mandatory. Without these tags, an applet will not be displayed.

Order of arguments within the tag is not significant.

The *WIDTH* and *HEIGHT* Tags

The WIDTH and HEIGHT tags specify, in pixels, how much space the browser should allocate to the applet for display. Be aware that other elements on the applet's HTML page may cause the browser to constrain the applet's size to some value other than what the HEIGHT and WIDTH tags requested.

An applet can determine at run time how much space the browser gave it by calling the getSize() method, which applets inherit from the java.awt.Component class.

WARNING Applets inherit the component method setSize(), but it is dangerous to rely on this method. The browser makes the ultimate decision on an applet's size and is free to ignore setSize() calls. Sun's appletviewer honors setSize(); Netscape browsers ignore it.

The *CODE* and *CODEBASE* Tags

The CODE tag is required. There are two ways to specify a value for CODE:

- A path on the page server, relative to the location of the calling HTML file
- An URL

In both cases, the value is case-sensitive and must include the `.class` extension. Note that if the value is specified as an URL, the applet can reside on any accessible machine.

An applet can determine the directory from which it came by calling `getCodeBase()`, and it can also determine the directory of the page that referenced it by calling `getDocumentBase()`. Both calls are methods of the `java.applet.Applet` class, and both return an instance of the `java.net.URL` class.

Many single-class applets reside in the same server directory as the page that references them. As the base of class files grows, however, it makes sense to organize classes into one directory structure, as shown in Figure 13.1.

FIGURE 13.1:

A class file directory

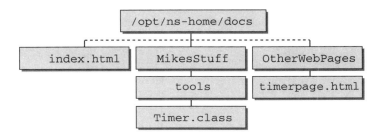

Calling an applet from `index.html` using just the CODE tag is straightforward:

```
1. <APPLET CODE="MikesStuff/tools/Timer.class" WIDTH=50 HEIGHT=50>
2. <APPLET>
```

However, if the applet is referenced from the `timerpage.html` file, things begin to get complicated:

```
1. <APPLET CODE="../MikesStuff/tools/Timer.class" HEIGHT=50 WIDTH=50>
2. </APPLET>
```

Line 1 certainly works, but as the file structure grows or changes, each affected HTML document must be modified according to its location. The CODEBASE tag lets you avoid that busy work by specifying the directory where the class files reside. CODEBASE lets you specify the URL of a directory; the CODE tag then provides a relative path within that directory. Here is how the example could be modified to specify a code base:

```
1. <APPLET CODE=tools/Timer.class CODEBASE=MikeStuff HEIGHT=50 WIDTH=50>
2. </APPLET>
```

As with the CODE tag, there are two ways to specify the value of CODEBASE:

- A path on the page server, relative to the location of the calling HTML file
- An URL

The *PARAM* Tag

The PARAM tag allows data to be passed from an HTML page to an applet on that page.

On the HTML side, matters are fairly simple. Consider a Thermostat applet that allows the Web page to select a label, the degree scale (Fahrenheit or Celsius), and the minimum supported change to setting (in degrees). The HTML might look like this:

```
1. <APPLET CODE=Thermostat.class WIDTH=200 HEIGHT=200>
2. <PARAM NAME=label VALUE="My Excellent Thermostat">
3. <PARAM NAME=scale VALUE=celsius>
4. <PARAM NAME=increment VALUE=2>
5. </APPLET>
```

This HTML specifies values for three parameters named `label`, `scale`, and `increment`. The corresponding values are all strings (even the value on line 4, which is clearly intended to be treated as a number). Notice the quotes in line 2, which delimit the value so that it can contain spaces.

NOTE   <PARAM> tags must appear between the <APPLET> tag and the </APPLET> tag.

When an applet wants to read the value of a parameter, it calls the `getParameter (String)` method. The string argument to the method is the name of the parameter to be read. This argument is case-insensitive: To read the scale parameter, you can call `getParameter("SCALE")`, `getParameter("scale")`, or any other combination of upper and lower case. The value returned by `getParameter()` is a string, and this time the string is case-sensitive; the value will be precisely the value as it appears in the PARAM tag.

The following applet fragment reads the three parameters from the HTML page and stores their values in instance variables:

```
 1. public class Thermostat extends Applet {
 2.   private String label;
 3.   private boolean isCelsius;
 4.   private int increment;
 5.
 6.   public void init() {
 7.     label = getParameter("LABEL");
 8.     isCelsius = getParameter("scale").equalsIgnoreCase("CELSIUS");
 9.     increment = Integer.parseInt(getParameter("INCREMENT"));
10.   }
11. }
```

On lines 7–9, the arguments to getParameter() are all upper case. This does no harm and makes the code a bit more readable. On line 7, the label value is simply read and stored. On line 8, the code determines whether or not the requested scale is Celsius. Since parameter values are returned exactly as they appear on the Web page (with case preserved), line 8 does its string comparison with equalsIgnoreCase() rather than equals(); this precaution allows the HTML author to specify a value of CELSIUS, Celsius, celsius, or even cELSIUS. On line 11, the increment value is received as a string and must be parsed to an int in order to be useful.

The code assumes that all three parameters really are defined in the HTML page and that the increment value string really represents an integer. To be truly robust, the code should test these assumptions. A missing parameter causes getParameter() to return null, which would crash a careless applet. The return value from getParameter() should always be checked. All variables whose values are derived from parameters should have default values to fall back on in case a parameter is missing or invalid.

```
 1. public class Thermostat extends Applet {
 2.   private String label = "Thermo";
 3.   private boolean isCelsius = false;
 4.   private integer increment = 1;
 5.
 6.   public void init() {
 7.     String val = getParameter("LABEL");
 8.     if (val != null)
 9.       label = val;
```

```
10.     try {
11.       isCelsius = getParameter("scale").equalsIgnoreCase("CELSIUS");
12.     } catch (NullPointerException e) { }
13.     try {
14.       increment = Integer.parseInt(getParameter("INCREMENT"));
15.     } catch (Exception e) { }     // Null pointer or number format
16.   }
17. }
```

Lines 7–9 make sure the label parameter value is non-null before assigning it to label. Line 11 will throw a null-pointer exception if the scale parameter is absent from the HTML page; if this happens, no assignment is made, and isCelsius retains its default value. Line 14 will throw a null-pointer exception if the increment parameter is absent, and it will throw a number format exception if the parameter is present but not valid; in both cases, the value of increment retains its default value.

The *ALT* Tag and Alternate HTML

The <ALT> tag is a face-saving mechanism for browsers that understand what the <APPLET> tag means but do not actually support applets. Such a browser will display the alternate text supplied by the <ALT> tag, in the space where the applet would normally appear.

Here is an example of the <ALT> tag:

```
1. <APPLET CODE= Thermostat.class WIDTH=200 HEIGHT=200
2.   ALT="Get another browser!">
3. </APPLET>
```

If a browser is completely Java-ignorant, it will not even understand the <APPLET> tag and will not know what to do with alternate text. However, such a browser will correctly display any non-Java HTML that appears between the <APPLET> and </APPLET> tags.

The *HSPACE*, *VSPACE*, and *ALIGN* Tags

The HSPACE, VSPACE, and ALIGN tags control the position of an applet as it appears on its page.

The value of HSPACE specifies the distance in pixels between the applet's left and right boundaries and any adjacent HTML elements. The value of VSPACE specifies the distance in pixels between the applet's top and bottom boundaries and any adjacent HTML elements.

The value of ALIGN specifies the alignment of the applet with respect to the surrounding HTML elements. The Certification Exam does not require you to know these, but for interest's sake they are: LEFT, RIGHT, BOTTOM, TOP, TEXTTOP, ABSBOTTOM, ABSMIDDLE, MIDDLE, and BASELINE.

The *NAME* Tag

The NAME tag supports inter-applet communication. If an applet has a name, then another applet on the same HTML page can use the name to get a reference to the first applet. The second applet can then make method calls to the first applet. Inter-applet communication is beyond the scope of the Certification Exam.

The *ARCHIVE* Tag

Version 1.1 of the JDK introduced *JAR* files. A JAR (Java ARchive) file is a zipped collection of files. The ARCHIVE tag identifies any JAR files on the server that the browser should download.

JAR files greatly speed remote class loading. There is a significant time penalty for downloading a file. If an applet defines 10 classes, then ordinarily the penalty is incurred 10 times. With JAR technology, all 10 class files can be bundled into a single JAR file, and the per-file penalty is only incurred once.

The CODE tag is still required to name the class file that begins execution of the applet, so a sample tag might look like

```
1. <APPLET CODE=Timer.class WIDTH=75 HEIGHT=75 ARCHIVE="bundle.jar">
2. </APPLET>
```

It is also possible to name multiple JARs for download simply by using a comma-separated list in place of a single entry:

```
<APPLET CODE=Timer.class WIDTH=75 HEIGHT=75
 ARCHIVE="a.jar,b.jar,c.jar"></APPLET>
```

Chapter Summary

The APPLET tag specifies applet information in an HTML page. You must explicitly close an <APPLET> tag with </APPLET>.

Within an APPLET tag, CODE, WIDTH, and HEIGHT tags are mandatory. Optional tags within the APPLET tag are

- CODEBASE
- ALT
- HSPACE
- VSPACE
- ALIGN
- NAME
- ARCHIVE

and between <APPLET> and </APPLET>

- PARAM

Test Yourself

1. Which line or lines of the following HTML code are erroneous?

   ```
   1. <APPLET WIDTH=50 HEIGHT=95 CODE=Thermostat.Class>
   2. <PARAM NAME=scale VALUE=Celsius>
   3. </APPLET>
   ```

2. True or False: The CODE value in an <APPLET> tag must name a class file that is in the same directory as the calling HTML page.

3. True or False: If getParameter() returns null, then assigning the return value to a variable of type String may cause an exception to be thrown.

4. True or False: Every ARCHIVE tag specifies exactly one JAR file.

5. Consider the following init() method from an applet:

```
1. public void init() {
2.    String val = "Primo";
3.    val = getParameter("XX").toUpperCase();
4.    System.out.println("val = " + val);
5. }
```

At line 4, what is the value of `val` if the applet's tag was the following:

```
1. <APPLET CODE=Q5.class WIDTH=100 HEIGHT=100>
2. <PARAM NAME=Xx VALUE=Secondo>
3. </APPLET>
```

A. null

B. "Primo"

C. "PRIMO"

D. "Secondo"

E. "SECONDO"

6. Consider the following `init()` method from an applet:

```
1. public void init() {
2.    int i = 100;
3.    String val = getParameter("YY");
4.    try {
5.      i = Integer.parseInt(val);
6.    } catch (Exception e) { }
7.    System.out.println("i = " + i);
8. }
```

At line 7, what is the value of i if the applet's tag was the following:

```
1. <APPLET CODE=Q6.class WIDTH=100 HEIGHT=100>
2. <PARAM NAME=yy VALUE=3a6>
3. </APPLET>
```

A. 0

B. 100

C. 3

D. 36

E. "3a6"

7. True or False: In the following tag, `WhereAmI.class` must be found in `big.jar`.

   ```
   1. <APPLET CODE=WhereAmI.class HEIGHT=200 WIDTH=75 ARCHIVE=big.jar>
   2. </APPLET>
   ```

8. The HTML below is part of the Web page located on `http://www.bar.com`. Will the HTML work?

   ```
   1. <APPLET CODE=bodies.Globe.class WIDTH=75 HEIGHT=75
   2. CODEBASE="http://www.foo.com/astronomy">
   3. </APPLET>
   ```

9. Suppose you have the following line within an `<APPLET>` tag:

   ```
   <PARAM NAME=gem VALUE=pearl>
   ```

   and the following line within the corresponding `init()` method:

   ```
   String gem = getParameter("pearl");
   ```

   What value is assigned to `gem`?

10. Consider the following `init()` method from an applet:

    ```
    1. public void init() {
    2.    int i = 100;
    3.    String val = getParameter("YY");
    4.    try {
    5.      i = Integer.parseInt(val);
    6.    } catch (NumberFormatException e) { i = 200; }
    7.      catch (NullPointerException e}  { i = 300; }
    8.    System.out.println("i = " + i);
    9. }
    ```

    At line 8, what is the value of i if the applet's tag was the following:

    ```
    1. <APPLET CODE=Q6.class WIDTH=100 HEIGHT=100>
    2. <PARAM NAME=aa VALUE=3a6>
    3. </APPLET>
    ```

    A. 0

    B. 100

    C. 200

    D. 300

    E. "3a6"

Input and Output

- Text representation and character encoding

- The File class

- The RandomAccessFile class

- Streams

- Readers and writers

In this chapter you will cover the following Java Certification Exam objectives:

- Write code that uses objects of the File class to navigate a file system.

- Write code that uses objects of the classes InputStreamReader and OutputStreamWriter to translate between Unicode and either platform default or ISO 8859-1 character encodings.

- Distinguish between conditions under which platform default encoding conversion should be used and conditions under which a specific conversion should be used.

- Select, from a list of classes in the java.io package, valid constructor arguments for FilterInputStream and FilterOutputStream subclasses.

- Write appropriate code to read, write, and update files using FileInputStream, FileOutputStream, and RandomAccessFile objects.

- Describe the permanent effects on the file system of constructing and using FileInputStream, FileOutputStream, and RandomAccessFile objects.

Java supports input and output with a flexible set of stream classes. File I/O requires a bit of additional support, which Java provides in the File and RandomAccessFile classes.

All I/O operations into and out of a Java Virtual Machine are contingent on approval by the security manager. Most browsers forbid all file access, so the File and RandomAccessFile classes are generally for use in applications.

All the classes discussed in this chapter reside in the java.io package.

File Input and Output

Java's File and RandomAccessFile classes provide functionality for navigating the local file system, describing files and directories, and accessing files in non-sequential order. (Accessing files sequentially is done with streams, readers, and writers, which are described later in this chapter.)

Files often contain text. Java's text representation goes far beyond traditional ASCII. Since the Certification Exam requires you to be familiar with how Java represents text, it is worthwhile to review this topic before looking at file I/O.

Text Representation and Character Encoding

Java uses two kinds of text representation:

- Unicode for internal representation of characters and strings

- UTF for input and output

Unicode uses 16 bits to represent each character. If the high-order 9 bits are all zeros, then the encoding is simply standard ASCII, with the low-order byte containing the character representation. Otherwise, the bits represent a character that is not represented in 7-bit ASCII. Java's `char` data type uses Unicode encoding, and the `String` class contains a collection of Java chars.

Unicode's 16 bits are sufficient to encode most alphabets, but pictographic Asian languages present a problem. Standards committees have developed compromises to allow limited but useful subsets of Chinese, Japanese, and Korean to be represented in Unicode, but it has become clear that an ideal global text representation scheme must use more than 16 bits per character.

The answer is *UTF*. The abbreviation stands for "UCS Transformation Format," and UCS stands for "Universal Character Set." Most people believe that UTF is short for "Universal Text Format," and while they are wrong, their version is more descriptive than the true version.

UTF encoding uses as many bits as needed to encode a character: fewer bits for smaller alphabets, more bits for the larger Asian alphabets. Since every character can be represented, UTF is a truly global encoding scheme.

A *character encoding* is a mapping between a character set and a range of binary numbers. Every Java platform has a default character encoding, which is used to interpret between internal Unicode and external bytes. The default character encoding reflects the local language and culture. Every encoding has a name. For example, "8859_1" is common ASCII, "8859_8" is ISO Latin/Hebrew, and "Cp1258" is Vietnamese.

When an I/O operation is performed in Java, the system needs to know which character encoding to use. The various I/O support classes use the local default encoding, unless they are explicitly instructed to use a different encoding. For most operations, the local default encoding is perfectly adequate. However, when communicating across a network with another computer, both machines need to use the same encoding, even if they reside in different countries. In such cases, it is a good idea to explicitly request "8859_1".

The *File* Class

The `java.io.File` class represents the name of a file or directory that might exist on the host machine's file system. The simplest form of the constructor for this class is

```
File(String pathname);
```

It is important to know that constructing an instance of `File` does not create a file on local file system. Calling the constructor simply creates an instance that encapsulates the specified string. Of course, if the instance is to be of any use, most likely it should encapsulate a string that represents an existing file or directory, or one that will shortly be created. However, at construction time no checks are made.

There are two other versions of the `File` constructor:

```
File(String dir, String subpath);
File(File dir, String subpath);
```

Both versions require you to provide a directory and a relative path (the `subpath` argument) within that directory. In one version you use a string to specify the directory; in the other, you use an instance of `File`. (Remember that the `File` class can represent a directory as well as a file.) You might, for example, execute the following code on a UNIX machine:

```
1. File f = new File("/tmp", "xyz");      // Assume /tmp is a directory
```

You might execute the following code on a Windows platform:

```
1. File f1 = new File("C:\a");            // Assume C:\a is a directory
2. File f2 = new File(f1, "Xyz.java");
```

Of course, there is no theoretical reason why you could not run the first example on a Windows machine and the second example on a UNIX platform. Up to this point you are doing nothing more than constructing objects that encapsulate strings. In practice, however, there is nothing to be gained from using the wrong pathname semantics.

After constructing an instance of `File`, you can make a number of method calls on it. Some of these calls simply do string manipulation on the file's pathname, while others access or modify the local file system.

The methods that support navigation are listed below:

- `boolean exists()`: This returns `true` if the file or directory exists, otherwise returns `false`.

- `String getAbsolutePath()`: This returns the absolute (i.e. not relative path of the file or directory.

- `String getCanonicalPath()`: This returns the canonical path of the file or directory. This is similar to `getAbsolutePath()`, but the symbols . and .. are resolved.

- `String getName()`: This returns the name of the file or directory. The name is the last element of the path.

- `String getParent()`: This returns the name of the directory that contains the `File`.

- `boolean isDirectory()`: This returns `true` if the `File` describes a directory that exists on the file system.

- `boolean isFile()`: This returns `true` if the `File` describes a file that exists on the file system.

- `String[] list()`: This returns an array containing the names of the files and directories within the `File`. The `File` must describe a directory, not a file.

The methods listed above are not the entirety of the class' methods. Some non-navigation methods are

- `boolean canRead()`: This returns `true` if the file or directory may be read.

- `boolean canWrite()`: This returns `true` if the file or directory may be modified.

- `boolean delete()`: This attempts to delete the file or directory.

- `long length()`: This returns the length of the file.

- `boolean mkdir()`: This attempts to create a directory whose path is described by the `File`.

- `boolean renameTo(File newname)`: This renames the file or directory. Returns `true` if the renaming succeeded, otherwise returns `false`.

The program listed below uses some of the navigation methods to create a recursive listing of a directory. The application expects the directory to be specified in the command line. The listing appears in a text area within a frame.

```
1. import java.awt.*;
2. import java.io.File;
3.
4. public class Lister extends Frame {
5.   TextArea      ta;
6.
7.   public static void main(String args[]) {
8.     // Get path or dir to be listed. Default to cwd if
9.     // no command line arg.
10.     String path = ".";
11.     if (args.length >= 1)
12.       path = args[0];
13.
14.     // Make sure path exists and is a directory.
15.     File f = new File(path);
16.     if (!f.isDirectory()) {
17.       System.out.println("Doesn't exist or not dir: " + path);
18.       System.exit(0);
19.     }
20.
21.     // Recursively list contents.
22.     Lister lister = new Lister(f);
23.     lister.setVisible(true);
24.   }
25.
26.   Lister(File f) {
27.     setSize(300, 450);
28.     ta = new TextArea();
29.     ta.setFont(new Font("Monospaced", Font.PLAIN, 14));
30.     add(BorderLayout.CENTER, ta);
31.     recurse(f, 0);
32.   }
33.
34.   //
35.   // Recursively list the contents of dirfile. Indent 5 spaces for
36.   // each level of depth.
37.   //
38.   void recurse(File dirfile, int depth) {
```

```
39.      String contents[] = dirfile.list();
40.      for (int i=0; i<contents.length; i++) {      // For each child...
41.        for (int spaces=0; spaces<depth; spaces++)    // Indent
42.          ta.append("    ");
43.        ta.append(contents[i] + "\n");                // Print name
44.        File child = new File(dirfile, contents[i]);
45.        if (child.isDirectory())
46.          recurse(child, depth+1);                    // Recurse if dir
47.      }
48.   }
49. }
```

Figure 14.1 shows a sample of this program's output.

FIGURE 14.1:

Sample listing

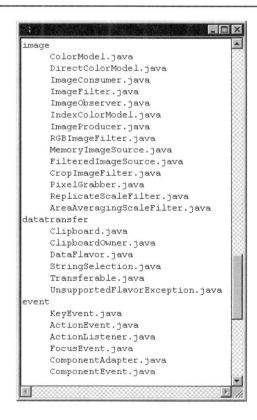

The program first checks for a command-line argument (lines 10–12). If one is supplied, it is assumed to be the name of the directory to be listed; if there is no argument, the current working directory will be listed. Note the call to isDirectory() on line 16. This call returns true only if path represents an existing directory.

After establishing that the thing to be listed really is a directory, the code constructs an instance of Lister, which makes a call to recurse(), passing in the File to be listed in the parameter dirfile.

The recurse() method makes a call to list() (line 39) to get a listing of the contents of the directory. Each file or subdirectory is printed (line 43) after appropriate indentation (5 spaces per level, lines 41 and 42). If the child is a directory (tested on line 45), its contents are listed recursively.

The Lister program shows one way to use the methods of the File class to navigate the local file system. These methods do not modify the contents of files in any way; to modify a file you must use either the RandomAccessFile class or Java's stream, reader, and writer facilities. All these topics are covered in the sections that follow, but first here is a summary of the key points concerning the File class:

- An instance of File describes a file or directory.

- The file or directory might or might not exist.

- Constructing/garbage collecting an instance of File has no effect on the local file system.

The *RandomAccessFile* Class

One way to read or modify a file is to use the java.io.RandomAccessFile class. This class presents a model of files that is incompatible with the stream/reader/ writer model described later in this chapter. The stream/reader/writer model was developed for general I/O, while the RandomAccessFile class takes advantage of a particular behavior of files that is not found in general I/O devices.

With a random-access file, you can seek to a desired position within a file, and then read or write a desired amount of data. The RandomAccessFile class provides methods that support seeking, reading, and writing.

The constructors for the class are

- RandomAccessFile(String file, String mode)

- RandomAccessFile(File file, String mode)

The mode string should be either "r" or "rw". Use "r" to open the file for reading only, and use "rw" to open for both reading and writing.

The second form of the constructor is useful when you want to use some of the methods of the File class before opening a random-access file, so that you already have an instance of File at hand when it comes time to call the RandomAccessFile constructor. For example, the code fragment below constructs an instance of File in order to verify that the string path represents a file that exists and may be written. If this is the case, the RandomAccessFile constructor is called; otherwise an exception is thrown.

```
1. File file = new File(path);
2. if (!file.isFile()  ||  !file.canRead()  ||  !file.canWrite()) {
3.    throw new IOException();
4. }
5. RandomAccessFile raf = new RandomAccessFile(file, "rw");
```

Constructing an instance of RandomAccessFile is like constructing an instance of File: No file is created on the file system. Similarly, destructing and garbage collecting an instance of RandomAccessFile does not cause deletion of the corresponding file on the file system.

After a random-access file is constructed, you can seek to any byte position within the file and then read or write. Pre-Java systems (the C standard I/O library, for example) have supported seeking to a position relative to the beginning of the file, the end of the file, or the current position within the file. Java's random-access files only support seeking relative to the beginning of the file, but there are methods that report the current position and the length of the file, so you can effectively perform the other kinds of seek as long as you are willing to do the arithmetic.

The methods that support seeking are

- long getFilePointer() throws IOException: This returns the current position within the file, in bytes. Subsequent reading and writing will take place starting at this position.

- long length() throws IOException: This returns the length of the file, in bytes.

- void seek(long position) throws IOException: This sets the current position within the file, in bytes. Subsequent reading and writing will take place starting at this position. Files start at position 0.

The code listed below is a subclass of RandomAccessFile that adds two new methods to support seeking from the current position or the end of the file. The code illustrates the use of the methods listed above.

```
1. class GeneralRAF extends RandomAccessFile {
2. public GeneralRAF(File path, String mode) throws IOException {
3.    super(path, mode);
4. }
5.
6.    public GeneralRAF(String path, String mode) throws IOException {
7.       super(path, mode);
8.    }
9.
10.    public void seekFromEnd(long offset) throws IOException {
11.       seek(length() - offset);
12.    }
13.
14.    public void seekFromCurrent(long offset) throws IOException {
15.       seek(getFilePointer() + offset);
16.    }
17. }
```

The whole point of seeking, of course, is to read from or write to a desired position within a file. Files are ordered collections of bytes, and the RandomAccessFile class has several methods that support reading and writing of bytes. However, the bytes in a file often combine to represent richer data formats. For example, two bytes could represent a Unicode character; four bytes could represent a float or an int. All the reading and writing methods advance the current file position.

The more common methods that support byte reading and writing are

- `int read() throws IOException`: This returns the next byte from the file (stored in the low-order 8 bits of an int), or -1 if at end of file.

- `int read(byte dest[]) throws IOException`: This attempts to read enough bytes to fill array dest[]. Returns the number of bytes read, or -1 if the file was at end of file.

- `int read(byte dest[], int offset, int len) throws IOException`: This attempts to read len bytes into array dest[], starting at offset. Returns the number of bytes read, or -1 if the file was at end of file.

- `void write(int b) throws IOException`: This writes the low-order byte of b.

- void write(int b[]) This throws IOException: writes all of byte array b[].

- void write(int b[], int offset, int len) throws IOException: This writes len bytes from byte array b[], starting at offset.

Random-access files support reading and writing of all primitive data types. Each read or write operation advances the current file position by the number of bytes read or written. Table 14.1 presents the various primitive-oriented methods, all of which throw IOException.

TABLE 14.1: Random-access file methods for primitive data types

Data Type	Read Method	Write Method
boolean	boolean readBoolean()	void writeBoolean(boolean b)
byte	byte readByte()	void writeByte(int b)
short	short readShort()	void writeShort(int s)
char	char readChar()	void writeChar(int c)
int	int readInt()	void writeInt(int i)
long	long readLong()	void writeLong(long l)
float	float readFloat()	void writeFloat(float f)
double	double readDouble()	void writeDouble(double d)
unsigned byte	int readUnsignedByte()	None
unsigned short	int readUnsignedShort()	None
line of text	String readLine()	None
UTF string	String readUTF()	void writeUTF(String s)

There are several more random access file methods to support reading and writing of not-quite-primitive data types. These methods deal with unsigned bytes, unsigned shorts, lines of text, and UTF strings, as shown in Table 14.1.

When a random-access file is no longer needed it should be closed:

- void close()throws IOException

The `close()` method releases non-memory system resources associated with the file.

To summarize, random-access files offer the following functionality:

- Seeking to any position within a file
- Reading and writing single or multiple bytes
- Reading and writing groups of bytes, treated as higher-level data types
- Closing

Streams, Readers, and Writers

Java's stream, reader, and writer classes view input and output as ordered sequences of bytes. Of course, dealing strictly with bytes would be tremendously bothersome, because data appears sometimes as bytes, sometimes as ints, sometimes as floats, and so on. You have already seen how the `RandomAccessFile` class allows you to read and write all of Java's primitive data types. The `readInt()` method, for example, reads four bytes from a file, pieces them together, and returns an int. Java's general I/O classes provide a similar structured approach:

- A low-level output stream receives bytes and writes bytes to an output device.
- A high-level *filter* output stream receives general-format data, such as primitives, and writes bytes to a low-level output stream or to another filter output stream.
- A *writer* is similar to a filter output stream but is specialized for writing Java strings in units of Unicode characters.
- A low-level input stream reads bytes from an input device and returns bytes to its caller.
- A high-level *filter* input stream reads bytes from a low-level input stream, or from another filter input stream, and returns general-format data to its caller.
- A *reader* is similar to a filter input stream but is specialized for reading UTF strings in units of Unicode characters.

The stream, reader, and writer classes are not very complicated. The easiest way to review them is to begin with the low-level streams.

Low-Level Streams

Low-level input streams have methods that read input and return the input as bytes. *Low-level output streams* have methods that are passed bytes, and write the bytes as output. The FileInputStream and FileOutputStream classes are excellent examples.

The two most common file input stream constructors are

- FileInputStream(String pathname)

- FileInputStream(File file)

After a file input stream has been constructed, you can call methods to read a single byte, an array of bytes, or a portion of an array of bytes. The functionality is similar to the byte-input methods you have already seen in the RandomAccessFile class:

- int read() throws IOException: This returns the next byte from the file (stored in the low-order 8 bits of an int) or -1 if at end of file.

- int read(byte dest[]) throws IOException: This attempts to read enough bytes to fill array dest[]. Returns the number of bytes read or -1 if the file was at end of file.

- int read(byte dest[], int offset, int len) throws IOException: This attempts to read len bytes into array dest[], starting at offset. Returns the number of bytes read, or -1 if the file was at end of file.

The code fragment below illustrates the use of these methods by reading a single byte into byte b, then enough bytes to fill byte array bytes[], and finally 20 bytes into the first 20 locations of byte array morebytes[].

```
 1. byte b;
 2. byte bytes[] = new byte[100];
 3. byte morebytes[] = new byte[50];
 4. try {
 5.   FileInputStream fis = new FileInputStream("some_file_name");
 6.   b = (byte) fis.read();      // Single byte
 7.   fis.read(bytes);                 // Fill the array
 8.   fis.read(morebytes, 0, 20);    // 1st 20 elements
 9.   fis.close();
10. } catch (IOException e) { }
```

The `FileInputStream` class has a few very useful utility methods:

- `int available() throws IOException`: This returns the number of bytes that can be read without blocking.

- `void close() throws IOException`: This releases non-memory system resources associated with the file. A file input stream should always be closed when no longer needed.

- `long skip(long nbytes) throws IOException`: This attempts to read and discard `nbytes` bytes. Returns the number of bytes actually skipped.

It is not surprising that file output streams are almost identical to file input streams. The commonly used constructors are

- `FileOutputStream(String pathname)`

- `FileOutputStream(File file)`

There are methods to support writing a single byte, an array of bytes, or a subset of an array of bytes:

- `void write(int b) throws IOException`: This writes the low-order byte of b.

- `void write(byte bytes[]) throws IOException`: This writes all members of byte array `bytes[]`.

- `void write(byte bytes[], int offset, int len) throws IOException`: This writes `len` bytes from array `bytes[]`, starting at `offset`.

The `FileOutputStream` class also has a `close()` method, which should always be called when a file output stream is no longer needed.

In addition to the two classes described above, the `java.io` package has a number of other low-level input and output stream classes:

- `InputStream` and `OutputStream`: These are the superclasses of the other low-level stream classes. They can be used for reading and writing network sockets.

- `ByteArrayInputStream` and `ByteArrayOutputStream`: These classes read and write arrays of bytes. Byte arrays are certainly not hardware I/O devices, but the classes are useful when you want to process or create sequences of bytes.

- `PipedInputStream` and `PipedOutputStream`: These classes provide a mechanism for thread communication.

High-Level Filter Streams

It is all very well to read bytes from input devices and write bytes to output devices, if bytes are the unit of information you are interested in. However, more often than not the bytes to be read or written constitute higher-level information such as ints or strings.

Java supports high-level I/O with high-level streams. The most common of these (and the ones covered in this chapter) extend from the abstract superclasses `FilterInputStream` and `FilterOutputStream`. *High-level input streams* do not read from input devices such as files or sockets; rather, they read from other streams. *High-level output streams* do not write to output devices, but to other streams.

A good example of a high-level input stream is the data input stream. There is only one constructor for this class:

- `DataInputStream(InputStream instream)`

The constructor requires you to pass in an input stream. This instance might be a file input stream (because `FileInputStream` extends `InputStream`), an input stream from a socket, or any other kind of input stream. When the instance of `DataInputStream` is called on to deliver data, it will make some number of `read()` calls on `instream`, process the bytes, and return an appropriate value. The commonly used input methods of the `DataInputStream` class are

- `boolean readBoolean() throws IOException`

- `byte readByte() throws IOException`

- `char readChar () throws IOException`

- `double readDouble () throws IOException`

- `float readFloat () throws IOException`

- `int readInt() throws IOException`

- `long readLong() throws IOException`

- `short readShort() throws IOException`

- `String readUTF() throws IOException`

There is, of course, a `close()` method.

> **NOTE** When creating chains of streams, it is recommended that you close all streams when you no longer need them, making sure to close in the opposite order of the order in which the streams were constructed.

The code fragment below illustrates a small input chain:

```
1. try {
2.    // Construct the chain
3.    FileInputStream fis = new FileInputStream("a_file");
4.    DataInputStream dis = new DataInputStream(fis);
5.
6.    // Read
7.    double d = dis.readDouble();
8.    int i = dis.readInt();
9.    String s = dis.readUTF();
10.
11.   // Close the chain
12.   dis.close();          // Close dis first, because it
13.   fis.close();          // Was created last
14. }
15. catch (IOException e) { }
```

Figure 14.2 shows the hierarchy of the input chain.

The code expects that the first eight bytes in the file represent a double, the next four bytes represent an int, and the next who-knows-how-many bytes represent a UTF string. This means that the code that originally created the file must have been writing a double, an int, and a UTF string. The file need not have been created by a Java program, but if it was, the easiest approach would be to use a data output stream.

The `DataOutputStream` class is the mirror image of the `DataInputStream` class. The constructor is

- `DataOutputStream(OutputStream ostream)`

The constructor requires you to pass in an output stream. When you write to the data output stream, it converts the parameters of the write methods to

FIGURE 14.2:

A chain of input
streams

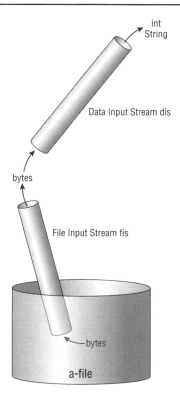

bytes, and writes them to `ostream`. The commonly used input methods of the
`DataOutputStream` class are

- void writeBoolean(boolean b) throws IOException

- void writeByte(int b) throws IOException

- void writeBytes(String s) throws IOException

- void writeChar(int c) throws IOException

- void writeDouble(double d) throws IOException

- void writeFloat(float b) throws IOException

- void writeInt(int i) throws IOException

- void writeLong(long l) throws IOException

- void writeShort(short s) throws IOException

- void writeUTF(String s) throws IOException

All these methods convert their input to bytes in the obvious way, with the exception of writeBytes(), which writes out only the low-order byte of each character in its string. As usual, there is a close() method. Again, chains of output streams should be closed in reverse order from their order of creation.

With the methods listed above in mind, you can now write code that creates a file like the one read in the previous example. In that example, the file contained a double, an int, and a string. The file might be created as follows:

```
1. try {
2.    // Create the chain
3.    FileOutputStream fos = new FileOutputStream("a_file");
4.    DataOutputStream dos = new DataOutputStream(fos);
5.
6.    // Write
7.    dos.writeDouble(123.456);
8.    dos.writeInt(55);
9.    dos.writeUTF("The moving finger writes");
10.
11.   // Close the chain
12.   dos.close();
13.   fos.close();
14. }
15. catch (IOException e) { }
```

In addition to data input streams and output streams, the java.io package offers several other high-level stream classes. The constructors for all high-level input streams require you to pass in the next-lower input stream in the chain; this will be the source of data read by the new object. Similarly, the constructors for the high-level output streams require you to pass in the next-lower output stream in the chain; the new object will write data to this stream. Some of the high-level streams are listed below:

- BufferedInputStream and BufferedOutputStream: These classes have internal buffers so that bytes can be read or written in large blocks, thus minimizing I/O overhead.

- PrintStream: This class can be asked to write text or primitives. Primitives are converted to character representations. The System.out and System.err objects are examples of this class.

- PushbackInputStream: This class allows the most recently read byte to be put back into the stream, as if it had not yet been read. This functionality is very useful for certain kinds of parser.

It is possible to create stream chains of arbitrary length. For example, the code fragment below implements a data input stream that reads from a buffered input stream, which in turn reads from a file input stream:

```
1. FileInputStream fis = new FileInputStream("read_this");
2. BufferedInputStream bis = new BufferedInputStream(fis);
3. DataInputStream dis = new DataInputStream(bis);
```

The chain that this code creates is shown in Figure 14.3.

FIGURE 14.3:

A longer chain

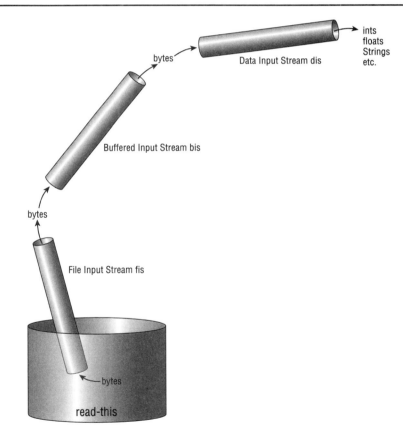

Readers and Writers

Readers and *writers* are like input and output streams: The low-level varieties communicate with I/O devices, while the high-level varieties communicate with low-level varieties. What makes readers and writers different is that they are exclusively oriented to Unicode characters.

A good example of a low-level reader is the `FileReader` class. Its commonly used constructors are

- `FileReader(String pathname)`
- `FileReader(File file)`

Of course, any file passed into these constructors must genuinely contain UTF strings.

The corresponding writer is the `FileWriter` class:

- `FileWriter(String pathname)`
- `FileWriter(File file)`

The other low-level reader and writer classes are

- `CharArrayReader` and `CharArrayWriter`: These classes read and write char arrays.

- `PipedReader` and `PipedWriter`: These classes provide a mechanism for thread communication.

- `StringReader` and `StringWriter`: These classes read and write strings.

The low-level readers all extend from the abstract `Reader` superclass. This class offers the now-familiar trio of `read()` methods for reading a single char, an array of chars, or a subset of an array of chars. Note, however, that the unit of information is now the char, not the byte. The three methods are

- `int read() throws IOException`: This returns the next char (stored in the low-order 16 bits of the int return value), or -1 if at end of input.

- `int read(char dest[]) throws IOException`: This attempts to read enough chars to fill array `dest[]`. Returns the number of chars read, or -1 if at end of input.

- `abstract int read(char dest[], int offset, int len) throws IOException`: This attempts to read `len` chars into array `dest[]`, starting at `offset`. Returns the number of chars read, or -1 if at end of input.

The low-level writers all extend from the abstract `Writer` superclass. This class provides methods that are a bit different from the standard trio of `write()` methods:

- `void write(int ch) throws IOException`: writes the char that appears in the low-order 16 bits of `ch`

- `void write(String str) throws IOException`: writes the string `str`

- `void write(String str, int offset, int len) throws IOException`: writes the substring of `str` that begins at `offset` and has length `len`

- `void write(char chars[]) throws IOException`: writes the char array `chars[]`

- `void write(char chars[], int offset, int len) throws IOException`: writes `len` chars from array `chars[]`, beginning at `offset`

The high-level readers and writers all inherit from the `Reader` or `Writer` superclass, so they also support the methods listed above. As with high-level streams, when you construct a high-level reader or writer you pass in the next-lower object in the chain. The high-level classes are

- `BufferedReader` and `BufferedWriter`: These classes have internal buffers so that data can be read or written in large blocks, thus minimizing I/O overhead. They are similar to buffered input streams and buffered output streams.

- `InputStreamReader` and `OutputStreamWriter`: These classes convert between streams of bytes and sequences of Unicode characters. By default, the classes assume that the streams use the platform's default character encoding; alternative constructors provide any desired encoding.

- `LineNumberReader`: This class views its input as a sequence of lines of text. A method called `readLine()` returns the next line, and the class keeps track of the current line number.

- `PrintWriter`: This class is similar to `PrintStream`, but it writes chars rather than bytes.

- `PushbackReader`: This class is similar to `PushbackInputStream`, but it reads chars rather than bytes.

The code fragment below chains a line number reader onto a file reader. The code prints each line of the file, preceded by a line number.

```
1. try {
2.    FileReader fr = new FileReader("data");
3.    LineNumberReader lnr = new LineNumberReader(fr);
4.    String s;
5.    int lineNum;
6.    while ((s = lnr.readLine()) != null) {
7.      System.out.println(lnr.getLineNumber() + ": " + s);
8.    }
9.    lnr.close();
10.   fr.close();
11. }
12. catch (IOException x) { }
```

Figure 14.4 shows the reader chain implemented by this code.

FIGURE 14.4:

A chain of readers

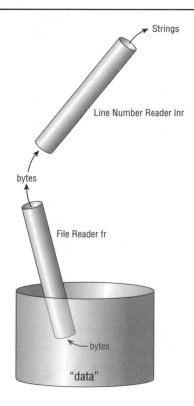

Chapter Summary

This chapter has covered the four big ideas of Java's I/O support:

- Inside a Java Virtual Machine, text is represented by 16-bit Unicode characters and strings. For I/O, text may alternately be represented by UTF strings.

- The File class is useful for navigating the local file system.

- The RandomAccessFile class lets you read and write at arbitrary places within a file.

- Input streams, output streams, readers, and writers provide a mechanism for creating input and output chains. Input and output streams operate on bytes; readers and writers operate on chars.

Test Yourself

1. Which of the statements below are true? (Chose none, some, or all.)

    A. UTF characters are all 8 bits.

    B. UTF characters are all 16 bits.

    C. UTF characters are all 24 bits.

    D. Unicode characters are all 16 bits.

    E. Bytecode characters are all 16 bits.

2. Which of the statements below are true? (Chose none, some, or all.)

    A. When you construct an instance of File, if you do not use the file-naming semantics of the local machine, the constructor will throw an IOException.

    B. When you construct an instance of File, if the corresponding file does not exist on the local file system, one will be created.

    C. When an instance of File is garbage collected, the corresponding file on the local file system is deleted.

3. True or False: The `File` class contains a method that changes the current working directory.

4. True or False: It is possible to use the `File` class to list the contents of the current working directory.

5. How many bytes does the following code write to file `destfile`?

```
1. try {
2.    FileOutputStream fos = new FileOutputStream("destfile");
3.    DataOutputStream dos = new DataOutputStream(fos);
4.    dos.writeInt(3);
5.    dos.writeDouble(0.0001);
6.    dos.close();
7.    fos.close();
8. }
9. catch (IOException e) { }
```

   A. 2

   B. 8

   C. 12

   D. 16

   E. The number of bytes depends on the underlying system.

6. What does the following code fragment print out at line 9?

```
1. FileOutputStream fos = new FileOutputStream("xx");
2. for (byte b=10; b<50; b++)
3.    fos.write(b);
4. fos.close();
5. RandomAccessFile raf = new RandomAccessFile("xx", "r");
6. raf.seek(10);
7. int i = raf.read();
8. raf.close()
9. System.out.println("i = " + i);
```

   A. The output is i = 30.

   B. The output is i = 20.

   C. The output is i = 10.

    D. There is no output because the code throws an exception at line 1.

    E. There is no output because the code throws an exception at line 5.

7. A file is created with the following code:

```
1. FileOutputStream fos = new FileOutputStream("datafile");
2. DataOutputStream dos = new DataOutputStream(fos);
3. for (int i=0; i<500; i++)
4.   dos.writeInt(i);
```

You would like to write code to read back the data from this file. Which solutions listed below will work? (Choose none, some, or all.)

    A. Construct a `FileInputStream`, passing the name of the file. Onto the `FileInputStream`, chain a `DataInputStream`, and call its `readInt()` method.

    B. Construct a `FileReader`, passing the name of the file. Call the file reader's `readInt()` method.

    C. Construct a `PipedInputStream`, passing the name of the file. Call the piped input stream's `readInt()` method.

    D. Construct a RandomAccessFile, passing the name of the file. Call the random access file's `readInt()` method.

    E. Construct a `FileReader`, passing the name of the file. Onto the `FileReader`, chain a `DataInputStream`, and call its `readInt()` method.

8. True or False: Readers have methods that can read and return floats and doubles.

9. You execute the code below in an empty directory. What is the result?

```
1. File f1 = new File("dirname");
2. File f2 = new File(f1, "filename");
```

    A. A new directory called `dirname` is created in the current working directory.

    B. A new directory called `dirname` is created in the current working directory. A new file called `filename` is created in directory `dirname`.

C. A new directory called di rname and a new file called filename are created, both in the current working directory.

D. A new file called filename is created in the current working directory.

E. No directory is created, and no file is created.

10. What is the result of attempting to compile and execute the code fragment below? Assume that the code fragment is part of an application that has write permission in the current working directory. Also assume that before execution, the current working directory does *not* contain a file called datafile.

```
1. try {
2.    RandomAccessFile raf = new RandomAccessFile("datafile") ,"rw";
3.    BufferedOutputStream bos = new BufferedOutputStream(raf);
4.    DataOutputStream dos = new DataOutputStream(bos);
5.    dos.writeDouble(Math.PI);
6.    dos.close();
7.    bos.close();
8.    raf.close();
9. } catch (IOException e) { }
```

A. The code fails to compile.

B. The code compiles, but throws an exception at line 3.

C. The code compiles and executes, but has no effect on the local file system.

D. The code compiles and executes; afterward, the current working directory contains a file called datafile.

APPENDIX

A

Answers

Chapter 1: Language Fundamentals

1. False. The range of negative numbers is greater by 1 than the range of positive numbers.

2. All of the identifiers are valid.

3. B and D are both acceptable. Answer A will compile but will not be called.

4. D is correct. This order must be strictly observed.

5. A and E are true. The array has 25 elements, indexed from 0 through 24. All elements are initialized to zero.

6. D is correct. A holder is constructed on line 6. A reference to that holder is passed into method bump() on line 5. Within the method call, the holder's held variable is bumped from 100 to 101.

7. C is correct. The decrement() method is passed a copy of the argument d; the copy gets decremented, but the original is untouched.

8. A is correct. Garbage collection cannot be forced. Calling System.gc() or Runtime.gc() is not 100 percent reliable, since the garbage-collection thread might defer to a thread of higher priority; thus B and D are incorrect. C is incorrect because the two gc() methods do not take arguments; in fact, if you still have a reference to pass into the method, the object is not yet eligible to be collected. E will make the object eligible for collection the next time the garbage collector runs.

9. D is correct. The range for a 16-bit short is -2^{15} through $2^{15} - 1$. This range is part of the Java specification, regardless of the underlying hardware.

10. D is correct. The range for an 8-bit short is -2^7 through $2^7 - 1$. Table 1.3 lists the ranges for Java's integral primitive data types.

Chapter 2: Operators and Assignments

1. C is correct. The assignment statement is evaluated as if it were

    ```
    x = a + b; a = a + 1; b = b + 1;
    ```

    Therefore the assignment to x is made using the sum of 6 + 7 giving 13. After the addition, the values of a and b are actually incremented, the new values, 7 and 8, are stored in the variables.

2. B and C are correct. In A the use of ! is inappropriate, since x is of int type, not boolean. This is a common mistake among C and C++ programmers, since the expression would be valid in those languages. In B, the comparison is inelegant (being a cumbersome equivalent of if (x <= 3), but valid, since the expression (x > 3) is a boolean type, and the ! operator can properly be applied to it. In C the bitwise inversion operator is applied to an integral type. The bit pattern of 6 looks like 0…0110 where the ellipsis represents 27 0 bits. The resulting bit pattern looks like 1…1001 where the ellipsis represents 27 1 bits.

3. A is correct. In every case, the bit pattern for –1 is "all ones." In A this is shifted five places to the right with the introduction of 0 bits at the most significant positions. The result is 27 1 bits in the less significant positions of the int value. Since the most significant bit is 0, this represents a positive value (actually 134217727). In B the shift value is 32 bits. This will result in no change at all to x, since the shift is actually performed by (32 mod 32) bits, which is 0. So in B the value of x is unchanged at –1. C is actually illegal since the result of x >>> 5 is of type int, and cannot be assigned into the byte variable x without explicit casting. Even if the cast were added, giving byte x = -1; x = (byte)(x >>> 5); the result of the expression x >>> 5 would be calculated like this:

    1. First promote x to an int. This gives a sign-extended result, that is an int –1 with 32 1 bits.

    2. Perform the shift; this behaves the same as in A above, giving 134217727,which is the value of 27 1 bits in the less significant positions.

    3. Casting the result of the expression simply "chops off" the less significant eight bits, since these are all ones, the resulting byte represents –1.

Finally, D performs a signed shift, which propagates 1 bits into the most significant position. So, in this case, the resulting value of x is unchanged at –1.

4.   A, C, and E are all legal. In A the use of += is treated as a shorthand for the expression in C. This attempts to "add" an int to a String which results in conversion of the int to a String—"9" in this case—and the concatenation of the two String objects. So in this case, the value of x after the code is executed is "Hello9".

In B the comparison (x == y) is not legal, since only the + operator performs implicit conversion to a String object. The variable y is an int type and cannot be compared with a reference value. Don't forget that comparison using == tests the values and that for objects, the "value" is the reference value and not the contents.

C is identical to A without the use of the shorthand assignment operator.

D calculates y + x, which is legal in itself, because it produces a String in the same way as did x + y. It then attempts to assign the result, which is "9Hello", into an int variable. Since the result of y + x is a String, this is not permitted.

E is rather different from the others. The important points are the use of the short-circuit operator && and the ternary operator ?:. The left-hand operand of the && operator is always evaluated and in this case the condition (x != null) is false. Because this is false, the right-hand part of the expression (x.length() > 0) need not be evaluated, as the result of the && operator is known to be false. This short-circuit effect neatly avoids executing the method call x.length(), which would fail with a NullPointerException at run time. This false result is then used in the evaluation of the ternary expression. As the boolean value is false, the result of the overall expression is the value to the right of the colon, that is 0.

5.   A and E are correct. Although int and float are not assignment compatible, they can generally be mixed on either side of an operator. Since == is not assignment but is a comparison operator, it simply causes normal promotion, so that the int value 9 is promoted to a float value 9.0 and compared successfully with the other float value 9.0F. For this reason A is true.

The code in B actually fails to compile. This is because of the mismatch between the int and the Integer object. The value of an object is its reference, and no conversions are ever possible between references and numeric types. This applies to any conversion, not just assignment compatibility.

In C, the code compiles successfully, since the comparison is between two object references. However, the test for equality compares the value of the references (the memory address typically) and since the variables x and y refer to two different objects, the test returns false. The code in D behaves exactly the same way.

Comparing E with D might persuade you that E should probably not print "Equal". In fact it does so because of a required optimization. Since String objects are immutable, literal strings are inevitably constant strings, so the compiler re-uses the same String object if it sees the same literal value occur more than once in the source. This means that the variables x and y actually do refer to the same object; so the test (x == y) is true and the "Equal" message is printed. It is particularly important that you do not allow this special behavior to persuade you that the == operator can be used to compare the contents of objects in any general way.

6. A is correct. The effect of the && operator is first to evaluate the left-hand operand. That is the expression (s.length() > 5). Since the length of the StringBuffer object s is actually 5, this test returns false. Using the logical identity false AND X = false, the value of the overall conditional is fully determined, and the && operator therefore skips evaluation of the right-hand operand. As a result, the value in the StringBuffer object is still simply "Hello" when it is printed out.

If the test on the left-hand side of && had returned true, as would have occurred had the StringBuffer contained a longer text segment, then the right-hand side would have been evaluated. Although it might look a little strange, that expression, (s.append(" there").equals("False")), is valid and returns a boolean. In fact, the value of the expression is guaranteed to be false, since it is clearly impossible for any StringBuffer to contain exactly "False" when it has just had the String " there" appended to it. This is irrelevant however—the essence of this expression is that, if it is evaluated, it has the side effect of changing the original StringBuffer by appending the text " there".

7. B is correct. The Exclusive-OR operator ^ works on the pairs of bits in equivalent positions in the two operands. In this example this produces:

```
      00001010
      00001111
XOR   --------
      00000101
```

Notice that the only 1 bits in the answer are in those columns where exactly one of the operands has a 1 bit. If neither, or both, of the operands has a 1, then a 0 bit results.

The value 00000101 binary corresponds to 5 decimal.

It is worth remembering that, although this example has been shown as a byte calculation, the actual working is done using int (32-bit) values. This is why the explicit cast is required before the result is assigned back into the variable b in line 5.

8. C is correct. In this code the optional result values for the ternary operator, 99.99 (a double) and 9 (an int), are of different types. The result type of a ternary operator must be fully determined at compile time, and in this case the type chosen, using the rules of promotion for binary operands, is double. Because the result is a double, the output value is printed in a floating point format.

The choice of which of the two values to output is made on the basis of the boolean value that precedes the ?. Since x is 4, the test (x > 4) is false. This causes the overall expression to take the second of the possible values, which is 9 rather than 99.99. Because the result type is promoted to a double, the output value is actually written as 9.0, rather than the more obvious 9.

If the two possible argument types had been entirely incompatible, for example (x > 4) ? "Hello" : 9, then the compiler would have issued an error at that line.

9. B shows the correct output. In this case, the calculation is relatively straightforward since only positive integers are involved. Dividing 10 by 3 gives 3 remainder 1, and this 1 forms the result of the modulo expression. Another

way to think of this calculation is $10 - 3 = 7, 7 - 3 = 4, 4 - 3 = 1, 1$ is less than 3 therefore the result is 1. The second approach is actually more general, since it handles floating-point calculations, too. Don't forget that for negative numbers, you should ignore the signs during the calculation part, and simply attach the sign of the left-hand operand to the result.

10. A is correct. The assignment operators of the form op= only evaluate the left-hand expression once. So the effect of decrementing x, in --x, occurs only once, resulting in a value of 0 and not –1. Therefore no out-of-bounds array accesses are attempted. The array element that is affected by this operation is "Fred", since the decrement occurs before the += operation is performed. Although String objects themselves are immutable, the references that are the array elements are not. It is entirely possible to cause the value name[0] to be modified to refer to a newly constructed String, which happens to be "Fred."

Chapter 3: Modifiers

1. A, D, and E are illegal. A is illegal because "friendly" is not a keyword. B is a legal transient declaration. C is strange but legal. D is illegal because only methods and classes may be abstract. E is illegal because abstract and final are contradictory.

2. B is true: A final class may not have any abstract methods. Any class with abstract methods must itself be abstract, and a class may not be both abstract and final. Statement A says that an abstract class may not have final methods, but there is nothing wrong with this. The abstract class will eventually be subclassed, and the subclass must avoid overriding the parent's final methods. Any other methods can be freely overridden.

3. A is the correct answer. The code will not compile because on line 1 class Aaa is declared final and may not be subclassed. Lines 10 and 15 are fine. The instance variable finalref is final, so it may not be modified; it can only reference the object created on line 10. However, the data within that object is not final, so there is nothing wrong with line 15.

4. E is correct. A, B, and C don't mean anything, because only variables may be transient, not methods or classes. D is false because transient variables may never be static. E is a good one-sentence definition of transient.

5. E is correct. Multiple static initializers (lines 5 and 12) are legal. All static initializer code is executed at class-load time, so before `main()` is ever run, the value of x is initialized to 10 (line 3), then bumped to 15 (line 5), then divided by 5 (line 12).

6. E is correct. The program compiles fine; the "static reference to a private variable" stuff in answers A and B is nonsense. The static variable x gets incremented four times, on lines 8, 10, 12, and 13.

7. On line 3, the method may be declared private. The method access of the subclass version (line 8) is friendly, and only a private or friendly method may be overridden to be friendly. The basic principle is that a method may not be overridden to be more private. (See Figure 3.2.) On line 8 (assuming line 3 is left alone), the superclass version is friendly, so the subclass version may stand as it is (and be friendly), or it may be declared protected or public.

8. The correct answer is D (`transient`). The other modifiers control access from other objects within the Java Virtual Machine. Answer E (`private transient`) also works but is not minimal.

9. C is correct: Static methods may not be overridden to be non-static. B is incorrect because it states the case backwards: Methods actually may be overridden to be more *private*, not more public. Answers A, D, and E make no sense.

10. A is correct. There is nothing wrong with `Nightingale`. The static `referenceCount` is bumped twice: once on line 4 of `Nightingale`, and once on line 5 of `Bird`. (The no-argument constructor of the superclass is always implicitly called at the beginning of a class' constructor, unless a different superclass constructor is requested. This has nothing to do with the topic of this chapter, but is covered in Chapter 6, *Objects and Classes*.) Since `referenceCount` is bumped twice and not just once, answer B is wrong. C says that statics cannot be overridden, but no static method is being overridden on line 4; all that is happening is an incre-ment of an inherited static variable. D is wrong, since `protected` is precisely the access modifier we want `Bird.fly()` to have: We are calling `Bird.fly()`

from a subclass in a different package. Answer E is ridiculous, but it uses credible terminology.

Chapter 4: Converting and Casting

1. D is correct. C is wrong because objects do not take part in arithmetic operations. E is wrong because only casting of object references potentially requires a runtime check.

2. Line 6 (b = s) will not compile because converting a short to a byte is a narrowing conversion, which requires an explicit cast. The other assignments in the code are widening conversions.

3. Surprisingly, the code will fail to compile at line 3. The two operands, which are originally bytes, are converted to ints before the multiplication. The result of the multiplication is an int, which cannot be assigned to byte b.

4. E is correct. The result of the calculation on line 2 is an int (because all arithmetic results are ints or wider). An int can be assigned to an int, long, float, or double.

5. D is correct. At line 8, the char argument ch is widened to type int (a method-call conversion), and passed to the int version of method crunch().

6. D is correct.

7. Line 7 will not compile. Changing an Object to a Float is going "down" the inheritance hierarchy tree, so an explicit cast is required.

8. D is correct. The code will compile and run; the cast in line 6 is required, because changing an Animal to a Dog is going "down" the tree.

9. E is correct. The cast in line 7 is required. Answer D is a preposterous statement expressed in a tone of authority.

10. B is correct. The conversion in line 6 is fine (class to interface), but the conversion in line 7 (interface to class) is not allowed. A cast in line 7 will fix the problem.

Chapter 5: Flow Control and Exceptions

1. B, C, D, and F are correct. The loops iterate i from 0 to 1 and j from 0 to 2. However, the inner loop executes a `continue` statement whenever the values of i and j are the same. Since the output is generated inside the inner loop, after the `continue` statement, this means that no output is generated when the values are the same. Therefore, the outputs suggested by answers A and E are skipped.

2. D is correct. The values of i appear set to take the values 0 to 1 and for each of these values, j takes values 0, 1 and 2. However, whenever i and j have the same value, the outer loop is continued before the output is generated. Since the outer loop is the target of the `continue` statement, the whole of the inner loop is abandoned. The only line to be output is that shown in D as the starting condition, i = 0 and j = 0 immediately causes i to take on the value 1, and as soon as both i and j are set to 1 after the first inner iteration, the `continue` again serves to terminate the remaining values.

3. C is correct. In A the variable declaration for i is illegal. This type of declaration is permitted only in the first part of a `for()` loop. The absence of initialization should also be a clue here. In B the loop control expression—the variable i in this case—is of type `int`. A `boolean` expression is required. C is valid. Despite the complexity of declaring one value inside the `for()` construction, and one outside (along with the use of the comma operator in the end part) this is entirely legitimate. D would have been correct, except that the label has been omitted from line 2 which should have read `loop: do {`.

4. D is correct. The first test at line 2 fails, which immediately causes control to skip to line 10, bypassing both the possible tests that might result in the output of `message one` or `message two`. So, even though the test at line 3 would be `true`, it is never made; A is not correct. At line 10, the test is again `false`, so the message at line 11 is skipped, but `message four`, at line 14, is output.

5. D is correct. A is incorrect because the code is legal despite the expression at line 5. This is because the expression itself is a constant. B is incorrect because it states that the `switch()` part can take a `long` argument. Only `byte`, `short`, `char`, and `int` are acceptable. The output results from the value 2 like this: First, the option `case 2:` is selected, which outputs `value is two`. However, there is no `break` statement between lines 4 and 5, so the execution falls into the next case and outputs `value is three` from line 6. The `default:` part of a `switch()` is only executed when no other options have been selected, or if there is no `break` preceding it. In this case, neither of these situations holds true, so the output consists only of the two messages listed in D.

6. B, E, and F are correct. The exception causes a jump out of the `try` block, so the message `Success` from line 4 is not printed. The first applicable catch is at line 6, which is an exact match for the thrown exception. This results in the message at line 7 being printed, so B is one of the required answers. Only one `catch` block is ever executed, so control passes to the `finally` block which results in the message at line 16 being output; so E is part of the correct answer. Since the exception was caught, it is considered to have been handled and execution continues after the `finally` block. This results in the output of the message at line 18, so F is also part of the correct answer.

7. A, E, and F are correct. With no exceptions the `try` block executes to completion, so the message `Success` from line 4 is printed and A is part of the correct answer. No `catch` is executed, so B, C, and D are incorrect. Control then passes to the `finally` block, which results in the message at line 16 being output, so E is part of the correct answer. Because no exception was thrown, execution continues after the `finally` block, resulting in the output of the message at line 18, so F is also part of the correct answer.

8. E is correct. The thrown error prevents completion of the `try` block, so the message `Success` from line 4 is not printed. No catch is appropriate, so B, C, and D are incorrect. Control then passes to the `finally` block, which results in the message at line 16 being output; so option E is part of the correct answer. Because the error was not caught, execution exits the method and the error is rethrown in the caller of this method, so F is not part of the correct answer.

9. B is correct. A would give misleading line number information in the stack trace of the exception, reporting that the exception arose at line 1, which is where the exception object was created. C is illegal since you must throw an object that is a subclass of java.lang.Throwable, and you cannot throw a class, only an object. D is also illegal, as it attempts to throw a String which is not a subclass of java.lang.Throwable. E is entirely legal, but it is not as good as B since E doesn't take the effort to clarify the nature of the problem by providing a string of explanation.

10. B and D are correct. A does not handle the exceptions, so the method aMethod might throw any of the exceptions that dodgy() might throw. However the exceptions are not declared with a throws construction. In B, declaring "throws IOException" is sufficient, because java.lang.RuntimeException is not a checked exception and because IOException is a superclass of MalformedURLException, it is unnecessary to mention the MalformedURLException explicitly (although it might make better "self-documentation" to do so). C is unacceptable because its throws declaration fails to mention the checked exceptions—it is not an error to declare the runtime exception, although it is strictly redundant. D is also acceptable, since the catch block handles IOException, which include MalformedURLException. RuntimeException will still be thrown by the method aMethod() if it is thrown by dodgy(), but as RuntimeException is not a checked exception, this is not an error. E is not acceptable, since the overriding method in anotherClass is declared as throwing IOException, while the overridden method in aClass was only declared as throwing MalformedURLException. It would have been correct for the base class to declare that it throws IOException and then the derived class to throw MalformedURLException, but as it is, the overriding method is attempting to throw exceptions not declared for the original method. The fact that the only exception that actually can arise is the MalformedURLException is not enough to rescue this, because the compiler only checks the declarations, not the semantics of the code.

Chapter 6: Objects and Classes

1. A, C, and E are correct. In each of these answers, the argument list differs from the original, so the method is an overload. Overloaded methods are effectively independent, and there are no constraints on the accessibility, return type, or exceptions that may be thrown. B would be a legal overriding method, except that it cannot be defined in the same class as the original method; rather, it must be declared in a subclass. D is also an override, since the *types* of its arguments are the same: Changing the parameter names is not sufficient to count as overloading.

2. B and D are correct. A is illegal because it is less accessible than the original method; the fact that it throws no exceptions is perfectly acceptable. B is legal because it overloads the method of the parent class, and as such it is not constrained by any rules governing its return value, accessibility, or argument list. The exception thrown by C is sufficient to make that method illegal. D is legal because the accessibility and return type are identical, and the method is an override because the types of the arguments are identical—remember that the names of the arguments are irrelevant. The absence of an exception list in D is not a problem: An overriding method may legitimately throw fewer exceptions than its original, but it may not throw more.

3. E and F are correct. The Cat class is a subclass of the Pet class, and as such should extend Pet, rather than containing an instance of Pet. B and C should be members of the Pet class and as such are inherited into the Cat class; therefore, they should not be declared in the Cat class. D would declare a reference to an instance of the Cat class, which is not generally appropriate inside the Cat class itself (unless, perhaps, you were asked to give the Cat a member that refers to its mother). Finally, the neutered flag and markings descriptions, E and F, are the items called for by the specification; these are correct items.

4. Answer: `public class Cat extends Pet`. The class should be `public` since it is to be used freely throughout the application. The statement "A cat is a pet" tells us that the Cat class should subclass Pet. The other words offered are required for the body of the definitions of either Cat or Pet—for use as member variables—but are not part of the opening declaration.

5. C is correct. The first message is produced by the Base class when b1 .method(5) is called and is therefore Value is 5. Despite variable b2 being declared as being of the Base class, the behavior that results when method() is invoked upon it is the behavior associated with class of the actual object, not with the type of the variable. Since the object is of class Sub, not of class Base, the second message is generated by line 3 of class Sub: This value is 6.

6. B and C are correct. Since the class has explicit constructors defined, the default constructor is suppressed, so A is not possible. B and C have argument lists that match the constructors defined at lines 2 and 4 respectively, and so are correct constructions. D has three integer arguments, but there are no constructors that take three arguments of any kind in the Test class, so D is incorrect. Finally, E is a syntax used for construction of inner classes and is therefore wrong.

7. A and C are correct. In the constructor at lines 2 and 3, there is no explicit call to either this() or super(), which means that the compiler will generate a call to the zero argument superclass constructor, as in A. The explicit call to super() at line 5 requires that the Base class must have a constructor as in C. This has two consequences. First, C must be one of the required constructors and therefore one of the answers. Second, the Base class must have at least that constructor defined explicitly, so the default constructor is not generated, but must be added explicitly. Therefore the constructor of A is also required and must be a correct answer. At no point in the Test class is there a call to either a superclass constructor with one or three arguments, so B and D need not explicitly exist.

8. A, B, and E are correct. Inner classes may be defined with any accessibility, so private is entirely acceptable and A is correct. Similarly, the static modifier is permitted on an inner class, which causes it not to be associated with any particular instance of the outer class. This means that B is also correct. Inner classes defined in methods may be anonymous—and indeed often are—but this is not required, so C is wrong. D is wrong because it is not possible for an inner class defined in a method to access the local variables of the method, except for those variables that are marked as final. Constructing an instance of a static inner class does not need an instance

of the enclosing object, but all non-static inner classes do require such a reference, and that reference must be available to the new operation. The reference to the enclosing object is commonly implied as this, which is why it is commonly not explicit. These points make E true.

9. A, B, C, and E are correct. Since Inner is not a static inner class, it has a reference to an enclosing object, and all the variables of that object are accessible. Therefore A and B are correct, despite the fact that b is marked private. Variables in the enclosing method are only accessible if those variables are marked final, so the method argument c is correct, but the variable d is not. Finally, the parameter e is of course accessible, since it is a parameter to the method containing line 8 itself.

10. A is correct. Construction of a normal (that is, a named and non-static) inner class requires an instance of the enclosing class. Often this enclosing instance is provided via the implied this reference, but an explicit reference may be used in front of the new operator, as shown in A.

Anonymous inner classes can only be instantiated at the same point they are declared, like this:

```
return new ActionListener() {
   public void actionPerformed(ActionEvent e); { }
};
```

Hence B is illegal—it actually attempts to instantiate the interface ActionListener as if that interface were itself an inner class inside Outer.

C is illegal since Inner is a non-static inner class, and so it requires a reference to an enclosing instance when it is constructed. The form shown suggests the implied this reference, but since the method is static, there is no this reference and the construction is illegal.

D is illegal since it attempts to use arguments to the constructor of an anonymous inner class that implements an interface. The clue is in the attempt to define a constructor at line 3. This would be a constructor for the interface MyInterface not for the inner class—this is wrong on two counts. First, interfaces do not define constructors, and second we need a constructor for our anonymous class, not for the interface.

Chapter 7: Threads

1. A is correct. The Runnable interface defines a run() method with void return type and no parameters. The method given in the problem has a String parameter, so the compiler will complain that class Greebo does not define void run() from interface Runnable. B is wrong, because you can definitely pass a parameter to a thread's constructor; the parameter becomes the thread's target. C, D, and E are nonsense.

2. C is correct. A is true on a preemptive platform, B is true on a time-sliced platform. The moral is that such code should be avoided, since it gives such different results on different platforms.

3. False. The yield() method is static and always causes the current thread to yield. In this case, ironically, it is the first thread that will yield.

4. True. The second thread will remain in the Suspended state until it receives a resume() call.

5. D is true. The thread will sleep for 100 milliseconds (more or less, given the resolution of the JVM being used). Then the thread will enter the Ready state; it will not actually run until the scheduler permits it to run.

6. E is correct. When you call notify() on a monitor, you have no control over which waiting thread gets notified.

7. D is correct. Although wait() and notify() must be called from synchronized code, there is no corresponding rule for suspend() and resume(). The code will run until line 4, at which point the executing thread will become suspended. Since it is suspended, it will never be able to execute line 5. A suspended thread can never resume itself, since to do so it has to be running; a suspended thread can only be resumed by a different thread.

8. This time E is correct. The only difference between this problem and the previous one is that line 4 yields rather than suspending. The executing thread moves into the Ready state; soon afterward, the scheduler moves it back into the Running state. It then executes line 5, making a resume() call to itself. This call has no effect, because the thread was not suspended.

9. Yes. The call to xxx() occurs before the thread is registered with the thread scheduler, so the question has nothing to do with threads.

10. False. A monitor is an instance of any class that has synchronized code.

Chapter 8: The *java.lang* Package

1. None of the answers is correct. Strings are immutable.

2. C is correct. Since s1 and s2 are references to two different objects, the == test fails. However, the strings contained within the two string objects are identical, so the equals() test passes.

3. D is correct. The java.lang.Math class is final, so it cannot be subclassed.

4. A is correct. The constructor for the Math class is private, so it cannot be called. The Math class methods are static, so it is never necessary to construct an instance. The import at line 1 is not required, since all classes of the java.lang package are automatically imported.

5. E is correct. A is wrong because line 1 is a perfectly acceptable way to create a string, and is actually more efficient than explicitly calling the constructor. B is wrong because the argument to the equals() method is of type Object; thus any object reference or array variable may be passed. The calls on lines 3 and 5 return false without throwing exceptions.

6. The code compiles, and line 2 executes.

7. True. The StringBuffer class is mutable. After execution of line 2, sbuf refers to the same object, although the object has been modified.

8. True. See answer 7 above.

9. True. Line 1 constructs a new instance of String and stores it in the string pool. In line 2, ≤xyz≤ is already represented in the pool, so no new instance is constructed.

10. False. Line 1 constructs a new instance of String and stores it in the string pool. Line 2 explicitly constructs another instance.

Chapter 9: Components

1. E is correct. Since the button does not specify a background, it gets the same background as the applet: blue. The button's foreground color and font are explicitly set to white and 64-point bold serif, so these settings take effect rather than the applet's values.

2. B and E are correct. Since you have not explicitly set a font for the check box, it uses the font of its immediate container.

3. C, D, and E are correct. The panel does not explicitly get its font set, so it uses the applet's font. The check box does not explicitly get its font set, so it uses the panel's font, which is the applet's font.

4. B. The number of rows comes first, then the number of columns.

5. C, D, and E are correct. The first parameter (10) specifies the number of *visible* items. The second parameter (`false`) specifies whether multiple selection is supported. A list always acquires a vertical scroll bar if the number of items exceeds the number of visible items.

6. C is correct. If a text field is too narrow to display its contents, you need to scroll using the arrow keys.

7. A and C are correct. A menu may contain menu items, check-box menu items (*not* check boxes!), separators, and (sub)menus.

8. B is correct. Only a frame may contain a menu bar.

9. E is correct. A newly constructed frame has zero-by-zero size and is not visible. You have to call both `setSize()` (or `setBounds()`) and `setVisible()`.

10. False. The `java.awt.CheckboxGroup` class is not a kind of component.

Chapter 10: Layout Managers

1. E is correct. Java makes no guarantees about component size from platform to platform, because it uses each platform's own fonts and component appearance. The whole point of layout managers is that you don't have to worry about platform-to-platform differences in component appearance.

2. E is correct. A is wrong because the constructor is called from within its own class; the application would compile even if the constructor were private. B is wrong because the frame has a default layout manager, which is an instance of `BorderLayout`. If you `add()` a component to a container that uses a Border layout manager, and you don't specify a region as a second parameter, then the component is added at Center, just as if you had specified `BorderLayout.CENTER` as a second parameter. (Note, however, that explicitly providing the parameter is much better programming style than relying on default behavior.) C is wrong because the button does appear; it takes up the entire frame, as described in E. Answer D would be true if frames used Flow layout managers by default.

3. C is correct. A is wrong because *any* container's default layout manager can be replaced; that is the only way to get things done if the default manager isn't what you want. B is wrong because there is no restriction against having a single row or a single column. What really happens is this: The frame contains two panels—p1 occupies the entire left half of the frame and p2 occupies the entire right half (because the frame uses a grid with one row and two columns). Each panel uses a Flow layout manager, so within the panels every component gets to be its preferred size. Thus the two buttons are just big enough to encompass their labels. Panel p1 uses a right-aligning Flow layout manager, so its single component is aligned to the far right of that panel, just left of the vertical center line. Panel p2 uses a left-aligning Flow layout manager, so its single component is aligned to the far left of that panel, just right of the vertical center line. The two buttons end up as described in answer C. D and E are incorrect because the buttons get to be their preferred sizes.

4. B is correct. The frame is laid out in a grid with three rows and one column. Thus each of the three panels p1, p2, and p3 is as wide as the frame and ⅓ as high. The "Alpha" button goes at North of the top panel, so it is as wide as

the panel itself (thus as wide as the frame), and it gets to be its preferred height. The "Beta" button goes at Center of the middle panel, so it occupies the entire panel (since there is nothing else in the panel). The "Gamma" button goes at South of the bottom panel, so it is as wide as the panel itself (thus as wide as the frame), and it gets to be its preferred height.

5. D is correct. A is wrong because every frame gets a default Border layout manager. Since the button is placed at South, it is always as wide as the frame, and it gets resized when the frame gets resized. Its height is always its preferred height. Note that of the three plausible answers (C, D, and E), the correct answer is the simplest. The point of this question is that when a container gets resized, its layout manager lays out all the components again.

6. A is correct. The only lines of code that matter are 9, 10, and 16. The button is added to a panel that uses a Flow layout manager. Therefore the button gets to be its preferred size.

7. With a Border layout manager, any component at North (or South) is as wide as the container and as high as its own preferred height. A vertical scroll bar needs plenty of play in the vertical direction, but it does not need to be very wide. The problem produces a scroll bar that is both too wide and too short to be useful, so the correct answer is C. With a Border layout manager, vertical scroll bars are most useful at East and West; horizontal scroll bars are most useful at North and South.

8. The default layout manager for panels and applets is Flow. The default for frames is Border.

9. True. The Grid layout manager ignores the preferred size of its components and makes all components the same size. If the frame contained any panels, then the components within those panels would be likely to be smaller than those directly contained by the panel. However, the question explicitly states that the frame does not contain any panels.

10. False. The default layout manager is Border. Components at North and South will be the same width; components at East and West will be the same height. No other generalizations are possible.

11. False. Almost, but not quite. The component at Center gets all the space that is left over, after the components at North, South, *East and West* have been considered.

12. False. The question describes a hodgepodge of layout manager attributes.

Chapter 11: Events

1. False. The two event models are incompatible, and they should not appear in the same program.

2. A, B and E are correct. Since the class is public, it must reside in a file whose name corresponds to the class name. If the call to `super(nrows, ncols)` is omitted, the no-arguments constructor for `TextArea` will be invoked, and the desired number of rows and columns will be ignored. C and D are attempts to create confusion by introducing concepts from the 1.0 model; in the delegation model, all event handlers have `void` return type. E is correct because if the suggested line is omitted, text listeners will be ignored.

3. C and D are correct. The code will compile and execute cleanly. However, without a call to `super.processWindowEvent(we)`, the component will fail to notify its window listeners.

4. C is correct. Lines 2 and 3 construct instances of the listener classes, and store references to those instances in variables with interface types; such assignment is perfectly legal. The implication of answer B is that adding a second listener might create a problem; however, the delegation model supports multiple listeners. The code compiles cleanly and runs without throwing an exception.

5. E is correct. This problem is just like the previous one, with the addition of a perfectly legal `removeFocusListener()` call.

6. A and C are correct. Since the class extends `MouseAdapter`, and `MouseAdapter` implements the `MouseListener` interface, the `MyListener` class implicitly implements the interface as well; it does no harm to declare the implementation explicitly. The class can serve as a mouse

listener. In response to mouse events other than mouse entered, the listener executes the handler methods that it inherits from its superclass; these methods do nothing.

7. A is correct. Multiple interface implementation is legal in Java. The class must implement all methods of both interfaces, and this is indeed the case. Since the class implements the ActionListener interface, it is a legal action listener; since it also implements the ItemListener interface, it is also a legal item listener.

8. A is correct. This class attempts multiple class inheritance, which is illegal in Java.

9. False. A component, whether or not it has explicitly called enableEvents(), can have an unlimited number of listeners, and those listeners may be adapter subclasses.

10. E is correct. There are no guarantees about the order of invocation of event listeners.

Chapter 12: Painting

1. A is correct. The 13 pre-defined colors are static variables in class Color, so you access them via the class name as you would any other static variable. The name of the color-setting method is setColor(), not setCurrentColor().

2. D (cyan) is correct. This question tests your knowledge of static variables as well as the Color class. The Color class has 13 final static variables, named red, green, yellow, and so on. These variables happen to be of type Color. So Color.red is the name of an instance of Color. Recall from Chapter 3 (*Modifiers*) that there are two ways to access a static variable: via the class name, which is the preferred way, or via a reference to any instance of the class. Thus one (non-preferred) way to access the green static variable is via Color.red, because Color.red is a reference to an instance. Thus Color.red.green is a legal way to refer to the green static variable. Similarly, the preferred way to refer to the yellow static variable is Color.yellow, but it is legal (although very strange) to reference it as Color.red.green.yellow,

because `Color.red.green` is a reference to an instance. And so on. The answer would still be cyan if the color were set to `Color.red.white.red` `.black.cyan.magenta.blue.pink.orange.cyan`.

3. B is correct (a black vertical line that is 40 pixels long, and a red square with sides of 150 pixels). The `setColor()` method affects only *subsequently drawn* graphics; it does not affect *previously drawn* graphics. Thus the line is black and the square is red. The arguments to `setLine()` are coordinates of end-points, so the line goes from (10, 10) to (10, 50) and its length is 40 pixels. The arguments to `drawRect()` are x position, y position, width, and height, so the square's side is 150 pixels.

    Some readers may feel that a different answer is appropriate: "None of the above, because you never said that g was an instance of `Graphics`." This is legitimate; the real issue is what to do when you have this reaction during the Certification Exam. Always bear in mind that the exam questions are about Java, not about rhetoric. The exam tests your knowledge of Java, not your ability to see through tricky phrasing.

4. A is correct. The `fillArc()` method draws pie pieces, not chords.

5. B, D, and E are correct. A polyline is never filled or closed; it is just an open run of line segments. A polygon may be filled (the `fillPolygon()` method) or not filled (the `drawPolygon()` method).

6. False. When there is damage to be repaired, the GUI thread passes to `paint()` a graphics context whose clip region is already set to the damaged region. Java was built this way to make sure that programmers never have to determine damaged clip regions. In fact, programmers never have to do anything at all about exposure damage, provided all drawing is done in `paint()` or in methods called by `paint()`.

7. D is correct, and is a standard technique whenever you don't want `update()` to wipe the screen before calling `paint()`. All the diagonal cyan lines will remain on the screen; the effect will be like drawing with a calligraphy pen. Answers A and B (on line 4, replace `repaint()` with `paint()` or `repaint()`) will not compile, because both `paint()` and `repaint()` require a `Graphics` as an input. Answer C is serious trouble: `super.update(g)` will clear the screen and call `paint(g)`, which will call `super.update(g)`, and so on forever.

8. D is correct. The signature for the Font constructor is Font(String fontname, int style, int size). The font name can be one of "Serif", "SansSerif", or "Monospaced". The style should be one of Font.PLAIN, Font.BOLD, or Font.ITALIC.

9. B is correct. The y-coordinate parameter passed into drawString() is the vertical position of the baseline of the text. Since the baseline is at 0 (that is, the top of the component) only descenders will be visible. The string "question #9" contains one descender, so only a single descending squiggle from the *q* will be seen.

10. D is correct. The signature for drawOval() is drawOval(int x, int y, int width, int height), where x and y define the upper-left corner of the oval's bounding box, and width and height define the bounding box's size. The question points out the common misconception that x and y define the center of the oval.

Chapter 13: Applets and HTML

1. There is a problem in line 1. The value of CODE is case-sensitive, so capitalizing the first letter of the .class extension is not valid. The browser will ignore the entire applet tag.

2. False. If the value is an URL, then the class file could even reside on a different machine.

3. False. A String variable can be assigned a value of null.

4. False. An ARCHIVE tag may specify a comma-separated list of JAR files.

5. E is correct. The call to getParameter() ignores the case of its argument and returns "Secondo", which is the exact value from the HTML page, with capitalization intact. The call to toUpperCase() converts to upper case.

6. B is correct. The call to getParameter() ignores the case of its argument, and returns "3a6", which is the exact value from the HTML page, with capitalization intact. The parseInt() call throws a number-format exception,

so the assignment to i on line 5 never happens. Thus i retains its original value of 100.

7. False. The class file might reside in big.jar, or it might reside in the same directory as the HTML file.

8. Yes. The value of CODEBASE may be an URL.

9. The value is null. The getParameter() call is looking for a parameter named "pearl", and no such parameter is defined in the HTML code. The only parameter defined in the HTML is "gem".

10. D is correct. Since the parameter aa is not defined, null is passed into the parseInt() call at line 5, resulting in a null-pointer exception. The null-pointer exception handler assigns a value of 300 to i.

Chapter 14: Input and Output

1. Only D is correct. UTF characters are as big as they need to be. Unicode characters are all 16 bits. There is no such thing as a Bytecode character; bytecode is the format generated by the Java compiler.

2. All three statements are false. Construction and garbage collection of a File have no effect on the local file system.

3. False. The File class does not provide a way to change the current working directory.

4. True. The code below shows how this is done:

```
1. File f = new File(".");
2. String contents[] = f.list();
```

5. C is correct. The writeInt() call writes out an int, which is 4 bytes long; the writeDouble() call writes out a double, which is 8 bytes long, for a total of 12 bytes.

6. B is correct. All the code is perfectly legal, so no exceptions are thrown. The first byte in the file is 10, the next byte is 11, the next is 12, and so on. The byte at file position 10 is 20, so the output is i = 20.

7. A and D are correct. Solution A chains a data input stream onto a file input stream. Solution D simply uses the RandomAccessFile class. B fails because the FileReader class has no readInt() method; readers and writers only handle text. Solution C fails because the PipedInputStream class has nothing to do with file I/O. (Piped input and output streams are used in inter-thread communication.) Solution E fails because you cannot chain a data input stream onto a file reader. Readers read chars, and input streams handle bytes.

8. False. Readers and writers only deal with character I/O.

9. E is correct. Constructing an instance of the File class has no effect on the local file system.

10. A is correct. Compilation fails at line 3, because there is no constructor for BufferedOutputStream that takes a RandomAccessFile object as a parameter. You can be sure of this even if you are not familiar with buffered output streams, because random-access files are completely incompatible with the stream/reader/writer model.

APPENDIX

B

The 1.1.3 APIs

T his appendix lists the APIs of all the classes and interfaces of the Java Developer's Kit 1.1.3. This chapter is intended as a reference, not as instructional material, so data and method signatures are given without additional textual explanation. (Sun's online API web pages are freely distrubuted, and the explanations go into decent depth. To repeat that information here would require several hundred additional pages.)

The packages are presented in alphabetical order. Within each package, the classes and interfaces are presented in alphabetical order. Within each class and interface, the public data, public constructors, and public methods are presented in alphabetical order. In the data section, static variables appear first, followed by instance variables. In the methods section, static methods appear first, followed by non-static methods. Non-public data and methods are omitted, again in the spirit of creating a useful reference rather than a complete manual that would require hundreds more pages.

NOTE These APIs were generated by software that read and parsed the source code for the JDK 1.1.3. (The software is available for a licensing fee; please send email to authorph@sgsware.com for more details.) Everything from here down comes directly from the source.

The *java.applet* Package

The *Applet* Class

```
public Class Applet extends Panel
```

Methods

```
public void destroy();
public AppletContext getAppletContext();
public String getAppletInfo();
public AudioClip getAudioClip(URL url);
public AudioClip getAudioClip(URL url, String name);
public URL getCodeBase();
public URL getDocumentBase();
```

```
public Image getImage(URL url);
public Image getImage(URL url, String name);
public Locale getLocale();
public String getParameter(String name);
public String[][] getParameterInfo();
public void init();
public boolean isActive();
public void play(URL url);
public void play(URL url, String name);
public void resize(Dimension d);
public void resize(int width, int height);
public final void setStub(AppletStub stub);
public void showStatus(String msg);
public void start();
public void stop();
```

The *AppletContext* Interface

```
public Interface AppletContext
```

Methods

```
Applet getApplet(String name);
Enumeration getApplets();
AudioClip getAudioClip(URL url);
Image getImage(URL url);
void showDocument(URL url);
public void showDocument(URL url, String target);
void showStatus(String status);
```

The *AppletStub* Interface

```
public Interface AppletStub
```

Methods

```
void appletResize(int width, int height);
AppletContext getAppletContext();
URL getCodeBase();
URL getDocumentBase();
String getParameter(String name);
boolean isActive();
```

The *AudioClip* Interface

```
public Interface AudioClip
```

Methods

```
void loop();
void play();
void stop();
```

The *java.awt* Package

The *AWTError* Class

```
public Class AWTError extends Error
```

Constructors

```
public AWTError(String msg);
```

The *AWTEvent* Class

```
public abstract Class AWTEvent extends EventObject
```

Data

```
public final static long ACTION_EVENT_MASK = 0x80;
public final static long ADJUSTMENT_EVENT_MASK = 0x100;
public final static long COMPONENT_EVENT_MASK = 0x01;
public final static long CONTAINER_EVENT_MASK = 0x02;
public final static long FOCUS_EVENT_MASK = 0x04;
public final static long ITEM_EVENT_MASK = 0x200;
public final static long KEY_EVENT_MASK = 0x08;
public final static long MOUSE_EVENT_MASK = 0x10;
public final static long MOUSE_MOTION_EVENT_MASK = 0x20;
public final static int RESERVED_ID_MAX = 1999;
public final static long TEXT_EVENT_MASK = 0x400;
public final static long WINDOW_EVENT_MASK = 0x40;
```

Constructors

```
public AWTEvent(Event event);
public AWTEvent(Object source, int id);
```

Methods

```
public int getID();
public String paramString();
public String toString();
```

The *AWTEventMulticaster* Class

```
public Class AWTEventMulticaster extends Object implements
  ComponentListener, ContainerListener, FocusListener, KeyListener,
  MouseListener, MouseMotionListener, WindowListener, ActionListener,
  ItemListener, AdjustmentListener, TextListener
```

Methods

```
public static ActionListener add(ActionListener a, ActionListener b);
public static AdjustmentListener add(AdjustmentListener a,
  AdjustmentListener b);
public static ComponentListener add(ComponentListener a,
  ComponentListener b);
public static ContainerListener add(ContainerListener a,
  ContainerListener b);
public static FocusListener add(FocusListener a, FocusListener b);
public static ItemListener add(ItemListener a, ItemListener b);
public static KeyListener add(KeyListener a, KeyListener b);
public static MouseListener add(MouseListener a, MouseListener b);
public static MouseMotionListener add(MouseMotionListener a,
  MouseMotionListener b);
public static TextListener add(TextListener a, TextListener b);
public static WindowListener add(WindowListener a, WindowListener b);
public static ActionListener remove(ActionListener l, ActionListener
  oldl);
public static AdjustmentListener remove(AdjustmentListener l,
  AdjustmentListener oldl);
public static ComponentListener remove(ComponentListener l,
  ComponentListener oldl);
public static ContainerListener remove(ContainerListener l,
  ContainerListener oldl);
```

```
public static FocusListener remove(FocusListener l, FocusListener
    oldl);
public static ItemListener remove(ItemListener l, ItemListener oldl);
public static KeyListener remove(KeyListener l, KeyListener oldl);
public static MouseListener remove(MouseListener l, MouseListener
    oldl);
public static MouseMotionListener remove(MouseMotionListener l,
    MouseMotionListener oldl);
public static TextListener remove(TextListener l, TextListener oldl);
public static WindowListener remove(WindowListener l, WindowListener
    oldl);
public void actionPerformed(ActionEvent e);
public void adjustmentValueChanged(AdjustmentEvent e);
public void componentAdded(ContainerEvent e);
public void componentHidden(ComponentEvent e);
public void componentMoved(ComponentEvent e);
public void componentRemoved(ContainerEvent e);
public void componentResized(ComponentEvent e);
public void componentShown(ComponentEvent e);
public void focusGained(FocusEvent e);
public void focusLost(FocusEvent e);
public void itemStateChanged(ItemEvent e);
public void keyPressed(KeyEvent e);
public void keyReleased(KeyEvent e);
public void keyTyped(KeyEvent e);
public void mouseClicked(MouseEvent e);
public void mouseDragged(MouseEvent e);
public void mouseEntered(MouseEvent e);
public void mouseExited(MouseEvent e);
public void mouseMoved(MouseEvent e);
public void mousePressed(MouseEvent e);
public void mouseReleased(MouseEvent e);
public void textValueChanged(TextEvent e);
public void windowActivated(WindowEvent e);
public void windowClosed(WindowEvent e);
public void windowClosing(WindowEvent e);
public void windowDeactivated(WindowEvent e);
public void windowDeiconified(WindowEvent e);
public void windowIconified(WindowEvent e);
public void windowOpened(WindowEvent e);
```

The *AWTException* Class

```
public Class AWTException extends Exception
```

Constructors

```
public AWTException(String msg);
```

The *Adjustable* Interface

```
public Interface Adjustable
```

Data

```
public static final int HORIZONTAL = 0;
public static final int VERTICAL = 1;
```

Methods

```
void addAdjustmentListener(AdjustmentListener l);
int getBlockIncrement();
int getMaximum();
int getMinimum();
int getOrientation();
int getUnitIncrement();
int getValue();
int getVisibleAmount();
void removeAdjustmentListener(AdjustmentListener l);
void setBlockIncrement(int b);
void setMaximum(int max);
void setMinimum(int min);
void setUnitIncrement(int u);
void setValue(int v);
void setVisibleAmount(int v);
```

The *BorderLayout* Class

```
public Class BorderLayout extends Object implements LayoutManager2,
    java.io.Serializable
```

Data

```
public static final String CENTER = "Center";
public static final String EAST = "East";
```

```
public static final String NORTH = "North";
public static final String SOUTH = "South";
public static final String WEST = "West";
```

Constructors

```
public BorderLayout();
public BorderLayout(int hgap, int vgap);
```

Methods

```
public void addLayoutComponent(Component comp, Object constraints);
public void addLayoutComponent(String name, Component comp);
public int getHgap();
public float getLayoutAlignmentX(Container parent);
public float getLayoutAlignmentY(Container parent);
public int getVgap();
public void invalidateLayout(Container target);
public void layoutContainer(Container target);
public Dimension maximumLayoutSize(Container target);
public Dimension minimumLayoutSize(Container target);
public Dimension preferredLayoutSize(Container target);
public void removeLayoutComponent(Component comp);
public void setHgap(int hgap);
public void setVgap(int vgap);
public String toString();
```

The *Button* Class

```
public Class Button extends Component
```

Constructors

```
public Button();
public Button(String label);
```

Methods

```
public synchronized void addActionListener(ActionListener l);
public void addNotify();
public String getActionCommand();
public String getLabel();
public synchronized void removeActionListener(ActionListener l);
public void setActionCommand(String command);
public synchronized void setLabel(String label);
```

The *Canvas* Class

```
public Class Canvas extends Component
```

Constructors

```
public Canvas();
```

Methods

```
public void addNotify();
public void paint(Graphics g);
```

The *CardLayout* Class

```
public Class CardLayout extends Object implements LayoutManager2,
    java.io.Serializable
```

Constructors

```
public CardLayout();
public CardLayout(int hgap, int vgap);
```

Methods

```
public void addLayoutComponent(Component comp, Object constraints);
public void addLayoutComponent(String name, Component comp);
public void first(Container parent);
public int getHgap();
public float getLayoutAlignmentX(Container parent);
public float getLayoutAlignmentY(Container parent);
public int getVgap();
public void invalidateLayout(Container target);
public void last(Container parent);
public void layoutContainer(Container parent);
public Dimension maximumLayoutSize(Container target);
public Dimension minimumLayoutSize(Container parent);
public void next(Container parent);
public Dimension preferredLayoutSize(Container parent);
public void previous(Container parent);
public void removeLayoutComponent(Component comp);
public void setHgap(int hgap);
public void setVgap(int vgap);
public void show(Container parent, String name);
public String toString();
```

The *Checkbox* Class

```
public Class Checkbox extends Component implements ItemSelectable
```

Constructors

```
public Checkbox();
public Checkbox(String label);
public Checkbox(String label, boolean state);
public Checkbox(String label, boolean state, CheckboxGroup group);
public Checkbox(String label, CheckboxGroup group, boolean state);
```

Methods

```
public synchronized void addItemListener(ItemListener l);
public void addNotify();
public CheckboxGroup getCheckboxGroup();
public String getLabel();
public Object[] getSelectedObjects();
public boolean getState();
public synchronized void removeItemListener(ItemListener l);
public void setCheckboxGroup(CheckboxGroup g);
public synchronized void setLabel(String label);
public void setState(boolean state);
```

The *CheckboxGroup* Class

```
public Class CheckboxGroup extends Object implements
    java.io.Serializable
```

Constructors

```
public CheckboxGroup();
```

Methods

```
public Checkbox getCurrent();
public Checkbox getSelectedCheckbox();
public synchronized void setCurrent(Checkbox box);
public synchronized void setSelectedCheckbox(Checkbox box);
public String toString();
```

The *CheckboxMenuItem* Class

```
public Class CheckboxMenuItem extends MenuItem implements
   ItemSelectable
```

Constructors

```
public CheckboxMenuItem();
public CheckboxMenuItem(String label);
public CheckboxMenuItem(String label, boolean state);
```

Methods

```
public synchronized void addItemListener(ItemListener l);
public void addNotify();
public synchronized Object[] getSelectedObjects();
public boolean getState();
public String paramString();
public synchronized void removeItemListener(ItemListener l);
public synchronized void setState(boolean b);
```

The *Choice* Class

```
public Class Choice extends Component implements ItemSelectable
```

Constructors

```
public Choice();
```

Methods

```
public synchronized void add(String item);
public synchronized void addItem(String item);
public synchronized void addItemListener(ItemListener l);
public void addNotify();
public int countItems();
public String getItem(int index);
public int getItemCount();
public int getSelectedIndex();
public synchronized String getSelectedItem();
public synchronized Object[] getSelectedObjects();
public synchronized void insert(String item, int index);
public synchronized void remove(int position);
public synchronized void remove(String item);
```

```
public synchronized void removeAll();
public synchronized void removeItemListener(ItemListener l);
public synchronized void select(int pos);
public synchronized void select(String str);
```

The *Color* Class

```
public Class Color extends Object implements java.io.Serializable
```

Data

```
public final static Color black = new Color(0, 0, 0);
public final static Color blue = new Color(0, 0, 255);
public final static Color cyan = new Color(0, 255, 255);
public final static Color darkGray = new Color(64, 64, 64);
public final static Color gray = new Color(128, 128, 128);
public final static Color green = new Color(0, 255, 0);
public final static Color lightGray = new Color(192, 192, 192);
public final static Color magenta = new Color(255, 0, 255);
public final static Color orange = new Color(255, 200, 0);
public final static Color pink = new Color(255, 175, 175);
public final static Color red = new Color(255, 0, 0);
public final static Color white = new Color(255, 255, 255);
public final static Color yellow = new Color(255, 255, 0);
```

Constructors

```
public Color(int r, int g, int b);
public Color(int rgb);
public Color(float r, float g, float b);
```

Methods

```
public static Color decode(String nm) throws NumberFormatException;
public static Color getColor(String nm);
public static Color getColor(String nm, Color v);
public static Color getColor(String nm, int v);
public static Color getHSBColor(float h, float s, float b);
public static int HSBtoRGB(float hue, float saturation, float bright-
    ness);
public static float[] RGBtoHSB(int r, int g, int b, float[] hsbvals);
public Color brighter();
public Color darker();
public boolean equals(Object obj);
```

```
public int getBlue();
public int getGreen();
public int getRed();
public int getRGB();
public int hashCode();
public String toString();
```

The *Component* Class

```
public abstract Class Component extends Object implements
   ImageObserver, MenuContainer, Serializable
```

Data

```
public static final float BOTTOM_ALIGNMENT = 1.0f;
public static final float CENTER_ALIGNMENT = 0.5f;
public static final float LEFT_ALIGNMENT = 0.0f;
public static final float RIGHT_ALIGNMENT = 1.0f;
public static final float TOP_ALIGNMENT = 0.0f;
```

Methods

```
public boolean action(Event evt, Object what);
public synchronized void add(PopupMenu popup);
public synchronized void addComponentListener(ComponentListener l);
public synchronized void addFocusListener(FocusListener l);
public synchronized void addKeyListener(KeyListener l);
public synchronized void addMouseListener(MouseListener l);
public synchronized void addMouseMotionListener(MouseMotionListener l);
public void addNotify();
public Rectangle bounds();
public int checkImage(Image image, ImageObserver observer);
public int checkImage(Image image, int width, int height, ImageObserver
   observer);
public boolean contains(int x, int y);
public boolean contains(Point p);
public Image createImage(ImageProducer producer);
public Image createImage(int width, int height);
public void deliverEvent(Event e);
public void disable();
public final void dispatchEvent(AWTEvent e);
public void doLayout();
public void enable();
```

```java
public void enable(boolean b);
public float getAlignmentX();
public float getAlignmentY();
public Color getBackground();
public Rectangle getBounds();
public ColorModel getColorModel();
public Component getComponentAt(int x, int y);
public Component getComponentAt(Point p);
public Cursor getCursor();
public Font getFont();
public FontMetrics getFontMetrics(Font font);
public Color getForeground();
public Graphics getGraphics();
public Locale getLocale();
public Point getLocation();
public Point getLocationOnScreen();
public Dimension getMaximumSize();
public Dimension getMinimumSize();
public String getName();
public Container getParent();
public ComponentPeer getPeer();
public Dimension getPreferredSize();
public Dimension getSize();
public Toolkit getToolkit();
public final Object getTreeLock();
public boolean gotFocus(Event evt, Object what);
public boolean handleEvent(Event evt);
public void hide();
public boolean imageUpdate(Image img, int flags, int x, int y, int w,
   int h);
public boolean inside(int x, int y);
public void invalidate();
public boolean isEnabled();
public boolean isFocusTraversable();
public boolean isShowing();
public boolean isValid();
public boolean isVisible();
public boolean keyDown(Event evt, int key);
public boolean keyUp(Event evt, int key);
public void layout();
public void list();
public void list(PrintStream out);
```

```
public void list(PrintStream out, int indent);
public void list(PrintWriter out);
public void list(PrintWriter out, int indent);
public Component locate(int x, int y);
public Point location();
public boolean lostFocus(Event evt, Object what);
public Dimension minimumSize();
public boolean mouseDown(Event evt, int x, int y);
public boolean mouseDrag(Event evt, int x, int y);
public boolean mouseEnter(Event evt, int x, int y);
public boolean mouseExit(Event evt, int x, int y);
public boolean mouseMove(Event evt, int x, int y);
public boolean mouseUp(Event evt, int x, int y);
public void move(int x, int y);
public void nextFocus();
public void paint(Graphics g);
public void paintAll(Graphics g);
public boolean postEvent(Event e);
public Dimension preferredSize();
public boolean prepareImage(Image image, ImageObserver observer);
public boolean prepareImage(Image image, int width, int height,
  ImageObserver observer);
public void print(Graphics g);
public void printAll(Graphics g);
public synchronized void remove(MenuComponent popup);
public synchronized void removeComponentListener(ComponentListener l);
public synchronized void removeFocusListener(FocusListener l);
public synchronized void removeKeyListener(KeyListener l);
public synchronized void removeMouseListener(MouseListener l);
public synchronized void removeMouseMotionListener(MouseMotionListener l);
public void removeNotify();
public void repaint();
public void repaint(int x, int y, int width, int height);
public void repaint(long tm);
public void repaint(long tm, int x, int y, int width, int height);
public void requestFocus();
public void reshape(int x, int y, int width, int height);
public void resize(Dimension d);
public void resize(int width, int height);
public void setBackground(Color c);
public void setBounds(int x, int y, int width, int height);
public void setBounds(Rectangle r);
```

```
public synchronized void setCursor(Cursor cursor);
public void setEnabled(boolean b);
public synchronized void setFont(Font f);
public void setForeground(Color c);
public void setLocale(Locale l);
public void setLocation(int x, int y);
public void setLocation(Point p);
public void setName(String name);
public void setSize(Dimension d);
public void setSize(int width, int height);
public void setVisible(boolean b);
public void show();
public void show(boolean b);
public Dimension size();
public String toString();
public void transferFocus();
public void update(Graphics g);
public void validate();
```

The *Container* Class

```
public abstract Class Container extends Component
```

Methods

```
public Component add(Component comp);
public Component add(Component comp, int index);
public void add(Component comp, Object constraints);
public void add(Component comp, Object constraints, int index);
public Component add(String name, Component comp);
public synchronized void addContainerListener(ContainerListener l);
public void addNotify();
public int countComponents();
public void deliverEvent(Event e);
public void doLayout();
public float getAlignmentX();
public float getAlignmentY();
public Component getComponent(int n);
public Component getComponentAt(int x, int y);
public Component getComponentAt(Point p);
public int getComponentCount();
public Component[] getComponents();
```

```
public Insets getInsets();
public LayoutManager getLayout();
public Dimension getMaximumSize();
public Dimension getMinimumSize();
public Dimension getPreferredSize();
public Insets insets();
public void invalidate();
public boolean isAncestorOf(Component c);
public void layout();
public void list(PrintStream out, int indent);
public void list(PrintWriter out, int indent);
public Component locate(int x, int y);
public Dimension minimumSize();
public void paint(Graphics g);
public void paintComponents(Graphics g);
public Dimension preferredSize();
public void print(Graphics g);
public void printComponents(Graphics g);
public void remove(Component comp);
public void remove(int index);
public void removeAll();
public void removeContainerListener(ContainerListener l);
public void removeNotify();
public void setLayout(LayoutManager mgr);
public void validate();
```

The *Cursor* Class

```
public Class Cursor extends Object implements java.io.Serializable
```

Data

```
public static final int CROSSHAIR_CURSOR = 1;
public static final int DEFAULT_CURSOR = 0;
public static final int E_RESIZE_CURSOR = 11;
public static final int HAND_CURSOR = 12;
public static final int MOVE_CURSOR = 13;
public static final int N_RESIZE_CURSOR = 8;
public static final int NE_RESIZE_CURSOR = 7;
public static final int NW_RESIZE_CURSOR = 6;
public static final int S_RESIZE_CURSOR = 9;
public static final int SE_RESIZE_CURSOR = 5;
```

```
public static final int SW_RESIZE_CURSOR = 4;
public static final int TEXT_CURSOR = 2;
public static final int W_RESIZE_CURSOR = 10;
public static final int WAIT_CURSOR = 3;
```

Constructors

```
public Cursor(int type);
```

Methods

```
static public Cursor getDefaultCursor();
static public Cursor getPredefinedCursor(int type);
public int getType();
```

The *Dialog* Class

```
public Class Dialog extends Window
```

Constructors

```
public Dialog(Frame parent);
public Dialog(Frame parent, boolean modal);
public Dialog(Frame parent, String title);
public Dialog(Frame parent, String title, boolean modal);
```

Methods

```
public void addNotify();
public String getTitle();
public boolean isModal();
public boolean isResizable();
public void setModal(boolean b);
public synchronized void setResizable(boolean resizable);
public synchronized void setTitle(String title);
public void show();
```

The *Dimension* Class

```
public Class Dimension extends Object implements java.io.Serializable
```

Data

```
public int height;
public int width;
```

Constructors

```
public Dimension();
public Dimension(Dimension d);
public Dimension(int width, int height);
```

Methods

```
public boolean equals(Object obj);
public Dimension getSize();
public void setSize(Dimension d);
public void setSize(int width, int height);
public String toString();
```

The *Event* Class

```
public Class Event extends Object implements java.io.Serializable
```

Data

```
public static final int ACTION_EVENT = 1 + MISC_EVENT;
public static final int ALT_MASK = 1 << 3;
public static final int BACK_SPACE = '\b';
public static final int CAPS_LOCK = 1022;
public static final int CTRL_MASK = 1 << 1;
public static final int DELETE = 127;
public static final int DOWN = 1005;
public static final int END = 1001;
public static final int ENTER = '\n';
public static final int ESCAPE = 27;
public static final int F1 = 1008;
public static final int F10 = 1017;
public static final int F11 = 1018;
public static final int F12 = 1019;
public static final int F2 = 1009;
public static final int F3 = 1010;
public static final int F4 = 1011;
public static final int F5 = 1012;
public static final int F6 = 1013;
public static final int F7 = 1014;
public static final int F8 = 1015;
public static final int F9 = 1016;
public static final int GOT_FOCUS = 4 + MISC_EVENT;
```

```
public static final int HOME = 1000;
public static final int INSERT = 1025;
public static final int KEY_ACTION = 3 + KEY_EVENT;
public static final int KEY_ACTION_RELEASE = 4 + KEY_EVENT;
public static final int KEY_PRESS = 1 + KEY_EVENT;
public static final int KEY_RELEASE = 2 + KEY_EVENT;
public static final int LEFT = 1006;
public static final int LIST_DESELECT = 2 + LIST_EVENT;
public static final int LIST_SELECT = 1 + LIST_EVENT;
public static final int LOAD_FILE = 2 + MISC_EVENT;
public static final int LOST_FOCUS = 5 + MISC_EVENT;
public static final int META_MASK = 1 << 2;
public static final int MOUSE_DOWN = 1 + MOUSE_EVENT;
public static final int MOUSE_DRAG = 6 + MOUSE_EVENT;
public static final int MOUSE_ENTER = 4 + MOUSE_EVENT;
public static final int MOUSE_EXIT = 5 + MOUSE_EVENT;
public static final int MOUSE_MOVE = 3 + MOUSE_EVENT;
public static final int MOUSE_UP = 2 + MOUSE_EVENT;
public static final int NUM_LOCK = 1023;
public static final int PAUSE = 1024;
public static final int PGDN = 1003;
public static final int PGUP = 1002;
public static final int PRINT_SCREEN = 1020;
public static final int RIGHT = 1007;
public static final int SAVE_FILE = 3 + MISC_EVENT;
public static final int SCROLL_ABSOLUTE = 5 + SCROLL_EVENT;
public static final int SCROLL_BEGIN = 6 + SCROLL_EVENT;
public static final int SCROLL_END = 7 + SCROLL_EVENT;
public static final int SCROLL_LINE_DOWN = 2 + SCROLL_EVENT;
public static final int SCROLL_LINE_UP = 1 + SCROLL_EVENT;
public static final int SCROLL_LOCK = 1021;
public static final int SCROLL_PAGE_DOWN = 4 + SCROLL_EVENT;
public static final int SCROLL_PAGE_UP = 3 + SCROLL_EVENT;
public static final int SHIFT_MASK = 1 << 0;
public static final int TAB = '\t';
public static final int UP = 1004;
public static final int WINDOW_DEICONIFY = 4 + WINDOW_EVENT;
public static final int WINDOW_DESTROY = 1 + WINDOW_EVENT;
public static final int WINDOW_EXPOSE = 2 + WINDOW_EVENT;
public static final int WINDOW_ICONIFY = 3 + WINDOW_EVENT;
public static final int WINDOW_MOVED = 5 + WINDOW_EVENT;
public Object arg;
```

```
public int clickCount;
public Event evt;
public int id;
public int key;
public int modifiers;
public Object target;
public long when;
public int x;
public int y;
```

Constructors

```
public Event(Object target, long when, int id, int x, int y, int key,
   int modifiers, Object arg);
public Event(Object target, long when, int id, int x, int y, int key,
   int modifiers);
public Event(Object target, int id, Object arg);
```

Methods

```
public boolean controlDown();
public boolean metaDown();
public boolean shiftDown();
public String toString();
public void translate(int x, int y);
```

The *EventQueue* Class

```
public Class EventQueue extends Object
```

Constructors

```
public EventQueue();
```

Methods

```
public synchronized AWTEvent getNextEvent() throws
   InterruptedException;
public synchronized AWTEvent peekEvent();
public synchronized AWTEvent peekEvent(int id);
public synchronized void postEvent(AWTEvent theEvent);
```

The *FileDialog* Class

```
public Class FileDialog extends Dialog
```

Data

```
public static final int LOAD = 0;
public static final int SAVE = 1;
```

Constructors

```
public FileDialog(Frame parent);
public FileDialog(Frame parent, String title);
public FileDialog(Frame parent, String title, int mode);
```

Methods

```
public void addNotify();
public String getDirectory();
public String getFile();
public FilenameFilter getFilenameFilter();
public int getMode();
public synchronized void setDirectory(String dir);
public synchronized void setFile(String file);
public synchronized void setFilenameFilter(FilenameFilter filter);
public void setMode(int mode);
```

The *FlowLayout* Class

```
public Class FlowLayout extends Object implements LayoutManager,
    java.io.Serializable
```

Data

```
public static final int CENTER = 1;
public static final int LEFT = 0;
public static final int RIGHT = 2;
```

Constructors

```
public FlowLayout();
public FlowLayout(int align);
public FlowLayout(int align, int hgap, int vgap);
```

Methods

```
public void addLayoutComponent(String name, Component comp);
public int getAlignment();
public int getHgap();
public int getVgap();
public void layoutContainer(Container target);
public Dimension minimumLayoutSize(Container target);
public Dimension preferredLayoutSize(Container target);
public void removeLayoutComponent(Component comp);
public void setAlignment(int align);
public void setHgap(int hgap);
public void setVgap(int vgap);
public String toString();
```

The *Font* Class

```
public Class Font extends Object implements java.io.Serializable
```

Data

```
public static final int BOLD = 1;
public static final int ITALIC = 2;
public static final int PLAIN = 0;
```

Constructors

```
public Font(String name, int style, int size);
```

Methods

```
public static Font decode(String str);
public static Font getFont(String nm);
public static Font getFont(String nm, Font font);
public boolean equals(Object obj);
public String getFamily();
public String getName();
public FontPeer getPeer();
public int getSize();
public int getStyle();
public int hashCode();
public boolean isBold();
public boolean isItalic();
public boolean isPlain();
public String toString();
```

The *FontMetrics* Class

```
public abstract Class FontMetrics extends Object implements
    java.io.Serializable
```

Methods

```
public int bytesWidth(byte data[], int off, int len);
public int charsWidth(char data[], int off, int len);
public int charWidth(char ch);
public int charWidth(int ch);
public int getAscent();
public int getDescent();
public Font getFont();
public int getHeight();
public int getLeading();
public int getMaxAdvance();
public int getMaxAscent();
public int getMaxDecent();
public int getMaxDescent();
public int[] getWidths();
public int stringWidth(String str);
public String toString();
```

The *Frame* Class

```
public Class Frame extends Window implements MenuContainer
```

Data

```
public static final int CROSSHAIR_CURSOR = Cursor.CROSSHAIR_CURSOR;
public static final int DEFAULT_CURSOR = Cursor.DEFAULT_CURSOR;
public static final int E_RESIZE_CURSOR = Cursor.E_RESIZE_CURSOR;
public static final int HAND_CURSOR = Cursor.HAND_CURSOR;
public static final int MOVE_CURSOR = Cursor.MOVE_CURSOR;
public static final int N_RESIZE_CURSOR = Cursor.N_RESIZE_CURSOR;
public static final int NE_RESIZE_CURSOR = Cursor.NE_RESIZE_CURSOR;
public static final int NW_RESIZE_CURSOR = Cursor.NW_RESIZE_CURSOR;
public static final int S_RESIZE_CURSOR = Cursor.S_RESIZE_CURSOR;
public static final int SE_RESIZE_CURSOR = Cursor.SE_RESIZE_CURSOR;
public static final int SW_RESIZE_CURSOR = Cursor.SW_RESIZE_CURSOR;
public static final int TEXT_CURSOR = Cursor.TEXT_CURSOR;
public static final int W_RESIZE_CURSOR = Cursor.W_RESIZE_CURSOR;
public static final int WAIT_CURSOR = Cursor.WAIT_CURSOR;
```

Constructors

```
public Frame();
public Frame(String title);
```

Methods

```
public void addNotify();
public synchronized void dispose();
public int getCursorType();
public Image getIconImage();
public MenuBar getMenuBar();
public String getTitle();
public boolean isResizable();
public synchronized void remove(MenuComponent m);
public synchronized void setCursor(int cursorType);
public synchronized void setIconImage(Image image);
public synchronized void setMenuBar(MenuBar mb);
public synchronized void setResizable(boolean resizable);
public synchronized void setTitle(String title);
```

The *Graphics* Class

```
public abstract Class Graphics extends Object
```

Methods

```
public abstract void clearRect(int x, int y, int width, int height);
public abstract void clipRect(int x, int y, int width, int height);
public abstract void copyArea(int x, int y, int width, int height, int
   dx, int dy);
public abstract Graphics create();
public abstract void dispose();
public abstract void drawArc(int x, int y, int width, int height, int
   startAngle, int arcAngle);
public abstract boolean drawImage(Image img, int x, int y,
   ImageObserver observer);
public abstract boolean drawImage(Image img, int x, int y, int width,
   int height, ImageObserver observer);
public abstract boolean drawImage(Image img, int x, int y, Color
   bgcolor, ImageObserver observer);
public abstract boolean drawImage(Image img, int x, int y, int width,
   int height, Color bgcolor, ImageObserver observer);
```

```
public abstract boolean drawImage(Image img, int dx1, int dy1, int dx2,
    int dy2, int sx1, int sy1, int sx2, int sy2, ImageObserver observer);
public abstract boolean drawImage(Image img, int dx1, int dy1, int dx2,
    int dy2, int sx1, int sy1, int sx2, int sy2, Color bgcolor,
    ImageObserver observer);
public abstract void drawLine(int x1, int y1, int x2, int y2);
public abstract void drawOval(int x, int y, int width, int height);
public abstract void drawPolygon(int xPoints[], int yPoints[], int
    nPoints);
public abstract void drawPolyline(int xPoints[], int yPoints[], int
    nPoints);
public abstract void drawRoundRect(int x, int y, int width, int height,
    int arcWidth, int arcHeight);
public abstract void drawString(String str, int x, int y);
public abstract void fillArc(int x, int y, int width, int height, int
    startAngle, int arcAngle);
public abstract void fillOval(int x, int y, int width, int height);
public abstract void fillPolygon(int xPoints[], int yPoints[], int
    nPoints);
public abstract void fillRect(int x, int y, int width, int height);
public abstract void fillRoundRect(int x, int y, int width, int height,
    int arcWidth, int arcHeight);
public abstract Shape getClip();
public abstract Rectangle getClipBounds();
public abstract Color getColor();
public abstract Font getFont();
public abstract FontMetrics getFontMetrics(Font f);
public abstract void setClip(int x, int y, int width, int height);
public abstract void setClip(Shape clip);
public abstract void setColor(Color c);
public abstract void setFont(Font font);
public abstract void setPaintMode();
public abstract void setXORMode(Color c1);
public abstract void translate(int x, int y);
public Graphics create(int x, int y, int width, int height);
public void draw3DRect(int x, int y, int width, int height, boolean
    raised);
public void drawBytes(byte data[], int offset, int length, int x, int y);
public void drawChars(char data[], int offset, int length, int x, int y);
public void drawPolygon(Polygon p);
public void drawRect(int x, int y, int width, int height);
```

```
public void fill3DRect(int x, int y, int width, int height, boolean
    raised);
public void fillPolygon(Polygon p);
public void finalize();
public Rectangle getClipRect();
public FontMetrics getFontMetrics();
public String toString();
```

The *GridBagConstraints* Class

```
public Class GridBagConstraints extends Object implements Cloneable,
    java.io.Serializable
```

Data

```
public static final int BOTH = 1;
public static final int CENTER = 10;
public static final int EAST = 13;
public static final int HORIZONTAL = 2;
public static final int NONE = 0;
public static final int NORTH = 11;
public static final int NORTHEAST = 12;
public static final int NORTHWEST = 18;
public static final int RELATIVE = -1;
public static final int REMAINDER = 0;
public static final int SOUTH = 15;
public static final int SOUTHEAST = 14;
public static final int SOUTHWEST = 16;
public static final int VERTICAL = 3;
public static final int WEST = 17;
public int anchor, fill;
public int gridx, gridy, gridwidth, gridheight;
public Insets insets;
public int ipadx, ipady;
public double weightx, weighty;
```

Methods

```
public GridBagConstraints ();
public Object clone ();
```

The *GridLayout* Class

```
public Class GridLayout extends Object implements LayoutManager,
    java.io.Serializable
```

Constructors

```
public GridLayout();
public GridLayout(int rows, int cols);
public GridLayout(int rows, int cols, int hgap, int vgap);
```

Methods

```
public void addLayoutComponent(String name, Component comp);
public int getColumns();
public int getHgap();
public int getRows();
public int getVgap();
public void layoutContainer(Container parent);
public Dimension minimumLayoutSize(Container parent);
public Dimension preferredLayoutSize(Container parent);
public void removeLayoutComponent(Component comp);
public void setColumns(int cols);
public void setHgap(int hgap);
public void setRows(int rows);
public void setVgap(int vgap);
public String toString();
```

The *IllegalComponentStateException* Class

```
public Class IllegalComponentStateException extends
    IllegalStateException
```

Constructors

```
public IllegalComponentStateException();
public IllegalComponentStateException(String s);
```

The *Image* Class

```
public abstract Class Image extends Object
```

Data

```
public static final int SCALE_AREA_AVERAGING = 16;
public static final int SCALE_DEFAULT = 1;
public static final int SCALE_FAST = 2;
public static final int SCALE_REPLICATE = 8;
public static final int SCALE_SMOOTH = 4;
public static final Object UndefinedProperty = new Object();
```

Methods

```
public abstract void flush();
public abstract Graphics getGraphics();
public abstract int getHeight(ImageObserver observer);
public abstract Object getProperty(String name, ImageObserver
    observer);
public abstract ImageProducer getSource();
public abstract int getWidth(ImageObserver observer);
public Image getScaledInstance(int width, int height, int hints);
```

The *Insets* Class

```
public Class Insets extends Object implements Cloneable,
    java.io.Serializable
```

Data

```
public int bottom;
public int left;
public int right;
public int top;
```

Constructors

```
public Insets(int top, int left, int bottom, int right);
```

Methods

```
public Object clone();
public boolean equals(Object obj);
public String toString();
```

The *ItemSelectable* Interface

```
public Interface ItemSelectable
```

Methods

```
public void addItemListener(ItemListener l);
public Object[] getSelectedObjects();
public void removeItemListener(ItemListener l);
```

The *Label* Class

```
public Class Label extends Component
```

Data

```
public static final int CENTER = 1;
public static final int LEFT = 0;
public static final int RIGHT = 2;
```

Constructors

```
public Label();
public Label(String text);
public Label(String text, int alignment);
```

Methods

```
public void addNotify();
public int getAlignment();
public String getText();
public synchronized void setAlignment(int alignment);
public synchronized void setText(String text);
```

The *LayoutManager* Interface

```
public Interface LayoutManager
```

Methods

```
void addLayoutComponent(String name, Component comp);
void layoutContainer(Container parent);
Dimension minimumLayoutSize(Container parent);
Dimension preferredLayoutSize(Container parent);
void removeLayoutComponent(Component comp);
```

The *LayoutManager2* Interface

```
public Interface LayoutManager2 extends LayoutManager
```

Methods

```
void addLayoutComponent(Component comp, Object constraints);
public float getLayoutAlignmentX(Container target);
public float getLayoutAlignmentY(Container target);
public void invalidateLayout(Container target);
public Dimension maximumLayoutSize(Container target);
```

The *List* Class

```
public Class List extends Component implements ItemSelectable
```

Constructors

```
public List();
public List(int rows);
public List(int rows, boolean multipleMode);
```

Methods

```
public void add(String item);
public synchronized void add(String item, int index);
public synchronized void addActionListener(ActionListener l);
public void addItem(String item);
public synchronized void addItem(String item, int index);
public synchronized void addItemListener(ItemListener l);
public void addNotify();
public boolean allowsMultipleSelections();
public synchronized void clear();
public int countItems();
public synchronized void delItem(int position);
public synchronized void delItems(int start, int end);
public synchronized void deselect(int index);
public String getItem(int index);
public int getItemCount();
public synchronized String[] getItems();
public Dimension getMinimumSize();
public Dimension getMinimumSize(int rows);
public Dimension getPreferredSize();
public Dimension getPreferredSize(int rows);
```

```
public int getRows();
public synchronized int getSelectedIndex();
public synchronized int[] getSelectedIndexes();
public synchronized String getSelectedItem();
public synchronized String[] getSelectedItems();
public Object[] getSelectedObjects();
public int getVisibleIndex();
public boolean isIndexSelected(int index);
public boolean isMultipleMode();
public boolean isSelected(int index);
public synchronized void makeVisible(int index);
public Dimension minimumSize();
public Dimension minimumSize(int rows);
public Dimension preferredSize();
public Dimension preferredSize(int rows);
public synchronized void remove(int position);
public synchronized void remove(String item);
public synchronized void removeActionListener(ActionListener l);
public synchronized void removeAll();
public synchronized void removeItemListener(ItemListener l);
public void removeNotify();
public synchronized void replaceItem(String newValue, int index);
public synchronized void select(int index);
public synchronized void setMultipleMode(boolean b);
public synchronized void setMultipleSelections(boolean b);
```

The *MediaTracker* Class

```
public Class MediaTracker extends Object implements
  java.io.Serializable
```

Data

```
public static final int ABORTED = 2;
public static final int COMPLETE = 8;
public static final int ERRORED = 4;
public static final int LOADING = 1;
```

Constructors

```
public MediaTracker(Component comp);
```

Methods

```
public void addImage(Image image, int id);
public synchronized void addImage(Image image, int id, int w, int h);
public boolean checkAll();
public boolean checkAll(boolean load);
public boolean checkID(int id);
public boolean checkID(int id, boolean load);
public synchronized Object[] getErrorsAny();
public synchronized Object[] getErrorsID(int id);
public synchronized boolean isErrorAny();
public synchronized boolean isErrorID(int id);
public synchronized void removeImage(Image image);
public synchronized void removeImage(Image image, int id);
public synchronized void removeImage(Image image, int id, int width,
    int height);
public int statusAll(boolean load);
public int statusID(int id, boolean load);
public void waitForAll() throws InterruptedException;
public synchronized boolean waitForAll(long ms) throws
    InterruptedException;
public void waitForID(int id) throws InterruptedException;
public synchronized boolean waitForID(int id, long ms) throws
    InterruptedException;
```

The *Menu* Class

```
public Class Menu extends MenuItem implements MenuContainer
```

Constructors

```
public Menu();
public Menu(String label);
public Menu(String label, boolean tearOff);
```

Methods

```
public synchronized MenuItem add(MenuItem mi);
public void add(String label);
public void addNotify();
public void addSeparator();
public int countItems();
public MenuItem getItem(int index);
```

```
public int getItemCount();
public synchronized void insert(MenuItem menuitem, int index);
public void insert(String label, int index);
public void insertSeparator(int index);
public boolean isTearOff();
public String paramString();
public synchronized void remove(int index);
public synchronized void remove(MenuComponent item);
public synchronized void removeAll();
public void removeNotify();
```

The *MenuBar* Class

```
public Class MenuBar extends MenuComponent implements MenuContainer
```

Constructors

```
public MenuBar();
```

Methods

```
public synchronized Menu add(Menu m);
public void addNotify();
public int countMenus();
public void deleteShortcut(MenuShortcut s);
public Menu getHelpMenu();
public Menu getMenu(int i);
public int getMenuCount();
public MenuItem getShortcutMenuItem(MenuShortcut s);
public synchronized void remove(int index);
public synchronized void remove(MenuComponent m);
public void removeNotify();
public synchronized void setHelpMenu(Menu m);
public synchronized Enumeration shortcuts();
```

The *MenuComponent* Class

```
public abstract Class MenuComponent extends Object implements
    java.io.Serializable
```

Methods

```
public final void dispatchEvent(AWTEvent e);
public Font getFont();
```

```
public String getName();
public MenuContainer getParent();
public MenuComponentPeer getPeer();
public boolean postEvent(Event evt);
public void removeNotify();
public void setFont(Font f);
public void setName(String name);
public String toString();
```

The *MenuContainer* Interface

```
public Interface MenuContainer
```

Methods

```
Font getFont();
boolean postEvent(Event evt);
void remove(MenuComponent comp);
```

The *MenuItem* Class

```
public Class MenuItem extends MenuComponent
```

Constructors

```
public MenuItem();
public MenuItem(String label);
public MenuItem(String label, MenuShortcut s);
```

Methods

```
public synchronized void addActionListener(ActionListener l);
public void addNotify();
public void deleteShortcut();
public synchronized void disable();
public synchronized void enable();
public void enable(boolean b);
public String getActionCommand();
public String getLabel();
public MenuShortcut getShortcut();
public boolean isEnabled();
public String paramString();
public synchronized void removeActionListener(ActionListener l);
public void setActionCommand(String command);
```

```
public synchronized void setEnabled(boolean b);
public synchronized void setLabel(String label);
public void setShortcut(MenuShortcut s);
```

The *MenuShortcut* Class

```
public Class MenuShortcut extends Object implements
  java.io.Serializable
```

Constructors

```
public MenuShortcut(int key);
public MenuShortcut(int key, boolean useShiftModifier);
```

Methods

```
public boolean equals(MenuShortcut s);
public int getKey();
public String toString();
public boolean usesShiftModifier();
```

The *Panel* Class

```
public Class Panel extends Container
```

Constructors

```
public Panel();
public Panel(LayoutManager layout);
```

Methods

```
public void addNotify();
```

The *Point* Class

```
public Class Point extends Object implements java.io.Serializable
```

Data

```
public int x;
public int y;
```

Constructors

```
public Point();
public Point(Point p);
public Point(int x, int y);
```

Methods

```
public boolean equals(Object obj);
public Point getLocation();
public int hashCode();
public void move(int x, int y);
public void setLocation(int x, int y);
public void setLocation(Point p);
public String toString();
public void translate(int x, int y);
```

The *Polygon* Class

```
public Class Polygon extends Object implements Shape,
    java.io.Serializable
```

Data

```
public int npoints = 0;
public int xpoints[] = new int[4];
public int ypoints[] = new int[4];
```

Constructors

```
public Polygon();
public Polygon(int xpoints[], int ypoints[], int npoints);
```

Methods

```
public void addPoint(int x, int y);
public boolean contains(int x, int y);
public boolean contains(Point p);
public Rectangle getBoundingBox();
public Rectangle getBounds();
public boolean inside(int x, int y);
public void translate(int deltaX, int deltaY);
```

The *PopupMenu* Class

```
public Class PopupMenu extends Menu
```

Constructors

```
public PopupMenu();
public PopupMenu(String label);
```

Methods

```
public synchronized void addNotify();
public void show(Component origin, int x, int y);
```

The *PrintGraphics* Interface

```
public Interface PrintGraphics
```

Methods

```
public PrintJob getPrintJob();
```

The *PrintJob* Class

```
public abstract Class PrintJob extends Object
```

Methods

```
public abstract void end();
public abstract Graphics getGraphics();
public abstract Dimension getPageDimension();
public abstract int getPageResolution();
public abstract boolean lastPageFirst();
public void finalize();
```

The *Rectangle* Class

```
public Class Rectangle extends Object implements Shape,
    java.io.Serializable
```

Data

```
public int height;
public int width;
```

```
public int x;
public int y;
```

Constructors

```
public Rectangle();
public Rectangle(Rectangle r);
public Rectangle(int x, int y, int width, int height);
public Rectangle(int width, int height);
public Rectangle(Point p, Dimension d);
public Rectangle(Point p);
public Rectangle(Dimension d);
```

Methods

```
public void add(int newx, int newy);
public void add(Point pt);
public void add(Rectangle r);
public boolean contains(int x, int y);
public boolean contains(Point p);
public boolean equals(Object obj);
public Rectangle getBounds();
public Point getLocation();
public Dimension getSize();
public void grow(int h, int v);
public int hashCode();
public boolean inside(int x, int y);
public Rectangle intersection(Rectangle r);
public boolean intersects(Rectangle r);
public boolean isEmpty();
public void move(int x, int y);
public void reshape(int x, int y, int width, int height);
public void resize(int width, int height);
public void setBounds(int x, int y, int width, int height);
public void setBounds(Rectangle r);
public void setLocation(int x, int y);
public void setLocation(Point p);
public void setSize(Dimension d);
public void setSize(int width, int height);
public String toString();
public void translate(int x, int y);
public Rectangle union(Rectangle r);
```

The *ScrollPane* Class

```
public Class ScrollPane extends Container
```

Data

```
public static final int SCROLLBARS_ALWAYS = 1;
public static final int SCROLLBARS_AS_NEEDED = 0;
public static final int SCROLLBARS_NEVER = 2;
```

Constructors

```
public ScrollPane();
public ScrollPane(int scrollbarDisplayPolicy);
```

Methods

```
public void addNotify();
public void doLayout();
public Adjustable getHAdjustable();
public int getHScrollbarHeight();
public int getScrollbarDisplayPolicy();
public Point getScrollPosition();
public Adjustable getVAdjustable();
public Dimension getViewportSize();
public int getVScrollbarWidth();
public void layout();
public String paramString();
public void printComponents(Graphics g);
public final void setLayout(LayoutManager mgr);
public void setScrollPosition(int x, int y);
public void setScrollPosition(Point p);
```

The *Scrollbar* Class

```
public Class Scrollbar extends Component implements Adjustable
```

Data

```
public static final int HORIZONTAL = 0;
public static final int VERTICAL = 1;
```

Constructors

```
public Scrollbar();
public Scrollbar(int orientation);
public Scrollbar(int orientation, int value, int visible, int minimum,
   int maximum);
```

Methods

```
public synchronized void addAdjustmentListener(AdjustmentListener l);
public void addNotify();
public int getBlockIncrement();
public int getLineIncrement();
public int getMaximum();
public int getMinimum();
public int getOrientation();
public int getPageIncrement();
public int getUnitIncrement();
public int getValue();
public int getVisible();
public int getVisibleAmount();
public synchronized void removeAdjustmentListener(AdjustmentListener l);
public synchronized void setBlockIncrement(int v);
public void setLineIncrement(int v);
public synchronized void setMaximum(int newMaximum);
public synchronized void setMinimum(int newMinimum);
public synchronized void setOrientation(int orientation);
public void setPageIncrement(int v);
public synchronized void setUnitIncrement(int v);
public synchronized void setValue(int newValue);
public synchronized void setValues(int value, int visible, int minimum,
   int maximum);
public synchronized void setVisibleAmount(int newAmount);
```

The *Shape* Interface

```
public Interface Shape
```

Methods

```
public Rectangle getBounds();
```

The *SystemColor* Class

```
public Class SystemColor extends Color implements java.io.Serializable
```

Data

```
public final static int ACTIVE_CAPTION = 1;
public final static int ACTIVE_CAPTION_BORDER = 3;
public final static int ACTIVE_CAPTION_TEXT = 2;
public final static SystemColor activeCaption = new
   SystemColor((byte)ACTIVE_CAPTION);
public final static SystemColor activeCaptionBorder = new
   SystemColor((byte)ACTIVE_CAPTION_BORDER);
public final static SystemColor activeCaptionText = new
   SystemColor((byte)ACTIVE_CAPTION_TEXT);
public final static int CONTROL = 17;
public final static SystemColor control = new SystemColor((byte)CONTROL);
public final static int CONTROL_DK_SHADOW = 22;
public final static int CONTROL_HIGHLIGHT = 19;
public final static int CONTROL_LT_HIGHLIGHT = 20;
public final static int CONTROL_SHADOW = 21;
public final static int CONTROL_TEXT = 18;
public final static SystemColor controlDkShadow = new
   SystemColor((byte)CONTROL_DK_SHADOW);
public final static SystemColor controlHighlight = new
   SystemColor((byte)CONTROL_HIGHLIGHT);
public final static SystemColor controlLtHighlight = new
   SystemColor((byte)CONTROL_LT_HIGHLIGHT);
public final static SystemColor controlShadow = new
   SystemColor((byte)CONTROL_SHADOW);
public final static SystemColor controlText = new
   SystemColor((byte)CONTROL_TEXT);
public final static int DESKTOP = 0;
public final static SystemColor desktop = new SystemColor((byte)DESKTOP);
public final static int INACTIVE_CAPTION = 4;
public final static int INACTIVE_CAPTION_BORDER = 6;
public final static int INACTIVE_CAPTION_TEXT = 5;
public final static SystemColor inactiveCaption = new
   SystemColor((byte)INACTIVE_CAPTION);
public final static SystemColor inactiveCaptionBorder = new
   SystemColor((byte)INACTIVE_CAPTION_BORDER);
public final static SystemColor inactiveCaptionText = new
   SystemColor((byte)INACTIVE_CAPTION_TEXT);
```

```
public final static int INFO = 24;
public final static SystemColor info = new SystemColor((byte)INFO);
public final static int INFO_TEXT = 25;
public final static SystemColor infoText = new
   SystemColor((byte)INFO_TEXT);
public final static int MENU = 10;
public final static SystemColor menu = new SystemColor((byte)MENU);
public final static int MENU_TEXT = 11;
public final static SystemColor menuText = new
   SystemColor((byte)MENU_TEXT);
public final static int NUM_COLORS = 26;
public final static int SCROLLBAR = 23;
public final static SystemColor scrollbar = new
   SystemColor((byte)SCROLLBAR);
public final static int TEXT = 12;
public final static SystemColor text = new SystemColor((byte)TEXT);
public final static int TEXT_HIGHLIGHT = 14;
public final static int TEXT_HIGHLIGHT_TEXT = 15;
public final static int TEXT_INACTIVE_TEXT = 16;
public final static int TEXT_TEXT = 13;
public final static SystemColor textHighlight = new
   SystemColor((byte)TEXT_HIGHLIGHT);
public final static SystemColor textHighlightText = new
   SystemColor((byte)TEXT_HIGHLIGHT_TEXT);
public final static SystemColor textInactiveText = new
   SystemColor((byte)TEXT_INACTIVE_TEXT);
public final static SystemColor textText = new
   SystemColor((byte)TEXT_TEXT);
public final static int WINDOW = 7;
public final static SystemColor window = new SystemColor((byte)WINDOW);
public final static int WINDOW_BORDER = 8;
public final static int WINDOW_TEXT = 9;
public final static SystemColor windowBorder = new
   SystemColor((byte)WINDOW_BORDER);
public final static SystemColor windowText = new
   SystemColor((byte)WINDOW_TEXT);
```

Methods

```
public int getRGB();
public String toString();
```

The *TextArea* Class

```
public Class TextArea extends TextComponent
```

Data

```
public static final int SCROLLBARS_BOTH = 0;
public static final int SCROLLBARS_HORIZONTAL_ONLY = 2;
public static final int SCROLLBARS_NONE = 3;
public static final int SCROLLBARS_VERTICAL_ONLY = 1;
```

Constructors

```
public TextArea();
public TextArea(String text);
public TextArea(int rows, int columns);
public TextArea(String text, int rows, int columns);
public TextArea(String text, int rows, int columns, int scrollbars);
```

Methods

```
public void addNotify();
public synchronized void append(String str);
public void appendText(String str);
public int getColumns();
public Dimension getMinimumSize();
public Dimension getMinimumSize(int rows, int columns);
public Dimension getPreferredSize();
public Dimension getPreferredSize(int rows, int columns);
public int getRows();
public int getScrollbarVisibility();
public synchronized void insert(String str, int pos);
public void insertText(String str, int pos);
public Dimension minimumSize();
public Dimension minimumSize(int rows, int columns);
public Dimension preferredSize();
public Dimension preferredSize(int rows, int columns);
public synchronized void replaceRange(String str, int start, int end);
public void replaceText(String str, int start, int end);
public void setColumns(int columns);
public void setRows(int rows);
```

The *TextComponent* Class

```
public Class TextComponent extends Component
```

Methods

```
public synchronized void addTextListener(TextListener l);
public int getCaretPosition();
public synchronized String getSelectedText();
public synchronized int getSelectionEnd();
public synchronized int getSelectionStart();
public synchronized String getText();
public boolean isEditable();
public void removeNotify();
public void removeTextListener(TextListener l);
public synchronized void select(int selectionStart, int selectionEnd);
public synchronized void selectAll();
public void setCaretPosition(int position);
public synchronized void setEditable(boolean b);
public synchronized void setSelectionEnd(int selectionEnd);
public synchronized void setSelectionStart(int selectionStart);
public synchronized void setText(String t);
```

The *TextField* Class

```
public Class TextField extends TextComponent
```

Constructors

```
public TextField();
public TextField(String text);
public TextField(int columns);
public TextField(String text, int columns);
```

Methods

```
public synchronized void addActionListener(ActionListener l);
public void addNotify();
public boolean echoCharIsSet();
public int getColumns();
public char getEchoChar();
public Dimension getMinimumSize();
public Dimension getMinimumSize(int columns);
public Dimension getPreferredSize();
```

```
public Dimension getPreferredSize(int columns);
public Dimension minimumSize();
public Dimension minimumSize(int columns);
public Dimension preferredSize();
public Dimension preferredSize(int columns);
public synchronized void removeActionListener(ActionListener l);
public void setColumns(int columns);
public void setEchoChar(char c);
public void setEchoCharacter(char c);
```

The *Toolkit* Class

```
public abstract Class Toolkit extends Object
```

Methods

```
public static synchronized Toolkit getDefaultToolkit();
public static String getProperty(String key, String defaultValue);
public abstract void beep();
public abstract int checkImage(Image image, int width, int height,
    ImageObserver observer);
protected abstract ButtonPeer createButton(Button target);
protected abstract CanvasPeer createCanvas(Canvas target);
protected abstract CheckboxPeer createCheckbox(Checkbox target);
protected abstract CheckboxMenuItemPeer
    createCheckboxMenuItem(CheckboxMenuItem target);
protected abstract ChoicePeer createChoice(Choice target);
protected abstract DialogPeer createDialog(Dialog target);
protected abstract FileDialogPeer createFileDialog(FileDialog target);
protected abstract FramePeer createFrame(Frame target);
public abstract Image createImage(byte[] imagedata, int imageoffset,
    int imagelength);
public abstract Image createImage(ImageProducer producer);
protected abstract LabelPeer createLabel(Label target);
protected abstract ListPeer createList(List target);
protected abstract MenuPeer createMenu(Menu target);
protected abstract MenuBarPeer createMenuBar(MenuBar target);
protected abstract MenuItemPeer createMenuItem(MenuItem target);
protected abstract PanelPeer createPanel(Panel target);
protected abstract PopupMenuPeer createPopupMenu(PopupMenu target);
protected abstract ScrollbarPeer createScrollbar(Scrollbar target);
protected abstract ScrollPanePeer createScrollPane(ScrollPane target);
```

```
protected abstract TextAreaPeer createTextArea(TextArea target);
protected abstract TextFieldPeer createTextField(TextField target);
protected abstract WindowPeer createWindow(Window target);
public abstract ColorModel getColorModel();
public abstract String[] getFontList();
public abstract FontMetrics getFontMetrics(Font font);
protected abstract FontPeer getFontPeer(String name, int style);
public abstract Image getImage(String filename);
public abstract Image getImage(URL url);
public abstract PrintJob getPrintJob(Frame frame, String jobtitle,
    Properties props);
public abstract int getScreenResolution();
public abstract Dimension getScreenSize();
public abstract Clipboard getSystemClipboard();
protected abstract EventQueue getSystemEventQueueImpl();
public abstract boolean prepareImage(Image image, int width, int
    height, ImageObserver observer);
public abstract void sync();
public Image createImage(byte[] imagedata);
public int getMenuShortcutKeyMask();
public final EventQueue getSystemEventQueue();
```

The *Window* Class

```
public Class Window extends Container
```

Constructors

```
public Window(Frame parent);
```

Methods

```
public void addNotify();
public synchronized void addWindowListener(WindowListener l);
public void dispose();
public Component getFocusOwner();
public Locale getLocale();
public Toolkit getToolkit();
public final String getWarningString();
public boolean isShowing();
public void pack();
public boolean postEvent(Event e);
public synchronized void removeWindowListener(WindowListener l);
```

```
public void show();
public void toBack();
public void toFront();
```

The *java.awt.datatransfer* Package

The *Clipboard* Class

```
public Class Clipboard extends Object
```

Constructors

```
public Clipboard(String name);
```

Methods

```
public synchronized Transferable getContents(Object requestor);
public String getName();
public synchronized void setContents(Transferable contents,
  ClipboardOwner owner);
```

The *ClipboardOwner* Interface

```
public Interface ClipboardOwner
```

Methods

```
public void lostOwnership(Clipboard clipboard, Transferable contents);
```

The *DataFlavor* Class

```
public Class DataFlavor extends Object
```

Data

```
public static DataFlavor plainTextFlavor;
public static DataFlavor stringFlavor;
```

Constructors

```
public DataFlavor(Class representationClass, String
  humanPresentableName);
public DataFlavor(String mimeType, String humanPresentableName);
```

Methods

```
public boolean equals(DataFlavor dataFlavor);
public String getHumanPresentableName();
public String getMimeType();
public Class getRepresentationClass();
public final boolean isMimeTypeEqual(DataFlavor dataFlavor);
public boolean isMimeTypeEqual(String mimeType);
public void setHumanPresentableName(String humanPresentableName);
```

The *StringSelection* Class

```
public Class StringSelection extends Object implements Transferable,
  ClipboardOwner
```

Constructors

```
public StringSelection(String data);
```

Methods

```
public synchronized Object getTransferData(DataFlavor flavor) throws
  UnsupportedFlavorException, IOException;
public synchronized DataFlavor[] getTransferDataFlavors();
public boolean isDataFlavorSupported(DataFlavor flavor);
public void lostOwnership(Clipboard clipboard, Transferable contents);
```

The *Transferable* Interface

```
public Interface Transferable
```

Methods

```
public Object getTransferData(DataFlavor flavor) throws
  UnsupportedFlavorException, IOException;
public DataFlavor[] getTransferDataFlavors();
public boolean isDataFlavorSupported(DataFlavor flavor);
```

The *UnsupportedFlavorException* Class

```
public Class UnsupportedFlavorException extends Exception
```

Constructors

```
public UnsupportedFlavorException(DataFlavor flavor);
```

The *java.awt.event* Package

The *ActionEvent* Class

```
public Class ActionEvent extends AWTEvent
```

Data

```
public static final int ACTION_FIRST = 1001;
public static final int ACTION_LAST = 1001;
public static final int ACTION_PERFORMED = ACTION_FIRST;
public static final int ALT_MASK = Event.ALT_MASK;
public static final int CTRL_MASK = Event.CTRL_MASK;
public static final int META_MASK = Event.META_MASK;
public static final int SHIFT_MASK = Event.SHIFT_MASK;
```

Constructors

```
public ActionEvent(Object source, int id, String command);
public ActionEvent(Object source, int id, String command, int
  modifiers);
```

Methods

```
public String getActionCommand();
public int getModifiers();
public String paramString();
```

The *ActionListener* Interface

```
public Interface ActionListener extends EventListener
```

Methods

```
public void actionPerformed(ActionEvent e);
```

The *AdjustmentEvent* Class

```
public Class AdjustmentEvent extends AWTEvent
```

Data

```
public static final int ADJUSTMENT_FIRST = 601;
public static final int ADJUSTMENT_LAST = 601;
public static final int ADJUSTMENT_VALUE_CHANGED = ADJUSTMENT_FIRST;
public static final int BLOCK_DECREMENT = 3;
public static final int BLOCK_INCREMENT = 4;
public static final int TRACK = 5;
public static final int UNIT_DECREMENT = 2;
public static final int UNIT_INCREMENT = 1;
```

Constructors

```
public AdjustmentEvent(Adjustable source, int id, int type, int value);
```

Methods

```
public Adjustable getAdjustable();
public int getAdjustmentType();
public int getValue();
public String paramString();
```

The *AdjustmentListener* Interface

```
public Interface AdjustmentListener extends EventListener
```

Methods

```
public void adjustmentValueChanged(AdjustmentEvent e);
```

The *ComponentAdapter* Class

```
public abstract Class ComponentAdapter extends Object implements
  ComponentListener
```

Methods

```
public void componentHidden(ComponentEvent e);
public void componentMoved(ComponentEvent e);
public void componentResized(ComponentEvent e);
public void componentShown(ComponentEvent e);
```

The *ComponentEvent* Class

```
public Class ComponentEvent extends AWTEvent
```

Data

```
public static final int COMPONENT_FIRST = 100;
public static final int COMPONENT_HIDDEN = 3 + COMPONENT_FIRST;
public static final int COMPONENT_LAST = 103;
public static final int COMPONENT_MOVED = COMPONENT_FIRST;
public static final int COMPONENT_RESIZED = 1 + COMPONENT_FIRST;
public static final int COMPONENT_SHOWN = 2 + COMPONENT_FIRST;
```

Constructors

```
public ComponentEvent(Component source, int id);
```

Methods

```
public Component getComponent();
public String paramString();
```

The *ComponentListener* Interface

```
public Interface ComponentListener extends EventListener
```

Methods

```
public void componentHidden(ComponentEvent e);
public void componentMoved(ComponentEvent e);
public void componentResized(ComponentEvent e);
public void componentShown(ComponentEvent e);
```

The *ContainerAdapter* Class

```
public abstract Class ContainerAdapter extends Object implements
  ContainerListener
```

Methods

```
public void componentAdded(ContainerEvent e);
public void componentRemoved(ContainerEvent e);
```

The *ContainerEvent* Class

```
public Class ContainerEvent extends ComponentEvent
```

Data

```
public static final int COMPONENT_ADDED = CONTAINER_FIRST;
public static final int COMPONENT_REMOVED = 1 + CONTAINER_FIRST;
public static final int CONTAINER_FIRST = 300;
public static final int CONTAINER_LAST = 301;
```

Constructors

```
public ContainerEvent(Component source, int id, Component child);
```

Methods

```
public Component getChild();
public Container getContainer();
public String paramString();
```

The *ContainerListener* Interface

```
public Interface ContainerListener extends EventListener
```

Methods

```
public void componentAdded(ContainerEvent e);
public void componentRemoved(ContainerEvent e);
```

The *FocusAdapter* Class

```
public abstract Class FocusAdapter extends Object implements
    FocusListener
```

Methods

```
public void focusGained(FocusEvent e);
public void focusLost(FocusEvent e);
```

The *FocusEvent* Class

```
public Class FocusEvent extends ComponentEvent
```

Data

```
public static final int FOCUS_FIRST = 1004;
public static final int FOCUS_GAINED = FOCUS_FIRST;
public static final int FOCUS_LAST = 1005;
public static final int FOCUS_LOST = 1 + FOCUS_FIRST;
```

Constructors

```
public FocusEvent(Component source, int id, boolean temporary);
public FocusEvent(Component source, int id);
```

Methods

```
public boolean isTemporary();
public String paramString();
```

The *FocusListener* Interface

```
public Interface FocusListener extends EventListener
```

Methods

```
public void focusGained(FocusEvent e);
public void focusLost(FocusEvent e);
```

The *InputEvent* Class

```
public abstract Class InputEvent extends ComponentEvent
```

Data

```
public static final int ALT_MASK = Event.ALT_MASK;
public static final int BUTTON1_MASK = 1 << 4;
public static final int BUTTON2_MASK = Event.ALT_MASK;
public static final int BUTTON3_MASK = Event.META_MASK;
public static final int CTRL_MASK = Event.CTRL_MASK;
public static final int META_MASK = Event.META_MASK;
public static final int SHIFT_MASK = Event.SHIFT_MASK;
```

Methods

```
public void consume();
public int getModifiers();
public long getWhen();
public boolean isAltDown();
```

```
public boolean isConsumed();
public boolean isControlDown();
public boolean isMetaDown();
public boolean isShiftDown();
```

The *ItemEvent* Class

```
public Class ItemEvent extends AWTEvent
```

Data

```
public static final int DESELECTED = 2;
public static final int ITEM_FIRST = 701;
public static final int ITEM_LAST = 701;
public static final int ITEM_STATE_CHANGED = ITEM_FIRST;
public static final int SELECTED = 1;
```

Constructors

```
public ItemEvent(ItemSelectable source, int id, Object item, int
  stateChange);
```

Methods

```
public Object getItem();
public ItemSelectable getItemSelectable();
public int getStateChange();
public String paramString();
```

The *ItemListener* Interface

```
public Interface ItemListener extends EventListener
```

Methods

```
void itemStateChanged(ItemEvent e);
```

The *KeyAdapter* Class

```
public abstract Class KeyAdapter extends Object implements KeyListener
```

Methods

```
public void keyPressed(KeyEvent e);
public void keyReleased(KeyEvent e);
public void keyTyped(KeyEvent e);
```

The *KeyEvent* Class

```
public Class KeyEvent extends InputEvent
```

Data

```
public static final char CHAR_UNDEFINED = 0x0;
public static final int KEY_FIRST = 400;
public static final int KEY_LAST = 402;
public static final int KEY_PRESSED = 1 + KEY_FIRST;
public static final int KEY_RELEASED = 2 + KEY_FIRST;
public static final int KEY_TYPED = KEY_FIRST;
public static final int VK_0 = 0x30;
public static final int VK_1 = 0x31;
public static final int VK_2 = 0x32;
public static final int VK_3 = 0x33;
public static final int VK_4 = 0x34;
public static final int VK_5 = 0x35;
public static final int VK_6 = 0x36;
public static final int VK_7 = 0x37;
public static final int VK_8 = 0x38;
public static final int VK_9 = 0x39;
public static final int VK_A = 0x41;
public static final int VK_ACCEPT = 0x1E;
public static final int VK_ADD = 0x6B;
public static final int VK_ALT = 0x12;
public static final int VK_B = 0x42;
public static final int VK_BACK_QUOTE = 0xC0;
public static final int VK_BACK_SLASH = 0x5C;
public static final int VK_BACK_SPACE = '\b';
public static final int VK_C = 0x43;
public static final int VK_CANCEL = 0x03;
public static final int VK_CAPS_LOCK = 0x14;
public static final int VK_CLEAR = 0x0C;
public static final int VK_CLOSE_BRACKET = 0x5D;
public static final int VK_COMMA = 0x2C;
public static final int VK_CONTROL = 0x11;
public static final int VK_CONVERT = 0x1C;
public static final int VK_D = 0x44;
public static final int VK_DECIMAL = 0x6E;
public static final int VK_DELETE = 0x7F;
public static final int VK_DIVIDE = 0x6F;
public static final int VK_DOWN = 0x28;
```

```
public static final int VK_E = 0x45;
public static final int VK_END = 0x23;
public static final int VK_ENTER = '\n';
public static final int VK_EQUALS = 0x3D;
public static final int VK_ESCAPE = 0x1B;
public static final int VK_F = 0x46;
public static final int VK_F1 = 0x70;
public static final int VK_F10 = 0x79;
public static final int VK_F11 = 0x7A;
public static final int VK_F12 = 0x7B;
public static final int VK_F2 = 0x71;
public static final int VK_F3 = 0x72;
public static final int VK_F4 = 0x73;
public static final int VK_F5 = 0x74;
public static final int VK_F6 = 0x75;
public static final int VK_F7 = 0x76;
public static final int VK_F8 = 0x77;
public static final int VK_F9 = 0x78;
public static final int VK_FINAL = 0x18;
public static final int VK_G = 0x47;
public static final int VK_H = 0x48;
public static final int VK_HELP = 0x9C;
public static final int VK_HOME = 0x24;
public static final int VK_I = 0x49;
public static final int VK_INSERT = 0x9B;
public static final int VK_J = 0x4A;
public static final int VK_K = 0x4B;
public static final int VK_KANA = 0x15;
public static final int VK_KANJI = 0x19;
public static final int VK_L = 0x4C;
public static final int VK_LEFT = 0x25;
public static final int VK_M = 0x4D;
public static final int VK_META = 0x9D;
public static final int VK_MODECHANGE = 0x1F;
public static final int VK_MULTIPLY = 0x6A;
public static final int VK_N = 0x4E;
public static final int VK_NONCONVERT = 0x1D;
public static final int VK_NUM_LOCK = 0x90;
public static final int VK_NUMPAD0 = 0x60;
public static final int VK_NUMPAD1 = 0x61;
public static final int VK_NUMPAD2 = 0x62;
public static final int VK_NUMPAD3 = 0x63;
```

```
public static final int VK_NUMPAD4 = 0x64;
public static final int VK_NUMPAD5 = 0x65;
public static final int VK_NUMPAD6 = 0x66;
public static final int VK_NUMPAD7 = 0x67;
public static final int VK_NUMPAD8 = 0x68;
public static final int VK_NUMPAD9 = 0x69;
public static final int VK_O = 0x4F;
public static final int VK_OPEN_BRACKET = 0x5B;
public static final int VK_P = 0x50;
public static final int VK_PAGE_DOWN = 0x22;
public static final int VK_PAGE_UP = 0x21;
public static final int VK_PAUSE = 0x13;
public static final int VK_PERIOD = 0x2E;
public static final int VK_PRINTSCREEN = 0x9A;
public static final int VK_Q = 0x51;
public static final int VK_QUOTE = 0xDE;
public static final int VK_R = 0x52;
public static final int VK_RIGHT = 0x27;
public static final int VK_S = 0x53;
public static final int VK_SCROLL_LOCK = 0x91;
public static final int VK_SEMICOLON = 0x3B;
public static final int VK_SEPARATER = 0x6C;
public static final int VK_SHIFT = 0x10;
public static final int VK_SLASH = 0x2F;
public static final int VK_SPACE = 0x20;
public static final int VK_SUBTRACT = 0x6D;
public static final int VK_T = 0x54;
public static final int VK_TAB = '\t';
public static final int VK_U = 0x55;
public static final int VK_UNDEFINED = 0x0;
public static final int VK_UP = 0x26;
public static final int VK_V = 0x56;
public static final int VK_W = 0x57;
public static final int VK_X = 0x58;
public static final int VK_Y = 0x59;
public static final int VK_Z = 0x5A;
```

Constructors

```
public KeyEvent(Component source, int id, long when, int modifiers, int
    keyCode, char keyChar);
public KeyEvent(Component source, int id, long when, int modifiers, int
    keyCode);
```

Methods

```
public static String getKeyModifiersText(int modifiers);
public static String getKeyText(int keyCode);
public char getKeyChar();
public int getKeyCode();
public boolean isActionKey();
public String paramString();
public void setKeyChar(char keyChar);
public void setKeyCode(int keyCode);
public void setModifiers(int modifiers);
```

The *KeyListener* Interface

```
public Interface KeyListener extends EventListener
```

Methods

```
public void keyPressed(KeyEvent e);
public void keyReleased(KeyEvent e);
public void keyTyped(KeyEvent e);
```

The *MouseAdapter* Class

```
public abstract Class MouseAdapter extends Object implements
  MouseListener
```

Methods

```
public void mouseClicked(MouseEvent e);
public void mouseEntered(MouseEvent e);
public void mouseExited(MouseEvent e);
public void mousePressed(MouseEvent e);
public void mouseReleased(MouseEvent e);
```

The *MouseEvent* Class

```
public Class MouseEvent extends InputEvent
```

Data

```
public static final int MOUSE_CLICKED = MOUSE_FIRST;
public static final int MOUSE_DRAGGED = 6 + MOUSE_FIRST;
public static final int MOUSE_ENTERED = 4 + MOUSE_FIRST;
```

```
public static final int MOUSE_EXITED = 5 + MOUSE_FIRST;
public static final int MOUSE_FIRST = 500;
public static final int MOUSE_LAST = 506;
public static final int MOUSE_MOVED = 3 + MOUSE_FIRST;
public static final int MOUSE_PRESSED = 1 + MOUSE_FIRST;
public static final int MOUSE_RELEASED = 2 + MOUSE_FIRST;
```

Constructors

```
public MouseEvent(Component source, int id, long when, int modifiers,
    int x, int y, int clickCount, boolean popupTrigger);
```

Methods

```
public int getClickCount();
public Point getPoint();
public int getX();
public int getY();
public boolean isPopupTrigger();
public String paramString();
public synchronized void translatePoint(int x, int y);
```

The *MouseListener* Interface

```
public Interface MouseListener extends EventListener
```

Methods

```
public void mouseClicked(MouseEvent e);
public void mouseEntered(MouseEvent e);
public void mouseExited(MouseEvent e);
public void mousePressed(MouseEvent e);
public void mouseReleased(MouseEvent e);
```

The *MouseMotionAdapter* Class

```
public abstract Class MouseMotionAdapter extends Object implements
  MouseMotionListener
```

Methods

```
public void mouseDragged(MouseEvent e);
public void mouseMoved(MouseEvent e);
```

The *MouseMotionListener* Interface

```
public Interface MouseMotionListener extends EventListener
```

Methods

```
public void mouseDragged(MouseEvent e);
public void mouseMoved(MouseEvent e);
```

The *PaintEvent* Class

```
public Class PaintEvent extends ComponentEvent
```

Data

```
public static final int PAINT = PAINT_FIRST;
public static final int PAINT_FIRST = 800;
public static final int PAINT_LAST = 801;
public static final int UPDATE = PAINT_FIRST + 1;
```

Constructors

```
public PaintEvent(Component source, int id, Rectangle updateRect);
```

Methods

```
public Rectangle getUpdateRect();
public String paramString();
public void setUpdateRect(Rectangle updateRect);
```

The *TextEvent* Class

```
public Class TextEvent extends AWTEvent
```

Data

```
public static final int TEXT_FIRST = 900;
public static final int TEXT_LAST = 900;
public static final int TEXT_VALUE_CHANGED = TEXT_FIRST;
```

Constructors

```
public TextEvent(Object source, int id);
```

Methods

```
public String paramString();
```

The *TextListener* Interface

```
public Interface TextListener extends EventListener
```

Methods

```
public void textValueChanged(TextEvent e);
```

The *WindowAdapter* Class

```
public abstract Class WindowAdapter extends Object implements
    WindowListener
```

Methods

```
public void windowActivated(WindowEvent e);
public void windowClosed(WindowEvent e);
public void windowClosing(WindowEvent e);
public void windowDeactivated(WindowEvent e);
public void windowDeiconified(WindowEvent e);
public void windowIconified(WindowEvent e);
public void windowOpened(WindowEvent e);
```

The *WindowEvent* Class

```
public Class WindowEvent extends ComponentEvent
```

Data

```
public static final int WINDOW_ACTIVATED = 5 + WINDOW_FIRST;
public static final int WINDOW_CLOSED = 2 + WINDOW_FIRST;
public static final int WINDOW_CLOSING = 1 + WINDOW_FIRST;
public static final int WINDOW_DEACTIVATED = 6 + WINDOW_FIRST;
public static final int WINDOW_DEICONIFIED = 4 + WINDOW_FIRST;
public static final int WINDOW_FIRST = 200;
public static final int WINDOW_ICONIFIED = 3 + WINDOW_FIRST;
public static final int WINDOW_LAST = 206;
public static final int WINDOW_OPENED = WINDOW_FIRST;
```

Constructors

```
public WindowEvent(Window source, int id);
```

Methods

```
public Window getWindow();
public String paramString();
```

The *WindowListener* Interface

```
public Interface WindowListener extends EventListener
```

Methods

```
public void windowActivated(WindowEvent e);
public void windowClosed(WindowEvent e);
public void windowClosing(WindowEvent e);
public void windowDeactivated(WindowEvent e);
public void windowDeiconified(WindowEvent e);
public void windowIconified(WindowEvent e);
public void windowOpened(WindowEvent e);
```

The *java.awt.image* Package

The *AreaAveragingScaleFilter* Class

```
public Class AreaAveragingScaleFilter extends ReplicateScaleFilter
```

Constructors

```
public AreaAveragingScaleFilter(int width, int height);
```

Methods

```
public void setHints(int hints);
public void setPixels(int x, int y, int w, int h, ColorModel model,
   byte pixels[], int off, int scansize);
public void setPixels(int x, int y, int w, int h, ColorModel model, int
   pixels[], int off, int scansize);
```

The *ColorModel* Class

```
public abstract Class ColorModel extends Object
```

Constructors

```
public ColorModel(int bits);
```

Methods

```
public static ColorModel getRGBdefault();
public abstract int getAlpha(int pixel);
public abstract int getBlue(int pixel);
public abstract int getGreen(int pixel);
public abstract int getRed(int pixel);
private native void deletepData();
public void finalize();
public int getPixelSize();
public int getRGB(int pixel);
```

The *CropImageFilter* Class

```
public Class CropImageFilter extends ImageFilter
```

Constructors

```
public CropImageFilter(int x, int y, int w, int h);
```

Methods

```
public void setDimensions(int w, int h);
public void setPixels(int x, int y, int w, int h, ColorModel model,
  byte pixels[], int off, int scansize);
public void setPixels(int x, int y, int w, int h, ColorModel model, int
  pixels[], int off, int scansize);
public void setProperties(Hashtable props);
```

The *DirectColorModel* Class

```
public Class DirectColorModel extends ColorModel
```

Constructors

```
public DirectColorModel(int bits, int rmask, int gmask, int bmask);
```

```
public DirectColorModel(int bits, int rmask, int gmask, int bmask, int
  amask);
```

Methods

```
final public int getAlpha(int pixel);
final public int getAlphaMask();
final public int getBlue(int pixel);
final public int getBlueMask();
final public int getGreen(int pixel);
final public int getGreenMask();
final public int getRed(int pixel);
final public int getRedMask();
final public int getRGB(int pixel);
```

The *FilteredImageSource* Class

```
public Class FilteredImageSource extends Object implements
  ImageProducer
```

Constructors

```
public FilteredImageSource(ImageProducer orig, ImageFilter imgf);
```

Methods

```
public synchronized void addConsumer(ImageConsumer ic);
public synchronized boolean isConsumer(ImageConsumer ic);
public synchronized void removeConsumer(ImageConsumer ic);
public void requestTopDownLeftRightResend(ImageConsumer ic);
public void startProduction(ImageConsumer ic);
```

The *ImageConsumer* Interface

```
public Interface ImageConsumer
```

Methods

```
void imageComplete(int status);
void setColorModel(ColorModel model);
void setDimensions(int width, int height);
void setHints(int hintflags);
void setPixels(int x, int y, int w, int h, ColorModel model, byte
  pixels[], int off, int scansize);
```

```
void setPixels(int x, int y, int w, int h, ColorModel model, int
    pixels[], int off, int scansize);
void setProperties(Hashtable props);
```

The *ImageFilter* Class

```
public Class ImageFilter extends Object implements ImageConsumer,
    Cloneable
```

Methods

```
public Object clone();
public ImageFilter getFilterInstance(ImageConsumer ic);
public void imageComplete(int status);
public void resendTopDownLeftRight(ImageProducer ip);
public void setColorModel(ColorModel model);
public void setDimensions(int width, int height);
public void setHints(int hints);
public void setPixels(int x, int y, int w, int h, ColorModel model,
    byte pixels[], int off, int scansize);
public void setPixels(int x, int y, int w, int h, ColorModel model, int
    pixels[], int off, int scansize);
public void setProperties(Hashtable props);
```

The *ImageObserver* Interface

```
public Interface ImageObserver
```

Data

```
public static final int ABORT = 128;
public static final int ALLBITS = 32;
public static final int ERROR = 64;
public static final int FRAMEBITS = 16;
public static final int HEIGHT = 2;
public static final int PROPERTIES = 4;
public static final int SOMEBITS = 8;
public static final int WIDTH = 1;
```

Methods

```
public boolean imageUpdate(Image img, int infoflags, int x, int y, int
    width, int height);
```

The *ImageProducer* Interface

```
public Interface ImageProducer
```

Methods

```
public void addConsumer(ImageConsumer ic);
public boolean isConsumer(ImageConsumer ic);
public void removeConsumer(ImageConsumer ic);
public void requestTopDownLeftRightResend(ImageConsumer ic);
public void startProduction(ImageConsumer ic);
```

The *IndexColorModel* Class

```
public Class IndexColorModel extends ColorModel
```

Constructors

```
public IndexColorModel(int bits, int size, byte r[], byte g[], byte
  b[]);
public IndexColorModel(int bits, int size, byte r[], byte g[], byte
  b[], int trans);
public IndexColorModel(int bits, int size, byte r[], byte g[], byte
  b[], byte a[]);
public IndexColorModel(int bits, int size, byte cmap[], int start,
  boolean hasalpha);
public IndexColorModel(int bits, int size, byte cmap[], int start,
  boolean hasalpha, int trans);
```

Methods

```
final public int getAlpha(int pixel);
final public void getAlphas(byte a[]);
final public int getBlue(int pixel);
final public void getBlues(byte b[]);
final public int getGreen(int pixel);
final public void getGreens(byte g[]);
final public int getMapSize();
final public int getRed(int pixel);
final public void getReds(byte r[]);
final public int getRGB(int pixel);
final public int getTransparentPixel();
```

The *MemoryImageSource* Class

```
public Class MemoryImageSource extends Object implements ImageProducer
```

Constructors

```
public MemoryImageSource(int w, int h, ColorModel cm, byte[] pix, int
    off, int scan);
public MemoryImageSource(int w, int h, ColorModel cm, byte[] pix, int
    off, int scan, Hashtable props);
public MemoryImageSource(int w, int h, ColorModel cm, int[] pix, int
    off, int scan);
public MemoryImageSource(int w, int h, ColorModel cm, int[] pix, int
    off, int scan, Hashtable props);
public MemoryImageSource(int w, int h, int pix[], int off, int scan);
public MemoryImageSource(int w, int h, int pix[], int off, int scan,
    Hashtable props);
```

Methods

```
public synchronized void addConsumer(ImageConsumer ic);
public synchronized boolean isConsumer(ImageConsumer ic);
public void newPixels();
public synchronized void newPixels(byte[] newpix, ColorModel newmodel,
    int offset, int scansize);
public synchronized void newPixels(int x, int y, int w, int h);
public synchronized void newPixels(int x, int y, int w, int h, boolean
    framenotify);
public synchronized void newPixels(int[] newpix, ColorModel newmodel,
    int offset, int scansize);
public synchronized void removeConsumer(ImageConsumer ic);
public void requestTopDownLeftRightResend(ImageConsumer ic);
public synchronized void setAnimated(boolean animated);
public synchronized void setFullBufferUpdates(boolean fullbuffers);
public void startProduction(ImageConsumer ic);
```

The *PixelGrabber* Class

```
public Class PixelGrabber extends Object implements ImageConsumer
```

Constructors

```
public PixelGrabber(Image img, int x, int y, int w, int h, int[] pix,
    int off, int scansize);
```

```
public PixelGrabber(ImageProducer ip, int x, int y, int w, int h, int[]
    pix, int off, int scansize);
public PixelGrabber(Image img, int x, int y, int w, int h, boolean
    forceRGB);
```

Methods

```
public synchronized void abortGrabbing();
public synchronized ColorModel getColorModel();
public synchronized int getHeight();
public synchronized Object getPixels();
public synchronized int getStatus();
public synchronized int getWidth();
public boolean grabPixels() throws InterruptedException;
public synchronized boolean grabPixels(long ms) throws
    InterruptedException;
public synchronized void imageComplete(int status);
public void setColorModel(ColorModel model);
public void setDimensions(int width, int height);
public void setHints(int hints);
public void setPixels(int srcX, int srcY, int srcW, int srcH,
    ColorModel model, byte pixels[], int srcOff, int srcScan);
public void setPixels(int srcX, int srcY, int srcW, int srcH,
    ColorModel model, int pixels[], int srcOff, int srcScan);
public void setProperties(Hashtable props);
public synchronized void startGrabbing();
public synchronized int status();
```

The *RGBImageFilter* Class

```
public abstract Class RGBImageFilter extends ImageFilter
```

Methods

```
public abstract int filterRGB(int x, int y, int rgb);
public IndexColorModel filterIndexColorModel(IndexColorModel icm);
public void filterRGBPixels(int x, int y, int w, int h, int pixels[],
    int off, int scansize);
public void setColorModel(ColorModel model);
public void setPixels(int x, int y, int w, int h, ColorModel model,
    byte pixels[], int off, int scansize);
public void setPixels(int x, int y, int w, int h, ColorModel model, int
    pixels[], int off, int scansize);
```

```
public void substituteColorModel(ColorModel oldcm, ColorModel newcm);
```

The *ReplicateScaleFilter* Class

```
public Class ReplicateScaleFilter extends ImageFilter
```

Constructors

```
public ReplicateScaleFilter(int width, int height);
```

Methods

```
public void setDimensions(int w, int h);
public void setPixels(int x, int y, int w, int h, ColorModel model,
    byte pixels[], int off, int scansize);
public void setPixels(int x, int y, int w, int h, ColorModel model, int
    pixels[], int off, int scansize);
public void setProperties(Hashtable props);
```

The *java.awt.peer* Package

The *ActiveEvent* Interface

```
public Interface ActiveEvent
```

Methods

```
public void dispatch();
```

The *ButtonPeer* Interface

```
public Interface ButtonPeer extends ComponentPeer
```

Methods

```
void setLabel(String label);
```

The *CanvasPeer* Interface

```
public Interface CanvasPeer extends ComponentPeer
```

The *CheckboxMenuItemPeer* Interface

public Interface CheckboxMenuItemPeer extends MenuItemPeer

Methods

void setState(boolean t);

The *CheckboxPeer* Interface

public Interface CheckboxPeer extends ComponentPeer

Methods

void setCheckboxGroup(CheckboxGroup g);
void setLabel(String label);
void setState(boolean state);

The *ChoicePeer* Interface

public Interface ChoicePeer extends ComponentPeer

Methods

void add(String item, int index);
void addItem(String item, int index);
void remove(int index);
void select(int index);

The *ComponentPeer* Interface

public Interface ComponentPeer

Methods

int checkImage(Image img, int w, int h, ImageObserver o);
Image createImage(ImageProducer producer);
Image createImage(int width, int height);
void disable();
void dispose();
void enable();
ColorModel getColorModel();
FontMetrics getFontMetrics(Font font);
Graphics getGraphics();

```
Point getLocationOnScreen();
Dimension getMinimumSize();
Dimension getPreferredSize();
java.awt.Toolkit getToolkit();
void handleEvent(AWTEvent e);
void hide();
boolean isFocusTraversable();
Dimension minimumSize();
void paint(Graphics g);
Dimension preferredSize();
boolean prepareImage(Image img, int w, int h, ImageObserver o);
void print(Graphics g);
void repaint(long tm, int x, int y, int width, int height);
void requestFocus();
void reshape(int x, int y, int width, int height);
void setBackground(Color c);
void setBounds(int x, int y, int width, int height);
void setCursor(Cursor cursor);
void setEnabled(boolean b);
void setFont(Font f);
void setForeground(Color c);
void setVisible(boolean b);
void show();
```

The *ContainerPeer* Interface

```
public Interface ContainerPeer extends ComponentPeer
```

Methods

```
void beginValidate();
void endValidate();
Insets getInsets();
Insets insets();
```

The *DialogPeer* Interface

```
public Interface DialogPeer extends WindowPeer
```

Methods

```
void setResizable(boolean resizeable);
void setTitle(String title);
```

The *FileDialogPeer* Interface

```
public Interface FileDialogPeer extends DialogPeer
```

Methods

```
void setDirectory(String dir);
void setFile(String file);
void setFilenameFilter(FilenameFilter filter);
```

The *FontPeer* Interface

```
public Interface FontPeer
```

The *FramePeer* Interface

```
public Interface FramePeer extends WindowPeer
```

Methods

```
void setIconImage(Image im);
void setMenuBar(MenuBar mb);
void setResizable(boolean resizeable);
void setTitle(String title);
```

The *LabelPeer* Interface

```
public Interface LabelPeer extends ComponentPeer
```

Methods

```
void setAlignment(int alignment);
void setText(String label);
```

The *LightweightPeer* Interface

```
public Interface LightweightPeer extends ComponentPeer
```

The *ListPeer* Interface

```
public Interface ListPeer extends ComponentPeer
```

Methods

```
void add(String item, int index);
void addItem(String item, int index);
```

```
void clear();
void delItems(int start, int end);
void deselect(int index);
Dimension getMinimumSize(int rows);
Dimension getPreferredSize(int rows);
int[] getSelectedIndexes();
void makeVisible(int index);
Dimension minimumSize(int v);
Dimension preferredSize(int v);
void removeAll();
void select(int index);
void setMultipleMode(boolean b);
void setMultipleSelections(boolean v);
```

The *MenuBarPeer* Interface

```
public Interface MenuBarPeer extends MenuComponentPeer
```

Methods

```
void addHelpMenu(Menu m);
void addMenu(Menu m);
void delMenu(int index);
```

The *MenuComponentPeer* Interface

```
public Interface MenuComponentPeer
```

Methods

```
void dispose();
```

The *MenuItemPeer* Interface

```
public Interface MenuItemPeer extends MenuComponentPeer
```

Methods

```
void disable();
void enable();
void setEnabled(boolean b);
void setLabel(String label);
```

The *MenuPeer* Interface

```
public Interface MenuPeer extends MenuItemPeer
```

Methods

```
void addItem(MenuItem item);
void addSeparator();
void delItem(int index);
```

The *PanelPeer* Interface

```
public Interface PanelPeer extends ContainerPeer
```

The *PopupMenuPeer* Interface

```
public Interface PopupMenuPeer extends MenuPeer
```

Methods

```
void show(Event e);
```

The *ScrollPanePeer* Interface

```
public Interface ScrollPanePeer extends ContainerPeer
```

Methods

```
void childResized(int w, int h);
int getHScrollbarHeight();
int getVScrollbarWidth();
void setScrollPosition(int x, int y);
void setUnitIncrement(Adjustable adj, int u);
void setValue(Adjustable adj, int v);
```

The *ScrollbarPeer* Interface

```
public Interface ScrollbarPeer extends ComponentPeer
```

Methods

```
void setLineIncrement(int l);
void setPageIncrement(int l);
void setValues(int value, int visible, int minimum, int maximum);
```

The *TextAreaPeer* Interface

```
public Interface TextAreaPeer extends TextComponentPeer
```

Methods

```
Dimension getMinimumSize(int rows, int columns);
Dimension getPreferredSize(int rows, int columns);
void insert(String text, int pos);
void insertText(String txt, int pos);
Dimension minimumSize(int rows, int cols);
Dimension preferredSize(int rows, int cols);
void replaceRange(String text, int start, int end);
void replaceText(String txt, int start, int end);
```

The *TextComponentPeer* Interface

```
public Interface TextComponentPeer extends ComponentPeer
```

Methods

```
int getCaretPosition();
int getSelectionEnd();
int getSelectionStart();
String getText();
void select(int selStart, int selEnd);
void setCaretPosition(int pos);
void setEditable(boolean editable);
void setText(String l);
```

The *TextFieldPeer* Interface

```
public Interface TextFieldPeer extends TextComponentPeer
```

Methods

```
Dimension getMinimumSize(int columns);
Dimension getPreferredSize(int columns);
Dimension minimumSize(int cols);
Dimension preferredSize(int cols);
void setEchoChar(char echoChar);
void setEchoCharacter(char c);
```

The *WindowPeer* Interface

```
public Interface WindowPeer extends ContainerPeer
```

Methods

```
void toBack();
void toFront();
```

The *java.beans* Package

The *BeanDescriptor* Class

```
public Class BeanDescriptor extends FeatureDescriptor
```

Constructors

```
public BeanDescriptor(Class beanClass);
public BeanDescriptor(Class beanClass, Class customizerClass);
```

Methods

```
public Class getBeanClass();
public Class getCustomizerClass();
```

The *BeanInfo* Interface

```
public Interface BeanInfo
```

Methods

```
BeanInfo[] getAdditionalBeanInfo();
BeanDescriptor getBeanDescriptor();
int getDefaultEventIndex();
int getDefaultPropertyIndex();
EventSetDescriptor[] getEventSetDescriptors();
java.awt.Image getIcon(int iconKind);
MethodDescriptor[] getMethodDescriptors();
PropertyDescriptor[] getPropertyDescriptors();
```

The *Beans* Class

```
public Class Beans extends Object
```

Methods

```
public static Object getInstanceOf(Object bean, Class targetType);
public static Object instantiate(ClassLoader cls, String beanName)
    throws java.io.IOException, ClassNotFoundException;
public static boolean isDesignTime();
public static boolean isGuiAvailable();
public static boolean isInstanceOf(Object bean, Class targetType);
public static void setDesignTime(boolean isDesignTime) throws
    SecurityException;
public static void setGuiAvailable(boolean isGuiAvailable) throws
    SecurityException;
```

The *Customizer* Interface

```
public Interface Customizer
```

Methods

```
void addPropertyChangeListener(PropertyChangeListener listener);
void removePropertyChangeListener(PropertyChangeListener listener);
void setObject(Object bean);
```

The *EventSetDescriptor* Class

```
public Class EventSetDescriptor extends FeatureDescriptor
```

Constructors

```
public EventSetDescriptor(Class sourceClass, String eventSetName, Class
    listenerType, String listenerMethodName) throws
    IntrospectionException;
public EventSetDescriptor(Class sourceClass, String eventSetName, Class
    listenerType, String listenerMethodNames[], String
    addListenerMethodName, String removeListenerMethodName) throws
    IntrospectionException;
public EventSetDescriptor(String eventSetName, Class listenerType,
    Method listenerMethods[], Method addListenerMethod, Method
    removeListenerMethod) throws IntrospectionException;
```

```
public EventSetDescriptor(String eventSetName, Class listenerType,
  MethodDescriptor listenerMethodDescriptors[], Method
  addListenerMethod, Method removeListenerMethod) throws
  IntrospectionException;
```

Methods

```
public Method getAddListenerMethod();
public MethodDescriptor[] getListenerMethodDescriptors();
public Method[] getListenerMethods();
public Class getListenerType();
public Method getRemoveListenerMethod();
public boolean isInDefaultEventSet();
public boolean isUnicast();
public void setInDefaultEventSet(boolean inDefaultEventSet);
public void setUnicast(boolean unicast);
```

The *FeatureDescriptor* Class

```
public Class FeatureDescriptor extends Object
```

Constructors

```
public FeatureDescriptor();
```

Methods

```
public java.util.Enumeration attributeNames();
public String getDisplayName();
public String getName();
public String getShortDescription();
public Object getValue(String attributeName);
public boolean isExpert();
public boolean isHidden();
public void setDisplayName(String displayName);
public void setExpert(boolean expert);
public void setHidden(boolean hidden);
public void setName(String name);
public void setShortDescription(String text);
public void setValue(String attributeName, Object value);
```

The *IndexedPropertyDescriptor* Class

```
public Class IndexedPropertyDescriptor extends PropertyDescriptor
```

Constructors

```
public IndexedPropertyDescriptor(String propertyName, Class beanClass)
  throws IntrospectionException;
public IndexedPropertyDescriptor(String propertyName, Class beanClass,
  String getterName, String setterName, String indexedGetterName,
  String indexedSetterName) throws IntrospectionException;
public IndexedPropertyDescriptor(String propertyName, Method getter,
  Method setter, Method indexedGetter, Method indexedSetter) throws
  IntrospectionException;
```

Methods

```
public Class getIndexedPropertyType();
public Method getIndexedReadMethod();
public Method getIndexedWriteMethod();
```

The *IntrospectionException* Class

```
public Class IntrospectionException extends Exception
```

Constructors

```
public IntrospectionException(String mess);
```

The *Introspector* Class

```
public Class Introspector extends Object
```

Methods

```
public static String decapitalize(String name);
public static BeanInfo getBeanInfo(Class beanClass) throws
  IntrospectionException;
public static BeanInfo getBeanInfo(Class beanClass, Class stopClass)
  throws IntrospectionException;
public static String[] getBeanInfoSearchPath();
public static void setBeanInfoSearchPath(String path[]);
```

The *MethodDescriptor* Class

```
public Class MethodDescriptor extends FeatureDescriptor
```

Constructors

```
public MethodDescriptor(Method method);
public MethodDescriptor(Method method, ParameterDescriptor
  parameterDescriptors[]);
```

Methods

```
public Method getMethod();
public ParameterDescriptor[] getParameterDescriptors();
```

The *ParameterDescriptor* Class

```
public Class ParameterDescriptor extends FeatureDescriptor
```

The *PropertyChangeEvent* Class

```
public Class PropertyChangeEvent extends java.util.EventObject
```

Constructors

```
public PropertyChangeEvent(Object source, String propertyName, Object
  oldValue, Object newValue);
```

Methods

```
public Object getNewValue();
public Object getOldValue();
public Object getPropagationId();
public String getPropertyName();
public void setPropagationId(Object propagationId);
```

The *PropertyChangeListener* Interface

```
public Interface PropertyChangeListener extends java.util.EventListener
```

Methods

```
void propertyChange(PropertyChangeEvent evt);
```

The *PropertyChangeSupport* Class

```
public Class PropertyChangeSupport extends Object implements
    java.io.Serializable
```

Constructors

```
public PropertyChangeSupport(Object sourceBean);
```

Methods

```
public synchronized void addPropertyChangeListener(
    PropertyChangeListener listener);
public void firePropertyChange(String propertyName, Object oldValue,
    Object newValue);
public synchronized void removePropertyChangeListener(
    PropertyChangeListener listener);
```

The *PropertyDescriptor* Class

```
public Class PropertyDescriptor extends FeatureDescriptor
```

Constructors

```
public PropertyDescriptor(String propertyName, Class beanClass) throws
    IntrospectionException;
public PropertyDescriptor(String propertyName, Class beanClass, String
    getterName, String setterName) throws IntrospectionException;
public PropertyDescriptor(String propertyName, Method getter, Method
    setter) throws IntrospectionException;
```

Methods

```
public Class getPropertyEditorClass();
public Class getPropertyType();
public Method getReadMethod();
public Method getWriteMethod();
public boolean isBound();
public boolean isConstrained();
public void setBound(boolean bound);
public void setConstrained(boolean constrained);
public void setPropertyEditorClass(Class propertyEditorClass);
```

The *PropertyEditor* Interface

```
public Interface PropertyEditor
```

Methods

```
void addPropertyChangeListener(PropertyChangeListener listener);
String getAsText();
java.awt.Component getCustomEditor();
String getJavaInitializationString();
String[] getTags();
Object getValue();
boolean isPaintable();
void paintValue(java.awt.Graphics gfx, java.awt.Rectangle box);
void removePropertyChangeListener(PropertyChangeListener listener);
void setAsText(String text) throws java.lang.IllegalArgumentException;
void setValue(Object value);
boolean supportsCustomEditor();
```

The *PropertyEditorManager* Class

```
public Class PropertyEditorManager extends Object
```

Methods

```
public static PropertyEditor findEditor(Class targetType);
public static String[] getEditorSearchPath();
public static void registerEditor(Class targetType, Class editorClass);
public static void setEditorSearchPath(String path[]);
```

The *PropertyEditorSupport* Class

```
public Class PropertyEditorSupport extends Object implements
  PropertyEditor
```

Methods

```
public synchronized void addPropertyChangeListener(
  PropertyChangeListener listener);
public void firePropertyChange();
public String getAsText();
public java.awt.Component getCustomEditor();
public String getJavaInitializationString();
public String[] getTags();
public Object getValue();
```

```
public boolean isPaintable();
public void paintValue(java.awt.Graphics gfx, java.awt.Rectangle box);
public synchronized void removePropertyChangeListener(
  PropertyChangeListener listener);
public void setAsText(String text) throws
  java.lang.IllegalArgumentException;
public void setValue(Object value);
public boolean supportsCustomEditor();
```

The *PropertyVetoException* Class

```
public Class PropertyVetoException extends Exception
```

Constructors

```
public PropertyVetoException(String mess, PropertyChangeEvent evt);
```

Methods

```
public PropertyChangeEvent getPropertyChangeEvent();
```

The *SimpleBeanInfo* Class

```
public Class SimpleBeanInfo extends Object implements BeanInfo
```

Methods

```
public BeanInfo[] getAdditionalBeanInfo();
public BeanDescriptor getBeanDescriptor();
public int getDefaultEventIndex();
public int getDefaultPropertyIndex();
public EventSetDescriptor[] getEventSetDescriptors();
public java.awt.Image getIcon(int iconKind);
public MethodDescriptor[] getMethodDescriptors();
public PropertyDescriptor[] getPropertyDescriptors();
public java.awt.Image loadImage(String resourceName);
```

The *VetoableChangeListener* Interface

```
public Interface VetoableChangeListener extends java.util.EventListener
```

Methods

```
void vetoableChange(PropertyChangeEvent evt) throws
  PropertyVetoException;
```

The *VetoableChangeSupport* Class

```
public Class VetoableChangeSupport extends Object implements
   java.io.Serializable
```

Constructors

```
public VetoableChangeSupport(Object sourceBean);
```

Methods

```
public synchronized void addVetoableChangeListener(
   VetoableChangeListener listener);
public void fireVetoableChange(String propertyName, Object oldValue,
   Object newValue) throws PropertyVetoException;
public synchronized void removeVetoableChangeListener(
   VetoableChangeListener listener);
```

The *Visibility* Interface

```
public Interface Visibility
```

Methods

```
boolean avoidingGui();
void dontUseGui();
boolean needsGui();
void okToUseGui();
```

The *java.io* Package

The *BufferedInputStream* Class

```
public Class BufferedInputStream extends FilterInputStream
```

Constructors

```
public BufferedInputStream(InputStream in);
public BufferedInputStream(InputStream in, int size);
```

Methods

```
public synchronized int available() throws IOException;
public synchronized void mark(int readlimit);
public boolean markSupported();
public synchronized int read() throws IOException;
public synchronized int read(byte b[], int off, int len) throws
    IOException;
public synchronized void reset() throws IOException;
public synchronized long skip(long n) throws IOException;
```

The *BufferedOutputStream* Class

```
public Class BufferedOutputStream extends FilterOutputStream
```

Constructors

```
public BufferedOutputStream(OutputStream out);
public BufferedOutputStream(OutputStream out, int size);
```

Methods

```
public synchronized void flush() throws IOException;
public synchronized void write(byte b[], int off, int len) throws
    IOException;
public synchronized void write(int b) throws IOException;
```

The *BufferedReader* Class

```
public Class BufferedReader extends Reader
```

Constructors

```
public BufferedReader(Reader in, int sz);
public BufferedReader(Reader in);
```

Methods

```
public void close() throws IOException;
public void mark(int readAheadLimit) throws IOException;
public boolean markSupported();
public int read() throws IOException;
public int read(char cbuf[], int off, int len) throws IOException;
public String readLine() throws IOException;
```

```
public boolean ready() throws IOException;
public void reset() throws IOException;
public long skip(long n) throws IOException;
```

The *BufferedWriter* Class

```
public Class BufferedWriter extends Writer
```

Constructors

```
public BufferedWriter(Writer out);
public BufferedWriter(Writer out, int sz);
```

Methods

```
public void close() throws IOException;
public void flush() throws IOException;
public void newLine() throws IOException;
public void write(char cbuf[], int off, int len) throws IOException;
public void write(int c) throws IOException;
public void write(String s, int off, int len) throws IOException;
```

The *ByteArrayInputStream* Class

```
public Class ByteArrayInputStream extends InputStream
```

Constructors

```
public ByteArrayInputStream(byte buf[]);
public ByteArrayInputStream(byte buf[], int offset, int length);
```

Methods

```
public synchronized int available();
public void mark(int markpos);
public boolean markSupported();
public synchronized int read();
public synchronized int read(byte b[], int off, int len);
public synchronized void reset();
public synchronized long skip(long n);
```

The *ByteArrayOutputStream* Class

```
public Class ByteArrayOutputStream extends OutputStream
```

Constructors

```
public ByteArrayOutputStream();
public ByteArrayOutputStream(int size);
```

Methods

```
public synchronized void reset();
public int size();
public synchronized byte toByteArray()[];
public String toString();
public String toString(int hibyte);
public String toString(String enc) throws UnsupportedEncodingException;
public synchronized void write(byte b[], int off, int len);
public synchronized void write(int b);
public synchronized void writeTo(OutputStream out) throws IOException;
```

The *CharArrayReader* Class

```
public Class CharArrayReader extends Reader
```

Constructors

```
public CharArrayReader(char buf[]);
public CharArrayReader(char buf[], int offset, int length);
```

Methods

```
public void close();
public void mark(int readAheadLimit) throws IOException;
public boolean markSupported();
public int read() throws IOException;
public int read(char b[], int off, int len) throws IOException;
public boolean ready() throws IOException;
public void reset() throws IOException;
public long skip(long n) throws IOException;
```

The *CharArrayWriter* Class

```
public Class CharArrayWriter extends Writer
```

Constructors

```
public CharArrayWriter();
public CharArrayWriter(int initialSize);
```

Methods

```
public void close();
public void flush();
public void reset();
public int size();
public char toCharArray()[];
public String toString();
public void write(char c[], int off, int len);
public void write(int c);
public void write(String str, int off, int len);
public void writeTo(Writer out) throws IOException;
```

The *CharConversionException* Class

```
public Class CharConversionException extends java.io.IOException
```

Constructors

```
public CharConversionException();
public CharConversionException(String s);
```

The *DataInput* Interface

```
public Interface DataInput
```

Methods

```
boolean readBoolean() throws IOException;
byte readByte() throws IOException;
char readChar() throws IOException;
double readDouble() throws IOException;
float readFloat() throws IOException;
void readFully(byte b[]) throws IOException;
void readFully(byte b[], int off, int len) throws IOException;
```

```
int readInt() throws IOException;
String readLine() throws IOException;
long readLong() throws IOException;
short readShort() throws IOException;
int readUnsignedByte() throws IOException;
int readUnsignedShort() throws IOException;
String readUTF() throws IOException;
int skipBytes(int n) throws IOException;
```

The *DataInputStream* Class

```
public Class DataInputStream extends FilterInputStream implements
    DataInput
```

Constructors

```
public DataInputStream(InputStream in);
```

Methods

```
public final static String readUTF(DataInput in) throws IOException;
public final int read(byte b[]) throws IOException;
public final int read(byte b[], int off, int len) throws IOException;
public final boolean readBoolean() throws IOException;
public final byte readByte() throws IOException;
public final char readChar() throws IOException;
public final double readDouble() throws IOException;
public final float readFloat() throws IOException;
public final void readFully(byte b[]) throws IOException;
public final void readFully(byte b[], int off, int len) throws
    IOException;
public final int readInt() throws IOException;
public final String readLine() throws IOException;
public final long readLong() throws IOException;
public final short readShort() throws IOException;
public final int readUnsignedByte() throws IOException;
public final int readUnsignedShort() throws IOException;
public final String readUTF() throws IOException;
public final int skipBytes(int n) throws IOException;
```

The *DataOutput* Interface

```
public Interface DataOutput
```

Methods

```
void write(byte b[]) throws IOException;
void write(byte b[], int off, int len) throws IOException;
void write(int b) throws IOException;
void writeBoolean(boolean v) throws IOException;
void writeByte(int v) throws IOException;
void writeBytes(String s) throws IOException;
void writeChar(int v) throws IOException;
void writeChars(String s) throws IOException;
void writeDouble(double v) throws IOException;
void writeFloat(float v) throws IOException;
void writeInt(int v) throws IOException;
void writeLong(long v) throws IOException;
void writeShort(int v) throws IOException;
void writeUTF(String str) throws IOException;
```

The *DataOutputStream* Class

```
public Class DataOutputStream extends FilterOutputStream implements
  DataOutput
```

Constructors

```
public DataOutputStream(OutputStream out);
```

Methods

```
public void flush() throws IOException;
public final int size();
public synchronized void write(byte b[], int off, int len) throws
  IOException;
public synchronized void write(int b) throws IOException;
public final void writeBoolean(boolean v) throws IOException;
public final void writeByte(int v) throws IOException;
public final void writeBytes(String s) throws IOException;
public final void writeChar(int v) throws IOException;
public final void writeChars(String s) throws IOException;
public final void writeDouble(double v) throws IOException;
public final void writeFloat(float v) throws IOException;
```

```
public final void writeInt(int v) throws IOException;
public final void writeLong(long v) throws IOException;
public final void writeShort(int v) throws IOException;
public final void writeUTF(String str) throws IOException;
```

The *EOFException* Class

```
public Class EOFException extends IOException
```

Constructors

```
public EOFException();
public EOFException(String s);
```

The *Externalizable* Interface

```
public Interface Externalizable extends java.io.Serializable
```

Methods

```
void readExternal(ObjectInput in) throws IOException,
  ClassNotFoundException;
void writeExternal(ObjectOutput out) throws IOException;
```

The *File* Class

```
public Class File extends Object implements java.io.Serializable
```

Data

```
public static final String pathSeparator =
  System.getProperty("path.separator");
public static final char pathSeparatorChar = pathSeparator.charAt(0);
public static final String separator = System.getProperty("file.
  separator");
public static final char separatorChar = separator.charAt(0);
```

Constructors

```
public File(String path);
public File(String path, String name);
public File(File dir, String name);
```

Methods

```
private native String canonPath(String p) throws IOException;
public boolean canRead();
private native boolean canRead0();
public boolean canWrite();
private native boolean canWrite0();
public boolean delete();
private native boolean delete0();
public boolean equals(Object obj);
public boolean exists();
private native boolean exists0();
public String getAbsolutePath();
public String getCanonicalPath() throws IOException;
public String getName();
public String getParent();
public String getPath();
public int hashCode();
public native boolean isAbsolute();
public boolean isDirectory();
private native boolean isDirectory0();
public boolean isFile();
private native boolean isFile0();
public long lastModified();
private native long lastModified0();
public long length();
private native long length0();
public String[] list();
public String[] list(FilenameFilter filter);
private native String[] list0();
public boolean mkdir();
private native boolean mkdir0();
public boolean mkdirs();
public boolean renameTo(File dest);
private native boolean renameTo0(File dest);
private native boolean rmdir0();
public String toString();
```

The *FileDescriptor* Class

```
public Class FileDescriptor extends Object
```

Data

```
public static final FileDescriptor err = initSystemFD(new
    FileDescriptor(),2);
public static final FileDescriptor in = initSystemFD(new
    FileDescriptor(),0);
public static final FileDescriptor out = initSystemFD(new
    FileDescriptor(),1);
```

Methods

```
private static native FileDescriptor initSystemFD(FileDescriptor fdObj,
    int desc);
public native void sync() throws SyncFailedException;
public native boolean valid();
```

The *FileInputStream* Class

```
public Class FileInputStream extends InputStream
```

Constructors

```
public FileInputStream(String name) throws FileNotFoundException;
public FileInputStream(File file) throws FileNotFoundException;
public FileInputStream(FileDescriptor fdObj);
```

Methods

```
public native int available() throws IOException;
public native void close() throws IOException;
public final FileDescriptor getFD() throws IOException;
private native void open(String name) throws IOException;
public native int read() throws IOException;
public int read(byte b[]) throws IOException;
public int read(byte b[], int off, int len) throws IOException;
private native int readBytes(byte b[], int off, int len) throws
    IOException;
public native long skip(long n) throws IOException;
```

The *FileNotFoundException* Class

```
public Class FileNotFoundException extends IOException
```

Constructors

```
public FileNotFoundException();
public FileNotFoundException(String s);
```

The *FileOutputStream* Class

```
public Class FileOutputStream extends OutputStream
```

Constructors

```
public FileOutputStream(String name) throws IOException;
public FileOutputStream(String name, boolean append) throws
  IOException;
public FileOutputStream(File file) throws IOException;
public FileOutputStream(FileDescriptor fdObj);
```

Methods

```
public native void close() throws IOException;
public final FileDescriptor getFD() throws IOException;
private native void open(String name) throws IOException;
private native void openAppend(String name) throws IOException;
public void write(byte b[]) throws IOException;
public void write(byte b[], int off, int len) throws IOException;
public native void write(int b) throws IOException;
private native void writeBytes(byte b[], int off, int len) throws
  IOException;
```

The *FileReader* Class

```
public Class FileReader extends InputStreamReader
```

Constructors

```
public FileReader(String fileName) throws FileNotFoundException;
public FileReader(File file) throws FileNotFoundException;
public FileReader(FileDescriptor fd);
```

The *FileWriter* Class

```
public Class FileWriter extends OutputStreamWriter
```

Constructors

```
public FileWriter(String fileName) throws IOException;
public FileWriter(String fileName, boolean append) throws IOException;
public FileWriter(File file) throws IOException;
public FileWriter(FileDescriptor fd);
```

The *FilenameFilter* Interface

```
public Interface FilenameFilter
```

Methods

```
boolean accept(File dir, String name);
```

The *FilterInputStream* Class

```
public Class FilterInputStream extends InputStream
```

Methods

```
public int available() throws IOException;
public void close() throws IOException;
public synchronized void mark(int readlimit);
public boolean markSupported();
public int read() throws IOException;
public int read(byte b[]) throws IOException;
public int read(byte b[], int off, int len) throws IOException;
public synchronized void reset() throws IOException;
public long skip(long n) throws IOException;
```

The *FilterOutputStream* Class

```
public Class FilterOutputStream extends OutputStream
```

Constructors

```
public FilterOutputStream(OutputStream out);
```

Methods

```
public void close() throws IOException;
public void flush() throws IOException;
public void write(byte b[]) throws IOException;
public void write(byte b[], int off, int len) throws IOException;
public void write(int b) throws IOException;
```

The *FilterReader* Class

```
public abstract Class FilterReader extends Reader
```

Methods

```
public void close() throws IOException;
public void mark(int readAheadLimit) throws IOException;
public boolean markSupported();
public int read() throws IOException;
public int read(char cbuf[], int off, int len) throws IOException;
public boolean ready() throws IOException;
public void reset() throws IOException;
public long skip(long n) throws IOException;
```

The *FilterWriter* Class

```
public abstract Class FilterWriter extends Writer
```

Methods

```
public void close() throws IOException;
public void flush() throws IOException;
public void write(char cbuf[], int off, int len) throws IOException;
public void write(int c) throws IOException;
public void write(String str, int off, int len) throws IOException;
```

The *IOException* Class

```
public Class IOException extends Exception
```

Constructors

```
public IOException();
public IOException(String s);
```

The *InputStream* Class

```
public abstract Class InputStream extends Object
```

Methods

```
public abstract int read() throws IOException;
public int available() throws IOException;
public void close() throws IOException;
public synchronized void mark(int readlimit);
public boolean markSupported();
public int read(byte b[]) throws IOException;
public int read(byte b[], int off, int len) throws IOException;
public synchronized void reset() throws IOException;
public long skip(long n) throws IOException;
```

The *InputStreamReader* Class

```
public Class InputStreamReader extends Reader
```

Constructors

```
public InputStreamReader(InputStream in);
public InputStreamReader(InputStream in, String enc) throws
    UnsupportedEncodingException;
```

Methods

```
public void close() throws IOException;
public String getEncoding();
public int read() throws IOException;
public int read(char cbuf[], int off, int len) throws IOException;
public boolean ready() throws IOException;
```

The *InterruptedIOException* Class

```
public Class InterruptedIOException extends IOException
```

Data

```
public int bytesTransferred = 0;
```

Constructors

```
public InterruptedIOException();
public InterruptedIOException(String s);
```

The *InvalidClassException* Class

```
public Class InvalidClassException extends ObjectStreamException
```

Data

```
public String classname;
```

Constructors

```
public InvalidClassException(String reason);
public InvalidClassException(String cname, String reason);
```

Methods

```
public String getMessage();
```

The *InvalidObjectException* Class

```
public Class InvalidObjectException extends ObjectStreamException
```

Constructors

```
public InvalidObjectException(String reason);
```

The *LineNumberInputStream* Class

```
public Class LineNumberInputStream extends FilterInputStream
```

Constructors

```
public LineNumberInputStream(InputStream in);
```

Methods

```
public int available() throws IOException;
public int getLineNumber();
public void mark(int readlimit);
public int read() throws IOException;
public int read(byte b[], int off, int len) throws IOException;
public void reset() throws IOException;
public void setLineNumber(int lineNumber);
public long skip(long n) throws IOException;
```

The *LineNumberReader* Class

```
public Class LineNumberReader extends BufferedReader
```

Constructors

```
public LineNumberReader(Reader in);
public LineNumberReader(Reader in, int sz);
```

Methods

```
public int getLineNumber();
public void mark(int readAheadLimit) throws IOException;
public int read() throws IOException;
public int read(char cbuf[], int off, int len) throws IOException;
public String readLine() throws IOException;
public void reset() throws IOException;
public void setLineNumber(int lineNumber);
public long skip(long n) throws IOException;
```

The *NotActiveException* Class

```
public Class NotActiveException extends ObjectStreamException
```

Constructors

```
public NotActiveException(String reason);
public NotActiveException();
```

The *NotSerializableException* Class

```
public Class NotSerializableException extends ObjectStreamException
```

Constructors

```
public NotSerializableException(String classname);
public NotSerializableException();
```

The *ObjectInput* Interface

```
public Interface ObjectInput extends DataInput
```

Methods

```
public int available() throws IOException;
public void close() throws IOException;
```

```
public int read() throws IOException;
public int read(byte b[]) throws IOException;
public int read(byte b[], int off, int len) throws IOException;
public Object readObject() throws ClassNotFoundException, IOException;
public long skip(long n) throws IOException;
```

The *ObjectInputStream* Class

```
public Class ObjectInputStream extends InputStream implements
   ObjectInput, ObjectStreamConstants
```

Constructors

```
public ObjectInputStream(InputStream in) throws IOException,
   StreamCorruptedException;
```

Methods

```
private static native Object allocateNewArray(Class aclass, int
   length);
private static native Object allocateNewObject(Class aclass, Class
   initclass) throws InstantiationException, IllegalAccessException;
public int available() throws IOException;
public void close() throws IOException;
public final void defaultReadObject() throws IOException,
   ClassNotFoundException, NotActiveException;
private native void inputClassFields(Object o, Class cl, int[]
   fieldSequence) throws InvalidClassException,
   StreamCorruptedException, ClassNotFoundException, IOException;
private native boolean invokeObjectReader(Object o, Class aclass)
   throws InvalidClassException, StreamCorruptedException,
   ClassNotFoundException, IOException;
private native Class loadClass0(Class cl, String classname) throws
   ClassNotFoundException;
public int read() throws IOException;
public int read(byte[] data, int offset, int length) throws
   IOException;
public boolean readBoolean() throws IOException;
public byte readByte() throws IOException;
public char readChar() throws IOException;
public double readDouble() throws IOException;
public float readFloat() throws IOException;
public void readFully(byte[] data) throws IOException;
```

```
public void readFully(byte[] data, int offset, int size) throws
    IOException;
public int readInt() throws IOException;
public String readLine() throws IOException;
public long readLong() throws IOException;
public final Object readObject() throws OptionalDataException,
    ClassNotFoundException, IOException;
public short readShort() throws IOException;
public int readUnsignedByte() throws IOException;
public int readUnsignedShort() throws IOException;
public String readUTF() throws IOException;
public synchronized void registerValidation(ObjectInputValidation obj,
    int prio) throws NotActiveException, InvalidObjectException;
public int skipBytes(int len) throws IOException;
```

The *ObjectInputValidation* Interface

```
public Interface ObjectInputValidation
```

Methods

```
public void validateObject() throws InvalidObjectException;
```

The *ObjectOutput* Interface

```
public Interface ObjectOutput extends DataOutput
```

Methods

```
public void close() throws IOException;
public void flush() throws IOException;
public void write(byte b[]) throws IOException;
public void write(byte b[], int off, int len) throws IOException;
public void write(int b) throws IOException;
public void writeObject(Object obj) throws IOException;
```

The *ObjectOutputStream* Class

```
public Class ObjectOutputStream extends OutputStream implements
    ObjectOutput, ObjectStreamConstants
```

Constructors

```
public ObjectOutputStream(OutputStream out) throws IOException;
```

Methods

```
public void close() throws IOException;
public final void defaultWriteObject() throws IOException;
public void flush() throws IOException;
private native boolean invokeObjectWriter(Object o, Class c) throws
  IOException;
private native void outputClassFields(Object o, Class cl, int[]
  fieldSequence) throws IOException, InvalidClassException;
public void reset() throws IOException;
public void write(byte b[]) throws IOException;
public void write(byte b[], int off, int len) throws IOException;
public void write(int data) throws IOException;
public void writeBoolean(boolean data) throws IOException;
public void writeByte(int data) throws IOException;
public void writeBytes(String data) throws IOException;
public void writeChar(int data) throws IOException;
public void writeChars(String data) throws IOException;
public void writeDouble(double data) throws IOException;
public void writeFloat(float data) throws IOException;
public void writeInt(int data) throws IOException;
public void writeLong(long data) throws IOException;
public final void writeObject(Object obj) throws IOException;
public void writeShort(int data) throws IOException;
public void writeUTF(String data) throws IOException;
```

The *ObjectStreamClass* Class

```
public Class ObjectStreamClass extends Object implements
  java.io.Serializable
```

Methods

```
private static native int getClassAccess(Class aclass);
private static native int getFieldAccess(Class aclass, String field-
  sig);
private static native String[] getFieldSignatures(Class aclass);
private static native int getMethodAccess(Class aclass, String
  methodsig);
private static native String[] getMethodsignatures(Class aclass);
private static native long getSerialVersionUID(Class cl);
private static native boolean hasWriteObject(Class cl);
public static ObjectStreamClass lookup(Class cl);
```

```
public Class forClass();
private native ObjectStreamField[] getFields0(Class cl);
public String getName();
public long getSerialVersionUID();
public String toString();
```

The *ObjectStreamException* Class

```
public abstract Class ObjectStreamException extends IOException
```

The *OptionalDataException* Class

```
public Class OptionalDataException extends ObjectStreamException
```

Data

```
public boolean eof;
public int length;
```

The *OutputStream* Class

```
public abstract Class OutputStream extends Object
```

Methods

```
public abstract void write(int b) throws IOException;
public void close() throws IOException;
public void flush() throws IOException;
public void write(byte b[]) throws IOException;
public void write(byte b[], int off, int len) throws IOException;
```

The *OutputStreamWriter* Class

```
public Class OutputStreamWriter extends Writer
```

Constructors

```
public OutputStreamWriter(OutputStream out, String enc) throws
    UnsupportedEncodingException;
public OutputStreamWriter(OutputStream out);
```

Methods

```
public void close() throws IOException;
public void flush() throws IOException;
public String getEncoding();
public void write(char cbuf[], int off, int len) throws IOException;
public void write(int c) throws IOException;
public void write(String str, int off, int len) throws IOException;
```

The *PipedInputStream* Class

```
public Class PipedInputStream extends InputStream
```

Constructors

```
public PipedInputStream(PipedOutputStream src) throws IOException;
public PipedInputStream();
```

Methods

```
public synchronized int available() throws IOException;
public void close() throws IOException;
public void connect(PipedOutputStream src) throws IOException;
public synchronized int read() throws IOException;
public synchronized int read(byte b[], int off, int len) throws
  IOException;
```

The *PipedOutputStream* Class

```
public Class PipedOutputStream extends OutputStream
```

Constructors

```
public PipedOutputStream(PipedInputStream snk) throws IOException;
public PipedOutputStream();
```

Methods

```
public void close() throws IOException;
public void connect(PipedInputStream snk) throws IOException;
public synchronized void flush() throws IOException;
public void write(byte b[], int off, int len) throws IOException;
public void write(int b) throws IOException;
```

The *PipedReader* Class

```
public Class PipedReader extends Reader
```

Constructors

```
public PipedReader();
public PipedReader(PipedWriter src) throws IOException;
```

Methods

```
public void close() throws IOException;
public void connect(PipedWriter src) throws IOException;
public int read(char cbuf[], int off, int len) throws IOException;
```

The *PipedWriter* Class

```
public Class PipedWriter extends Writer
```

Constructors

```
public PipedWriter();
public PipedWriter(PipedReader sink) throws IOException;
```

Methods

```
public void close() throws IOException;
public void connect(PipedReader sink) throws IOException;
public void flush() throws IOException;
public void write(char cbuf[], int off, int len) throws IOException;
```

The *PrintStream* Class

```
public Class PrintStream extends FilterOutputStream
```

Constructors

```
public PrintStream(OutputStream out);
public PrintStream(OutputStream out, boolean autoFlush);
```

Methods

```
public boolean checkError();
public void close();
```

```
public void flush();
public void print(char c);
public void print(char s[]);
public void print(double d);
public void print(float f);
public void print(int i);
public void print(long l);
public void print(Object obj);
public void print(String s);
public void println(boolean x);
public void println(char x);
public void println(char x[]);
public void println(double x);
public void println(float x);
public void println(int x);
public void println(long x);
public void println(Object x);
public void println(String x);
public void write(int b);
public void print(boolean b);
public void println();
public void write(byte buf[], int off, int len);
```

The *PrintWriter* Class

```
public Class PrintWriter extends Writer
```

Constructors

```
public PrintWriter(Writer out, boolean autoFlush);
public PrintWriter(OutputStream out);
public PrintWriter(OutputStream out, boolean autoFlush);
```

Methods

```
public PrintWriter (Writer out);
public boolean checkError();
public void close();
public void flush();
public void print(char c);
public void print(char s[]);
public void print(double d);
```

```
public void print(float f);
public void print(int i);
public void print(long l);
public void print(Object obj);
public void print(String s);
public void println(boolean x);
public void println(char x);
public void println(char x[]);
public void println(double x);
public void println(float x);
public void println(int x);
public void println(long x);
public void println(Object x);
public void println(String x);
public void write(int c);
public void print(boolean b);
public void println();
public void write(char buf[], int off, int len);
public void write(char buf[]);
public void write(String s, int off, int len);
public void write(String s);
```

The *PushbackInputStream* Class

```
public Class PushbackInputStream extends FilterInputStream
```

Constructors

```
public PushbackInputStream(InputStream in, int size);
public PushbackInputStream(InputStream in);
```

Methods

```
public int available() throws IOException;
public boolean markSupported();
public int read() throws IOException;
public int read(byte[] b, int off, int len) throws IOException;
public void unread(byte[] b, int off, int len) throws IOException;
public void unread(byte[] b) throws IOException;
public void unread(int b) throws IOException;
```

The *PushbackReader* Class

```
public Class PushbackReader extends FilterReader
```

Constructors

```
public PushbackReader(Reader in, int size);
public PushbackReader(Reader in);
```

Methods

```
public void close() throws IOException;
public boolean markSupported();
public int read() throws IOException;
public int read(char cbuf[], int off, int len) throws IOException;
public boolean ready() throws IOException;
public void unread(char cbuf[], int off, int len) throws IOException;
public void unread(char cbuf[]) throws IOException;
public void unread(int c) throws IOException;
```

The *RandomAccessFile* Class

```
public Class RandomAccessFile extends Object implements DataOutput,
  DataInput
```

Constructors

```
public RandomAccessFile(String name, String mode) throws IOException;
public RandomAccessFile(File file, String mode) throws IOException;
```

Methods

```
public native void close() throws IOException;
public final FileDescriptor getFD() throws IOException;
public native long getFilePointer() throws IOException;
public native long length() throws IOException;
private native void open(String name, boolean writeable) throws
  IOException;
public native int read() throws IOException;
public int read(byte b[], int off, int len) throws IOException;
public int read(byte b[]) throws IOException;
public final boolean readBoolean() throws IOException;
public final byte readByte() throws IOException;
```

```
private native int readBytes(byte b[], int off, int len) throws
    IOException;
public final char readChar() throws IOException;
public final double readDouble() throws IOException;
public final float readFloat() throws IOException;
public final void readFully(byte b[]) throws IOException;
public final void readFully(byte b[], int off, int len) throws
    IOException;
public final int readInt() throws IOException;
public final String readLine() throws IOException;
public final long readLong() throws IOException;
public final short readShort() throws IOException;
public final int readUnsignedByte() throws IOException;
public final int readUnsignedShort() throws IOException;
public final String readUTF() throws IOException;
public native void seek(long pos) throws IOException;
public int skipBytes(int n) throws IOException;
public void write(byte b[]) throws IOException;
public void write(byte b[], int off, int len) throws IOException;
public native void write(int b) throws IOException;
public final void writeBoolean(boolean v) throws IOException;
public final void writeByte(int v) throws IOException;
private native void writeBytes(byte b[], int off, int len) throws
    IOException;
public final void writeBytes(String s) throws IOException;
public final void writeChar(int v) throws IOException;
public final void writeChars(String s) throws IOException;
public final void writeDouble(double v) throws IOException;
public final void writeFloat(float v) throws IOException;
public final void writeInt(int v) throws IOException;
public final void writeLong(long v) throws IOException;
public final void writeShort(int v) throws IOException;
public final void writeUTF(String str) throws IOException;
```

The *Reader* Class

```
public abstract Class Reader extends Object
```

Methods

```
abstract public void close() throws IOException;
abstract public int read(char cbuf[], int off, int len) throws
    IOException;
```

```
public void mark(int readAheadLimit) throws IOException;
public boolean markSupported();
public int read() throws IOException;
public int read(char cbuf[]) throws IOException;
public boolean ready() throws IOException;
public void reset() throws IOException;
public long skip(long n) throws IOException;
```

The *SequenceInputStream* Class

```
public Class SequenceInputStream extends InputStream
```

Constructors

```
public SequenceInputStream(Enumeration e);
public SequenceInputStream(InputStream s1, InputStream s2);
```

Methods

```
public int available() throws IOException;
public void close() throws IOException;
public int read() throws IOException;
public int read(byte buf[], int pos, int len) throws IOException;
```

The *Serializable* Interface

```
public Interface Serializable
```

The *StreamCorruptedException* Class

```
public Class StreamCorruptedException extends ObjectStreamException
```

Constructors

```
public StreamCorruptedException(String reason);
public StreamCorruptedException();
```

The *StreamTokenizer* Class

```
public Class StreamTokenizer extends Object
```

Data

```
public static final int TT_EOF = -1;
public static final int TT_EOL = '\n';
```

```
public static final int TT_NUMBER = -2;
public static final int TT_WORD = -3;
public double nval;
public String sval;
public int ttype = TT_NOTHING;
```

The *StringBufferInputStream* Class

```
public Class StringBufferInputStream extends InputStream
```

Constructors

```
public StringBufferInputStream(String s);
```

Methods

```
public synchronized int available();
public synchronized int read();
public synchronized int read(byte b[], int off, int len);
public synchronized void reset();
public synchronized long skip(long n);
```

The *StringReader* Class

```
public Class StringReader extends Reader
```

Constructors

```
public StringReader(String s);
```

Methods

```
public void close();
public void mark(int readAheadLimit) throws IOException;
public boolean markSupported();
public int read() throws IOException;
public int read(char cbuf[], int off, int len) throws IOException;
public boolean ready();
public void reset() throws IOException;
public long skip(long ns) throws IOException;
```

The *StringWriter* Class

```
public Class StringWriter extends Writer
```

Constructors

```
public StringWriter();
```

Methods

```
public void close();
public void flush();
public StringBuffer getBuffer();
public String toString();
public void write(char cbuf[], int off, int len);
public void write(int c);
public void write(String str);
public void write(String str, int off, int len);
```

The *SyncFailedException* Class

```
public Class SyncFailedException extends IOException
```

Constructors

```
public SyncFailedException(String desc);
```

The *UTFDataFormatException* Class

```
public Class UTFDataFormatException extends IOException
```

Constructors

```
public UTFDataFormatException();
public UTFDataFormatException(String s);
```

The *UnsupportedEncodingException* Class

```
public Class UnsupportedEncodingException extends IOException
```

Constructors

```
public UnsupportedEncodingException();
public UnsupportedEncodingException(String s);
```

The *WriteAbortedException* Class

```
public Class WriteAbortedException extends ObjectStreamException
```

Data

```
public Exception detail;
```

Constructors

```
public WriteAbortedException(String s, Exception ex);
```

Methods

```
public String getMessage();
```

The *Writer* Class

```
public abstract Class Writer extends Object
```

Methods

```
abstract public void close() throws IOException;
abstract public void flush() throws IOException;
abstract public void write(char cbuf[], int off, int len) throws
    IOException;
public void write(char cbuf[]) throws IOException;
public void write(int c) throws IOException;
public void write(String str) throws IOException;
public void write(String str, int off, int len) throws IOException;
```

The *java.lang* Package

The *AbstractMethodError* Class

```
public Class AbstractMethodError extends IncompatibleClassChangeError
```

Constructors

```
public AbstractMethodError();
public AbstractMethodError(String s);
```

The *ArithmeticException* Class

```
public Class ArithmeticException extends RuntimeException
```

Constructors

```
public ArithmeticException();
public ArithmeticException(String s);
```

The *ArrayIndexOutOfBoundsException* Class

```
public Class ArrayIndexOutOfBoundsException extends
    IndexOutOfBoundsException
```

Constructors

```
public ArrayIndexOutOfBoundsException();
public ArrayIndexOutOfBoundsException(int index);
public ArrayIndexOutOfBoundsException(String s);
```

The *ArrayStoreException* Class

```
public Class ArrayStoreException extends RuntimeException
```

Constructors

```
public ArrayStoreException();
public ArrayStoreException(String s);
```

The *Boolean* Class

```
public Class Boolean extends Object implements java.io.Serializable
```

Data

```
public static final Boolean FALSE = new Boolean(false);
public static final Boolean TRUE = new Boolean(true);
public static final Class TYPE = Class.getPrimitiveClass("boolean");
```

Constructors

```
public Boolean(boolean value);
public Boolean(String s);
```

Methods

```
public static boolean getBoolean(String name);
public static Boolean valueOf(String s);
public boolean booleanValue();
public boolean equals(Object obj);
public int hashCode();
public String toString();
```

The *Byte* Class

```
public Class Byte extends Number
```

Data

```
public static final byte MAX_VALUE = 127;
public static final byte MIN_VALUE = -128;
public static final Class TYPE = Class.getPrimitiveClass("byte");
```

Constructors

```
public Byte(byte value);
public Byte(String s) throws NumberFormatException;
```

Methods

```
public static Byte decode(String nm) throws NumberFormatException;
public static byte parseByte(String s) throws NumberFormatException;
public static byte parseByte(String s, int radix) throws
   NumberFormatException;
public static String toString(byte b);
public static Byte valueOf(String s, int radix) throws
   NumberFormatException;
public static Byte valueOf(String s) throws NumberFormatException;
public byte byteValue();
public double doubleValue();
public boolean equals(Object obj);
public float floatValue();
public int hashCode();
public int intValue();
public long longValue();
public short shortValue();
public String toString();
```

The *Character* Class

```
public Class Character extends Object implements java.io.Serializable
```

Data

```
public static final int MAX_RADIX = 36;
public static final char MAX_VALUE = '\uffff';
public static final int MIN_RADIX = 2;
public static final char MIN_VALUE = '\u0000';
public static final Class TYPE = Class.getPrimitiveClass("char");
public static final byte UNASSIGNED = 0, UPPERCASE_LETTER = 1,
    LOWERCASE_LETTER = 2, TITLECASE_LETTER = 3, MODIFIER_LETTER = 4,
    OTHER_LETTER = 5, NON_SPACING_MARK = 6, ENCLOSING_MARK = 7,
    COMBINING_SPACING_MARK = 8, DECIMAL_DIGIT_NUMBER = 9, LETTER_NUMBER = 10,
    OTHER_NUMBER = 11, SPACE_SEPARATOR = 12, LINE_SEPARATOR = 13,
    PARAGRAPH_SEPARATOR = 14, CONTROL = 15, FORMAT = 16, PRIVATE_USE = 18,
    SURROGATE = 19, DASH_PUNCTUATION = 20, START_PUNCTUATION = 21,
    END_PUNCTUATION = 22, CONNECTOR_PUNCTUATION = 23, OTHER_PUNCTUATION = 24,
    MATH_SYMBOL = 25, CURRENCY_SYMBOL = 26, MODIFIER_SYMBOL = 27,
    OTHER_SYMBOL = 28;
```

Constructors

```
public Character(char value);
```

Methods

```
public static int digit(char ch, int radix);
public static char forDigit(int digit, int radix);
public static int getNumericValue(char ch);
public static int getType(char ch);
public static boolean isDefined(char ch);
public static boolean isDigit(char ch);
public static boolean isIdentifierIgnorable(char ch);
public static boolean isISOControl(char ch);
public static boolean isJavaIdentifierPart(char ch);
public static boolean isJavaIdentifierStart(char ch);
public static boolean isJavaLetter(char ch);
public static boolean isJavaLetterOrDigit(char ch);
public static boolean isLetter(char ch);
public static boolean isLetterOrDigit(char ch);
public static boolean isLowerCase(char ch);
```

```
public static boolean isSpace(char ch);
public static boolean isSpaceChar(char ch);
public static boolean isTitleCase(char ch);
public static boolean isUnicodeIdentifierPart(char ch);
public static boolean isUnicodeIdentifierStart(char ch);
public static boolean isUpperCase(char ch);
public static boolean isWhitespace(char ch);
public static char toLowerCase(char ch);
public static char toTitleCase(char ch);
public static char toUpperCase(char ch);
public char charValue();
public boolean equals(Object obj);
public int hashCode();
public String toString();
```

The *Class* Class

```
public Class Class extends Object implements java.io.Serializable
```

Methods

```
public static native Class forName(String className) throws
    ClassNotFoundException;
static native Class getPrimitiveClass(String name);
public Class[] getClasses();
public native ClassLoader getClassLoader();
public native Class getComponentType();
public Constructor getConstructor(Class[] parameterTypes) throws
    NoSuchMethodException, SecurityException;
private native Constructor getConstructor0(Class[] parameterTypes, int
    which);
public Constructor[] getConstructors() throws SecurityException;
private native Constructor[] getConstructors0(int which);
public Class[] getDeclaredClasses() throws SecurityException;
public Constructor getDeclaredConstructor(Class[] parameterTypes)
    throws NoSuchMethodException, SecurityException;
public Constructor[] getDeclaredConstructors() throws
    SecurityException;
public Field getDeclaredField(String name) throws NoSuchFieldException,
    SecurityException;
public Field[] getDeclaredFields() throws SecurityException;
```

```
public Method getDeclaredMethod(String name, Class[] parameterTypes)
    throws NoSuchMethodException, SecurityException;
public Method[] getDeclaredMethods() throws SecurityException;
public Class getDeclaringClass();
public Field getField(String name) throws NoSuchFieldException,
    SecurityException;
private native Field getField0(String name, int which);
public Field[] getFields() throws SecurityException;
private native Field[] getFields0(int which);
public native Class[] getInterfaces();
public Method getMethod(String name, Class[] parameterTypes) throws
    NoSuchMethodException, SecurityException;
private native Method getMethod0(String name, Class[] parameterTypes,
    int which);
public Method[] getMethods() throws SecurityException;
private native Method[] getMethods0(int which);
public native int getModifiers();
public native String getName();
public java.net.URL getResource(String name);
public InputStream getResourceAsStream(String name);
public native Object[] getSigners();
public native Class getSuperclass();
public native boolean isArray();
public native boolean isAssignableFrom(Class cls);
public native boolean isInstance(Object obj);
public native boolean isInterface();
public native boolean isPrimitive();
public native Object newInstance() throws InstantiationException,
    IllegalAccessException;
native void setSigners(Object[] signers);
public String toString();
```

The *ClassCastException* Class

```
public Class ClassCastException extends RuntimeException
```

Constructors

```
public ClassCastException();
public ClassCastException(String s);
```

The *ClassCircularityError* Class

```
public Class ClassCircularityError extends LinkageError
```

Constructors

```
public ClassCircularityError();
public ClassCircularityError(String s);
```

The *ClassFormatError* Class

```
public Class ClassFormatError extends LinkageError
```

Constructors

```
public ClassFormatError();
public ClassFormatError(String s);
```

The *ClassLoader* Class

```
public abstract Class ClassLoader extends Object
```

Methods

```
public static final java.net.URL getSystemResource(String name);
private static native String getSystemResourceAsName0(String name);
public static final InputStream getSystemResourceAsStream(String name);
private static native InputStream getSystemResourceAsStream0(String
  name);
protected abstract Class loadClass(String name, boolean resolve) throws
  ClassNotFoundException;
private native Class defineClass0(String name, byte data[], int offset,
  int length);
private native Class findSystemClass0(String name) throws
  ClassNotFoundException;
public java.net.URL getResource(String name);
public InputStream getResourceAsStream(String name);
private native void init();
public Class loadClass(String name) throws ClassNotFoundException;
private native void resolveClass0(Class c);
```

The *ClassNotFoundException* Class

```
public Class ClassNotFoundException extends Exception
```

Constructors

```
public ClassNotFoundException();
public ClassNotFoundException(String s);
```

The *CloneNotSupportedException* Class

```
public Class CloneNotSupportedException extends Exception
```

Constructors

```
public CloneNotSupportedException();
public CloneNotSupportedException(String s);
```

The *Cloneable* Interface

```
public Interface Cloneable
```

The *Compiler* Class

```
public Class Compiler extends Object
```

Methods

```
public static native Object command(Object any);
public static native boolean compileClass(Class clazz);
public static native boolean compileClasses(String string);
public static native void disable();
public static native void enable();
private static native void initialize();
```

The *Double* Class

```
public Class Double extends Number
```

Data

```
public static final double MAX_VALUE = 1.79769313486231570e+308;
public static final double MIN_VALUE = longBitsToDouble(1L);
```

```
public static final double NaN = 0.0d / 0.0;
public static final double NEGATIVE_INFINITY = -1.0 / 0.0;
public static final double POSITIVE_INFINITY = 1.0 / 0.0;
public static final Class TYPE = Class.getPrimitiveClass("double");
```

Constructors

```
public Double(double value);
public Double(String s) throws NumberFormatException;
```

Methods

```
public static native long doubleToLongBits(double value);
static public boolean isInfinite(double v);
static public boolean isNaN(double v);
public static native double longBitsToDouble(long bits);
public static String toString(double d);
public static Double valueOf(String s) throws NumberFormatException;
static native double valueOf0(String s) throws NumberFormatException;
public byte byteValue();
public double doubleValue();
public boolean equals(Object obj);
public float floatValue();
public int hashCode();
public int intValue();
public boolean isInfinite();
public boolean isNaN();
public long longValue();
public short shortValue();
public String toString();
```

The *Error* Class

```
public Class Error extends Throwable
```

Constructors

```
public Error();
public Error(String s);
```

The *Exception* Class

```
public Class Exception extends Throwable
```

Constructors

```
public Exception();
public Exception(String s);
```

The *ExceptionInInitializerError* Class

```
public Class ExceptionInInitializerError extends LinkageError
```

Constructors

```
public ExceptionInInitializerError();
public ExceptionInInitializerError(Throwable thrown);
public ExceptionInInitializerError(String s);
```

Methods

```
public Throwable getException();
```

The *Float* Class

```
public Class Float extends Number
```

Data

```
public static final float MAX_VALUE = 3.40282346638528860e+38f;
public static final float MIN_VALUE = 1.40129846432481707e-45f;
public static final float NaN = 0.0f / 0.0f;
public static final float NEGATIVE_INFINITY = -1.0f / 0.0f;
public static final float POSITIVE_INFINITY = 1.0f / 0.0f;
public static final Class TYPE = Class.getPrimitiveClass("float");
```

Constructors

```
public Float(float value);
public Float(double value);
public Float(String s) throws NumberFormatException;
```

Methods

```
public static native int floatToIntBits(float value);
public static native float intBitsToFloat(int bits);
```

```
static public boolean isInfinite(float v);
static public boolean isNaN(float v);
public static String toString(float f);
public static Float valueOf(String s) throws NumberFormatException;
public byte byteValue();
public double doubleValue();
public boolean equals(Object obj);
public float floatValue();
public int hashCode();
public int intValue();
public boolean isInfinite();
public boolean isNaN();
public long longValue();
public short shortValue();
public String toString();
```

The *IllegalAccessError* Class

```
public Class IllegalAccessError extends IncompatibleClassChangeError
```

Constructors

```
public IllegalAccessError();
public IllegalAccessError(String s);
```

The *IllegalAccessException* Class

```
public Class IllegalAccessException extends Exception
```

Constructors

```
public IllegalAccessException();
public IllegalAccessException(String s);
```

The *IllegalArgumentException* Class

```
public Class IllegalArgumentException extends RuntimeException
```

Constructors

```
public IllegalArgumentException();
public IllegalArgumentException(String s);
```

The *IllegalMonitorStateException* Class

```
public Class IllegalMonitorStateException extends RuntimeException
```

Constructors

```
public IllegalMonitorStateException();
public IllegalMonitorStateException(String s);
```

The *IllegalStateException* Class

```
public Class IllegalStateException extends RuntimeException
```

Constructors

```
public IllegalStateException();
public IllegalStateException(String s);
```

The *IllegalThreadStateException* Class

```
public Class IllegalThreadStateException extends
    IllegalArgumentException
```

Constructors

```
public IllegalThreadStateException();
public IllegalThreadStateException(String s);
```

The *IncompatibleClassChangeError* Class

```
public Class IncompatibleClassChangeError extends LinkageError
```

Constructors

```
public IncompatibleClassChangeError(String s);
```

Methods

```
public IncompatibleClassChangeError ();
```

The *IndexOutOfBoundsException* Class

```
public Class IndexOutOfBoundsException extends RuntimeException
```

Constructors

```
public IndexOutOfBoundsException();
public IndexOutOfBoundsException(String s);
```

The *InstantiationError* Class

```
public Class InstantiationError extends IncompatibleClassChangeError
```

Constructors

```
public InstantiationError();
public InstantiationError(String s);
```

The *InstantiationException* Class

```
public Class InstantiationException extends Exception
```

Constructors

```
public InstantiationException();
public InstantiationException(String s);
```

The *Integer* Class

```
public Class Integer extends Number
```

Data

```
public static final int MAX_VALUE = 0x7fffffff;
public static final int MIN_VALUE = 0x80000000;
public static final Class TYPE = Class.getPrimitiveClass("int");
```

Constructors

```
public Integer(int value);
public Integer(String s) throws NumberFormatException;
```

Methods

```
public static Integer decode(String nm) throws NumberFormatException;
public static Integer getInteger(String nm);
public static Integer getInteger(String nm, int val);
public static Integer getInteger(String nm, Integer val);
public static int parseInt(String s, int radix) throws
  NumberFormatException;
public static int parseInt(String s) throws NumberFormatException;
public static String toBinaryString(int i);
public static String toHexString(int i);
public static String toOctalString(int i);
public static String toString(int i, int radix);
public static String toString(int i);
public static Integer valueOf(String s, int radix) throws
  NumberFormatException;
public static Integer valueOf(String s) throws NumberFormatException;
public byte byteValue();
public double doubleValue();
public boolean equals(Object obj);
public float floatValue();
public int hashCode();
public int intValue();
public long longValue();
public short shortValue();
public String toString();
```

The *InternalError* Class

```
public Class InternalError extends VirtualMachineError
```

Constructors

```
public InternalError();
public InternalError(String s);
```

The *InterruptedException* Class

```
public Class InterruptedException extends Exception
```

Constructors

```
public InterruptedException();
public InterruptedException(String s);
```

The *LinkageError* Class

```
public Class LinkageError extends Error
```

Constructors

```
public LinkageError();
public LinkageError(String s);
```

The *Long* Class

```
public Class Long extends Number
```

Data

```
public static final long MAX_VALUE = 0x7fffffffffffffffL;
public static final long MIN_VALUE = 0x8000000000000000L;
public static final Class TYPE = Class.getPrimitiveClass("long");
```

Constructors

```
public Long(long value);
public Long(String s) throws NumberFormatException;
```

Methods

```
public static Long getLong(String nm);
public static Long getLong(String nm, long val);
public static Long getLong(String nm, Long val);
public static long parseLong(String s, int radix) throws
  NumberFormatException;
public static long parseLong(String s) throws NumberFormatException;
public static String toBinaryString(long i);
public static String toHexString(long i);
public static String toOctalString(long i);
public static String toString(long i, int radix);
public static String toString(long i);
public static Long valueOf(String s, int radix) throws
  NumberFormatException;
public static Long valueOf(String s) throws NumberFormatException;
public byte byteValue();
public double doubleValue();
public boolean equals(Object obj);
public float floatValue();
```

```
public int hashCode();
public int intValue();
public long longValue();
public short shortValue();
public String toString();
```

The *Math* Class

```
public Class Math extends Object
```

Data

```
public static final double E = 2.7182818284590452354;
public static final double PI = 3.14159265358979323846;
```

Methods

```
public static double abs(double a);
public static float abs(float a);
public static int abs(int a);
public static long abs(long a);
public static native double acos(double a);
public static native double asin(double a);
public static native double atan(double a);
public static native double atan2(double a, double b);
public static native double ceil(double a);
public static native double cos(double a);
public static native double exp(double a);
public static native double floor(double a);
public static native double IEEEremainder(double f1, double f2);
public static native double log(double a);
public static double max(double a, double b);
public static float max(float a, float b);
public static int max(int a, int b);
public static long max(long a, long b);
public static double min(double a, double b);
public static float min(float a, float b);
public static int min(int a, int b);
public static long min(long a, long b);
public static native double pow(double a, double b);
public static synchronized double random();
public static native double rint(double a);
public static long round(double a);
```

```
public static int round(float a);
public static native double sin(double a);
public static native double sqrt(double a);
public static native double tan(double a);
```

The *NegativeArraySizeException* Class

```
public Class NegativeArraySizeException extends RuntimeException
```

Constructors

```
public NegativeArraySizeException();
public NegativeArraySizeException(String s);
```

The *NoClassDefFoundError* Class

```
public Class NoClassDefFoundError extends LinkageError
```

Constructors

```
public NoClassDefFoundError();
public NoClassDefFoundError(String s);
```

The *NoSuchFieldError* Class

```
public Class NoSuchFieldError extends IncompatibleClassChangeError
```

Constructors

```
public NoSuchFieldError();
public NoSuchFieldError(String s);
```

The *NoSuchFieldException* Class

```
public Class NoSuchFieldException extends Exception
```

Constructors

```
public NoSuchFieldException();
public NoSuchFieldException(String s);
```

The *NoSuchMethodError* Class

```
public Class NoSuchMethodError extends IncompatibleClassChangeError
```

Constructors

```
public NoSuchMethodError();
public NoSuchMethodError(String s);
```

The *NoSuchMethodException* Class

```
public Class NoSuchMethodException extends Exception
```

Constructors

```
public NoSuchMethodException();
public NoSuchMethodException(String s);
```

The *NullPointerException* Class

```
public Class NullPointerException extends RuntimeException
```

Constructors

```
public NullPointerException();
public NullPointerException(String s);
```

The *Number* Class

```
public abstract Class Number extends Object implements
    java.io.Serializable
```

Methods

```
public abstract double doubleValue();
public abstract float floatValue();
public abstract int intValue();
public abstract long longValue();
public byte byteValue();
public short shortValue();
```

The *NumberFormatException* Class

```
public Class NumberFormatException extends IllegalArgumentException
```

Methods

```
public NumberFormatException ();
public NumberFormatException (String s);
```

The *Object* Class

```
public Class Object extends Object
```

Methods

```
protected native Object clone() throws CloneNotSupportedException;
public boolean equals(Object obj);
public final native Class getClass();
public native int hashCode();
public final native void notify();
public final native void notifyAll();
public String toString();
public final void wait() throws InterruptedException;
public final native void wait(long timeout) throws
   InterruptedException;
public final void wait(long timeout, int nanos) throws
   InterruptedException;
```

The *OutOfMemoryError* Class

```
public Class OutOfMemoryError extends VirtualMachineError
```

Constructors

```
public OutOfMemoryError();
public OutOfMemoryError(String s);
```

The *Process* Class

```
public abstract Class Process extends Object
```

Methods

```
abstract public void destroy();
abstract public int exitValue();
```

```
abstract public InputStream getErrorStream();
abstract public InputStream getInputStream();
abstract public OutputStream getOutputStream();
abstract public int waitFor() throws InterruptedException;
```

The *Runnable* Interface

```
public Interface Runnable
```

Methods

```
public abstract void run();
```

The *Runtime* Class

```
public Class Runtime extends Object
```

Methods

```
public static Runtime getRuntime();
public static void runFinalizersOnExit(boolean value);
private static native void runFinalizersOnExit0(boolean value);
private native String buildLibName(String pathname, String filename);
public Process exec(String command) throws IOException;
public Process exec(String command, String envp[]) throws IOException;
public Process exec(String cmdarray[]) throws IOException;
public Process exec(String cmdarray[], String envp[]) throws
  IOException;
private native Process execInternal(String cmdarray[], String envp[])
  throws IOException;
public void exit(int status);
private native void exitInternal(int status);
public native long freeMemory();
public native void gc();
public InputStream getLocalizedInputStream(InputStream in);
public OutputStream getLocalizedOutputStream(OutputStream out);
private synchronized native String initializeLinkerInternal();
public synchronized void load(String filename);
private native int loadFileInternal(String filename);
public synchronized void loadLibrary(String libname);
public native void runFinalization();
public native long totalMemory();
public native void traceInstructions(boolean on);
public native void traceMethodCalls(boolean on);
```

The *RuntimeException* Class

```
public Class RuntimeException extends Exception
```

Constructors

```
public RuntimeException();
public RuntimeException(String s);
```

The *SecurityException* Class

```
public Class SecurityException extends RuntimeException
```

Constructors

```
public SecurityException();
public SecurityException(String s);
```

The *SecurityManager* Class

```
public abstract Class SecurityManager extends Object
```

Methods

```
public void checkAccept(String host, int port);
public void checkAccess(Thread g);
public void checkAccess(ThreadGroup g);
public void checkAwtEventQueueAccess();
public void checkConnect(String host, int port);
public void checkConnect(String host, int port, Object context);
public void checkCreateClassLoader();
public void checkDelete(String file);
public void checkExec(String cmd);
public void checkExit(int status);
public void checkLink(String lib);
public void checkListen(int port);
public void checkMemberAccess(Class clazz, int which);
public void checkMulticast(InetAddress maddr);
public void checkMulticast(InetAddress maddr, byte ttl);
public void checkPackageAccess(String pkg);
public void checkPackageDefinition(String pkg);
public void checkPrintJobAccess();
public void checkPropertiesAccess();
public void checkPropertyAccess(String key);
```

```
public void checkRead(FileDescriptor fd);
public void checkRead(String file);
public void checkRead(String file, Object context);
public void checkSecurityAccess(String action);
public void checkSetFactory();
public void checkSystemClipboardAccess();
public boolean checkTopLevelWindow(Object window);
public void checkWrite(FileDescriptor fd);
public void checkWrite(String file);
protected native int classDepth(String name);
protected native int classLoaderDepth();
protected native ClassLoader currentClassLoader();
private native Class currentLoadedClass0();
protected native Class[] getClassContext();
public boolean getInCheck();
public Object getSecurityContext();
public ThreadGroup getThreadGroup();
```

The *Short* Class

```
public Class Short extends Number
```

Data

```
public static final short MAX_VALUE = 32767;
public static final short MIN_VALUE = -32768;
public static final Class TYPE = Class.getPrimitiveClass("short");
```

Constructors

```
public Short(short value);
public Short(String s) throws NumberFormatException;
```

Methods

```
public static Short decode(String nm) throws NumberFormatException;
public static short parseShort(String s) throws NumberFormatException;
public static short parseShort(String s, int radix) throws
  NumberFormatException;
public static String toString(short s);
public static Short valueOf(String s, int radix) throws
  NumberFormatException;
public static Short valueOf(String s) throws NumberFormatException;
public byte byteValue();
```

```
public double doubleValue();
public boolean equals(Object obj);
public float floatValue();
public int hashCode();
public int intValue();
public long longValue();
public short shortValue();
public String toString();
```

The *StackOverflowError* Class

```
public Class StackOverflowError extends VirtualMachineError
```

Constructors

```
public StackOverflowError();
public StackOverflowError(String s);
```

The *String* Class

```
public Class String extends Object implements java.io.Serializable
```

Constructors

```
public String();
public String(String value);
public String(char value[]);
public String(char value[], int offset, int count);
public String(byte ascii[], int hibyte, int offset, int count);
public String(byte ascii[], int hibyte);
public String(byte bytes[], int offset, int length, String enc) throws
    UnsupportedEncodingException;
public String(byte bytes[], String enc) throws
    UnsupportedEncodingException;
public String(byte bytes[], int offset, int length);
public String(byte bytes[]);
```

Methods

```
public static String copyValueOf(char data[], int offset, int count);
public static String copyValueOf(char data[]);
public static String valueOf(boolean b);
public static String valueOf(char data[]);
public static String valueOf(char data[], int offset, int count);
```

```
public static String valueOf(char c);
public static String valueOf(double d);
public static String valueOf(float f);
public static String valueOf(int i);
public static String valueOf(long l);
public static String valueOf(Object obj);
public String (StringBuffer buffer);
public char charAt(int index);
public int compareTo(String anotherString);
public String concat(String str);
public boolean endsWith(String suffix);
public boolean equals(Object anObject);
public boolean equalsIgnoreCase(String anotherString);
public byte[] getBytes();
public void getBytes(int srcBegin, int srcEnd, byte dst[], int
  dstBegin);
public byte[] getBytes(String enc) throws UnsupportedEncodingException;
public void getChars(int srcBegin, int srcEnd, char dst[], int
  dstBegin);
public int hashCode();
public int indexOf(int ch);
public int indexOf(int ch, int fromIndex);
public int indexOf(String str);
public int indexOf(String str, int fromIndex);
public native String intern();
public int lastIndexOf(int ch);
public int lastIndexOf(int ch, int fromIndex);
public int lastIndexOf(String str);
public int lastIndexOf(String str, int fromIndex);
public int length();
public boolean regionMatches(boolean ignoreCase, int toffset, String
  other, int ooffset, int len);
public boolean regionMatches(int toffset, String other, int ooffset,
  int len);
public String replace(char oldChar, char newChar);
public boolean startsWith(String prefix, int toffset);
public boolean startsWith(String prefix);
public String substring(int beginIndex);
public String substring(int beginIndex, int endIndex);
public char[] toCharArray();
public String toLowerCase( Locale locale );
public String toLowerCase();
```

```
public String toString();
public String toUpperCase( Locale locale );
public String toUpperCase();
public String trim();
```

The *StringBuffer* Class

```
public Class StringBuffer extends Object implements
    java.io.Serializable
```

Constructors

```
public StringBuffer();
public StringBuffer(int length);
public StringBuffer(String str);
```

Methods

```
public StringBuffer append(boolean b);
public synchronized StringBuffer append(char str[]);
public synchronized StringBuffer append(char str[], int offset, int
    len);
public synchronized StringBuffer append(char c);
public StringBuffer append(double d);
public StringBuffer append(float f);
public StringBuffer append(int i);
public StringBuffer append(long l);
public synchronized StringBuffer append(Object obj);
public synchronized StringBuffer append(String str);
public int capacity();
public synchronized char charAt(int index);
public synchronized void ensureCapacity(int minimumCapacity);
public synchronized void getChars(int srcBegin, int srcEnd, char dst[],
    int dstBegin);
public synchronized StringBuffer insert(int offset, Object obj);
public synchronized StringBuffer insert(int offset, String str);
public synchronized StringBuffer insert(int offset, char str[]);
public StringBuffer insert(int offset, boolean b);
public synchronized StringBuffer insert(int offset, char c);
public StringBuffer insert(int offset, int i);
public StringBuffer insert(int offset, long l);
public StringBuffer insert(int offset, float f);
public StringBuffer insert(int offset, double d);
```

```
public int length();
public synchronized StringBuffer reverse();
public synchronized void setCharAt(int index, char ch);
public synchronized void setLength(int newLength);
public String toString();
```

The *StringIndexOutOfBoundsException* Class

```
public Class StringIndexOutOfBoundsException extends
  IndexOutOfBoundsException
```

Constructors

```
public StringIndexOutOfBoundsException();
public StringIndexOutOfBoundsException(String s);
public StringIndexOutOfBoundsException(int index);
```

The *System* Class

```
public Class System extends Object
```

Data

```
public final static PrintStream err = nullPrintStream();
public final static InputStream in = nullInputStream();
public final static PrintStream out = nullPrintStream();
```

Methods

```
public static native void arraycopy(Object src, int src_position,
  Object dst, int dst_position, int length);
public static native long currentTimeMillis();
public static void exit(int status);
public static void gc();
public static String getenv(String name);
public static Properties getProperties();
public static String getProperty(String key);
public static String getProperty(String key, String def);
public static SecurityManager getSecurityManager();
public static native int identityHashCode(Object x);
private static native Properties initProperties(Properties props);
public static void load(String filename);
public static void loadLibrary(String libname);
public static void runFinalization();
```

```
public static void runFinalizersOnExit(boolean value);
public static void setErr(PrintStream err);
private static native void setErr0(PrintStream err);
public static void setIn(InputStream in);
private static native void setIn0(InputStream in);
public static void setOut(PrintStream out);
private static native void setOut0(PrintStream out);
public static void setProperties(Properties props);
public static void setSecurityManager(SecurityManager s);
```

The *Thread* Class

```
public Class Thread extends Object implements Runnable
```

Data

```
public final static int MAX_PRIORITY = 10;
public final static int MIN_PRIORITY = 1;
public final static int NORM_PRIORITY = 5;
```

Constructors

```
public Thread();
public Thread(Runnable target);
public Thread(ThreadGroup group, Runnable target);
public Thread(String name);
public Thread(ThreadGroup group, String name);
public Thread(Runnable target, String name);
public Thread(ThreadGroup group, Runnable target, String name);
```

Methods

```
public static int activeCount();
public static native Thread currentThread();
public static void dumpStack();
public static int enumerate(Thread tarray[]);
public static boolean interrupted();
public static native void sleep(long millis) throws
   InterruptedException;
public static void sleep(long millis, int nanos) throws
   InterruptedException;
public static native void yield();
public void checkAccess();
public native int countStackFrames();
```

```
public void destroy();
public final String getName();
public final int getPriority();
public final ThreadGroup getThreadGroup();
public void interrupt();
private native void interrupt0();
public final native boolean isAlive();
public final boolean isDaemon();
public boolean isInterrupted();
private native boolean isInterrupted(boolean ClearInterrupted);
public final void join() throws InterruptedException;
public final synchronized void join(long millis) throws
   InterruptedException;
public final synchronized void join(long millis, int nanos) throws
   InterruptedException;
public final void resume();
private native void resume0();
public void run();
public final void setDaemon(boolean on);
public final void setName(String name);
public final void setPriority(int newPriority);
private native void setPriority0(int newPriority);
public synchronized native void start();
public final void stop();
public final synchronized void stop(Throwable o);
private native void stop0(Object o);
public final void suspend();
private native void suspend0();
public String toString();
```

The *ThreadDeath* Class

```
public Class ThreadDeath extends Error
```

The *ThreadGroup* Class

```
public Class ThreadGroup extends Object
```

Constructors

```
public ThreadGroup(String name);
public ThreadGroup(ThreadGroup parent, String name);
```

Methods

```
public int activeCount();
public int activeGroupCount();
public boolean allowThreadSuspension(boolean b);
public final void checkAccess();
public final void destroy();
public int enumerate(Thread list[]);
public int enumerate(Thread list[], boolean recurse);
public int enumerate(ThreadGroup list[]);
public int enumerate(ThreadGroup list[], boolean recurse);
public final int getMaxPriority();
public final String getName();
public final ThreadGroup getParent();
public final boolean isDaemon();
public synchronized boolean isDestroyed();
public void list();
public final boolean parentOf(ThreadGroup g);
public final void resume();
public final void setDaemon(boolean daemon);
public final void setMaxPriority(int pri);
public final void stop();
public final void suspend();
public String toString();
public void uncaughtException(Thread t, Throwable e);
```

The *Throwable* Class

```
public Class Throwable extends Object implements java.io.Serializable
```

Constructors

```
public Throwable();
public Throwable(String message);
```

Methods

```
public native Throwable fillInStackTrace();
public String getLocalizedMessage();
public String getMessage();
public void printStackTrace();
```

```
public void printStackTrace(java.io.PrintStream s);
public void printStackTrace(java.io.PrintWriter s);
private native void printStackTrace0(Object s);
public String toString();
```

The *UnknownError* Class

```
public Class UnknownError extends VirtualMachineError
```

Constructors

```
public UnknownError();
public UnknownError(String s);
```

The *UnsatisfiedLinkError* Class

```
public Class UnsatisfiedLinkError extends LinkageError
```

Constructors

```
public UnsatisfiedLinkError();
public UnsatisfiedLinkError(String s);
```

The *VerifyError* Class

```
public Class VerifyError extends LinkageError
```

Constructors

```
public VerifyError();
public VerifyError(String s);
```

The *VirtualMachineError* Class

```
public abstract Class VirtualMachineError extends Error
```

Constructors

```
public VirtualMachineError();
public VirtualMachineError(String s);
```

The *Void* Class

```
public Class Void extends Object
```

Data

```
public static final Class TYPE = Class.getPrimitiveClass("void");
```

The *java.lang.reflect* Package

The *Array* Class

```
public Class Array extends Object
```

Methods

```
public static native Object get(Object array, int index) throws
    IllegalArgumentException, ArrayIndexOutOfBoundsException;
public static native boolean getBoolean(Object array, int index) throws
    IllegalArgumentException, ArrayIndexOutOfBoundsException;
public static native byte getByte(Object array, int index) throws
    IllegalArgumentException, ArrayIndexOutOfBoundsException;
public static native char getChar(Object array, int index) throws
    IllegalArgumentException, ArrayIndexOutOfBoundsException;
public static native double getDouble(Object array, int index) throws
    IllegalArgumentException, ArrayIndexOutOfBoundsException;
public static native float getFloat(Object array, int index) throws
    IllegalArgumentException, ArrayIndexOutOfBoundsException;
public static native int getInt(Object array, int index) throws
    IllegalArgumentException, ArrayIndexOutOfBoundsException;
public static native int getLength(Object array) throws
    IllegalArgumentException;
public static native long getLong(Object array, int index) throws
    IllegalArgumentException, ArrayIndexOutOfBoundsException;
public static native short getShort(Object array, int index) throws
    IllegalArgumentException, ArrayIndexOutOfBoundsException;
private static native Object multiNewArray(Class componentType, int[]
    dimensions) throws IllegalArgumentException,
    NegativeArraySizeException;
```

```
private static native Object newArray(Class componentType, int length)
  throws NegativeArraySizeException;
public static Object newInstance(Class componentType, int length)
  throws NegativeArraySizeException;
public static Object newInstance(Class componentType, int[] dimensions)
  throws IllegalArgumentException, NegativeArraySizeException;
public static native void set(Object array, int index, Object value)
  throws IllegalArgumentException, ArrayIndexOutOfBoundsException;
public static native void setBoolean(Object array, int index, boolean
  z) throws IllegalArgumentException, ArrayIndexOutOfBoundsException;
public static native void setByte(Object array, int index, byte b)
  throws IllegalArgumentException, ArrayIndexOutOfBoundsException;
public static native void setChar(Object array, int index, char c)
  throws IllegalArgumentException, ArrayIndexOutOfBoundsException;
public static native void setDouble(Object array, int index, double d)
  throws IllegalArgumentException, ArrayIndexOutOfBoundsException;
public static native void setFloat(Object array, int index, float f)
  throws IllegalArgumentException, ArrayIndexOutOfBoundsException;
public static native void setInt(Object array, int index, int i) throws
  IllegalArgumentException, ArrayIndexOutOfBoundsException;
public static native void setLong(Object array, int index, long l)
  throws IllegalArgumentException, ArrayIndexOutOfBoundsException;
public static native void setShort(Object array, int index, short s)
  throws IllegalArgumentException, ArrayIndexOutOfBoundsException;
```

The *Constructor* Class

```
public Class Constructor extends Object implements Member
```

Methods

```
public boolean equals(Object obj);
public Class getDeclaringClass();
public Class[] getExceptionTypes();
public native int getModifiers();
public String getName();
public Class[] getParameterTypes();
public int hashCode();
public native Object newInstance(Object[] initargs) throws
  InstantiationException, IllegalAccessException,
  IllegalArgumentException, InvocationTargetException;
public String toString();
```

The *Field* Class

```
public Class Field extends Object implements Member
```

Methods

```
public boolean equals(Object obj);
public native Object get(Object obj) throws IllegalArgumentException,
   IllegalAccessException;
public native boolean getBoolean(Object obj) throws
   IllegalArgumentException, IllegalAccessException;
public native byte getByte(Object obj) throws IllegalArgumentException,
   IllegalAccessException;
public native char getChar(Object obj) throws IllegalArgumentException,
   IllegalAccessException;
public Class getDeclaringClass();
public native double getDouble(Object obj) throws
   IllegalArgumentException, IllegalAccessException;
public native float getFloat(Object obj) throws
   IllegalArgumentException, IllegalAccessException;
public native int getInt(Object obj) throws IllegalArgumentException,
   IllegalAccessException;
public native long getLong(Object obj) throws IllegalArgumentException,
   IllegalAccessException;
public native int getModifiers();
public String getName();
public native short getShort(Object obj) throws
   IllegalArgumentException, IllegalAccessException;
public Class getType();
public int hashCode();
public native void set(Object obj, Object value) throws
   IllegalArgumentException, IllegalAccessException;
public native void setBoolean(Object obj, boolean z) throws
   IllegalArgumentException, IllegalAccessException;
public native void setByte(Object obj, byte b) throws
   IllegalArgumentException, IllegalAccessException;
public native void setChar(Object obj, char c) throws
   IllegalArgumentException, IllegalAccessException;
public native void setDouble(Object obj, double d) throws
   IllegalArgumentException, IllegalAccessException;
public native void setFloat(Object obj, float f) throws
   IllegalArgumentException, IllegalAccessException;
```

```
public native void setInt(Object obj, int i) throws
    IllegalArgumentException, IllegalAccessException;
public native void setLong(Object obj, long l) throws
    IllegalArgumentException, IllegalAccessException;
public native void setShort(Object obj, short s) throws
    IllegalArgumentException, IllegalAccessException;
public String toString();
```

The *InvocationTargetException* Class

```
public Class InvocationTargetException extends Exception
```

Constructors

```
public InvocationTargetException(Throwable target);
public InvocationTargetException(Throwable target, String s);
```

Methods

```
public Throwable getTargetException();
```

The *Member* Interface

```
public Interface Member
```

Data

```
public static final int DECLARED = 1;
public static final int PUBLIC = 0;
```

Methods

```
public Class getDeclaringClass();
public int getModifiers();
public String getName();
```

The *Method* Class

```
public Class Method extends Object implements Member
```

Methods

```
public boolean equals(Object obj);
public Class getDeclaringClass();
public Class[] getExceptionTypes();
```

```
public native int getModifiers();
public String getName();
public Class[] getParameterTypes();
public Class getReturnType();
public int hashCode();
public native Object invoke(Object obj, Object[] args) throws
   IllegalAccessException, IllegalArgumentException,
   InvocationTargetException;
public String toString();
```

The *Modifier* Class

```
public Class Modifier extends Object
```

Data

```
public static final int ABSTRACT = 0x00000400;
public static final int FINAL = 0x00000010;
public static final int INTERFACE = 0x00000200;
public static final int NATIVE = 0x00000100;
public static final int PRIVATE = 0x00000002;
public static final int PROTECTED = 0x00000004;
public static final int PUBLIC = 0x00000001;
public static final int STATIC = 0x00000008;
public static final int SYNCHRONIZED = 0x00000020;
public static final int TRANSIENT = 0x00000080;
public static final int VOLATILE = 0x00000040;
```

Methods

```
public static boolean isAbstract(int mod);
public static boolean isFinal(int mod);
public static boolean isInterface(int mod);
public static boolean isNative(int mod);
public static boolean isPrivate(int mod);
public static boolean isProtected(int mod);
public static boolean isPublic(int mod);
public static boolean isStatic(int mod);
public static boolean isSynchronized(int mod);
public static boolean isTransient(int mod);
public static boolean isVolatile(int mod);
public static String toString(int mod);
```

The *java.math* Package

The *BigDecimal* Class

```
public Class BigDecimal extends Number
```

Data

```
public final static int ROUND_CEILING = 2;
public final static int ROUND_DOWN = 1;
public final static int ROUND_FLOOR = 3;
public final static int ROUND_HALF_DOWN = 5;
public final static int ROUND_HALF_EVEN = 6;
public final static int ROUND_HALF_UP = 4;
public final static int ROUND_UNNECESSARY = 7;
public final static int ROUND_UP = 0;
```

Constructors

```
public BigDecimal(String val) throws NumberFormatException;
public BigDecimal(double val) throws NumberFormatException;
public BigDecimal(BigInteger val);
public BigDecimal(BigInteger val, int scale) throws
   NumberFormatException;
```

Methods

```
public static BigDecimal valueOf(long val, int scale) throws
   NumberFormatException;
public static BigDecimal valueOf(long val);
public BigDecimal abs();
public BigDecimal add(BigDecimal val);
public int compareTo(BigDecimal val);
public BigDecimal divide(BigDecimal val, int scale, int roundingMode)
   throws ArithmeticException, IllegalArgumentException;
public BigDecimal divide(BigDecimal val, int roundingMode) throws
   ArithmeticException, IllegalArgumentException;
public double doubleValue();
public boolean equals(Object x);
public float floatValue();
public int hashCode();
public int intValue();
```

```
public long longValue();
public BigDecimal max(BigDecimal val);
public BigDecimal min(BigDecimal val);
public BigDecimal movePointLeft(int n);
public BigDecimal movePointRight(int n);
public BigDecimal multiply(BigDecimal val);
public BigDecimal negate();
public int scale();
public BigDecimal setScale(int scale, int roundingMode) throws
   ArithmeticException, IllegalArgumentException;
public BigDecimal setScale(int scale) throws ArithmeticException,
   IllegalArgumentException;
public int signum();
public BigDecimal subtract(BigDecimal val);
public BigInteger toBigInteger();
public String toString();
```

The *BigInteger* Class

```
public Class BigInteger extends Number
```

Constructors

```
public BigInteger(byte[] val) throws NumberFormatException;
public BigInteger(int signum, byte[] magnitude) throws
   NumberFormatException;
public BigInteger(String val, int radix) throws NumberFormatException;
public BigInteger(String val) throws NumberFormatException;
public BigInteger(int numBits, Random rndSrc) throws
   IllegalArgumentException;
public BigInteger(int bitLength, int certainty, Random rnd);
```

Methods

```
private static native byte[] plumbAdd(byte[] a, byte[] b);
private static native byte[] plumbDivide(byte[] a, byte[] b);
private static native byte[][] plumbDivideAndRemainder(byte[] a,
   byte[] b);
private static native byte[] plumbGcd(byte[] a, byte[] b);
private static native byte[] plumbGeneratePrime(byte[] a);
private static native byte[] plumbModInverse(byte[] a, byte[] m);
private static native byte[] plumbModPow(byte[] a, byte[] b, byte[] m);
private static native byte[] plumbMultiply(byte[] a, byte[] b);
```

```
private static native byte[] plumbRemainder(byte[] a, byte[] b);
private static native byte[] plumbSquare(byte[] a);
private static native BigInteger plumbSubtract(byte[] a, byte[] b);
private static native void plumbInit();
public static BigInteger valueOf(long val);
public BigInteger abs();
public BigInteger add(BigInteger val) throws ArithmeticException;
public BigInteger and(BigInteger val);
public BigInteger andNot(BigInteger val);
public int bitCount();
public int bitLength();
public BigInteger clearBit(int n) throws ArithmeticException;
public int compareTo(BigInteger val);
public BigInteger divide(BigInteger val) throws ArithmeticException;
public BigInteger[] divideAndRemainder(BigInteger val) throws
  ArithmeticException;
public double doubleValue();
public boolean equals(Object x);
public BigInteger flipBit(int n) throws ArithmeticException;
public float floatValue();
public BigInteger gcd(BigInteger val);
public int getLowestSetBit();
public int hashCode();
public int intValue();
public boolean isProbablePrime(int certainty);
public long longValue();
public BigInteger max(BigInteger val);
public BigInteger min(BigInteger val);
public BigInteger mod(BigInteger m);
public BigInteger modInverse(BigInteger m) throws ArithmeticException;
public BigInteger modPow(BigInteger exponent, BigInteger m);
public BigInteger multiply(BigInteger val);
public BigInteger negate();
public BigInteger not();
public BigInteger or(BigInteger val);
public BigInteger pow(int exponent) throws ArithmeticException;
public BigInteger remainder(BigInteger val) throws ArithmeticException;
public BigInteger setBit(int n) throws ArithmeticException;
public BigInteger shiftLeft(int n);
public BigInteger shiftRight(int n);
public int signum();
public BigInteger subtract(BigInteger val);
```

```
public boolean testBit(int n) throws ArithmeticException;
public byte[] toByteArray();
public String toString();
public String toString(int radix);
public BigInteger xor(BigInteger val);
```

The *java.net* Package

The *BindException* Class

```
public Class BindException extends SocketException
```

Constructors

```
public BindException(String msg);
public BindException();
```

The *ConnectException* Class

```
public Class ConnectException extends SocketException
```

Constructors

```
public ConnectException(String msg);
public ConnectException();
```

The *ContentHandler* Class

```
public abstract Class ContentHandler extends Object
```

Methods

```
abstract public Object getContent(URLConnection urlc) throws
    IOException;
```

The *ContentHandlerFactory* Interface

```
public Interface ContentHandlerFactory
```

Methods

```
ContentHandler createContentHandler(String mimetype);
```

The *DatagramPacket* Class

```
public Class DatagramPacket extends Object
```

Constructors

```
public DatagramPacket(byte ibuf[], int ilength);
public DatagramPacket(byte ibuf[], int ilength, InetAddress iaddr, int
  iport);
```

Methods

```
public synchronized InetAddress getAddress();
public synchronized byte[] getData();
public synchronized int getLength();
public synchronized int getPort();
public synchronized void setAddress(InetAddress iaddr);
public synchronized void setData(byte[] ibuf);
public synchronized void setLength(int ilength);
public synchronized void setPort(int iport);
```

The *DatagramSocket* Class

```
public Class DatagramSocket extends Object
```

Constructors

```
public DatagramSocket() throws SocketException;
public DatagramSocket(int port) throws SocketException;
public DatagramSocket(int port, InetAddress laddr) throws
  SocketException;
```

Methods

```
public void close();
public InetAddress getLocalAddress();
public int getLocalPort();
public synchronized int getSoTimeout() throws SocketException;
public synchronized void receive(DatagramPacket p) throws IOException;
public void send(DatagramPacket p) throws IOException;
public synchronized void setSoTimeout(int timeout) throws
  SocketException;
```

The *DatagramSocketImpl* Class

```
public abstract Class DatagramSocketImpl extends Object implements
    SocketOptions
```

Methods

```
protected abstract void bind(int lport, InetAddress laddr) throws
    SocketException;
protected abstract void close();
protected abstract void create() throws SocketException;
protected abstract byte getTTL() throws IOException;
protected abstract void join(InetAddress inetaddr) throws IOException;
protected abstract void leave(InetAddress inetaddr) throws IOException;
protected abstract int peek(InetAddress i) throws IOException;
protected abstract void receive(DatagramPacket p) throws IOException;
protected abstract void send(DatagramPacket p) throws IOException;
protected abstract void setTTL(byte ttl) throws IOException;
```

The *FileNameMap* Interface

```
public Interface FileNameMap
```

Methods

```
public String getContentTypeFor(String fileName);
```

The *HttpURLConnection* Class

```
public abstract Class HttpURLConnection extends URLConnection
```

Data

```
public static final int HTTP_ACCEPTED = 202;
public static final int HTTP_BAD_GATEWAY = 502;
public static final int HTTP_BAD_METHOD = 405;
public static final int HTTP_BAD_REQUEST = 400;
public static final int HTTP_CLIENT_TIMEOUT = 408;
public static final int HTTP_CONFLICT = 409;
public static final int HTTP_CREATED = 201;
public static final int HTTP_ENTITY_TOO_LARGE = 413;
public static final int HTTP_FORBIDDEN = 403;
public static final int HTTP_GATEWAY_TIMEOUT = 504;
public static final int HTTP_GONE = 410;
public static final int HTTP_INTERNAL_ERROR = 501;
```

```
public static final int HTTP_LENGTH_REQUIRED = 411;
public static final int HTTP_MOVED_PERM = 301;
public static final int HTTP_MOVED_TEMP = 302;
public static final int HTTP_MULT_CHOICE = 300;
public static final int HTTP_NO_CONTENT = 204;
public static final int HTTP_NOT_ACCEPTABLE = 406;
public static final int HTTP_NOT_AUTHORITATIVE = 203;
public static final int HTTP_NOT_FOUND = 404;
public static final int HTTP_NOT_MODIFIED = 304;
public static final int HTTP_OK = 200;
public static final int HTTP_PARTIAL = 206;
public static final int HTTP_PAYMENT_REQUIRED = 402;
public static final int HTTP_PRECON_FAILED = 412;
public static final int HTTP_PROXY_AUTH = 407;
public static final int HTTP_REQ_TOO_LONG = 414;
public static final int HTTP_RESET = 205;
public static final int HTTP_SEE_OTHER = 303;
public static final int HTTP_SERVER_ERROR = 500;
public static final int HTTP_UNAUTHORIZED = 401;
public static final int HTTP_UNAVAILABLE = 503;
public static final int HTTP_UNSUPPORTED_TYPE = 415;
public static final int HTTP_USE_PROXY = 305;
public static final int HTTP_VERSION = 505;
```

Methods

```
public static boolean getFollowRedirects();
public static void setFollowRedirects(boolean set);
public abstract void disconnect();
public abstract boolean usingProxy();
public String getRequestMethod();
public int getResponseCode() throws IOException;
public String getResponseMessage() throws IOException;
public void setRequestMethod(String method) throws ProtocolException;
```

The *InetAddress* Class

```
public Class InetAddress extends Object implements java.io.Serializable
```

Methods

```
public static InetAddress getAllByName(String host)[] throws
  UnknownHostException;
```

```
public static InetAddress getByName(String host) throws
  UnknownHostException;
public static InetAddress getLocalHost() throws UnknownHostException;
public boolean equals(Object obj);
public byte[] getAddress();
public String getHostAddress();
public String getHostName();
public int hashCode();
public boolean isMulticastAddress();
public String toString();
```

The *MalformedURLException* Class

```
public Class MalformedURLException extends IOException
```

Constructors

```
public MalformedURLException();
public MalformedURLException(String msg);
```

The *MulticastSocket* Class

```
public Class MulticastSocket extends DatagramSocket
```

Constructors

```
public MulticastSocket() throws IOException;
public MulticastSocket(int port) throws IOException;
```

Methods

```
public InetAddress getInterface() throws SocketException;
public byte getTTL() throws IOException;
public void joinGroup(InetAddress mcastaddr) throws IOException;
public void leaveGroup(InetAddress mcastaddr) throws IOException;
public synchronized void send(DatagramPacket p, byte ttl) throws
  IOException;
public void setInterface(InetAddress inf) throws SocketException;
public void setTTL(byte ttl) throws IOException;
```

The *NoRouteToHostException* Class

```
public Class NoRouteToHostException extends SocketException
```

Constructors

```
public NoRouteToHostException(String msg);
public NoRouteToHostException();
```

The *ProtocolException* Class

```
public Class ProtocolException extends IOException
```

Constructors

```
public ProtocolException(String host);
public ProtocolException();
```

The *ServerSocket* Class

```
public Class ServerSocket extends Object
```

Constructors

```
public ServerSocket(int port) throws IOException;
public ServerSocket(int port, int backlog) throws IOException;
public ServerSocket(int port, int backlog, InetAddress bindAddr) throws
  IOException;
```

Methods

```
public static synchronized void setSocketFactory(SocketImplFactory fac)
  throws IOException;
public Socket accept() throws IOException;
public void close() throws IOException;
public InetAddress getInetAddress();
public int getLocalPort();
public synchronized int getSoTimeout() throws IOException;
public synchronized void setSoTimeout(int timeout) throws
  SocketException;
public String toString();
```

The *Socket* Class

```
public Class Socket extends Object
```

Constructors

```
public Socket(String host, int port) throws UnknownHostException,
    IOException;
public Socket(InetAddress address, int port) throws IOException;
public Socket(String host, int port, InetAddress localAddr, int
    localPort) throws IOException;
public Socket(InetAddress address, int port, InetAddress localAddr, int
    localPort) throws IOException;
public Socket(String host, int port, boolean stream) throws
    IOException;
public Socket(InetAddress host, int port, boolean stream) throws
    IOException;
```

Methods

```
public static synchronized void setSocketImplFactory(SocketImplFactory
    fac) throws IOException;
public synchronized void close() throws IOException;
public InetAddress getInetAddress();
public InputStream getInputStream() throws IOException;
public InetAddress getLocalAddress();
public int getLocalPort();
public OutputStream getOutputStream() throws IOException;
public int getPort();
public int getSoLinger() throws SocketException;
public synchronized int getSoTimeout() throws SocketException;
public boolean getTcpNoDelay() throws SocketException;
public void setSoLinger(boolean on, int val) throws SocketException;
public synchronized void setSoTimeout(int timeout) throws
    SocketException;
public void setTcpNoDelay(boolean on) throws SocketException;
public String toString();
```

The *SocketException* Class

```
public Class SocketException extends IOException
```

Constructors

```
public SocketException(String msg);
public SocketException();
```

The *SocketImpl* Class

```
public abstract Class SocketImpl extends Object implements
    SocketOptions
```

Methods

```
protected abstract void accept(SocketImpl s) throws IOException;
protected abstract int available() throws IOException;
protected abstract void bind(InetAddress host, int port) throws
    IOException;
protected abstract void close() throws IOException;
protected abstract void connect(InetAddress address, int port) throws
    IOException;
protected abstract void connect(String host, int port) throws
    IOException;
protected abstract void create(boolean stream) throws IOException;
protected abstract InputStream getInputStream() throws IOException;
protected abstract OutputStream getOutputStream() throws IOException;
protected abstract void listen(int backlog) throws IOException;
public String toString();
```

The *SocketImplFactory* Interface

```
public Interface SocketImplFactory
```

Methods

```
SocketImpl createSocketImpl();
```

The *URL* Class

```
public Class URL extends Object implements java.io.Serializable
```

Constructors

```
public URL(String protocol, String host, int port, String file) throws
  MalformedURLException;
public URL(String protocol, String host, String file) throws
  MalformedURLException;
public URL(String spec) throws MalformedURLException;
public URL(URL context, String spec) throws MalformedURLException;
```

Methods

```
public static synchronized void
  setURLStreamHandlerFactory(URLStreamHandlerFactory fac);
public boolean equals(Object obj);
public final Object getContent() throws java.io.IOException;
public String getFile();
public String getHost();
public int getPort();
public String getProtocol();
public String getRef();
public int hashCode();
public URLConnection openConnection() throws java.io.IOException;
public final InputStream openStream() throws java.io.IOException;
public boolean sameFile(URL other);
public String toExternalForm();
public String toString();
```

The *URLConnection* Class

```
public abstract Class URLConnection extends Object
```

Data

```
public static FileNameMap fileNameMap;
```

Methods

```
public static boolean getDefaultAllowUserInteraction();
public static String getDefaultRequestProperty(String key);
```

```
static public String guessContentTypeFromStream(InputStream is) throws
  IOException;
public static synchronized void
  setContentHandlerFactory(ContentHandlerFactory fac);
public static void setDefaultAllowUserInteraction(boolean
  defaultallowuserinteraction);
public static void setDefaultRequestProperty(String key, String value);
abstract public void connect() throws IOException;
public boolean getAllowUserInteraction();
public Object getContent() throws IOException;
public String getContentEncoding();
public int getContentLength();
public String getContentType();
public long getDate();
public boolean getDefaultUseCaches();
public boolean getDoInput();
public boolean getDoOutput();
public long getExpiration();
public String getHeaderField(int n);
public String getHeaderField(String name);
public long getHeaderFieldDate(String name, long Default);
public int getHeaderFieldInt(String name, int Default);
public String getHeaderFieldKey(int n);
public long getIfModifiedSince();
public InputStream getInputStream() throws IOException;
public long getLastModified();
public OutputStream getOutputStream() throws IOException;
public String getRequestProperty(String key);
public URL getURL();
public boolean getUseCaches();
public void setAllowUserInteraction(boolean allowuserinteraction);
public void setDefaultUseCaches(boolean defaultusecaches);
public void setDoInput(boolean doinput);
public void setDoOutput(boolean dooutput);
public void setIfModifiedSince(long ifmodifiedsince);
public void setRequestProperty(String key, String value);
public void setUseCaches(boolean usecaches);
public String toString();
```

The *URLEncoder* Class

```
public Class URLEncoder extends Object
```

Methods

```
public static String encode(String s);
```

The *URLStreamHandler* Class

```
public abstract Class URLStreamHandler extends Object
```

Methods

```
abstract protected URLConnection openConnection(URL u) throws
    IOException;
```

The *URLStreamHandlerFactory* Interface

```
public Interface URLStreamHandlerFactory
```

Methods

```
URLStreamHandler createURLStreamHandler(String protocol);
```

The *UnknownHostException* Class

```
public Class UnknownHostException extends IOException
```

Constructors

```
public UnknownHostException(String host);
public UnknownHostException();
```

The *UnknownServiceException* Class

```
public Class UnknownServiceException extends IOException
```

Constructors

```
public UnknownServiceException();
public UnknownServiceException(String msg);
```

The *java.rmi* Package

The *AccessException* Class

```
public Class AccessException extends java.rmi.RemoteException
```

Constructors

```
public AccessException(String s);
public AccessException(String s, Exception ex);
```

The *AlreadyBoundException* Class

```
public Class AlreadyBoundException extends java.lang.Exception
```

Constructors

```
public AlreadyBoundException();
public AlreadyBoundException(String s);
```

The *ConnectException* Class

```
public Class ConnectException extends RemoteException
```

Constructors

```
public ConnectException(String s);
public ConnectException(String s, Exception ex);
```

The *ConnectIOException* Class

```
public Class ConnectIOException extends RemoteException
```

Constructors

```
public ConnectIOException(String s);
public ConnectIOException(String s, Exception ex);
```

The *MarshalException* Class

```
public Class MarshalException extends RemoteException
```

Constructors

```
public MarshalException(String s);
public MarshalException(String s, Exception ex);
```

The *Naming* Class

```
public Class Naming extends Object
```

Methods

```
public static void bind(String name, Remote obj) throws
   AlreadyBoundException, java.net.MalformedURLException,
   UnknownHostException, RemoteException;
public static String[] list(String name) throws RemoteException,
   java.net.MalformedURLException, UnknownHostException;
public static Remote lookup(String name) throws NotBoundException,
   java.net.MalformedURLException, UnknownHostException,
   RemoteException;
public static void rebind(String name, Remote obj) throws
   RemoteException, java.net.MalformedURLException,
   UnknownHostException;
public static void unbind(String name) throws RemoteException,
   NotBoundException, java.net.MalformedURLException,
   UnknownHostException;
```

The *NoSuchObjectException* Class

```
public Class NoSuchObjectException extends java.rmi.RemoteException
```

Constructors

```
public NoSuchObjectException(String s);
```

The *NotBoundException* Class

```
public Class NotBoundException extends java.lang.Exception
```

Constructors

```
public NotBoundException();
public NotBoundException(String s);
```

The *RMISecurityException* Class

```
public Class RMISecurityException extends java.lang.SecurityException
```

Constructors

```
public RMISecurityException(String name);
public RMISecurityException(String name, String arg);
```

The *RMISecurityManager* Class

```
public Class RMISecurityManager extends SecurityManager
```

Constructors

```
public RMISecurityManager();
```

Methods

```
public synchronized void checkAccept(String host, int port);
public synchronized void checkAccess(Thread t);
public synchronized void checkAccess(ThreadGroup g);
public void checkAwtEventQueueAccess();
public synchronized void checkConnect(String host, int port);
public void checkConnect(String host, int port, Object context);
public synchronized void checkCreateClassLoader();
public void checkDelete(String file);
public synchronized void checkExec(String cmd);
public synchronized void checkExit(int status);
public synchronized void checkLink(String lib);
public synchronized void checkListen(int port);
public void checkMemberAccess(Class clazz, int which);
public void checkMulticast(InetAddress maddr);
public void checkMulticast(InetAddress maddr, byte ttl);
public synchronized void checkPackageAccess(String pkg);
public synchronized void checkPackageDefinition(String pkg);
public void checkPrintJobAccess();
```

```
public synchronized void checkPropertiesAccess();
public synchronized void checkPropertyAccess(String key);
public synchronized void checkRead(FileDescriptor fd);
public synchronized void checkRead(String file);
public void checkRead(String file, Object context);
public void checkSecurityAccess(String provider);
public synchronized void checkSetFactory();
public void checkSystemClipboardAccess();
public synchronized boolean checkTopLevelWindow(Object window);
public synchronized void checkWrite(FileDescriptor fd);
public synchronized void checkWrite(String file);
public Object getSecurityContext();
```

The *Remote* Interface

```
public Interface Remote
```

The *RemoteException* Class

```
public Class RemoteException extends java.io.IOException
```

Data

```
public Throwable detail;
```

Constructors

```
public RemoteException();
public RemoteException(String s);
public RemoteException(String s, Throwable ex);
```

Methods

```
public String getMessage();
```

The *ServerError* Class

```
public Class ServerError extends RemoteException
```

Constructors

```
public ServerError(String s, Error err);
```

The *ServerException* Class

```
public Class ServerException extends RemoteException
```

Constructors

```
public ServerException(String s);
public ServerException(String s, Exception ex);
```

The *ServerRuntimeException* Class

```
public Class ServerRuntimeException extends RemoteException
```

Constructors

```
public ServerRuntimeException(String s, Exception ex);
```

The *StubNotFoundException* Class

```
public Class StubNotFoundException extends RemoteException
```

Constructors

```
public StubNotFoundException(String s);
public StubNotFoundException(String s, Exception ex);
```

The *UnexpectedException* Class

```
public Class UnexpectedException extends RemoteException
```

Constructors

```
public UnexpectedException(String s);
public UnexpectedException(String s, Exception ex);
```

The *UnknownHostException* Class

```
public Class UnknownHostException extends RemoteException
```

Constructors

```
public UnknownHostException(String s);
public UnknownHostException(String s, Exception ex);
```

The *UnmarshalException* Class

```
public Class UnmarshalException extends RemoteException
```

Constructors

```
public UnmarshalException(String s);
public UnmarshalException(String s, Exception ex);
```

The *java.rmi.dgc* Package

The *DGC* Interface

```
public Interface DGC extends Remote
```

Methods

```
void clean(ObjID[] ids, long sequenceNum, VMID vmid, boolean strong)
  throws RemoteException;
Lease dirty(ObjID[] ids, long sequenceNum, Lease lease) throws
  RemoteException;
```

The *Lease* Class

```
public Class Lease extends Object implements java.io.Serializable
```

Constructors

```
public Lease(VMID id, long duration);
```

Methods

```
public long getValue();
public VMID getVMID();
```

The *VMID* Class

```
public Class VMID extends Object implements java.io.Serializable
```

Constructors

```
public VMID();
```

Methods

```
public static boolean isUnique();
public boolean equals(Object obj);
public int hashCode();
public String toString();
```

The *java.rmi.registry* Package

The *LocateRegistry* Class

```
public Class LocateRegistry extends Object
```

Methods

```
public static Registry createRegistry(int port) throws RemoteException;
public static Registry getRegistry() throws RemoteException;
public static Registry getRegistry(int port) throws RemoteException;
public static Registry getRegistry(String host) throws RemoteException,
    UnknownHostException;
public static Registry getRegistry(String host, int port) throws
    RemoteException, UnknownHostException;
```

The *Registry* Interface

```
public Interface Registry extends Remote
```

Data

```
public static final int REGISTRY_PORT = 1099;
```

Methods

```
public void bind(String name, Remote obj) throws RemoteException,
    AlreadyBoundException, AccessException;
public String[] list() throws RemoteException, AccessException;
public Remote lookup(String name) throws RemoteException,
    NotBoundException, AccessException;
public void rebind(String name, Remote obj) throws RemoteException,
    AccessException;
public void unbind(String name) throws RemoteException,
    NotBoundException, AccessException;
```

The *RegistryHandler* Interface

```
public Interface RegistryHandler
```

Methods

```
Registry registryImpl(int port) throws RemoteException;
Registry registryStub(String host, int port) throws RemoteException,
  UnknownHostException;
```

The *java.rmi.server* Package

The *ExportException* Class

```
public Class ExportException extends java.rmi.RemoteException
```

Constructors

```
public ExportException(String s);
public ExportException(String s, Exception ex);
```

The *LoaderHandler* Interface

```
public Interface LoaderHandler
```

Methods

```
Object getSecurityContext(ClassLoader loader);
Class loadClass(String name) throws MalformedURLException,
  ClassNotFoundException;
Class loadClass(URL codebase, String name) throws
  MalformedURLException, ClassNotFoundException;
```

The *LogStream* Class

```
public Class LogStream extends PrintStream
```

Data

```
public static final int BRIEF = 10;
public static final int SILENT = 0;
```

```
public static final int VERBOSE = 20;
```

Methods

```
public static synchronized PrintStream getDefaultStream();
public static LogStream log(String name);
public static int parseLevel(String s);
public static synchronized void setDefaultStream(PrintStream
  newDefault);
public synchronized OutputStream getOutputStream();
public synchronized void setOutputStream(OutputStream out);
public String toString();
public void write(byte b[], int off, int len);
public void write(int b);
```

The *ObjID* Class

```
public Class ObjID extends Object implements java.io.Serializable
```

Data

```
public static final int DGC_ID = 2;
public static final int REGISTRY_ID = 0;
```

Methods

```
public static ObjID read(ObjectInput in) throws java.io.IOException;
public ObjID ();
public ObjID (int num);
public boolean equals(Object obj);
public int hashCode();
public String toString();
public void write(ObjectOutput out) throws java.io.IOException;
```

The *Operation* Class

```
public Class Operation extends Object
```

Constructors

```
public Operation(String op);
```

Methods

```
public String getOperation();
public String toString();
```

The *RMIClassLoader* Class

```
public Class RMIClassLoader extends Object
```

Methods

```
public static Object getSecurityContext(ClassLoader loader);
public static Class loadClass(String name) throws
   MalformedURLException, ClassNotFoundException;
public static Class loadClass(URL codebase, String name) throws
   MalformedURLException, ClassNotFoundException;
```

The *RMIFailureHandler* Interface

```
public Interface RMIFailureHandler
```

Methods

```
public boolean failure(Exception ex);
```

The *RMISocketFactory* Class

```
public abstract Class RMISocketFactory extends Object
```

Methods

```
public static RMIFailureHandler getFailureHandler();
public static RMISocketFactory getSocketFactory();
public static void setFailureHandler(RMIFailureHandler fh);
public static void setSocketFactory(RMISocketFactory fac) throws
   IOException;
public abstract ServerSocket createServerSocket(int port) throws
   IOException;
public abstract Socket createSocket(String host, int port) throws
   IOException;
```

The *RemoteCall* Interface

```
public Interface RemoteCall
```

Methods

```
void done() throws IOException;
void executeCall() throws Exception;
```

```
ObjectInput getInputStream() throws IOException;
ObjectOutput getOutputStream() throws IOException;
ObjectOutput getResultStream(boolean success) throws IOException,
  StreamCorruptedException;
void releaseInputStream() throws IOException;
void releaseOutputStream() throws IOException;
```

The *RemoteObject* Class

```
public abstract Class RemoteObject extends Object implements Remote,
  java.io.Serializable
```

Methods

```
public boolean equals(Object obj);
public int hashCode();
public String toString();
```

The *RemoteRef* Interface

```
public Interface RemoteRef extends java.io.Externalizable
```

Methods

```
void done(RemoteCall call) throws RemoteException;
String getRefClass(java.io.ObjectOutput out);
void invoke(RemoteCall call) throws Exception;
RemoteCall newCall(RemoteObject obj, Operation[] op, int opnum, long
  hash) throws RemoteException;
boolean remoteEquals(RemoteRef obj);
int remoteHashCode();
String remoteToString();
```

The *RemoteServer* Class

```
public abstract Class RemoteServer extends RemoteObject
```

Methods

```
public static String getClientHost() throws ServerNotActiveException;
public static java.io.PrintStream getLog();
public static void setLog(java.io.OutputStream out);
```

The *RemoteStub* Class

```
public abstract Class RemoteStub extends RemoteObject
```

The *ServerCloneException* Class

```
public Class ServerCloneException extends CloneNotSupportedException
```

Data

```
public Exception detail;
```

Constructors

```
public ServerCloneException(String s);
public ServerCloneException(String s, Exception ex);
```

Methods

```
public String getMessage();
```

The *ServerNotActiveException* Class

```
public Class ServerNotActiveException extends java.lang.Exception
```

Constructors

```
public ServerNotActiveException();
public ServerNotActiveException(String s);
```

The *ServerRef* Interface

```
public Interface ServerRef extends RemoteRef
```

Methods

```
RemoteStub exportObject(Remote obj, Object data) throws
  RemoteException;
String getClientHost() throws ServerNotActiveException;
```

The *Skeleton* Interface

```
public Interface Skeleton
```

Methods

```
void dispatch(Remote obj, RemoteCall theCall, int opnum, long hash)
  throws Exception;
Operation[] getOperations();
```

The *SkeletonMismatchException* Class

```
public Class SkeletonMismatchException extends RemoteException
```

Constructors

```
public SkeletonMismatchException(String s);
```

The *SkeletonNotFoundException* Class

```
public Class SkeletonNotFoundException extends RemoteException
```

Constructors

```
public SkeletonNotFoundException(String s);
public SkeletonNotFoundException(String s, Exception ex);
```

The *SocketSecurityException* Class

```
public Class SocketSecurityException extends ExportException
```

Constructors

```
public SocketSecurityException(String s);
public SocketSecurityException(String s, Exception ex);
```

The *UID* Class

```
public Class UID extends Object implements java.io.Serializable
```

Constructors

```
public UID();
public UID(short num);
```

Methods

```
public static UID read(DataInput in) throws java.io.IOException;
public boolean equals(Object obj);
public int hashCode();
public String toString();
public void write(DataOutput out) throws java.io.IOException;
```

The *UnicastRemoteObject* Class

```
public Class UnicastRemoteObject extends RemoteServer
```

Methods

```
public static RemoteStub exportObject(Remote obj) throws
  RemoteException;
public Object clone() throws CloneNotSupportedException;
```

The *Unreferenced* Interface

```
public Interface Unreferenced
```

Methods

```
public void unreferenced();
```

The *java.security* Package

The *Certificate* Interface

```
public Interface Certificate
```

Methods

```
public abstract void decode(InputStream stream) throws KeyException,
  IOException;
public abstract void encode(OutputStream stream) throws KeyException,
  IOException;
public abstract String getFormat();
public abstract Principal getGuarantor();
public abstract Principal getPrincipal();
```

```
public abstract PublicKey getPublicKey();
public String toString(boolean detailed);
```

The *DigestException* Class

```
public Class DigestException extends Exception
```

Constructors

```
public DigestException();
public DigestException(String msg);
```

The *DigestInputStream* Class

```
public Class DigestInputStream extends FilterInputStream
```

Constructors

```
public DigestInputStream(InputStream stream, MessageDigest digest);
```

Methods

```
public MessageDigest getMessageDigest();
public void on(boolean on);
public int read() throws IOException;
public int read(byte[] b, int off, int len) throws IOException;
public void setMessageDigest(MessageDigest digest);
public String toString();
```

The *DigestOutputStream* Class

```
public Class DigestOutputStream extends FilterOutputStream
```

Constructors

```
public DigestOutputStream(OutputStream stream, MessageDigest digest);
```

Methods

```
public MessageDigest getMessageDigest();
public void on(boolean on);
public void setMessageDigest(MessageDigest digest);
public String toString();
public void write(byte[] b, int off, int len) throws IOException;
public void write(int b) throws IOException;
```

The *Identity* Class

```
public abstract Class Identity extends Object implements Principal,
    Serializable
```

Constructors

```
public Identity(String name, IdentityScope scope) throws
    KeyManagementException;
public Identity(String name);
```

Methods

```
public void addCertificate(Certificate certificate) throws
    KeyManagementException;
public Certificate[] certificates();
public final boolean equals(Object identity);
public String getInfo();
public final String getName();
public PublicKey getPublicKey();
public final IdentityScope getScope();
public int hashCode();
public void removeCertificate(Certificate certificate) throws
    KeyManagementException;
public void setInfo(String info);
public void setPublicKey(PublicKey key) throws KeyManagementException;
public String toString();
public String toString(boolean detailed);
```

The *IdentityScope* Class

```
public abstract Class IdentityScope extends Identity
```

Constructors

```
public IdentityScope(String name);
public IdentityScope(String name, IdentityScope scope) throws
    KeyManagementException;
```

Methods

```
public static IdentityScope getSystemScope();
public abstract void addIdentity(Identity identity) throws
    KeyManagementException;
```

```
public abstract Identity getIdentity(PublicKey key);
public abstract Identity getIdentity(String name);
public abstract Enumeration identities();
public abstract void removeIdentity(Identity identity) throws
  KeyManagementException;
public abstract int size();
public Identity getIdentity(Principal principal);
public String toString();
```

The *InvalidKeyException* Class

```
public Class InvalidKeyException extends KeyException
```

Constructors

```
public InvalidKeyException();
public InvalidKeyException(String msg);
```

The *InvalidParameterException* Class

```
public Class InvalidParameterException extends IllegalArgumentException
```

Constructors

```
public InvalidParameterException();
public InvalidParameterException(String msg);
```

The *Key* Interface

```
public Interface Key extends java.io.Serializable
```

Methods

```
public String getAlgorithm();
public byte[] getEncoded();
public String getFormat();
```

The *KeyException* Class

```
public Class KeyException extends Exception
```

Constructors

```
public KeyException();
public KeyException(String msg);
```

The *KeyManagementException* Class

```
public Class KeyManagementException extends KeyException
```

Constructors

```
public KeyManagementException();
public KeyManagementException(String msg);
```

The *KeyPair* Class

```
public Class KeyPair extends Object
```

Constructors

```
public KeyPair(PublicKey publicKey, PrivateKey privateKey);
```

Methods

```
public PrivateKey getPrivate();
public PublicKey getPublic();
```

The *KeyPairGenerator* Class

```
public abstract Class KeyPairGenerator extends Object
```

Methods

```
public static KeyPairGenerator getInstance(String algorithm) throws
   NoSuchAlgorithmException;
public static KeyPairGenerator getInstance(String algorithm, String
   provider) throws NoSuchAlgorithmException, NoSuchProviderException;
public abstract KeyPair generateKeyPair();
public abstract void initialize(int strength, SecureRandom random);
public String getAlgorithm();
public void initialize(int strength);
```

The *MessageDigest* Class

```
public abstract Class MessageDigest extends Object
```

Methods

```
public static MessageDigest getInstance(String algorithm) throws
   NoSuchAlgorithmException;
```

```
public static MessageDigest getInstance(String algorithm, String
    provider) throws NoSuchAlgorithmException, NoSuchProviderException;
public static boolean isEqual(byte digesta[], byte digestb[]);
protected abstract byte[] engineDigest();
protected abstract void engineReset();
protected abstract void engineUpdate(byte input);
protected abstract void engineUpdate(byte[] input, int offset,
    int len);
public Object clone() throws CloneNotSupportedException;
public byte[] digest();
public byte[] digest(byte[] input);
public final String getAlgorithm();
public void reset();
public String toString();
public void update(byte input);
public void update(byte[] input, int offset, int len);
public void update(byte[] input);
```

The *NoSuchAlgorithmException* Class

```
public Class NoSuchAlgorithmException extends Exception
```

Constructors

```
public NoSuchAlgorithmException();
public NoSuchAlgorithmException(String msg);
```

The *NoSuchProviderException* Class

```
public Class NoSuchProviderException extends Exception
```

Constructors

```
public NoSuchProviderException();
public NoSuchProviderException(String msg);
```

The *Principal* Interface

```
public Interface Principal
```

Methods

```
public boolean equals(Object another);
public String getName();
```

```
public int hashCode();
public String toString();
```

The *PrivateKey* Interface

```
public Interface PrivateKey extends Key
```

The *Provider* Class

```
public abstract Class Provider extends Properties
```

Methods

```
public String getInfo();
public String getName();
public double getVersion();
public String toString();
```

The *ProviderException* Class

```
public Class ProviderException extends RuntimeException
```

Constructors

```
public ProviderException();
public ProviderException(String s);
```

The *PublicKey* Interface

```
public Interface PublicKey extends Key
```

The *SecureRandom* Class

```
public Class SecureRandom extends Random
```

Constructors

```
public SecureRandom();
public SecureRandom(byte seed[]);
```

Methods

```
public static byte[] getSeed(int numBytes);
synchronized public void nextBytes(byte[] bytes);
```

```
synchronized public void setSeed(byte[] seed);
public void setSeed(long seed);
```

The *Security* Class

```
public Class Security extends Object
```

Methods

```
public static int addProvider(Provider provider);
public static String getAlgorithmProperty(String algName, String
  propName);
public static String getProperty(String key);
public static Provider getProvider(String name);
public static Provider[] getProviders();
public static int insertProviderAt(Provider provider, int position);
public static void removeProvider(String name);
public static void setProperty(String key, String datum);
```

The *Signature* Class

```
public abstract Class Signature extends Object
```

Methods

```
public static Signature getInstance(String algorithm) throws
  NoSuchAlgorithmException;
public static Signature getInstance(String algorithm, String provider)
  throws NoSuchAlgorithmException, NoSuchProviderException;
protected abstract Object engineGetParameter(String param) throws
  InvalidParameterException;
protected abstract void engineInitSign(PrivateKey privateKey) throws
  InvalidKeyException;
protected abstract void engineInitVerify(PublicKey publicKey) throws
  InvalidKeyException;
protected abstract void engineSetParameter(String param, Object value)
  throws InvalidParameterException;
protected abstract byte[] engineSign() throws SignatureException;
protected abstract void engineUpdate(byte b) throws SignatureException;
protected abstract void engineUpdate(byte[] b, int off, int len) throws
  SignatureException;
protected abstract boolean engineVerify(byte[] sigBytes) throws
  SignatureException;
```

```
public Object clone() throws CloneNotSupportedException;
public final String getAlgorithm();
public final Object getParameter(String param) throws
   InvalidParameterException;
public final void initSign(PrivateKey privateKey) throws
   InvalidKeyException;
public final void initVerify(PublicKey publicKey) throws
   InvalidKeyException;
public final void setParameter(String param, Object value) throws
   InvalidParameterException;
public final byte[] sign() throws SignatureException;
public String toString();
public final void update(byte b) throws SignatureException;
public final void update(byte[] data) throws SignatureException;
public final void update(byte[] data, int off, int len) throws
   SignatureException;
public final boolean verify(byte[] signature) throws
   SignatureException;
```

The *SignatureException* Class

```
public Class SignatureException extends Exception
```

Constructors

```
public SignatureException();
public SignatureException(String msg);
```

The *Signer* Class

```
public abstract Class Signer extends Identity
```

Constructors

```
public Signer(String name);
public Signer(String name, IdentityScope scope) throws
   KeyManagementException;
```

Methods

```
public PrivateKey getPrivateKey();
public final void setKeyPair(KeyPair pair) throws
   InvalidParameterException, KeyException;
public String toString();
```

The *java.security.acl* Package

The *Acl* Interface

```
public Interface Acl extends Owner
```

Methods

```
public boolean addEntry(Principal caller, AclEntry entry) throws
  NotOwnerException;
public boolean checkPermission(Principal principal, Permission
  permission);
public Enumeration entries();
public String getName();
public Enumeration getPermissions(Principal user);
public boolean removeEntry(Principal caller, AclEntry entry) throws
  NotOwnerException;
public void setName(Principal caller, String name) throws
  NotOwnerException;
public String toString();
```

The *AclEntry* Interface

```
public Interface AclEntry extends Cloneable
```

Methods

```
public boolean addPermission(Permission permission);
public boolean checkPermission(Permission permission);
public Object clone();
public Principal getPrincipal();
public boolean isNegative();
public Enumeration permissions();
public boolean removePermission(Permission permission);
public void setNegativePermissions();
public boolean setPrincipal(Principal user);
public String toString();
```

The *AclNotFoundException* Class

```
public Class AclNotFoundException extends Exception
```

Constructors

```
public AclNotFoundException();
```

The *Group* Interface

```
public Interface Group extends Principal
```

Methods

```
public boolean addMember(Principal user);
public boolean isMember(Principal member);
public Enumeration members();
public boolean removeMember(Principal user);
```

The *LastOwnerException* Class

```
public Class LastOwnerException extends Exception
```

Constructors

```
public LastOwnerException();
```

The *NotOwnerException* Class

```
public Class NotOwnerException extends Exception
```

Constructors

```
public NotOwnerException();
```

The *Owner* Interface

```
public Interface Owner
```

Methods

```
public boolean addOwner(Principal caller, Principal owner) throws
  NotOwnerException;
public boolean deleteOwner(Principal caller, Principal owner) throws
  NotOwnerException, LastOwnerException;
```

```
public boolean isOwner(Principal owner);
```

The *Permission* Interface

```
public Interface Permission
```

Methods

```
public boolean equals(Object another);
public String toString();
```

The *java.security.interfaces* Package

The *DSAKey* Interface

```
public Interface DSAKey
```

Methods

```
public DSAParams getParams();
```

The *DSAKeyPairGenerator* Interface

```
public Interface DSAKeyPairGenerator
```

Methods

```
public void initialize(DSAParams params, SecureRandom random) throws
    InvalidParameterException;
public void initialize(int modlen, boolean genParams, SecureRandom
    random) throws InvalidParameterException;
```

The *DSAParams* Interface

```
public Interface DSAParams
```

Methods

```
public BigInteger getG();
public BigInteger getP();
public BigInteger getQ();
```

The *DSAPrivateKey* Interface

```
public Interface DSAPrivateKey extends DSAKey,
```

Methods

```
public BigInteger getX();
```

The *DSAPublicKey* Interface

```
public Interface DSAPublicKey extends DSAKey,
```

Methods

```
public BigInteger getY();
```

The *java.sql* Package

The *CallableStatement* Interface

```
public Interface CallableStatement extends PreparedStatement
```

Methods

```
BigDecimal getBigDecimal(int parameterIndex, int scale) throws
    SQLException;
boolean getBoolean(int parameterIndex) throws SQLException;
byte getByte(int parameterIndex) throws SQLException;
byte[] getBytes(int parameterIndex) throws SQLException;
java.sql.Date getDate(int parameterIndex) throws SQLException;
double getDouble(int parameterIndex) throws SQLException;
float getFloat(int parameterIndex) throws SQLException;
int getInt(int parameterIndex) throws SQLException;
long getLong(int parameterIndex) throws SQLException;
Object getObject(int parameterIndex) throws SQLException;
short getShort(int parameterIndex) throws SQLException;
String getString(int parameterIndex) throws SQLException;
java.sql.Time getTime(int parameterIndex) throws SQLException;
java.sql.Timestamp getTimestamp(int parameterIndex) throws
    SQLException;
```

```
void registerOutParameter(int parameterIndex, int sqlType) throws
  SQLException;
void registerOutParameter(int parameterIndex, int sqlType, int scale)
  throws SQLException;
boolean wasNull() throws SQLException;
```

The *Connection* Interface

```
public Interface Connection
```

Methods

```
void clearWarnings() throws SQLException;
void close() throws SQLException;
void commit() throws SQLException;
Statement createStatement() throws SQLException;
boolean getAutoCommit() throws SQLException;
String getCatalog() throws SQLException;
DatabaseMetaData getMetaData() throws SQLException;
int getTransactionIsolation() throws SQLException;
SQLWarning getWarnings() throws SQLException;
boolean isClosed() throws SQLException;
boolean isReadOnly() throws SQLException;
String nativeSQL(String sql) throws SQLException;
CallableStatement prepareCall(String sql) throws SQLException;
PreparedStatement prepareStatement(String sql) throws SQLException;
void rollback() throws SQLException;
void setAutoCommit(boolean autoCommit) throws SQLException;
void setCatalog(String catalog) throws SQLException;
void setReadOnly(boolean readOnly) throws SQLException;
void setTransactionIsolation(int level) throws SQLException;
```

The *DataTruncation* Class

```
public Class DataTruncation extends SQLWarning
```

Constructors

```
public DataTruncation(int index, boolean parameter, boolean read, int
  dataSize, int transferSize);
```

Methods

```
public int getDataSize();
public int getIndex();
public boolean getParameter();
public boolean getRead();
public int getTransferSize();
```

The *DatabaseMetaData* Interface

```
public Interface DatabaseMetaData
```

Methods

```
boolean allProceduresAreCallable() throws SQLException;
boolean allTablesAreSelectable() throws SQLException;
boolean dataDefinitionCausesTransactionCommit() throws SQLException;
boolean dataDefinitionIgnoredInTransactions() throws SQLException;
boolean doesMaxRowSizeIncludeBlobs() throws SQLException;
ResultSet getBestRowIdentifier(String catalog, String schema, String
    table, int scope, boolean nullable) throws SQLException;
ResultSet getCatalogs() throws SQLException;
String getCatalogSeparator() throws SQLException;
String getCatalogTerm() throws SQLException;
ResultSet getColumnPrivileges(String catalog, String schema, String
    table, String columnNamePattern) throws SQLException;
ResultSet getColumns(String catalog, String schemaPattern, String
    tableNamePattern, String columnNamePattern) throws SQLException;
ResultSet getCrossReference( String primaryCatalog, String
    primarySchema, String primaryTable, String foreignCatalog, String
    foreignSchema, String foreignTable ) throws SQLException;
String getDatabaseProductName() throws SQLException;
String getDatabaseProductVersion() throws SQLException;
int getDefaultTransactionIsolation() throws SQLException;
int getDriverMajorVersion();
int getDriverMinorVersion();
String getDriverName() throws SQLException;
String getDriverVersion() throws SQLException;
ResultSet getExportedKeys(String catalog, String schema, String table)
    throws SQLException;
String getExtraNameCharacters() throws SQLException;
String getIdentifierQuoteString() throws SQLException;
```

```
ResultSet getImportedKeys(String catalog, String schema, String table)
  throws SQLException;
ResultSet getIndexInfo(String catalog, String schema, String table,
  boolean unique, boolean approximate) throws SQLException;
int getMaxBinaryLiteralLength() throws SQLException;
int getMaxCatalogNameLength() throws SQLException;
int getMaxCharLiteralLength() throws SQLException;
int getMaxColumnNameLength() throws SQLException;
int getMaxColumnsInGroupBy() throws SQLException;
int getMaxColumnsInIndex() throws SQLException;
int getMaxColumnsInOrderBy() throws SQLException;
int getMaxColumnsInSelect() throws SQLException;
int getMaxColumnsInTable() throws SQLException;
int getMaxConnections() throws SQLException;
int getMaxCursorNameLength() throws SQLException;
int getMaxIndexLength() throws SQLException;
int getMaxProcedureNameLength() throws SQLException;
int getMaxRowSize() throws SQLException;
int getMaxSchemaNameLength() throws SQLException;
int getMaxStatementLength() throws SQLException;
int getMaxStatements() throws SQLException;
int getMaxTableNameLength() throws SQLException;
int getMaxTablesInSelect() throws SQLException;
int getMaxUserNameLength() throws SQLException;
String getNumericFunctions() throws SQLException;
ResultSet getPrimaryKeys(String catalog, String schema, String table)
  throws SQLException;
ResultSet getProcedureColumns(String catalog, String schemaPattern,
  String procedureNamePattern, String columnNamePattern) throws
  SQLException;
ResultSet getProcedures(String catalog, String schemaPattern, String
  procedureNamePattern) throws SQLException;
String getProcedureTerm() throws SQLException;
ResultSet getSchemas() throws SQLException;
String getSchemaTerm() throws SQLException;
String getSearchStringEscape() throws SQLException;
String getSQLKeywords() throws SQLException;
String getStringFunctions() throws SQLException;
String getSystemFunctions() throws SQLException;
ResultSet getTablePrivileges(String catalog, String schemaPattern,
  String tableNamePattern) throws SQLException;
```

```
ResultSet getTables(String catalog, String schemaPattern, String
    tableNamePattern, String types[]) throws SQLException;
ResultSet getTableTypes() throws SQLException;
String getTimeDateFunctions() throws SQLException;
ResultSet getTypeInfo() throws SQLException;
String getURL() throws SQLException;
String getUserName() throws SQLException;
ResultSet getVersionColumns(String catalog, String schema, String
    table) throws SQLException;
boolean isCatalogAtStart() throws SQLException;
boolean isReadOnly() throws SQLException;
boolean nullPlusNonNullIsNull() throws SQLException;
boolean nullsAreSortedAtEnd() throws SQLException;
boolean nullsAreSortedAtStart() throws SQLException;
boolean nullsAreSortedHigh() throws SQLException;
boolean nullsAreSortedLow() throws SQLException;
boolean storesLowerCaseIdentifiers() throws SQLException;
boolean storesLowerCaseQuotedIdentifiers() throws SQLException;
boolean storesMixedCaseIdentifiers() throws SQLException;
boolean storesMixedCaseQuotedIdentifiers() throws SQLException;
boolean storesUpperCaseIdentifiers() throws SQLException;
boolean storesUpperCaseQuotedIdentifiers() throws SQLException;
boolean supportsAlterTableWithAddColumn() throws SQLException;
boolean supportsAlterTableWithDropColumn() throws SQLException;
boolean supportsANSI92EntryLevelSQL() throws SQLException;
boolean supportsANSI92FullSQL() throws SQLException;
boolean supportsANSI92IntermediateSQL() throws SQLException;
boolean supportsCatalogsInDataManipulation() throws SQLException;
boolean supportsCatalogsInIndexDefinitions() throws SQLException;
boolean supportsCatalogsInPrivilegeDefinitions() throws SQLException;
boolean supportsCatalogsInProcedureCalls() throws SQLException;
boolean supportsCatalogsInTableDefinitions() throws SQLException;
boolean supportsColumnAliasing() throws SQLException;
boolean supportsConvert() throws SQLException;
boolean supportsConvert(int fromType, int toType) throws SQLException;
boolean supportsCoreSQLGrammar() throws SQLException;
boolean supportsCorrelatedSubqueries() throws SQLException;
boolean supportsDataDefinitionAndDataManipulationTransactions() throws
    SQLException;
boolean supportsDataManipulationTransactionsOnly() throws SQLException;
boolean supportsDifferentTableCorrelationNames() throws SQLException;
boolean supportsExpressionsInOrderBy() throws SQLException;
```

```
boolean supportsExtendedSQLGrammar() throws SQLException;
boolean supportsFullOuterJoins() throws SQLException;
boolean supportsGroupBy() throws SQLException;
boolean supportsGroupByBeyondSelect() throws SQLException;
boolean supportsGroupByUnrelated() throws SQLException;
boolean supportsIntegrityEnhancementFacility() throws SQLException;
boolean supportsLikeEscapeClause() throws SQLException;
boolean supportsLimitedOuterJoins() throws SQLException;
boolean supportsMinimumSQLGrammar() throws SQLException;
boolean supportsMixedCaseIdentifiers() throws SQLException;
boolean supportsMixedCaseQuotedIdentifiers() throws SQLException;
boolean supportsMultipleResultSets() throws SQLException;
boolean supportsMultipleTransactions() throws SQLException;
boolean supportsNonNullableColumns() throws SQLException;
boolean supportsOpenCursorsAcrossCommit() throws SQLException;
boolean supportsOpenCursorsAcrossRollback() throws SQLException;
boolean supportsOpenStatementsAcrossCommit() throws SQLException;
boolean supportsOpenStatementsAcrossRollback() throws SQLException;
boolean supportsOrderByUnrelated() throws SQLException;
boolean supportsOuterJoins() throws SQLException;
boolean supportsPositionedDelete() throws SQLException;
boolean supportsPositionedUpdate() throws SQLException;
boolean supportsSchemasInDataManipulation() throws SQLException;
boolean supportsSchemasInIndexDefinitions() throws SQLException;
boolean supportsSchemasInPrivilegeDefinitions() throws SQLException;
boolean supportsSchemasInProcedureCalls() throws SQLException;
boolean supportsSchemasInTableDefinitions() throws SQLException;
boolean supportsSelectForUpdate() throws SQLException;
boolean supportsStoredProcedures() throws SQLException;
boolean supportsSubqueriesInComparisons() throws SQLException;
boolean supportsSubqueriesInExists() throws SQLException;
boolean supportsSubqueriesInIns() throws SQLException;
boolean supportsSubqueriesInQuantifieds() throws SQLException;
boolean supportsTableCorrelationNames() throws SQLException;
boolean supportsTransactionIsolationLevel(int level) throws
    SQLException;
boolean supportsTransactions() throws SQLException;
boolean supportsUnion() throws SQLException;
boolean supportsUnionAll() throws SQLException;
boolean usesLocalFilePerTable() throws SQLException;
boolean usesLocalFiles() throws SQLException;
```

The *Date* Class

```
public Class Date extends java.util.Date
```

Constructors

```
public Date(int year, int month, int day);
public Date(long date);
```

Methods

```
public static Date valueOf(String s);
public int getHours();
public int getMinutes();
public int getSeconds();
public void setHours(int i);
public void setMinutes(int i);
public void setSeconds(int i);
public void setTime(long date);
public String toString ();
```

The *Driver* Interface

```
public Interface Driver
```

Methods

```
boolean acceptsURL(String url) throws SQLException;
Connection connect(String url, java.util.Properties info) throws
    SQLException;
int getMajorVersion();
int getMinorVersion();
DriverPropertyInfo[] getPropertyInfo(String url, java.util.Properties
    info) throws SQLException;
boolean jdbcCompliant();
```

The *DriverManager* Class

```
public Class DriverManager extends Object
```

Methods

```
public static void deregisterDriver(Driver driver) throws SQLException;
public static synchronized Connection getConnection(String url,
    java.util.Properties info) throws SQLException;
```

```
public static synchronized Connection getConnection(String url, String
   user, String password) throws SQLException;
public static synchronized Connection getConnection(String url) throws
   SQLException;
public static Driver getDriver(String url) throws SQLException;
public static java.util.Enumeration getDrivers();
public static int getLoginTimeout();
public static java.io.PrintStream getLogStream();
public static void println(String message);
public static synchronized void registerDriver(java.sql.Driver driver)
   throws SQLException;
public static void setLoginTimeout(int seconds);
public static void setLogStream(java.io.PrintStream out);
```

The *DriverPropertyInfo* Class

```
public Class DriverPropertyInfo extends Object
```

Data

```
public String[] choices = null;
public String description = null;
public String name;
public boolean required = false;
public String value = null;
```

Constructors

```
public DriverPropertyInfo(String name, String value);
```

The *PreparedStatement* Interface

```
public Interface PreparedStatement extends Statement
```

Methods

```
void clearParameters() throws SQLException;
boolean execute() throws SQLException;
ResultSet executeQuery() throws SQLException;
int executeUpdate() throws SQLException;
void setAsciiStream(int parameterIndex, java.io.InputStream x, int
   length) throws SQLException;
void setBigDecimal(int parameterIndex, BigDecimal x) throws
   SQLException;
```

```
void setBinaryStream(int parameterIndex, java.io.InputStream x, int
    length) throws SQLException;
void setBoolean(int parameterIndex, boolean x) throws SQLException;
void setByte(int parameterIndex, byte x) throws SQLException;
void setBytes(int parameterIndex, byte x[]) throws SQLException;
void setDate(int parameterIndex, java.sql.Date x) throws SQLException;
void setDouble(int parameterIndex, double x) throws SQLException;
void setFloat(int parameterIndex, float x) throws SQLException;
void setInt(int parameterIndex, int x) throws SQLException;
void setLong(int parameterIndex, long x) throws SQLException;
void setNull(int parameterIndex, int sqlType) throws SQLException;
void setObject(int parameterIndex, Object x, int targetSqlType, int
    scale) throws SQLException;
void setObject(int parameterIndex, Object x, int targetSqlType) throws
    SQLException;
void setObject(int parameterIndex, Object x) throws SQLException;
void setShort(int parameterIndex, short x) throws SQLException;
void setString(int parameterIndex, String x) throws SQLException;
void setTime(int parameterIndex, java.sql.Time x) throws SQLException;
void setTimestamp(int parameterIndex, java.sql.Timestamp x) throws
    SQLException;
void setUnicodeStream(int parameterIndex, java.io.InputStream x, int
    length) throws SQLException;
```

The *ResultSet* Interface

```
public Interface ResultSet
```

Methods

```
void clearWarnings() throws SQLException;
void close() throws SQLException;
int findColumn(String columnName) throws SQLException;
java.io.InputStream getAsciiStream(int columnIndex) throws
    SQLException;
java.io.InputStream getAsciiStream(String columnName) throws
    SQLException;
BigDecimal getBigDecimal(int columnIndex, int scale) throws
    SQLException;
BigDecimal getBigDecimal(String columnName, int scale) throws
    SQLException;
```

```
java.io.InputStream getBinaryStream(int columnIndex) throws
    SQLException;
java.io.InputStream getBinaryStream(String columnName) throws
    SQLException;
boolean getBoolean(int columnIndex) throws SQLException;
boolean getBoolean(String columnName) throws SQLException;
byte getByte(int columnIndex) throws SQLException;
byte getByte(String columnName) throws SQLException;
byte[] getBytes(int columnIndex) throws SQLException;
byte[] getBytes(String columnName) throws SQLException;
String getCursorName() throws SQLException;
java.sql.Date getDate(int columnIndex) throws SQLException;
java.sql.Date getDate(String columnName) throws SQLException;
double getDouble(int columnIndex) throws SQLException;
double getDouble(String columnName) throws SQLException;
float getFloat(int columnIndex) throws SQLException;
float getFloat(String columnName) throws SQLException;
int getInt(int columnIndex) throws SQLException;
int getInt(String columnName) throws SQLException;
long getLong(int columnIndex) throws SQLException;
long getLong(String columnName) throws SQLException;
ResultSetMetaData getMetaData() throws SQLException;
Object getObject(int columnIndex) throws SQLException;
Object getObject(String columnName) throws SQLException;
short getShort(int columnIndex) throws SQLException;
short getShort(String columnName) throws SQLException;
String getString(int columnIndex) throws SQLException;
String getString(String columnName) throws SQLException;
java.sql.Time getTime(int columnIndex) throws SQLException;
java.sql.Time getTime(String columnName) throws SQLException;
java.sql.Timestamp getTimestamp(int columnIndex) throws SQLException;
java.sql.Timestamp getTimestamp(String columnName) throws SQLException;
java.io.InputStream getUnicodeStream(int columnIndex) throws
    SQLException;
java.io.InputStream getUnicodeStream(String columnName) throws
    SQLException;
SQLWarning getWarnings() throws SQLException;
boolean next() throws SQLException;
boolean wasNull() throws SQLException;
```

The *ResultSetMetaData* Interface

```
public Interface ResultSetMetaData
```

Methods

```
String getCatalogName(int column) throws SQLException;
int getColumnCount() throws SQLException;
int getColumnDisplaySize(int column) throws SQLException;
String getColumnLabel(int column) throws SQLException;
String getColumnName(int column) throws SQLException;
int getColumnType(int column) throws SQLException;
String getColumnTypeName(int column) throws SQLException;
int getPrecision(int column) throws SQLException;
int getScale(int column) throws SQLException;
String getSchemaName(int column) throws SQLException;
String getTableName(int column) throws SQLException;
boolean isAutoIncrement(int column) throws SQLException;
boolean isCaseSensitive(int column) throws SQLException;
boolean isCurrency(int column) throws SQLException;
boolean isDefinitelyWritable(int column) throws SQLException;
int isNullable(int column) throws SQLException;
boolean isReadOnly(int column) throws SQLException;
boolean isSearchable(int column) throws SQLException;
boolean isSigned(int column) throws SQLException;
boolean isWritable(int column) throws SQLException;
```

The *SQLException* Class

```
public Class SQLException extends java.lang.Exception
```

Constructors

```
public SQLException(String reason, String SQLState, int vendorCode);
public SQLException(String reason, String SQLState);
public SQLException(String reason);
public SQLException();
```

Methods

```
public int getErrorCode();
public SQLException getNextException();
```

```
public String getSQLState();
public synchronized void setNextException(SQLException ex);
```

The *SQLWarning* Class

```
public Class SQLWarning extends SQLException
```

Constructors

```
public SQLWarning(String reason, String SQLstate, int vendorCode);
public SQLWarning(String reason, String SQLstate);
public SQLWarning(String reason);
public SQLWarning();
```

Methods

```
public SQLWarning getNextWarning();
public void setNextWarning(SQLWarning w);
```

The *Statement* Interface

```
public Interface Statement
```

Methods

```
void cancel() throws SQLException;
void clearWarnings() throws SQLException;
void close() throws SQLException;
boolean execute(String sql) throws SQLException;
ResultSet executeQuery(String sql) throws SQLException;
int executeUpdate(String sql) throws SQLException;
int getMaxFieldSize() throws SQLException;
int getMaxRows() throws SQLException;
boolean getMoreResults() throws SQLException;
int getQueryTimeout() throws SQLException;
ResultSet getResultSet() throws SQLException;
int getUpdateCount() throws SQLException;
SQLWarning getWarnings() throws SQLException;
void setCursorName(String name) throws SQLException;
void setEscapeProcessing(boolean enable) throws SQLException;
void setMaxFieldSize(int max) throws SQLException;
void setMaxRows(int max) throws SQLException;
void setQueryTimeout(int seconds) throws SQLException;
```

The *Time* Class

```
public Class Time extends java.util.Date
```

Constructors

```
public Time(int hour, int minute, int second);
public Time(long time);
```

Methods

```
public static Time valueOf(String s);
public int getDate();
public int getDay();
public int getMonth();
public int getYear();
public void setDate(int i);
public void setMonth(int i);
public void setTime(long time);
public void setYear(int i);
public String toString ();
```

The *Timestamp* Class

```
public Class Timestamp extends java.util.Date
```

Constructors

```
public Timestamp(int year, int month, int date, int hour, int minute,
    int second, int nano);
public Timestamp(long time);
```

Methods

```
public static Timestamp valueOf(String s);
public boolean after(Timestamp ts);
public boolean before(Timestamp ts);
public boolean equals(Timestamp ts);
public int getNanos();
public void setNanos(int n);
public String toString ();
```

The *Types* Class

```
public Class Types extends Object
```

Data

```
public final static int BIGINT = -5;
public final static int BINARY = -2;
public final static int BIT = -7;
public final static int CHAR = 1;
public final static int DATE = 91;
public final static int DECIMAL = 3;
public final static int DOUBLE = 8;
public final static int FLOAT = 6;
public final static int INTEGER = 4;
public final static int LONGVARBINARY = -4;
public final static int LONGVARCHAR = -1;
public final static int NULL = 0;
public final static int NUMERIC = 2;
public final static int OTHER = 1111;
public final static int REAL = 7;
public final static int SMALLINT = 5;
public final static int TIME = 92;
public final static int TIMESTAMP = 93;
public final static int TINYINT = -6;
public final static int VARBINARY = -3;
public final static int VARCHAR = 12;
```

The *java.text* Package

The *BreakIterator* Class

```
public abstract Class BreakIterator extends Object implements
    Cloneable, java.io.Serializable
```

Data

```
public static final int DONE = -1;
```

Methods

```
public static synchronized Locale[] getAvailableLocales();
public static BreakIterator getCharacterInstance();
public static BreakIterator getCharacterInstance(Locale where);
public static BreakIterator getLineInstance();
public static BreakIterator getLineInstance(Locale where);
public static BreakIterator getSentenceInstance();
public static BreakIterator getSentenceInstance(Locale where);
public static BreakIterator getWordInstance();
public static BreakIterator getWordInstance(Locale where);
public abstract int current();
public abstract int first() ;
public abstract int following(int offset);
public abstract CharacterIterator getText();
public abstract int last();
public abstract int next();
public abstract int next(int n);
public abstract int previous();
public abstract void setText(CharacterIterator newText);
public Object clone();
public void setText(String newText);
```

The *CharacterIterator* Interface

```
public Interface CharacterIterator extends Cloneable
```

Data

```
public static final char DONE = '\uFFFF';
```

Methods

```
public Object clone();
public char current();
public char first();
public int getBeginIndex();
public int getEndIndex();
public int getIndex();
public char last();
public char next();
public char previous();
public char setIndex(int position);
```

The *ChoiceFormat* Class

```
public Class ChoiceFormat extends NumberFormat
```

Constructors

```
public ChoiceFormat(String newPattern);
public ChoiceFormat(double[] limits, String[] formats);
```

Methods

```
public static final double nextDouble (double d);
public static double nextDouble (double d, boolean positive);
public static final double previousDouble (double d);
public void applyPattern(String newPattern);
public Object clone();
public boolean equals(Object obj);
public StringBuffer format(double number, StringBuffer toAppendTo,
  FieldPosition status);
public StringBuffer format(long number, StringBuffer toAppendTo,
  FieldPosition status);
public Object[] getFormats();
public double[] getLimits();
public int hashCode();
public Number parse(String text, ParsePosition status);
public void setChoices(double[] limits, String formats[]);
public String toPattern();
```

The *CollationElementIterator* Class

```
public Class CollationElementIterator extends Object
```

Data

```
public final static int NULLORDER = 0xffffffff;
```

Methods

```
public final static int primaryOrder(int order);
public final static short secondaryOrder(int order);
public final static short tertiaryOrder(int order);
public int next();
public void reset();
```

The *CollationKey* Class

```
public Class CollationKey extends Object
```

Methods

```
public int compareTo(CollationKey target);
public boolean equals(Object target);
public String getSourceString();
public int hashCode();
public byte[] toByteArray();
```

The *Collator* Class

```
public abstract Class Collator extends Object implements Cloneable,
    Serializable
```

Data

```
public final static int CANONICAL_DECOMPOSITION = 1;
public final static int FULL_DECOMPOSITION = 2;
public final static int IDENTICAL = 3;
public final static int NO_DECOMPOSITION = 0;
public final static int PRIMARY = 0;
public final static int SECONDARY = 1;
public final static int TERTIARY = 2;
```

Methods

```
public static synchronized Locale[] getAvailableLocales();
public static synchronized Collator getInstance();
public static synchronized Collator getInstance(Locale desiredLocale);
public abstract int compare(String source, String target);
public abstract CollationKey getCollationKey(String source);
abstract public synchronized int hashCode();
public Object clone();
public boolean equals(Object that);
public boolean equals(String source, String target);
public synchronized int getDecomposition();
public synchronized int getStrength();
public synchronized void setDecomposition(int decompositionMode);
public synchronized void setStrength(int newStrength);
```

The *DateFormat* Class

```
public abstract Class DateFormat extends Format implements Cloneable
```

Data

```
public final static int AM_PM_FIELD = 14;
public final static int DATE_FIELD = 3;
public final static int DAY_OF_WEEK_FIELD = 9;
public final static int DAY_OF_WEEK_IN_MONTH_FIELD = 11;
public final static int DAY_OF_YEAR_FIELD = 10;
public static final int DEFAULT = MEDIUM;
public final static int ERA_FIELD = 0;
public static final int FULL = 0;
public final static int HOUR0_FIELD = 16;
public final static int HOUR1_FIELD = 15;
public final static int HOUR_OF_DAY0_FIELD = 5;
public final static int HOUR_OF_DAY1_FIELD = 4;
public static final int LONG = 1;
public static final int MEDIUM = 2;
public final static int MILLISECOND_FIELD = 8;
public final static int MINUTE_FIELD = 6;
public final static int MONTH_FIELD = 2;
public final static int SECOND_FIELD = 7;
public static final int SHORT = 3;
public final static int TIMEZONE_FIELD = 17;
public final static int WEEK_OF_MONTH_FIELD = 13;
public final static int WEEK_OF_YEAR_FIELD = 12;
public final static int YEAR_FIELD = 1;
```

Methods

```
public static Locale[] getAvailableLocales();
public final static DateFormat getDateInstance();
public final static DateFormat getDateInstance(int style);
public final static DateFormat getDateInstance(int style, Locale
  aLocale);
public final static DateFormat getDateTimeInstance();
public final static DateFormat getDateTimeInstance(int dateStyle, int
  timeStyle);
public final static DateFormat getDateTimeInstance(int dateStyle, int
  timeStyle, Locale aLocale);
public final static DateFormat getInstance();
```

```
public final static DateFormat getTimeInstance();
public final static DateFormat getTimeInstance(int style);
public final static DateFormat getTimeInstance(int style, Locale
    aLocale);
public abstract StringBuffer format(Date date, StringBuffer toAppendTo,
    FieldPosition fieldPosition);
public abstract Date parse(String text, ParsePosition pos);
public Object clone();
public boolean equals(Object obj);
public final String format(Date date);
public final StringBuffer format(Object obj, StringBuffer toAppendTo,
    FieldPosition fieldPosition);
public Calendar getCalendar();
public NumberFormat getNumberFormat();
public TimeZone getTimeZone();
public int hashCode();
public boolean isLenient();
public Date parse(String text) throws ParseException;
public Object parseObject (String source, ParsePosition pos);
public void setCalendar(Calendar newCalendar);
public void setLenient(boolean lenient);
public void setNumberFormat(NumberFormat newNumberFormat);
public void setTimeZone(TimeZone zone);
```

The *DateFormatSymbols* Class

```
public Class DateFormatSymbols extends Object implements Serializable,
    Cloneable
```

Constructors

```
public DateFormatSymbols();
public DateFormatSymbols(Locale locale);
```

Methods

```
public Object clone();
public boolean equals(Object obj);
public String[] getAmPmStrings();
public String[] getEras();
public String getLocalPatternChars();
public String[] getMonths();
public String[] getShortMonths();
```

```
public String[] getShortWeekdays();
public String[] getWeekdays();
public String[][] getZoneStrings();
public int hashCode();
public void setAmPmStrings(String[] newAmpms);
public void setEras(String[] newEras);
public void setLocalPatternChars(String newLocalPatternChars);
public void setMonths(String[] newMonths);
public void setShortMonths(String[] newShortMonths);
public void setShortWeekdays(String[] newShortWeekdays);
public void setWeekdays(String[] newWeekdays);
public void setZoneStrings(String[][] newZoneStrings);
```

The *DecimalFormat* Class

```
public Class DecimalFormat extends NumberFormat
```

Constructors

```
public DecimalFormat();
public DecimalFormat(String pattern);
```

Methods

```
public DecimalFormat (String pattern, DecimalFormatSymbols symbols);
public void applyLocalizedPattern( String pattern );
public void applyPattern( String pattern );
public Object clone();
public boolean equals(Object obj);
public StringBuffer format(double number, StringBuffer result,
  FieldPosition fieldPosition);
public StringBuffer format(long number, StringBuffer result,
  FieldPosition fieldPosition);
public DecimalFormatSymbols getDecimalFormatSymbols();
public int getGroupingSize ();
public int getMultiplier ();
public String getNegativePrefix ();
public String getNegativeSuffix ();
public String getPositivePrefix ();
public String getPositiveSuffix ();
public int hashCode();
public boolean isDecimalSeparatorAlwaysShown();
public Number parse(String text, ParsePosition status);
```

```
public void setDecimalFormatSymbols(DecimalFormatSymbols newSymbols);
public void setDecimalSeparatorAlwaysShown(boolean newValue);
public void setGroupingSize (int newValue);
public void setMultiplier (int newValue);
public void setNegativePrefix (String newValue);
public void setNegativeSuffix (String newValue);
public void setPositivePrefix (String newValue);
public void setPositiveSuffix (String newValue);
public String toLocalizedPattern();
public String toPattern();
```

The *DecimalFormatSymbols* Class

```
public Class DecimalFormatSymbols extends Object implements Cloneable,
    Serializable
```

Constructors

```
public DecimalFormatSymbols();
public DecimalFormatSymbols( Locale locale );
```

Methods

```
public Object clone();
public boolean equals(Object obj);
public char getDecimalSeparator();
public char getDigit();
public char getGroupingSeparator();
public String getInfinity();
public char getMinusSign();
public String getNaN();
public char getPatternSeparator();
public char getPercent();
public char getPerMill();
public char getZeroDigit();
public int hashCode();
public void setDecimalSeparator(char decimalSeparator);
public void setDigit(char digit);
public void setGroupingSeparator(char groupingSeparator);
public void setInfinity(String infinity);
public void setMinusSign(char minusSign);
public void setNaN(String NaN);
public void setPatternSeparator(char patternSeparator);
```

```
public void setPercent(char percent);
public void setPerMill(char perMill);
public void setZeroDigit(char zeroDigit);
```

The *FieldPosition* Class

```
public Class FieldPosition extends Object
```

Constructors

```
public FieldPosition(int field);
```

Methods

```
public int getBeginIndex();
public int getEndIndex();
public int getField();
```

The *Format* Class

```
public abstract Class Format extends Object implements Serializable,
  Cloneable
```

Methods

```
public abstract StringBuffer format(Object obj, StringBuffer
  toAppendTo, FieldPosition pos);
public abstract Object parseObject (String source, ParsePosition sta-
  tus);
public Object clone();
public final String format (Object obj);
public Object parseObject(String source) throws ParseException;
```

The *MessageFormat* Class

```
public Class MessageFormat extends Format
```

Constructors

```
public MessageFormat(String pattern);
```

Methods

```
public Locale getLocale();
public void setLocale(Locale theLocale);
```

The *NumberFormat* Class

```
public abstract Class NumberFormat extends Format implements Cloneable
```

Data

```
public static final int FRACTION_FIELD = 1;
public static final int INTEGER_FIELD = 0;
```

Methods

```
public static Locale[] getAvailableLocales();
public final static NumberFormat getCurrencyInstance();
public static NumberFormat getCurrencyInstance(Locale inLocale);
public final static NumberFormat getInstance();
public static NumberFormat getInstance(Locale inLocale);
public final static NumberFormat getNumberInstance();
public static NumberFormat getNumberInstance(Locale inLocale);
public final static NumberFormat getPercentInstance();
public static NumberFormat getPercentInstance(Locale inLocale);
public abstract StringBuffer format(double number, StringBuffer
  toAppendTo, FieldPosition pos);
public abstract StringBuffer format(long number, StringBuffer
  toAppendTo, FieldPosition pos);
public abstract Number parse(String text, ParsePosition parsePosition);
public Object clone();
public boolean equals(Object obj);
public final String format (double number);
public final String format (long number);
public final StringBuffer format(Object number, StringBuffer
  toAppendTo, FieldPosition pos);
public int getMaximumFractionDigits();
public int getMaximumIntegerDigits();
public int getMinimumFractionDigits();
public int getMinimumIntegerDigits();
public int hashCode();
public boolean isGroupingUsed();
public boolean isParseIntegerOnly();
public Number parse(String text) throws ParseException;
public final Object parseObject(String source, ParsePosition
  parsePosition);
public void setGroupingUsed(boolean newValue);
public void setMaximumFractionDigits(int newValue);
```

```
public void setMaximumIntegerDigits(int newValue);
public void setMinimumFractionDigits(int newValue);
public void setMinimumIntegerDigits(int newValue);
public void setParseIntegerOnly(boolean value);
```

The *ParseException* Class

```
public Class ParseException extends Exception
```

Constructors

```
public ParseException(String s, int errorOffset);
```

Methods

```
public int getErrorOffset ();
```

The *ParsePosition* Class

```
public Class ParsePosition extends Object
```

Constructors

```
public ParsePosition(int index);
```

Methods

```
public int getIndex();
public void setIndex(int index);
```

The *RuleBasedCollator* Class

```
public Class RuleBasedCollator extends Collator{
```

Constructors

```
public RuleBasedCollator(String rules) throws ParseException;
```

Methods

```
public Object clone();
public int compare(String source, String target);
public boolean equals(Object obj);
public CollationElementIterator getCollationElementIterator(String
  source);
```

```
public CollationKey getCollationKey(String source);
public String getRules();
public int hashCode();
```

The *SimpleDateFormat* Class

```
public Class SimpleDateFormat extends DateFormat
```

Constructors

```
public SimpleDateFormat();
public SimpleDateFormat(String pattern);
public SimpleDateFormat(String pattern, Locale loc);
public SimpleDateFormat(String pattern, DateFormatSymbols formatData);
```

Methods

```
public void applyLocalizedPattern(String pattern);
public void applyPattern (String pattern);
public Object clone();
public boolean equals(Object obj);
public StringBuffer format(Date date, StringBuffer toAppendTo,
  FieldPosition pos);
public DateFormatSymbols getDateFormatSymbols();
public int hashCode();
public Date parse(String text, ParsePosition pos);
public void setDateFormatSymbols(DateFormatSymbols newFormatSymbols);
public String toLocalizedPattern();
public String toPattern();
```

The *StringCharacterIterator* Class

```
public Class StringCharacterIterator extends Object implements
  CharacterIterator
```

Constructors

```
public StringCharacterIterator(String text);
public StringCharacterIterator(String text, int pos);
public StringCharacterIterator(String text, int begin, int end, int
  pos);
```

Methods

```
public Object clone();
public char current();
public boolean equals(Object obj);
public char first();
public int getBeginIndex();
public int getEndIndex();
public int getIndex();
public int hashCode();
public char last();
public char next();
public char previous();
public char setIndex(int p);
```

The *java.text.resources* Package

The *DateFormatZoneData* Class

```
public Class DateFormatZoneData extends ListResourceBundle
```

Methods

```
public Object[][] getContents();
```

The *DateFormatZoneData_ar* Class

```
public Class DateFormatZoneData_ar extends ListResourceBundle
```

Methods

```
public Object[][] getContents();
```

The *DateFormatZoneData_be* Class

```
public Class DateFormatZoneData_be extends ListResourceBundle
```

Methods

```
public Object[][] getContents();
```

The *DateFormatZoneData_bg* Class

```
public Class DateFormatZoneData_bg extends ListResourceBundle
```

Methods

```
public Object[][] getContents();
```

The *DateFormatZoneData_ca* Class

```
public Class DateFormatZoneData_ca extends ListResourceBundle
```

Methods

```
public Object[][] getContents();
```

The *DateFormatZoneData_cs* Class

```
public Class DateFormatZoneData_cs extends ListResourceBundle
```

Methods

```
public Object[][] getContents();
```

The *DateFormatZoneData_da* Class

```
public Class DateFormatZoneData_da extends ListResourceBundle
```

Methods

```
public Object[][] getContents();
```

The *DateFormatZoneData_de* Class

```
public Class DateFormatZoneData_de extends ListResourceBundle
```

Methods

```
public Object[][] getContents();
```

The *DateFormatZoneData_de_AT* Class

```
public Class DateFormatZoneData_de_AT extends ListResourceBundle
```

Methods

```
public Object[][] getContents();
```

The *DateFormatZoneData_de_CH* Class

```
public Class DateFormatZoneData_de_CH extends ListResourceBundle
```

Methods

```
public Object[][] getContents();
```

The *DateFormatZoneData_el* Class

```
public Class DateFormatZoneData_el extends ListResourceBundle
```

Methods

```
public Object[][] getContents();
```

The *DateFormatZoneData_en* Class

```
public Class DateFormatZoneData_en extends ListResourceBundle
```

Methods

```
public Object[][] getContents();
```

The *DateFormatZoneData_en_CA* Class

```
public Class DateFormatZoneData_en_CA extends ListResourceBundle
```

Methods

```
public Object[][] getContents();
```

The *DateFormatZoneData_en_GB* Class

```
public Class DateFormatZoneData_en_GB extends ListResourceBundle
```

Methods

```
public Object[][] getContents();
```

The *DateFormatZoneData_en_IE* Class

```
public Class DateFormatZoneData_en_IE extends ListResourceBundle
```

Methods

```
public Object[][] getContents();
```

The *DateFormatZoneData_es* Class

```
public Class DateFormatZoneData_es extends ListResourceBundle
```

Methods

```
public Object[][] getContents();
```

The *DateFormatZoneData_et* Class

```
public Class DateFormatZoneData_et extends ListResourceBundle
```

Methods

```
public Object[][] getContents();
```

The *DateFormatZoneData_fi* Class

```
public Class DateFormatZoneData_fi extends ListResourceBundle
```

Methods

```
public Object[][] getContents();
```

The *DateFormatZoneData_fr* Class

```
public Class DateFormatZoneData_fr extends ListResourceBundle
```

Methods

```
public Object[][] getContents();
```

The *DateFormatZoneData_fr_BE* Class

```
public Class DateFormatZoneData_fr_BE extends ListResourceBundle
```

Methods

```
public Object[][] getContents();
```

The *DateFormatZoneData_fr_CA* Class

```
public Class DateFormatZoneData_fr_CA extends ListResourceBundle
```

Methods

```
public Object[][] getContents();
```

The *DateFormatZoneData_fr_CH* Class

```
public Class DateFormatZoneData_fr_CH extends ListResourceBundle
```

Methods

```
public Object[][] getContents();
```

The *DateFormatZoneData_hr* Class

```
public Class DateFormatZoneData_hr extends ListResourceBundle
```

Methods

```
public Object[][] getContents();
```

The *DateFormatZoneData_hu* Class

```
public Class DateFormatZoneData_hu extends ListResourceBundle
```

Methods

```
public Object[][] getContents();
```

The *DateFormatZoneData_is* Class

```
public Class DateFormatZoneData_is extends ListResourceBundle
```

Methods

```
public Object[][] getContents();
```

The *DateFormatZoneData_it* Class

```
public Class DateFormatZoneData_it extends ListResourceBundle
```

Methods

```
public Object[][] getContents();
```

The *DateFormatZoneData_it_CH* Class

```
public Class DateFormatZoneData_it_CH extends ListResourceBundle
```

Methods

```
public Object[][] getContents();
```

The *DateFormatZoneData_iw* Class

```
public Class DateFormatZoneData_iw extends ListResourceBundle
```

Methods

```
public Object[][] getContents();
```

The *DateFormatZoneData_ja* Class

```
public Class DateFormatZoneData_ja extends ListResourceBundle
```

Methods

```
public Object[][] getContents();
```

The *DateFormatZoneData_ko* Class

```
public Class DateFormatZoneData_ko extends ListResourceBundle
```

Methods

```
public Object[][] getContents();
```

The *DateFormatZoneData_lt* Class

```
public Class DateFormatZoneData_lt extends ListResourceBundle
```

Methods

```
public Object[][] getContents();
```

The *DateFormatZoneData_lv* Class

```
public Class DateFormatZoneData_lv extends ListResourceBundle
```

Methods

```
public Object[][] getContents();
```

The *DateFormatZoneData_mk* Class

```
public Class DateFormatZoneData_mk extends ListResourceBundle
```

Methods

```
public Object[][] getContents();
```

The *DateFormatZoneData_nl* Class

```
public Class DateFormatZoneData_nl extends ListResourceBundle
```

Methods

```
public Object[][] getContents();
```

The *DateFormatZoneData_nl_BE* Class

```
public Class DateFormatZoneData_nl_BE extends ListResourceBundle
```

Methods

```
public Object[][] getContents();
```

The *DateFormatZoneData_no* Class

```
public Class DateFormatZoneData_no extends ListResourceBundle
```

Methods

```
public Object[][] getContents();
```

The *DateFormatZoneData_no_NO_NY* Class

```
public Class DateFormatZoneData_no_NO_NY extends ListResourceBundle
```

Methods

```
public Object[][] getContents();
```

The *DateFormatZoneData_pl* Class

```
public Class DateFormatZoneData_pl extends ListResourceBundle
```

Methods

```
public Object[][] getContents();
```

The *DateFormatZoneData_pt* Class

```
public Class DateFormatZoneData_pt extends ListResourceBundle
```

Methods

```
public Object[][] getContents();
```

The *DateFormatZoneData_ro* Class

```
public Class DateFormatZoneData_ro extends ListResourceBundle
```

Methods

```
public Object[][] getContents();
```

The *DateFormatZoneData_ru* Class

```
public Class DateFormatZoneData_ru extends ListResourceBundle
```

Methods

```
public Object[][] getContents();
```

The *DateFormatZoneData_sh* Class

```
public Class DateFormatZoneData_sh extends ListResourceBundle
```

Methods

```
public Object[][] getContents();
```

The *DateFormatZoneData_sk* Class

```
public Class DateFormatZoneData_sk extends ListResourceBundle
```

Methods

```
public Object[][] getContents();
```

The *DateFormatZoneData_sl* Class

```
public Class DateFormatZoneData_sl extends ListResourceBundle
```

Methods

```
public Object[][] getContents();
```

The *DateFormatZoneData_sq* Class

```
public Class DateFormatZoneData_sq extends ListResourceBundle
```

Methods

```
public Object[][] getContents();
```

The *DateFormatZoneData_sr* Class

```
public Class DateFormatZoneData_sr extends ListResourceBundle
```

Methods

```
public Object[][] getContents();
```

The *DateFormatZoneData_sv* Class

```
public Class DateFormatZoneData_sv extends ListResourceBundle
```

Methods

```
public Object[][] getContents();
```

The *DateFormatZoneData_tr* Class

```
public Class DateFormatZoneData_tr extends ListResourceBundle
```

Methods

```
public Object[][] getContents();
```

The *DateFormatZoneData_uk* Class

```
public Class DateFormatZoneData_uk extends ListResourceBundle
```

Methods

```
public Object[][] getContents();
```

The *DateFormatZoneData_zh* Class

```
public Class DateFormatZoneData_zh extends ListResourceBundle
```

Methods

```
public Object[][] getContents();
```

The *DateFormatZoneData_zh_TW* Class

```
public Class DateFormatZoneData_zh_TW extends ListResourceBundle
```

Methods

```
public Object[][] getContents();
```

The *LocaleData* Class

```
public Class LocaleData extends ResourceBundle
```

Methods

```
public static Locale[] getAvailableLocales(String key);
public Enumeration getKeys();
public Object handleGetObject(String key);
```

The *LocaleElements* Class

```
public Class LocaleElements extends LocaleData
```

Constructors

```
public LocaleElements();
```

The *LocaleElements_ar* Class

```
public Class LocaleElements_ar extends LocaleData
```

Constructors

```
public LocaleElements_ar();
```

The *LocaleElements_be* Class

```
public Class LocaleElements_be extends LocaleData
```

Constructors

```
public LocaleElements_be();
```

The *LocaleElements_bg* Class

```
public Class LocaleElements_bg extends LocaleData
```

Constructors

```
public LocaleElements_bg();
```

The *LocaleElements_ca* Class

```
public Class LocaleElements_ca extends LocaleData
```

Constructors

```
public LocaleElements_ca();
```

The *LocaleElements_cs* Class

```
public Class LocaleElements_cs extends LocaleData
```

Constructors

```
public LocaleElements_cs();
```

The *LocaleElements_da* Class

```
public Class LocaleElements_da extends LocaleData
```

Constructors

```
public LocaleElements_da();
```

The *LocaleElements_de* Class

```
public Class LocaleElements_de extends LocaleData
```

Constructors

```
public LocaleElements_de();
```

The *LocaleElements_de_AT* Class

```
public Class LocaleElements_de_AT extends LocaleData
```

Constructors

```
public LocaleElements_de_AT();
```

The *LocaleElements_de_CH* Class

```
public Class LocaleElements_de_CH extends LocaleData
```

Constructors

```
public LocaleElements_de_CH();
```

The *LocaleElements_el* Class

```
public Class LocaleElements_el extends LocaleData
```

Constructors

```
public LocaleElements_el();
```

The *LocaleElements_en* Class

```
public Class LocaleElements_en extends LocaleData
```

Constructors

```
public LocaleElements_en();
```

The *LocaleElements_en_CA* Class

```
public Class LocaleElements_en_CA extends LocaleData
```

Constructors

```
public LocaleElements_en_CA();
```

The *LocaleElements_en_GB* Class

```
public Class LocaleElements_en_GB extends LocaleData
```

Constructors

```
public LocaleElements_en_GB();
```

The *LocaleElements_en_IE* Class

```
public Class LocaleElements_en_IE extends LocaleData
```

Constructors

```
public LocaleElements_en_IE();
```

The *LocaleElements_es* Class

```
public Class LocaleElements_es extends LocaleData
```

Constructors

```
public LocaleElements_es();
```

The *LocaleElements_et* Class

```
public Class LocaleElements_et extends LocaleData
```

Constructors

```
public LocaleElements_et();
```

The *LocaleElements_fi* Class

```
public Class LocaleElements_fi extends LocaleData
```

Constructors

```
public LocaleElements_fi();
```

The *LocaleElements_fr* Class

```
public Class LocaleElements_fr extends LocaleData
```

Constructors

```
public LocaleElements_fr();
```

The *LocaleElements_fr_BE* Class

```
public Class LocaleElements_fr_BE extends LocaleData
```

Constructors

```
public LocaleElements_fr_BE();
```

The *LocaleElements_fr_CA* Class

```
public Class LocaleElements_fr_CA extends LocaleData
```

Constructors

```
public LocaleElements_fr_CA();
```

The *LocaleElements_fr_CH* Class

```
public Class LocaleElements_fr_CH extends LocaleData
```

Constructors

```
public LocaleElements_fr_CH();
```

The *LocaleElements_hr* Class

```
public Class LocaleElements_hr extends LocaleData
```

Constructors

```
public LocaleElements_hr();
```

The *LocaleElements_hu* Class

```
public Class LocaleElements_hu extends LocaleData
```

Constructors

```
public LocaleElements_hu();
```

The *LocaleElements_is* Class

```
public Class LocaleElements_is extends LocaleData
```

Constructors

```
public LocaleElements_is();
```

The *LocaleElements_it* Class

```
public Class LocaleElements_it extends LocaleData
```

Constructors

```
public LocaleElements_it();
```

The *LocaleElements_it_CH* Class

```
public Class LocaleElements_it_CH extends LocaleData
```

Constructors

```
public LocaleElements_it_CH();
```

The *LocaleElements_iw* Class

```
public Class LocaleElements_iw extends LocaleData
```

Constructors

```
public LocaleElements_iw();
```

The *LocaleElements_ja* Class

```
public Class LocaleElements_ja extends LocaleData
```

Constructors

```
public LocaleElements_ja();
```

The *LocaleElements_ko* Class

```
public Class LocaleElements_ko extends LocaleData
```

Constructors

```
public LocaleElements_ko();
```

The *LocaleElements_lt* Class

```
public Class LocaleElements_lt extends LocaleData
```

Constructors

```
public LocaleElements_lt();
```

The *LocaleElements_lv* Class

```
public Class LocaleElements_lv extends LocaleData
```

Constructors

```
public LocaleElements_lv();
```

The *LocaleElements_mk* Class

```
public Class LocaleElements_mk extends LocaleData
```

Constructors

```
public LocaleElements_mk();
```

The *LocaleElements_nl* Class

```
public Class LocaleElements_nl extends LocaleData
```

Constructors

```
public LocaleElements_nl();
```

The *LocaleElements_nl_BE* Class

```
public Class LocaleElements_nl_BE extends LocaleData
```

Constructors

```
public LocaleElements_nl_BE();
```

The *LocaleElements_no* Class

```
public Class LocaleElements_no extends LocaleData
```

Constructors

```
public LocaleElements_no();
```

The *LocaleElements_no_NO_NY* Class

```
public Class LocaleElements_no_NO_NY extends LocaleData
```

Constructors

```
public LocaleElements_no_NO_NY();
```

The *LocaleElements_pl* Class

```
public Class LocaleElements_pl extends LocaleData
```

Constructors

```
public LocaleElements_pl();
```

The *LocaleElements_pt* Class

```
public Class LocaleElements_pt extends LocaleData
```

Constructors

```
public LocaleElements_pt();
```

The *LocaleElements_ro* Class

```
public Class LocaleElements_ro extends LocaleData
```

Constructors

```
public LocaleElements_ro();
```

The *LocaleElements_ru* Class

```
public Class LocaleElements_ru extends LocaleData
```

Constructors

```
public LocaleElements_ru();
```

The *LocaleElements_sh* Class

```
public Class LocaleElements_sh extends LocaleData
```

Constructors

```
public LocaleElements_sh();
```

The *LocaleElements_sk* Class

```
public Class LocaleElements_sk extends LocaleData
```

Constructors

```
public LocaleElements_sk();
```

The *LocaleElements_sl* Class

```
public Class LocaleElements_sl extends LocaleData
```

Constructors

```
public LocaleElements_sl();
```

The *LocaleElements_sq* Class

```
public Class LocaleElements_sq extends LocaleData
```

Constructors

```
public LocaleElements_sq();
```

The *LocaleElements_sr* Class

```
public Class LocaleElements_sr extends LocaleData
```

Constructors

```
public LocaleElements_sr();
```

The *LocaleElements_sv* Class

```
public Class LocaleElements_sv extends LocaleData
```

Constructors

```
public LocaleElements_sv();
```

The *LocaleElements_tr* Class

```
public Class LocaleElements_tr extends LocaleData
```

Constructors

```
public LocaleElements_tr();
```

The *LocaleElements_uk* Class

```
public Class LocaleElements_uk extends LocaleData
```

Constructors

```
public LocaleElements_uk();
```

The *LocaleElements_zh* Class

```
public Class LocaleElements_zh extends LocaleData
```

Constructors

```
public LocaleElements_zh();
```

The *LocaleElements_zh_TW* Class

```
public Class LocaleElements_zh_TW extends LocaleData
```

Constructors

```
public LocaleElements_zh_TW();
```

The *java.util* Package

The *BitSet* Class

```
public Class BitSet extends Object implements Cloneable,
  java.io.Serializable
```

Constructors

```
public BitSet();
public BitSet(int nbits);
```

Methods

```
public void and(BitSet set);
public void clear(int bit);
public Object clone();
public boolean equals(Object obj);
public boolean get(int bit);
public int hashCode();
public void or(BitSet set);
public void set(int bit);
public int size();
public String toString();
public void xor(BitSet set);
```

The *Calendar* Class

```
public abstract Class Calendar extends Object implements Serializable,
  Cloneable
```

Data

```
public final static int AM = 0;
public final static int AM_PM = 9;
public final static int APRIL = 3;
public final static int AUGUST = 7;
public final static int DATE = 5;
public final static int DAY_OF_MONTH = 5;
public final static int DAY_OF_WEEK = 7;
public final static int DAY_OF_WEEK_IN_MONTH = 8;
public final static int DAY_OF_YEAR = 6;
```

```
public final static int DECEMBER = 11;
public final static int DST_OFFSET = 16;
public final static int ERA = 0;
public final static int FEBRUARY = 1;
public final static int FIELD_COUNT = 17;
public final static int FRIDAY = 6;
public final static int HOUR = 10;
public final static int HOUR_OF_DAY = 11;
public final static int JANUARY = 0;
public final static int JULY = 6;
public final static int JUNE = 5;
public final static int MARCH = 2;
public final static int MAY = 4;
public final static int MILLISECOND = 14;
public final static int MINUTE = 12;
public final static int MONDAY = 2;
public final static int MONTH = 2;
public final static int NOVEMBER = 10;
public final static int OCTOBER = 9;
public final static int PM = 1;
public final static int SATURDAY = 7;
public final static int SECOND = 13;
public final static int SEPTEMBER = 8;
public final static int SUNDAY = 1;
public final static int THURSDAY = 5;
public final static int TUESDAY = 3;
public final static int UNDECIMBER = 12;
public final static int WEDNESDAY = 4;
public final static int WEEK_OF_MONTH = 4;
public final static int WEEK_OF_YEAR = 3;
public final static int YEAR = 1;
public final static int ZONE_OFFSET = 15;
```

Methods

```
public static synchronized Locale[] getAvailableLocales();
public static synchronized Calendar getInstance();
public static synchronized Calendar getInstance(Locale aLocale);
public static synchronized Calendar getInstance(TimeZone zone);
public static synchronized Calendar getInstance(TimeZone zone, Locale
   aLocale);
abstract public void add(int field, int amount);
```

```
abstract public boolean after(Object when);
abstract public boolean before(Object when);
protected abstract void computeFields();
protected abstract void computeTime();
abstract public boolean equals(Object when);
abstract public int getGreatestMinimum(int field);
abstract public int getLeastMaximum(int field);
abstract public int getMaximum(int field);
abstract public int getMinimum(int field);
abstract public void roll(int field, boolean up);
public final void clear();
public final void clear(int field);
public Object clone();
public final int get(int field);
public int getFirstDayOfWeek();
public int getMinimalDaysInFirstWeek();
public final Date getTime();
public TimeZone getTimeZone();
public boolean isLenient();
public final boolean isSet(int field);
public final void set(int field, int value);
public final void set(int year, int month, int date);
public final void set(int year, int month, int date, int hour, int
    minute);
public final void set(int year, int month, int date, int hour, int
    minute, int second);
public void setFirstDayOfWeek(int value);
public void setLenient(boolean lenient);
public void setMinimalDaysInFirstWeek(int value);
public final void setTime(Date date);
public void setTimeZone(TimeZone value);
```

The *Date* Class

```
public Class Date extends Object implements java.io.Serializable,
    Cloneable
```

Constructors

```
public Date();
public Date(long date);
public Date(int year, int month, int date);
```

```
public Date(int year, int month, int date, int hrs, int min);
public Date(int year, int month, int date, int hrs, int min, int sec);
public Date(String s);
```

Methods

```
public static long parse(String s);
public static long UTC(int year, int month, int date, int hrs, int min,
    int sec);
public boolean after(Date when);
public boolean before(Date when);
public boolean equals(Object obj);
public int getDate();
public int getDay();
public int getHours();
public int getMinutes();
public int getMonth();
public int getSeconds();
public long getTime();
public int getTimezoneOffset();
public int getYear();
public int hashCode();
public void setDate(int date);
public void setHours(int hours);
public void setMinutes(int minutes);
public void setMonth(int month);
public void setSeconds(int seconds);
public void setTime(long time);
public void setYear(int year);
public String toGMTString();
public String toLocaleString();
public String toString();
```

The *Dictionary* Class

```
public abstract Class Dictionary extends Object
```

Methods

```
abstract public Enumeration elements();
abstract public Object get(Object key);
abstract public boolean isEmpty();
abstract public Enumeration keys();
```

```
abstract public Object put(Object key, Object value);
abstract public Object remove(Object key);
abstract public int size();
```

The *EmptyStackException* Class

```
public Class EmptyStackException extends RuntimeException
```

Constructors

```
public EmptyStackException();
```

The *Enumeration* Interface

```
public Interface Enumeration
```

Methods

```
boolean hasMoreElements();
Object nextElement();
```

The *EventListener* Interface

```
public Interface EventListener
```

The *EventObject* Class

```
public Class EventObject extends Object implements java.io.Serializable
```

Constructors

```
public EventObject(Object source);
```

Methods

```
public Object getSource();
public String toString();
```

The *GregorianCalendar* Class

```
public Class GregorianCalendar extends Calendar
```

Data

```
public static final int AD = 1;
public static final int BC = 0;
```

Constructors

```
public GregorianCalendar();
public GregorianCalendar(TimeZone zone);
public GregorianCalendar(Locale aLocale);
public GregorianCalendar(TimeZone zone, Locale aLocale);
public GregorianCalendar(int year, int month, int date);
public GregorianCalendar(int year, int month, int date, int hour, int
    minute);
public GregorianCalendar(int year, int month, int date, int hour, int
    minute, int second);
```

Methods

```
public void add(int field, int amount);
public boolean after(Object when);
public boolean before(Object when);
public Object clone();
public boolean equals(Object obj);
public int getGreatestMinimum(int field);
public final Date getGregorianChange();
public int getLeastMaximum(int field);
public int getMaximum(int field);
public int getMinimum(int field);
public synchronized int hashCode();
public boolean isLeapYear(int year);
public void roll(int field, boolean up);
public void setGregorianChange(Date date);
```

The *ListResourceBundle* Class

```
public abstract Class ListResourceBundle extends ResourceBundle
```

Methods

```
abstract protected Object[][] getContents();
public Enumeration getKeys();
public final Object handleGetObject(String key);
```

The *Locale* Class

```
public Class Locale extends Object implements Cloneable, Serializable
```

Data

```
static public final Locale CANADA = new Locale("en","CA","");
static public final Locale CANADA_FRENCH = new Locale("fr","CA","");
static public final Locale CHINA = new Locale("zh","CN","");
static public final Locale CHINESE = new Locale("zh","","");
static public final Locale ENGLISH = new Locale("en","","");
static public final Locale FRANCE = new Locale("fr","FR","");
static public final Locale FRENCH = new Locale("fr","","");
static public final Locale GERMAN = new Locale("de","","");
static public final Locale GERMANY = new Locale("de","DE","");
static public final Locale ITALIAN = new Locale("it","","");
static public final Locale ITALY = new Locale("it","IT","");
static public final Locale JAPAN = new Locale("ja","JP","");
static public final Locale JAPANESE = new Locale("ja","","");
static public final Locale KOREA = new Locale("ko","KR","");
static public final Locale KOREAN = new Locale("ko","","");
static public final Locale PRC = new Locale("zh","CN","");
static public final Locale SIMPLIFIED_CHINESE = new
   Locale("zh","CN","");
static public final Locale TAIWAN = new Locale("zh","TW","");
static public final Locale TRADITIONAL_CHINESE = new
   Locale("zh","TW","");
static public final Locale UK = new Locale("en","GB","");
static public final Locale US = new Locale("en","US","");
```

Constructors

```
public Locale(String language, String country, String variant);
public Locale(String language, String country);
```

Methods

```
public static synchronized Locale getDefault();
public static synchronized void setDefault(Locale newLocale);
public Object clone();
public boolean equals(Object obj);
public String getCountry();
public final String getDisplayCountry();
public String getDisplayCountry(Locale inLocale);
public final String getDisplayLanguage();
```

```
public String getDisplayLanguage(Locale inLocale);
public final String getDisplayName();
public String getDisplayName(Locale inLocale);
public final String getDisplayVariant();
public String getDisplayVariant(Locale inLocale);
public String getISO3Country() throws MissingResourceException;
public String getISO3Language() throws MissingResourceException;
public String getLanguage();
public String getVariant();
public synchronized int hashCode();
public final String toString();
```

The *MissingResourceException* Class

```
public Class MissingResourceException extends RuntimeException
```

Constructors

```
public MissingResourceException(String s, String className, String
    key);
```

Methods

```
public String getClassName();
public String getKey();
```

The *NoSuchElementException* Class

```
public Class NoSuchElementException extends RuntimeException
```

Constructors

```
public NoSuchElementException();
public NoSuchElementException(String s);
```

The *Observable* Class

```
public Class Observable extends Object
```

Constructors

```
public Observable();
```

Methods

```
public synchronized void addObserver(Observer o);
```

```
public synchronized int countObservers();
public synchronized void deleteObserver(Observer o);
public synchronized void deleteObservers();
public synchronized boolean hasChanged();
public void notifyObservers();
public void notifyObservers(Object arg);
```

The *Observer* Interface

```
public Interface Observer
```

Methods

```
void update(Observable o, Object arg);
```

The *Properties* Class

```
public Class Properties extends Hashtable
```

Constructors

```
public Properties();
public Properties(Properties defaults);
```

Methods

```
public String getProperty(String key);
public String getProperty(String key, String defaultValue);
public void list(PrintStream out);
public void list(PrintWriter out);
public synchronized void load(InputStream in) throws IOException;
public Enumeration propertyNames();
public synchronized void save(OutputStream out, String header);
```

The *PropertyResourceBundle* Class

```
public Class PropertyResourceBundle extends ResourceBundle
```

Methods

```
public PropertyResourceBundle (InputStream stream) throws IOException;
public Enumeration getKeys();
public Object handleGetObject(String key);
```

The *Random* Class

```
public Class Random extends Object implements java.io.Serializable
```

Constructors

```
public Random();
public Random(long seed);
```

Methods

```
public void nextBytes(byte[] bytes);
public double nextDouble();
public float nextFloat();
synchronized public double nextGaussian();
public int nextInt();
public long nextLong();
synchronized public void setSeed(long seed);
```

The *ResourceBundle* Class

```
public abstract Class ResourceBundle extends Object
```

Methods

```
public static final ResourceBundle getBundle(String baseName) throws
  MissingResourceException;
public static final ResourceBundle getBundle(String baseName, Locale
  locale);
private static native Class[] getClassContext();
public abstract Enumeration getKeys();
protected abstract Object handleGetObject(String key) throws
  MissingResourceException;
public final Object getObject(String key) throws
  MissingResourceException;
public final String getString(String key) throws
  MissingResourceException;
public final String[] getStringArray(String key) throws
  MissingResourceException;
```

The *SimpleTimeZone* Class

```
public Class SimpleTimeZone extends TimeZone
```

Constructors

```
public SimpleTimeZone(int rawOffset, String ID);
public SimpleTimeZone(int rawOffset, String ID, int startMonth, int
  startDayOfWeekInMonth, int startDayOfWeek, int startTime, int
  endMonth, int endDayOfWeekInMonth, int endDayOfWeek, int endTime);
```

Methods

```
public Object clone();
public boolean equals(Object obj);
public int getOffset(int era, int year, int month, int day, int
  dayOfWeek, int millis);
public int getRawOffset();
public synchronized int hashCode();
public boolean inDaylightTime(Date date);
public void setEndRule(int month, int dayOfWeekInMonth, int dayOfWeek,
  int time);
public void setRawOffset(int offsetMillis);
public void setStartRule(int month, int dayOfWeekInMonth, int
  dayOfWeek, int time);
public void setStartYear(int year);
public boolean useDaylightTime();
```

The *Stack* Class

```
public Class Stack extends Vector
```

Methods

```
public boolean empty();
public synchronized Object peek();
public synchronized Object pop();
public Object push(Object item);
public synchronized int search(Object o);
```

The *StringTokenizer* Class

```
public Class StringTokenizer extends Object implements Enumeration
```

Constructors

```
public StringTokenizer(String str, String delim, boolean returnTokens);
public StringTokenizer(String str, String delim);
public StringTokenizer(String str);
```

Methods

```
public int countTokens();
public boolean hasMoreElements();
public boolean hasMoreTokens();
public Object nextElement();
public String nextToken();
public String nextToken(String delim);
```

The *TimeZone* Class

```
public abstract Class TimeZone extends Object implements Serializable,
    Cloneable
```

Methods

```
public static synchronized String[] getAvailableIDs();
public static synchronized String[] getAvailableIDs(int rawOffset);
public static synchronized TimeZone getDefault();
public static synchronized TimeZone getTimeZone(String ID);
public static synchronized void setDefault(TimeZone zone);
abstract public int getOffset(int era, int year, int month, int day,
    int dayOfWeek, int milliseconds);
abstract public int getRawOffset();
abstract public boolean inDaylightTime(Date date);
abstract public void setRawOffset(int offsetMillis);
abstract public boolean useDaylightTime();
public Object clone();
public String getID();
public void setID(String ID);
```

The *TooManyListenersException* Class

```
public Class TooManyListenersException extends Exception
```

Constructors

```
public TooManyListenersException();
public TooManyListenersException(String s);
```

The *Vector* Class

```
public Class Vector extends Object implements Cloneable,
    java.io.Serializable
```

Constructors

```
public Vector(int initialCapacity, int capacityIncrement);
public Vector(int initialCapacity);
public Vector();
```

Methods

```
public final synchronized void addElement(Object obj);
public final int capacity();
public synchronized Object clone();
public final boolean contains(Object elem);
public final synchronized void copyInto(Object anArray[]);
public final synchronized Object elementAt(int index);
public final synchronized Enumeration elements();
public final synchronized void ensureCapacity(int minCapacity);
public final synchronized Object firstElement();
public final int indexOf(Object elem);
public final synchronized int indexOf(Object elem, int index);
public final synchronized void insertElementAt(Object obj, int index);
public final boolean isEmpty();
public final synchronized Object lastElement();
public final int lastIndexOf(Object elem);
public final synchronized int lastIndexOf(Object elem, int index);
public final synchronized void removeAllElements();
public final synchronized boolean removeElement(Object obj);
public final synchronized void removeElementAt(int index);
public final synchronized void setElementAt(Object obj, int index);
public final synchronized void setSize(int newSize);
public final int size();
```

```
public final synchronized String toString();
public final synchronized void trimToSize();
```

The *java.util.zip* Package

The *Adler32* Class

```
public Class Adler32 extends Object implements Checksum
```

Methods

```
public long getValue();
public void reset();
public native void update(byte[] b, int off, int len);
public void update(byte[] b);
public void update(int b);
private native void update1(int b);
```

The *CRC32* Class

```
public Class CRC32 extends Object implements Checksum
```

Methods

```
public long getValue();
public void reset();
public native void update(byte[] b, int off, int len);
public void update(byte[] b);
public void update(int b);
private native void update1(int b);
```

The *CheckedInputStream* Class

```
public Class CheckedInputStream extends FilterInputStream
```

Constructors

```
public CheckedInputStream(InputStream in, Checksum cksum);
```

Methods

```
public Checksum getChecksum();
public int read() throws IOException;
public int read(byte[] buf, int off, int len) throws IOException;
public long skip(long n) throws IOException;
```

The *CheckedOutputStream* Class

```
public Class CheckedOutputStream extends FilterOutputStream
```

Constructors

```
public CheckedOutputStream(OutputStream out, Checksum cksum);
```

Methods

```
public Checksum getChecksum();
public void write(byte[] b, int off, int len) throws IOException;
public void write(int b) throws IOException;
```

The *Checksum* Interface

```
public Interface Checksum
```

Methods

```
public long getValue();
public void reset();
public void update(byte[] b, int off, int len);
public void update(int b);
```

The *DataFormatException* Class

```
public Class DataFormatException extends Exception
```

Constructors

```
public DataFormatException();
public DataFormatException(String s);
```

The *Deflater* Class

```
public Class Deflater extends Object
```

Data

```
public static final int BEST_COMPRESSION = 9;
public static final int BEST_SPEED = 1;
public static final int DEFAULT_COMPRESSION = -1;
public static final int DEFAULT_STRATEGY = 0;
public static final int DEFLATED = 8;
public static final int FILTERED = 1;
public static final int HUFFMAN_ONLY = 2;
public static final int NO_COMPRESSION = 0;
```

Constructors

```
public Deflater(int level, boolean nowrap);
public Deflater(int level);
public Deflater();
```

Methods

```
public synchronized native int deflate(byte[] b, int off, int len);
public int deflate(byte[] b);
public synchronized native void end();
public synchronized void finish();
public synchronized boolean finished();
public synchronized native int getAdler();
public synchronized native int getTotalIn();
public synchronized native int getTotalOut();
private native void init(boolean nowrap);
public boolean needsInput();
public synchronized native void reset();
public synchronized native void setDictionary(byte[] b, int off, int
    len);
public void setDictionary(byte[] b);
public synchronized void setInput(byte[] b, int off, int len);
public void setInput(byte[] b);
public synchronized void setLevel(int Level);
public synchronized void setStrategy(int strategy);
```

The *DeflaterOutputStream* Class

```
public Class DeflaterOutputStream extends FilterOutputStream
```

Constructors

```
public DeflaterOutputStream(OutputStream out, Deflater def, int size);
public DeflaterOutputStream(OutputStream out, Deflater def);
public DeflaterOutputStream(OutputStream out);
```

Methods

```
public void close() throws IOException;
public void finish() throws IOException;
public void write(byte[] b, int off, int len) throws IOException;
public void write(int b) throws IOException;
```

The *GZIPInputStream* Class

```
public Class GZIPInputStream extends InflaterInputStream
```

Data

```
public final static int GZIP_MAGIC = 0x8b1f;
```

Constructors

```
public GZIPInputStream(InputStream in, int size) throws IOException;
public GZIPInputStream(InputStream in) throws IOException;
```

Methods

```
public void close() throws IOException;
public int read(byte[] buf, int off, int len) throws IOException;
```

The *GZIPOutputStream* Class

```
public Class GZIPOutputStream extends DeflaterOutputStream
```

Constructors

```
public GZIPOutputStream(OutputStream out, int size) throws IOException;
public GZIPOutputStream(OutputStream out) throws IOException;
```

Methods

```
public void close() throws IOException;
public void finish() throws IOException;
public synchronized void write(byte[] buf, int off, int len) throws
    IOException;
```

The *Inflater* Class

```
public Class Inflater extends Object
```

Constructors

```
public Inflater(boolean nowrap);
public Inflater();
```

Methods

```
public synchronized native void end();
public synchronized boolean finished();
public synchronized native int getAdler();
public synchronized int getRemaining();
public synchronized native int getTotalIn();
public synchronized native int getTotalOut();
public synchronized native int inflate(byte[] b, int off, int len)
    throws DataFormatException;
public int inflate(byte[] b) throws DataFormatException;
private native void init(boolean nowrap);
public synchronized boolean needsDictionary();
public synchronized boolean needsInput();
public synchronized native void reset();
public synchronized native void setDictionary(byte[] b, int off, int
    len);
public void setDictionary(byte[] b);
public synchronized void setInput(byte[] b, int off, int len);
public void setInput(byte[] b);
```

The *InflaterInputStream* Class

```
public Class InflaterInputStream extends FilterInputStream
```

Constructors

```
public InflaterInputStream(InputStream in, Inflater inf, int size);
```

```
public InflaterInputStream(InputStream in, Inflater inf);
public InflaterInputStream(InputStream in);
```

Methods

```
public int read() throws IOException;
public int read(byte[] b, int off, int len) throws IOException;
public long skip(long n) throws IOException;
```

The *ZipEntry* Class

```
public Class ZipEntry extends Object implements ZipConstants
```

Data

```
public static final int DEFLATED = 8;
public static final int STORED = 0;
```

Constructors

```
public ZipEntry(String name);
```

Methods

```
public String getComment();
public long getCompressedSize();
public long getCrc();
public byte[] getExtra();
public int getMethod();
public String getName();
public long getSize();
public long getTime();
public boolean isDirectory();
public void setComment(String comment);
public void setCrc(long crc);
public void setExtra(byte[] extra);
public void setMethod(int method);
public void setSize(long size);
public void setTime(long time);
public String toString();
```

The *ZipException* Class

```
public Class ZipException extends IOException
```

Constructors

```
public ZipException();
public ZipException(String s);
```

The *ZipFile* Class

```
public Class ZipFile extends Object implements ZipConstants
```

Constructors

```
public ZipFile(String name) throws IOException;
public ZipFile(File file) throws ZipException, IOException;
```

Methods

```
public void close() throws IOException;
public Enumeration entries();
public ZipEntry getEntry(String name);
public InputStream getInputStream(ZipEntry ze) throws IOException;
public String getName();
```

The *ZipInputStream* Class

```
public Class ZipInputStream extends InflaterInputStream implements
  ZipConstants
```

Constructors

```
public ZipInputStream(InputStream in);
```

Methods

```
public void close() throws IOException;
public void closeEntry() throws IOException;
public ZipEntry getNextEntry() throws IOException;
public int read(byte[] b, int off, int len) throws IOException;
public long skip(long n) throws IOException;
```

The *ZipOutputStream* Class

```
public Class ZipOutputStream extends DeflaterOutputStream implements
   ZipConstants
```

Data

```
public static final int DEFLATED = ZipEntry.DEFLATED;
public static final int STORED = ZipEntry.STORED;
```

Constructors

```
public ZipOutputStream(OutputStream out);
```

Methods

```
public void close() throws IOException;
public void closeEntry() throws IOException;
public void finish() throws IOException;
public void putNextEntry(ZipEntry e) throws IOException;
public void setComment(String comment);
public void setLevel(int level);
public void setMethod(int method);
public synchronized void write(byte[] b, int off, int len) throws
   IOException;
```

APPENDIX

C

Using the Test Program

The CD-ROM supplied with this book contains a Java program that allows you to test yourself. Our tester uses some of the questions from each chapter and allows you to simulate taking the real Java Certification Exam and to make a reasonable estimate of whether you are sufficiently prepared for the exam.

The Real Test

First, let's discuss the real test program, since it differs somewhat from the tester, but is the one you will have to use when you take the exam "for real." You will see immediately that the user interface is different. The real test uses a native Windows 3.1 interface which differs in appearance from any variation that the tester will offer. However, in addition to the inevitable differences of windowing system, the overall layout differs a little. We will take a little time to describe the overall appearance of the real test system.

The real test uses a single, scrollable area to present the question and the answer choices. This question area occupies most of the screen. Beneath the question area are three buttons: Next, Previous, and Help. The Help button gives help on using the test system, not on the questions. Next and Previous step between questions, but the Next button sometimes changes to More. This change occurs when a question is long enough to require scrolling for you to see the whole question and all the answers. After you have pressed the More button, or have scrolled down the page far enough to have seen the whole question with all its answers, the button changes back to Next. The diagram in Figure C.1 shows the approximate layout of the real test system's main screen.

When you have stepped through all the questions the real test system offers, you see a review page which shows all the questions and indicates any you have left unanswered. This page provides facilities for you to return to these unanswered questions to complete them.

Upon completion of the real test, which is strictly timed, you are presented with your mark on paper. You do not find out the correct answers, or even what specific questions you got wrong. The 1.1 version of the test does give you a breakdown of your scores by each group of objectives, so that you get some indication of the areas you should study further before you retake the exam.

FIGURE C.1

Sketch of the main
screen of the real test

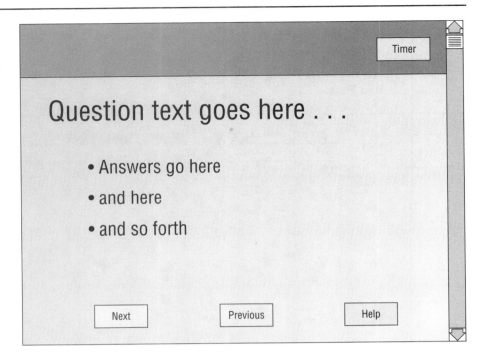

In addition to the main test system, the real test allows you to have a "trial run" working with the test system to become familiar with it. During that phase you are given questions that are entirely unrelated to Java, so do not worry about getting them right!

Another facility allows you to make comments about the questions if you wish, although you will probably want to concentrate on your answers.

Now that you have a sense of the format of the real test, let's discuss the tester that is provided on the CD with this book.

The Tester

There are several differences between the real program and the tester. First and foremost, the questions are different! While we have sought to cover the same ground as the real test, and to make the questions of comparable difficulty, you must appreciate that this is not the "real thing." There is no point in learning the answers to these questions by rote—that will only give you inappropriate confidence and will not provide you with actual answers to the real test.

The appearance of the tester main window on a Windows 95 system is shown in Figure C.2.

FIGURE C.2

Screen shot of the tester main screen

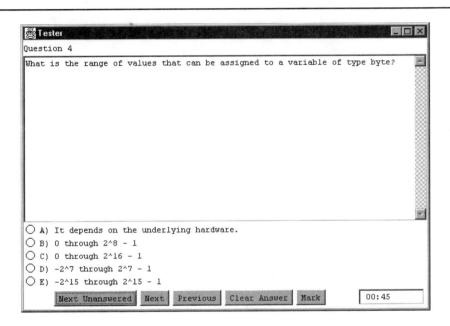

In the tester, the questions are presented in a scrollable text area in the upper part of the main window, with the answer options presented in the lower part.

The tester provides five buttons at the bottom of the window, and to the right is a timer. The timer can operate in either count-up mode, allowing you to determine how long you took to answer a set of questions, or in count-down mode, in which case it will force the tester into marking mode, preventing you from answering any more questions when the time reaches zero.

The buttons provided are marked Next Unanswered, Next, Previous, Clear Answer, and Mark. The first three of these buttons are for navigating the question set, Next and Previous are self-evident, while Next Unanswered checks the question set to find the next question that you have not yet answered.

The Clear Answer button removes all marks from a question so that the Next Unanswered button will consider it to be unanswered. You can use this if you decide to skip a question for now but want to be able to come back to it easily.

The Mark button stops the test and the timer and marks the questions. Unlike the real test, the tester gives you complete feedback on all the questions, including the correct answers and explanations. To give this feedback, the tester uses two additional windows. One pops up automatically when you press the Mark button. A screen shot of this window is shown in Figure C.3.

FIGURE C.3

The marking window

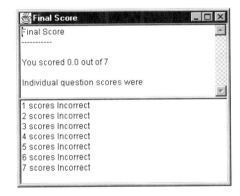

Notice that the marking window is divided into two regions. At the top is a text area that states your mark and the total number of questions you were asked. Beneath this is a scrollable list which indicates your score on a question-by-question basis. If you select one of the lines in this list, you are presented with a second window containing a text area which tells you either that you got the question correct, or what the correct answer is. An example of this is shown in Figure C.4.

FIGURE C.4

The explanation window

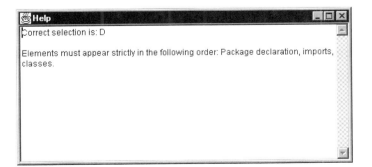

Notice how the first line indicates the correct answer or answers. If you got the question right, this line simply says so. The explanation text appears on the following lines.

Now that you know broadly what to expect when you run the tester, let's take a look at how to start the program and the options that it offers.

Running the Tester

To run the tester, first install it onto your hard disk. To do this, choose one of the archives (`test.zip`, `test.jar`) and expand it into a suitable place on your system, such as `C:\tester`. Next, select that directory as current and issue the command

```
java Test
```

from the system prompt. This starts the tester program, giving you unlimited time to complete the test and a random selection of about 65 questions. When you press the Mark button, the timer at the bottom right-hand corner of the display will stop, showing you how long you spent on the questions.

Imposing a Time Limit

You can also run the test in timed mode; the tester will move forcibly into marking mode if you take too long. To invoke this behavior in the tester, define the property `testTime` when you start the program. This value should be specified in minutes, and to approximate the conditions of the real exam you should give yourself between one-and-a-half and two minutes per question. To define this property, start the tester with a command like this:

```
java -DtestTime=90 Test
```

This would give you one-and-a-half hours to complete the test.

Controlling the Number of Questions

If for any reason you do not want to run a test with the default number of questions, you can specify a particular number by setting the property `questionCount`. So for example, to request only 20 questions start the tester like this:

```
java -DquestionCount=20 Test
```

Of course, you can ask for more questions than the default if you wish. If you ask for more questions than are available, however, you will only get each question once.

Controlling the Question Categories

By default, the tester reads all the questions from the file `Questions.ser`, which contains questions for all chapters, but you can direct it to specific files if you wish. The questions for each chapter are in separate files. The file names are the chapter number as a two-digit value followed by an underscore, a short hint at the chapter name, and finally the extension `.ser`. You can select one or more of these by specifying the property `questionFiles`. For example, to select questions from chapters 4 and 7 issue the command:

```
java -DquestionFiles="04_Cast.ser|07_Threads.ser" Test
```

Notice the use of the pipe character (|) to separate the files in the list. If you want questions from only one chapter, you don't need to use the pipe at all.

Answering the Questions

The questions presented by the tester are all multiple choice; some take only a single correct answer, and some allow zero or more selections. You can tell if you are allowed only a single answer to a question because the answers will be presented to you with round radio buttons.

If you see square check boxes, you can select any number of options, from none to all that are shown. You can think of this type of question as a collection of true/false questions based on the same topic. Because true/false is generally considered to be pretty easy—giving you a 50 percent chance of success simply by guessing—you will not be surprised to know that you must get *all* parts of the question correct to score the mark.

As with any test, you must read each question carefully. We have tried to make the questions unambiguous, but inevitably some uncertainties will remain. Although it is practically impossible to eliminate ambiguity from natural language (if it weren't, then lawyers would be unemployed), the questions on the

Java Certification Exam have been subjected to extensive review and correction by many people; therefore, you can reasonably expect your interpretation of a question to match the intended one.

Good luck!

APPENDIX
D

Glossary

Abstract An abstract class may not be directly instantiated. Abstract classes are intended to be subclassed, with non-abstract methods overriding abstract methods.

Arithmetic Promotion Conversion of data to a wider type, in the course of an arithmetic operation.

Assignment Conversion Conversion of data from one type to another, in the course of assigning a value of one type to a variable of a different type.

AWT Java's Abstract Windowing Toolkit.

Bytecode The code format of Java class files.

Casting Explicit conversion from one data type to another.

Character Encoding A mapping from characters to bit sequences.

Clipping Restriction of the set of pixels that are affected by the `drawXXX()` methods of the `java.awt.Graphics` class.

Clip Region The region within a component that is affected by the `drawXXX()` methods of the `java.awt.Graphics` class.

Container A GUI component that can contain other components.

Deep Comparison Comparison of some or all of the instance variables of two objects.

Event Listener An object that is delegated to handle events of a certain type originating from a source object.

Feature An element of a class that can be modified by a modifier such as `private` or `static`. A class' features are its data, its methods, and the class itself.

Final A final member variable may not be modified. A final method may not be overridden. A final class may not be extended.

Friendly A friendly feature may be accessed from the class itself, or from any member of the class' package. Unlike `private`, `protected`, and `public`, "friendly" is not a Java keyword.

Garbage Collection Automatic de-allocation of unused memory.

GUI Graphical User Interface.

GUI Thread A thread that handles GUI input and responds to `repaint()` calls.

Inner Class A class that is defined within, and can only be used by another class.

Instance A single example or occurrence of a class.

JAR Acronym for Java ARchive file.

JDK Java Developer's Kit.

JVM Java Virtual Machine.

Layout Manager A class that dictates the size and location of components within a container.

Method A function associated with a class.

Method-Call Conversion
Conversion of data from one type to another, in the course of passing a value of one type into a method call that expects a variable of a different type.

Modal A modal dialog consumes all input directed at its parent component. Normal input dispatching resumes once a modal dialog is dismissed.

Monitor An object that can block and revive threads. In Java, monitors have synchronized code.

Narrowing Conversion Conversion to a new data type that encompasses a narrower range than the original data type.

Native A native method calls code that resides in a library that is loaded on the local computer.

Overload Overloaded methods of a class have the same method name but different argument lists and possibly different return types.

Override A class overrides an inherited method by providing a method with the same name, argument list, and return type.

Package A collection of classes.

Polygon A closed, connected sequence of line segments.

Polyline An open, connected sequence of line segments.

Preemptive Scheduling A thread-scheduling algorithm in which a thread may be kicked out of the CPU at any moment.

Primitive A primitive data type is a basic data type (as contrasted to an object reference or an array). Java's primitive types are `boolean`, `char`, `byte`, `short`, `int`, `long`, `float`, and `double`.

Private A private feature of a class may only be accessed by an instance of that class.

Protected A protected feature of a class may be accessed from the class itself, from any subclass of the class, or from any member of the class' package.

Public A public feature of a class may be accessed from any class whatsoever.

Repair Re-drawing of pixels in response to exposure.

Scope The scope of a variable is the portion of code within which the variable is defined.

Shallow Comparison Comparison of two object references.

Static A static feature is associated with a class rather than with an individual instance of the class. A static method may not access non-static variables.

Synchronized Synchronized code requires the executing thread to obtain the lock of the executing object.

Thread Scheduler Portion of a Java Virtual Machine that is responsible for determining which thread gets to execute.

Time-Sliced Scheduling A thread-scheduling algorithm in which threads take turns to use the CPU.

Transient A transient variable is never serialized.

Unicode A 16-bit encoding for representing characters. Java's char and String classes use Unicode encoding.

Widening Conversion Conversion to a new data type that encompasses a wider range than the original data type.

Wrapper A class that encapsulates a single primitive value. Java's wrapper classes reside in the java.lang package.

Index

Note to the Reader: Throughout this index **boldface** page numbers indicate primary discussions of a topic. *Italicized* page numbers indicate illustrations.

Symbols

& (ampersands)
   for bitwise operators, **51–56**
   for logical operators, **56–58**
* (asterisks), **34–36**
\ (backslashes)
   for escape sequences, 8
   for unicode characters, 7
^ (carets), **51–56**
: (colons), 58–59
, (commas)
   in for loops, **131**
   in throws statements, 141
{} (curly braces)
   for arrays, 10
   for synchronized blocks, 208
   for while() loops, 127–128
$ (dollar signs)
   in identifiers, 4
   for inner classes, 175
" (double quotes)
   escape sequences for, 8
   for string literals, 9
= (equal signs)
   for assignment operators, 59–60
   for comparison operators, 48–49
   for equality operators, **50–51**
! (exclamation points)
   for complement operators, **32–33**
   for equality operators, **50–51**
> (greater than signs)
   for comparison operators, 48–49
   for shift operators, 42–45
< (less than signs)
   for comparison operators, 48–49
   for shift operators, 42–45
- (minus signs)
   in increment operators, 30–31
   for subtraction, **37–40**
   as unary operators, **31–32**
() (parentheses)
   for casting, **33–34**, 98
   in for loops, 129
% (percent signs), **36–37**
+ (plus signs)
   for addition, **37–40**
   in increment operators, 30–31
   for string concatenation, **38–39**, **239–240**
   as unary operators, **31–32**
? (question marks)
   escape sequences for, 8
   for ternary operators, 58–59
' (single quotes)
   for char literals, 7
   escape sequences for, 8
[] (square brackets), 10
~t (tildes), **32**
_ (underscores), 4
| (vertical bars)
   for bitwise operators, **51–56**
   for logical operators, **56–58**

A

abs() method, 228
abstract modifier, **80–81**, *80*, 690
AbstractMethodError class, 540
access modifiers, **71–72**
   friendly, **74–75**, *75*

E

J

K

L

Q

R

Java© Development Kit Version 1.1 Binary Code License

1. This binary code license ("License") contains rights and restrictions associated with use of the accompanying software and documentation ("Software"). Read the License carefully before installing the Software. By installing the Software you agree to the terms and conditions of this License.

2. **Limited License Grant.** Sun grants to you ("Licensee") a non-exclusive, non-transferable limited license to use the Software without fee for evaluation of the Software and for development of Java© compatible applets and applications. Licensee may make one archival copy of the Software. Licensee may not re-distribute the Software in whole or in part, either separately or included with a product. Refer to the Java Runtime Environment Version 1.1 binary code license (http://www.javasoft.com/products/JDK/1.1/index.html) for the availability of runtime code which may be distributed with Java compatible applets and applications.

3. **Java Platform Interface.** Licensee may not modify the Java Platform Interface ("JPI", identified as classes contained within the "java" package or any subpackages of the "java" package), by creating additional classes within the JPI or otherwise causing the addition to or modification of the classes in the JPI. In the event that Licensee creates any Java-related API and distributes such API to others for applet or application development, Licensee must promptly publish an accurate specification for such API for free use by all developers of Java-based software.

4. **Restrictions.** Software is confidential copyrighted information of Sun and title to all copies is retained by Sun and/or its licensors. Licensee shall not modify, decompile, disassemble, decrypt, extract, or otherwise reverse engineer Software. Software may not be leased, assigned, or sublicensed, in whole or in any part. **Software is not designed or intended for use in on-line control of aircraft, air traffic, aircraft navigation or aircraft communications; or in the design, construction, operation or maintenance of any nuclear facility. Licensee warrants that it will not use of redistribute the Software for such purposes.**

5. **Trademarks and Logos.** This License does not authorize Licensee to use any Sun name, trademark, or logo. Licensee acknowledges that Sun owns the Java trademark and all Java-related trademarks, logos and icons including the Coffee Cup and Duke ("Java Marks") and agrees to: (i) to comply with the Java Trademark Guidelines at http://java.com/trademarks.html; (ii) assist Sun in protecting those rights, including assigning to Sun any rights acquired by Licensee in any Java Mark.

6. **Disclaimer of Warranty.** Software is provided "AS IS," without a warranty of any kind. ALL EXPRESS OR IMPLIED REPRESENTATIONS AND WARRANTIES, INCLUDING ANY IMPLIED WARRANTY OF MERCHANTABILITY, FITNESS FOR A PARTICULAR PURPOSE OR NON-INFRINGEMENT, ARE HEREBY EXCLUDED.

7. **Limitation of Liability.** SUN AND ITS LICENSORS SHALL NOT BE LIABLE FOR ANY DAMAGES SUFFERED BY LICENSEE OR ANY THIRD PARTY AS A RESULT OF USING OR DISTRIBUTING SOFTWARE. IN NO EVENT WILL SUN OR ITS LICENSORS BE LIABLE FOR ANY LOST REVENUE, PROFIT OR DATA, OR FOR DIRECT, INDIRECT, SPECIAL, CONSEQUENTIAL, INCIDENTAL OR PUNITIVE DAMAGES, HOWEVER CAUSED AND REGARDLESS OF THE THEORY OF LIABILITY, ARISING OUT OF THE USE OF OR INABILITY TO USE SOFTWARE, EVEN IF SUN HAS BEEN ADVISED OF THE POSSIBILITY OF SUCH DAMAGES.

8. **Termination.** Licensee may terminate this License at any time by destroying all copies of Software. This License will terminate immediately without notice from Sun if Licensee fails to comply with any provision of this License. Upon such termination, Licensee must destroy all copies of Software.

9. **Export Regulations.** Software, including technical data, is subject to U.S. export control laws, including the U.S. Export Administration Act and its associated regulations, and may be subject to export or import regulations in other countries. Licensee agrees to comply strictly with all such regulations and acknowledges that it has the responsibility to

obtain licenses to export, re-export, or import Software. Software may not be downloaded, or otherwise exported or re-exported (i) into, or to a national or resident of, Cuba, Iraq, Iran, North Korea, Libya, Sudan, Syria or any country to which the U.S. has embargoed goods; or (ii) to anyone on the U.S. Treasury Department's list of Specially Designated Nations of the U.S. Commerce Department's Table of Denial Orders.

10. **Restricted Rights.** Use, duplication or disclosure by the United States government is subject to the restrictions as set forth in the Rights in Technical Data and Computer Software Clauses in DFARS 252.227-7013(c) (1) (ii) and FAR 52.227-19(c) (2) as applicable.

11. **Governing Law.** Any action related to this License will be governed by California law and controlling U.S. federal law. No choice of law rules of any jurisdiction will apply.

12. **Severability.** If any of the above provisions are held to be in violation of applicable law, void, or unenforceable in any jurisdiction, then such provisions are herewith waived to the extent necessary for the License to be otherwise enforceable in such jurisdiction. However, if in Sun's opinion deletion of any provisions of the License by operation of this paragraph unreasonably compromises the rights or increase the liabilities of Sun or its licensors, Sun reserves the right to terminate the License and refund the fee paid by Licensee, if any, as Licensee's sole and exclusive remedy.

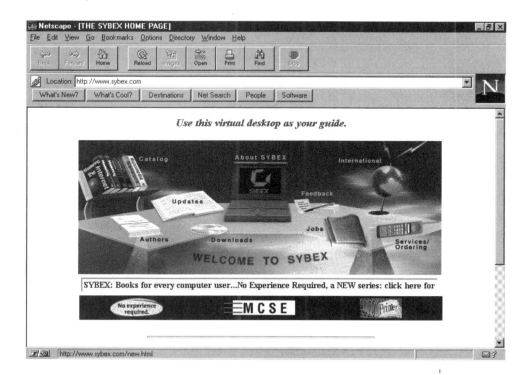

Objectives for the Sun Certified Java Programmer Examination for the JDK 1.1

Language Fundamentals

- Use standard "javadoc" format documentation to identify and use variables and methods in classes. Employ such documentation to identify variables and methods that are inherited from a superclass.
- Distinguish legal and illegal orderings of package declarations, import statements, public class declarations, and non-public class declarations.
- State the correct declaration for a main() method.
- Select specific elements from the command line arguments of the main() method by using the correct array subscript value.
- Identify Java keywords from a list of keywords and non-keywords.
- Determine the value of a member variable of any type when no explicit assignment has been made to it.
- Determine the value of an element of an array of any base type, when the array has been constructed but no explicit assignment has been made to the element.
- Recognize source code that fails to ensure definite initialization before use of method automatic variables and modify that code to correct the error.
- State the range of primitive data types byte, short, int, long and char.
- Distinguish between legal and illegal identifiers.
- Construct literal numeric values using decimal, octal and hexadecimal formats.
- Construct literal String values using quoted format.
- Construct a literal value of char type using Java's unicode escape format for a specified character code.

Operators and Assignments

- Determine the result, in terms of a bit pattern, of applying the '>>', '>>>', and '<<' operators to an int value specified as a bit pattern.
- Determine the result of the + operator applied to a combination of variables or constants of any type.
- Determine the result of applying the '==' comparison operator to any two objects of any type.
- Determine the result of applying the equals() method to any combination of objects of the classes java.lang.String, java.lang.Boolean, and java.lang.Object.
- In an expression involving the operators &, |, &&, and || , state which operands are evaluated and determine the resulting value of the expression.
- Determine if an assignment is permitted between any two variables of possibly different types.
- Determine the effect of assignment and modification operations upon variables of any type.
- Determine the effect upon objects and primitive variables of passing variables into methods and performing assignments and other modifying operations in that method.

Declarations and Access Control

- Declare variables of type "array of X" for any type X. Identify the legal positions for the "{ }" part of an array declaration.
- Construct arrays of any type.
- Write code to initialize an array using loop iteration.
- Write code to initialize an array using the combined declaration and initialization format.

- Define cases, including member variables and member methods.
- Declare classes using the modifiers public, abstract, or final.
- Declare variables using the modifiers private, protected, public, static, final, native, or abstract.
- State the prototype of the default constructor. List the circumstances which govern creation of a default constructor.
- State the consequences, in terms of the results of an assignment to a variable, of the qualifiers static or final being applied to that variable.
- State the effects on scope and accessibility of an instance variable or method of these factors:
  - The calling method is static.
  - the calling method is non-static.
  - The calling method is in the same class as the target.
  - The calling method is in a subclass of the class containing the target.
  - The calling method is in a class which is in the same package as the class containing the target.
  - No special relationship exists between the class of the caller and the class of the target.
  - The target declaration is qualified by any of private, protected, public static, final, or abstract.

Flow Control and Exception Handling

- Write nested conditional code using the if, else, and switch constructs.
- Identifying the legal expression types for the argument of if() and switch().
- Write nested loops to iterate blocks with specific values in loop counter variables.
- Demonstrate the use of both the labeled and unlabeled versions of the break and continue keywords to modify normal loop behavior.
- Demonstrate the flow of control that occurs in try, catch(), and finally constructions under conditions of normal execution, caught exception and uncaught exception.
- Write code that correctly uses the throws clause in a method declaration where that method contains code that might throw exceptions.
- State what exceptions may be legitimately thrown from an overriding method in a subclass, based on the declaration of the overidden superclass method.
- Write code to create and throw a specified exception.

Overloading, Overriding, Runtime Type, and Object Orientation

- Write classes that implement object oriented relationships specified using the clauses 'is a' and 'has a.'
- Determine at run time if an object is an instance of a specified class or some subclass of that class using the instanceof operator.
- Distinguish between overloaded and overridden methods.
- State the legal return types for an overloading method given the origin method declaration.
- State legal return types for an overriding method given the original method declaration.
- Describe the effect of invoking overridden method in base and derived classes.
- Write code for any overidden method that invokes the parental method using super.
- Write constructor bodies using this() and super() to access overloaded or parent-class constructors.
- Define a non-static inner class either in a class or method scope.